Kant's Reason

Kant's Reason

The Unity of Reason and the Limits of Comprehension in Kant

KARL SCHAFER

Great Clarendon Street, Oxford, OX2 6DP,
United Kingdom

Oxford University Press is a department of the University of Oxford.
It furthers the University's objective of excellence in research, scholarship,
and education by publishing worldwide. Oxford is a registered trade mark of
Oxford University Press in the UK and in certain other countries

© Karl Schafer 2023

The moral rights of the author have been asserted

All rights reserved. No part of this publication may be reproduced, stored in
a retrieval system, or transmitted, in any form or by any means, without the
prior permission in writing of Oxford University Press, or as expressly permitted
by law, by licence or under terms agreed with the appropriate reprographics
rights organization. Enquiries concerning reproduction outside the scope of the
above should be sent to the Rights Department, Oxford University Press, at the
address above

You must not circulate this work in any other form
and you must impose this same condition on any acquirer

Published in the United States of America by Oxford University Press
198 Madison Avenue, New York, NY 10016, United States of America

British Library Cataloguing in Publication Data
Data available

Library of Congress Control Number: 2023935829

ISBN 978–0–19–286853–4

DOI: 10.1093/oso/9780192868534.001.0001

Printed and bound by
CPI Group (UK) Ltd, Croydon, CR0 4YY

Links to third party websites are provided by Oxford in good faith and
for information only. Oxford disclaims any responsibility for the materials
contained in any third party website referenced in this work.

Contents

Acknowledgments	vii
List of Abbreviations	xi
Introduction: The Unity of Reason in Kant and Today	1

I. KANT'S RATIONAL CONSTITUTIVISM

1. Transcendental Philosophy and the Self-Consciousness of Reason	31
2. Self-Consciousness, Cognition, and the Taking Condition	56
3. Kant's Rational Constitutivism	91

II. THE UNITY OF REASON

4. Reason: The Capacity for Comprehension	119
5. Theoretical Reason's Supreme Principle and the Principle of Sufficient Reason	149
6. Practical Reason's Supreme Principle, the Moral Law, and the Highest Good	183
7. The Autonomy of Reason and the Capacity for Autonomy	211
Conclusion: Reason, Reasons, and the Future of the Critical Project	235
References	253
Index	269

Acknowledgments

For me at least, philosophical work is always a collaborative process, and there is very little in the pages that follow that I have not learned from someone else—indeed, more often than not, from *many* others *many* times over. The ideas that follow were developed over years of conversation with friends and colleagues, and I regard (at least the good parts of) what follows to be as much their work as it is mine. At the same time, I know from *repeated* experience that my memory for the sources and inspirations of my ideas is often *very imperfect*. So let me begin by apologizing to those I have forgotten and by acknowledging that my debts in this regard almost certainly far outstrip the acknowledgments here and in what follows.

Such remarks would be apt with respect to any of my philosophical work. But they are especially true here since these are ideas that, in some sense, I've been thinking about almost since I began to study philosophy. Indeed, elements of what follows are descended in some sense from the BA thesis on Kant and Hegel I wrote at the University of Chicago under the direction of Michael Forster. After leaving Chicago, I spent a year in Berlin on a Fulbright Fellowship working on German philosophy with Rolf-Peter Horstmann and Dina Emundts. After Berlin, I returned to the US to do a PhD at NYU under the direction of Thomas Nagel, Béatrice Longuenesse, Don Garrett, and David Velleman (as well as Sharon Street and Derek Parfit). Although my official PhD project was on contemporary moral psychology, in those years, I was also already working on the reading of Kant that follows, and my work here is deeply influenced by all of them, and especially by Béatrice and Tom. Indeed, what follows might be viewed as my attempt to think through some basic commitments in the latter's philosophy using the framework for thinking about Kant that the former's work provides.

A version of Chapter 6 served as my job talk at many institutions—including Pittsburgh, where I was lucky enough to join the faculty upon completion of my PhD. There, I was exposed to an extremely stimulating environment for thinking about the continuing relevance of Kant's philosophy, so much so that I might be reasonably regarded as a fellow traveler of the "Pittsburgh school." After leaving Pittsburgh, I then spent a very happy six years as a professor at UC Irvine, where my work on this project began in earnest, before leaving for Texas last year. All of these institutions have my thanks for their support during the development of this project, as does the Princeton University Center for Human Values, where I also spent an extremely productive year early on in this process.

The largest influence on this project has surely been the group of other Kant scholars and philosophers in conversation with whom I developed these ideas. Most notable in this respect is surely Nicholas Stang, whose influence on what follows can hardly be overstated. But much of the work that follows is deeply influenced by feedback I've received from other members of this group. Here I would single out for special acknowledgment *at least* the following (in alphabetical order): Lucy Allais, Rosalind Chaplin, Andrew Chignell, Steve Engstrom, Stefanie Grüne, Matthias Haase, Dai Heide, Aaron James, Jim Kreines, Kathryn Lindeman, Barry Maguire, Colin Marshall, Samantha Mathrene, Colin McLear, Melissa Merritt, Sasha Newton, Tyke Nunez, Andrews Reath, Tobias Rosefeldt, Tim Rosenkoetter, Kieran Setiya, Houston Smit, Andrew Stephenson, Sergio Tenenbaum, Clinton Tolley, Eric Watkins, and Jack Woods.

But along the way, my work on these topics has also benefited greatly from many, many others, including *at least* the following: Uygar Abaci, Alp Aker, Karl Ameriks, Fatmea Amijee, Caroline Arruda, Yuval Avnur, Ralf Bader, Carla Bagnoli, David Barnett, Ian Belcher, John Bengson, Sven Bernecker, Selim Berker, Chris Benzenberg, Simon Blackburn, Jochen Bojanowski, Bob Brandom, Claudi Brink, Matt Boyle, Angela Breitenbach, Sarah Buss, Justin Clarke-Doane, Alix Cohen, Annalisa Coliva, Jim Conant, Jonathan Dancy, Stephen Darwall, Janelle DeWitt, Catharine Diehl, Sinan Dogramaci, Daniela Dover, Casey Doyle, Julia Driver, Max Edwards, Sonny Elizondo, David Enoch, Patricio Fernandez, Luca Ferraro, Jeremey Fix, Anton Ford, Christopher Frey, Jennifer Frey, Michael Friedman, Patrick Frierson, Kim Frost, Markus Gabriel, Aaron Garrett, Gabriele Gava, Samuel Gavin, Allan Gibbard, Margaret Gilbert, Laura Gillespie, Jonathan Gingerich, Hannah Ginsborg, Wolfram Gobusch, Chuck Goldhaber, Anil Gomes, Sean Greenberg, Alex Gregory, Alex Guerrero, Paul Guyer, Adrian Haddock, Reza Hadisi, Gary Hatfield, Jeremy Heis, Jeff Helmreich, Boris Hennig, Tim Henning, Allison Hills, Alex Hinshelwood, Ulf Hlobil, Thomas Hoffman, Des Hogan, Ulf Hölbel, David Horst, Thomas Hurka, David Hunter, Paul Hurley, Alexander Jackson, Anja Jauerning, Karen Jones, Patrick Kain, Paul Katsafanas, Antti Kauppinen, Andrea Kern, Thomas Khurana, Irad Kimhi, Sari Kisilevsky, Patricia Kitcher, Franz Knappik, Karen Koch, Christine Marion Korsgaard, Mathis Koschel, Robbie Kubala, Doug Lavin, Thomas Land, David Landy, Andre Lebrun, Ben Lennertz, Jessica Leech, Jed Lewinsohn, Eliza Little, Errol Lord, Rudolf Makkreel, Anna-Sara Malmgren, Susanne Mantel, Eric Marcus, Julia Markovits, Berislav Marušić, Michela Massimi, Erasmus Mayr, John McDowell, Jake McNulty, Tristram McPherson, Michaela McSweeney, Neil Mehta, James Messina, Eliot Michaelson, Joe Milburn, John Morrison, Beau Madison Mount, Evgenia Mylonaki, Michael Nelson, Ram Neta, Karin Nisenbaum, Rory O'Connell. Dawa Ometto, Onora O'Neill, Lara Ostaric, Michael Otsuka, Hille Paakkunainen, Japa Pallikkathayil, Sarah Paul, Carlotta Pavese, Christopher Peacocke, David Plunkett, Duncan Pritchard, Ian Proops, Hsueh Qu, Peter

Railton, Michael Rescorla, Mike Ridge, Nick Riggle, Arthur Ripstein, Sebastian Rödl, Michael Rohlf, Connie Rosati, Wendy Salkin, Jack Samuel, Joe Saunders, David Saurez, Geoff Sayre-McCord, Tim Scanlon, Tamar Schapiro, Mark Schroeder, Francois Schroeter, Laura Schroeter, Jeff Sebo, Janum Sethi, Lisa Shabel, James Shaw, Matthew Silverstein, Daniel J. Singer, Neil Sinhababu. Jamsheed Siyar, Will Small, Matthew Smith, Michael Smith, Declan Smithies, Curtis Sommerlatte, David Sosa, Robert Steel, Martin Sticker, Myriam Stihl, Thomas Sturm, Daniel Sutherland, Sigrún Svavarsdóttir, Kurt Sylvan, Kathryn Tabb, Larry Temkin, Peter Thielke, Michael Thompson, Evan Tiffany, Markus Valaris, Mark van Roojen, Kenny Walden, Anik Waldow, R. Jay Wallace, Owen Ware, Daniel Warren, Sebastian Watzl, Wayne Waxman, Jonathan Way, Ralph Wedgwood, Peter Wiersbinski, Eric Wiland, Marcus Willaschek, Vanessa Wills, Daniel Wodak, Allen Wood, Melissa Zinkin, and Ariel Zylberman.

This work has also benefited greatly from two manuscript workshops on it at UCSD and Toronto, organized by Eric Watkins and Nicholas Stang, respectively. I also received a great deal of incredibly insightful feedback on this material from the participants in the 10. Kant Kurs in Berlin, convened by Tobias Rosefeldt, although unfortunately that took place too late for me to take full advantage of that feedback here. Thanks are also due to audiences at Simon Fraser University, New York University, University of Pennsylvania, Harvard University, Boston University, Humboldt Universität zu Berlin, University of Miami, University of Wisconsin, Immanuel Kant Baltic Federal University, Southampton University, University of California, San Diego, University of California, Irvine, New York University: Abu Dhabi, University of Toronto, National University of Singapore, Erlangen Universität, Universität Leipzig, Iowa State University, Potsdam Universität, Oxford University, University of Edinburgh, St. Andrews University, University of Michigan, University of Pittsburgh, and Cambridge University. I also received helpful feedback on related work at the summer school in German philosophy at Bonn, the NAKS Pacific Study Group, the Eastern, Central, and Pacific APA, the Conference on Unity in German Philosophy in Mainz and Cologne, the online workshop on Kant's fundamental assumptions, an online conference on epistemic autonomy hosted by Sasha Mudd, the California Philosophy Workshop, the Conference on Agency and Rationality at University of Campinas (Brazil), the Midsummer Philosophy Workshop at Cambridge University, the Conference on Construction, Constitution, and Normativity in Berlin, the Workshop on Ethics and Practical Reasoning at Dartmouth University, and SPAWN (Normative Realism) at Syracuse University.

Parts of what follows was developed with the support of a Charles A. Ryskamp Research Fellowship from the ACLS/Mellon Foundation, an Alexander von Humboldt Research Fellowship, and a Lawrence S. Rockefeller Faculty Fellowship at the Princeton University Center for Human Values, as well as the institutions above.

Special thanks are due to Max Edwards, whose wonderful copy-editing and incisive philosophical comments have made what follows much less painful to read than it would otherwise be. Many thanks also to Peter Momtchiloff for his consistent support and sure and experienced editorship of this project, and to Henry Clarke for his hard work as production editor Thanks as well to Dolarine Sonia Fonceca for directing the copy-editing process.

Finally, I would like to thank my wife Maura Murnane for her quite profound support throughout this process. This book was completed during what were easily the most challenging, but also ultimately most rewarding, years of my life. Against that background, it is completely true that I wouldn't be here to complete this project if it wasn't for Maura's support. I owe literally everything to her, not least of all the image on the cover.

This book is dedicated to the memory of my mother, who would have gracefully (if regretfully) accepted my desire never to discuss it with her.

I would also like to thank the publishers of the following articles for permission to reprint material from them in what follows:

"Kant on Method," in *The Oxford Handbook of Kant*, ed. A Stephenson and A. Gomes. Oxford: Oxford University Press, forthcoming.

"Practical Cognition and Knowledge of Things-in-Themselves," in *Kantian Freedom*, ed. D. Heide and E. Tiffany. Oxford: Oxford University Press, forthcoming.

"Kant on Reason as the Capacity for Comprehension." *Australasian Journal of Philosophy*, forthcoming.

"Kant's Conception of Cognition and Our Knowledge of Things in Themselves," in *The Sensible and Intelligible Worlds*, ed. N. Stang and K. Schafer. Oxford: Oxford University Press, 2022.

"A System of Faculties: Additive or Transformative?" *European Journal of Philosophy* 29.4 (2021): 918–36.

"Transcendental Philosophy as Capacities-First Philosophy." *Philosophy and Phenomenological Research* 103.3 (2021): 661–86.

"A Kantian Virtue Epistemology: Rational Capacities and Transcendental Arguments." *Synthese* 198 (2021): 3113–36.

"The Scenic Route? On Errol Lord's *The Importance of Being Rational*." *Philosophy and Phenomenological Research* 100.2 (2020): 469–75.

"Kant: Constitutivism as Capacities-First Philosophy." *Philosophical Explorations* 22.2 (2019): 177–93.

"Constitutivism about Reasons: Autonomy and Understanding," in *The Many Moral Rationalisms*, ed. K. Jones and F. Schroeter. Oxford: Oxford University Press, 2018.

List of Abbreviations

Titles of works of Kant are abbreviated according to their German titles and in the style recommended by *Kant-Studien*. Except as noted otherwise, citations are to volume and page of the *Akademie Ausgabe* (AA):

Immanuel Kant, *Gesammelte Schriften*, ed.: Vols 1–22 *Preussische Akademie der Wissenschaften*, Vol. 23 Deutsche *Akademie der Wissenschaften zu Berlin*, from Vol. 24 *Akademie der Wissenschaften zu Göttingen*. Berlin: Reimer then De Gruyter, 1900–.

Unless noted otherwise, Kant is quoted according to the Cambridge translations of the works of Kant specified below. Where no translation is listed, the Cambridge series does not include one.

References to Hume and Hegel are similarly formatted as noted below.

Abbreviations of Kant's Works

A/B	*Kritik der reinen Vernunft*, A edition (AA 4), B edition (AA 3). *Critique of Pure Reason*. Trans. and ed. Paul Guyer and Allen Wood. Cambridge: Cambridge University Press, 1998.
Anth	*Anthropologie in pragmatischer Hinsicht* (AA 7). *Anthropology from a pragmatic point of view*. Trans. R. Louden. In *Anthropology, History, and Education*. Ed. G. Zöller and R. Louden. Cambridge: Cambridge University Press, 2007.
B	*Briefwechsel* (AA 10–13). *Correspondence*. Trans. and ed. A. Zweig. Cambridge: Cambridge University Press, 1999.
EEKU	*Erste Einleitung in die Kritik der Urteilskraft* (AA 20). *First Introduction to the Critique of the Power of Judgment*. In *Critique of the Power of Judgment*. Trans. and ed. P. Guyer and E. Matthews. Cambridge: Cambridge University Press, 2000.
GMS	*Grundlegung zur Metaphysik der Sitten* (AA 4). *Groundwork of the Metaphysics of Morals*. In *Practical Philosophy*. Trans. and ed. M. J. Gregor. Cambridge: Cambridge University Press, 1996.
HN	*Handschriftlicher Nachlass* (AA 14–23).
IAG	*Idee zu einer allgemeinen Geschichte in weltbürgerlicher Absicht* (AA 8). Translation in *Anthropology, History, and Education*.

LIST OF ABBREVIATIONS

Log
: *Jäsche Logik* (AA 9).
Jäsche Logic. In *Lectures on Logic.* Trans. and ed. J. M. Young. Cambridge: Cambridge University Press, 1992.

KpV
: *Kritik der praktischen Vernunft* (AA 5).
Critique of Practical Reason. In *Practical Philosophy.*

KU
: *Kritik der Urteilskraft* (AA 5).
Critique of the Power of Judgment. Trans. and ed. P. Guyer and E. Matthews. Cambridge: Cambridge University Press, 2000.

MAN
: *Metaphysische Anfangsgründe der Naturwissenschaften* (AA 4).
Metaphysical Foundations of Natural Science. In *Theoretical Philosophy after 1781.* Trans. and ed. H. Allison and P. Heath. Cambridge: Cambridge University Press, 2002.

MS
: *Die Metaphysik der Sitten* (AA 6).
The Metaphysics of Morals. In *Practical Philosophy.*

O
: *What Does It Mean to Orient Oneself in Thinking?* (AA 8).
In *Religion within the Boundaries of Mere Reason.* In *Religion and Rational Theology.* Trans. and ed. A. Wood and G. di Giovanni. Cambridge: Cambridge University Press, 1996.

OP
: *Opus Postumum* (AA 21–2).
Opus Postumum. Trans. and ed. E. Förster and M. Rosen. Cambridge: Cambridge University Press, 1993.

Prol
: *Prolegomena zu einer jeden künftigen Metaphysik* (AA 4).
Prolegomena to any Future Metaphysics. In *Theoretical Philosophy after 1781.*

Refl
: *Reflexionen* (AA 14–19).
Selections in *Notes and Fragments.* Trans. and ed. P. Guyer, C. Bowman, and F. Rauscher. Cambridge: Cambridge University Press, 2005.

RGV
: *Die Religion innerhalb der Grenzen der bloßen Vernunft* (AA 6).
Religion within the Boundaries of Mere Reason. In *Religion and Rational Theology.* Trans. and ed. A. Wood and G. di Giovanni. Cambridge: Cambridge University Press, 1996.

SF
: *Der Streit der Fakultäten* (AA 07).
The Conflict of the Faculties. In *Practical Philosophy.*

V-Anth/Collins
: *Vorlesungen Wintersemester* 1772/3 Collins (AA 25).
Translation in *Lectures on Anthropology.* Trans. and ed. A. Wood and R. Louden. Cambridge: Cambridge University Press, 2012.

V-Lo/Blomberg
: *Logik Blomberg* (AA 24).
Translation in *Lectures on Logic.*

V-Lo/Dohna
: *Logik Dohna-Wundlacken.*
Translation in *Lectures on Logic.*

V-Lo/Wiener
: *Wiener Logik.*
Translation in *Lectures on Logic.*

V-Met/Dohna
: *Metaphysik Dohna* (AA 28).
Selections translated in *Lectures on Metaphysics.* Trans. and ed. K. Ameriks and S. Naragon. Cambridge: Cambridge University Press, 1997.

V-Met/Herder   *Metaphysik Herder* (AA 28).
                Selections translated in *Lectures on Metaphysics*.
V-Met/Mron   *Metaphysik Mrongovius* (AA 29).
                Translation in *Lectures on Metaphysics*.
V-Phil-Th/Pölitz *Philosophische Religionslehre nach Pölitz* (AA 28).
                Lectures on Philosophical Doctrine of Religion. In *Religion and Rational Theology*.

Abbreviations of Hegel's Works

PR   *Grundlinien der Philosophie des Rechts.*
      Elements of the Philosophy of Right. Trans. and ed. A. Wood and H. Nisbet. Cambridge: Cambridge University Press, 1991.
PS   *Phänomenologie des Geistes.*
      The Phenomenology of Spirit. Trans. and ed. M. Baur and T. Pinkard. Cambridge: Cambridge University Press, 2018.

Abbreviations of Hume's Works

T   *A Treatise of Human Nature*. Ed. D. Norton and M. Norton. Oxford: Clarendon Press, 2007.

Introduction

The Unity of Reason in Kant and Today

> ...they rightly occasion the expectation of perhaps being able some day to attain insight into the unity of the whole pure rational faculty (theoretical as well as practical) and to derive everything from one principle—the undeniable need of human reason, which finds complete satisfaction only in a complete systematic unity of its cognitions.
> (KpV 5:91)

Kant's influence on contemporary debates about reason and rationality would be difficult to overstate, and there is surely no shortage of interpretative work on Kant's views about reason, rationality, and related topics, or of contemporary treatments of these topics in a broadly Kantian vein. One could thus be forgiven for wondering whether there is much left for Kant to teach us about these questions. But despite this vast literature, I believe that Kant's views about reason still have the capacity to surprise us, and to do so in philosophically productive ways. It seems to me that, in many ways, we still lack a systematic account of some of the most philosophically vital aspects of Kant's account of reason; indeed, some of the most compelling aspects of this account were not fully developed by Kant himself. So there remains much work to be done in understanding the philosophical significance of Kant's conception of reason in both a historical and a contemporary context.

In the chapters to follow, I hope to develop a reading of Kant's conception of reason, its unity, and its significance for his philosophy that helps to bring out some of these aspects of his account. In doing so, my focus will ultimately be on two topics. First, I will argue that Kant presents us with a powerful model for understanding the *unity* of theoretical and practical reason as two manifestations of a unified capacity for *understanding* (or what Kant calls "comprehension") of both a theoretical and practical sort. As we will see, thinking of reason in this "understanding-first" or "comprehension-first" manner allows us to do justice to the deep commonalities between theoretical and practical rationality, without reducing either to the other in the manner that many attempts to explain the "unity of reason" implicitly do. For example, by thinking of reason in these terms, we can see why the activities of *both* theoretical and practical reason are governed by a version of the *Principle of Sufficient Reason*, and that Kant's various formulations of the moral law are best understood as attempts to express this principle as it appears in the context of practical reason. But through approaching reason in this way, we can also see why we should be cautious about the use that (say) rationalist metaphysicians have made of this principle in attempting to construct a fully determinate conception of the fundamental nature of reality. Thus, by investigating these issues through the lens provided by the idea of reason as the faculty for comprehension, we can better understand *both* the robust principles for theoretical and practical thought that follow from the nature of reason *and* the limits that Kant's critical philosophy places on our use of these principles.

At the same time, and this will be my second main theme, I will argue that Kant also presents us with a compelling model of the role that reason (as a capacity or power) should play in developing a systematic approach to foundational questions in philosophy. In making this point, I will focus primarily on what is now called "metaethics"—that is, foundational questions about the normative domain. More precisely, I will argue that by thinking through Kant's meta-normative commitments, we can arrive at an account of the fundamental norms that apply to us as rational beings that treats as explanatorily fundamental, not a substantive conception of the *objective reasons and values* that exist "out there" in the world, nor a *merely structural or formal* conception of the "requirements of rationality", but instead a robust conception of reason as a power or capacity—namely, reason as the capacity for understanding (both theoretical and practical).

I believe that this sort of "reason-first" or "understanding-first" perspective on the normative domain in many ways represents the most important legacy of Kant's philosophy in metaethics, a legacy that contemporary forms of constructivism, expressivism, *and* constitutivism all draw from, albeit in different ways.[1] While I have discussed Kant's relationship to expressivism and constructivism elsewhere, in my discussion here I will focus mainly on Kant's relationship to constitutivism, arguing that Kant defends a form of what we might call "reason-first constitutivism" or "rational constitutivism" about the fundamental norms that apply to us.[2]

As I will explain, I believe that this form of constitutivism more elegantly expresses Kant's core philosophical commitments in this area than do the forms of agency-first constitutivism that have dominated the contemporary debate. But the resulting "reason-first" approach to meta-normative questions may also be contrasted with the contemporary vogue for forms of "reason*s* fundamentalism"—that is, for views that take the notion of a reason *qua* (roughly)

---

[1] For more discussion of these connections, see (Schafer 2014a, 2015b, 2015c, 2018b).
[2] Compare the defense of a "dialectic-first" approach to the first *Critique* in (Kreines 2022).

a "consideration that counts in favor" as foundational for normative philosophy.[3] In this way, the conception of reason and its place in philosophy I will be defending represents a return to a more traditional view of these questions, one that seems to me less mysterious from a metaphysical and an epistemological perspective than contemporary forms of "reasons fundamentalism." In doing so, one of my aims will be to vindicate Kant's insistence that his philosophy is nothing more or less than the effort to bring reason's implicit self-understanding to explicit and systematic self-consciousness—the idea, that is, that Kant's form of "constitutivism" simply represents the normative self-consciousness of reason, as the power for understanding, in a philosophical form.

If this is right, then Kant's conception of reason challenges contemporary philosophical orthodoxy along several dimensions. First, in developing a systematic picture of the normative domain, it treats as fundamental, not *reasons* or *values* or *rationality* or (say) *fittingness*, but rather *reason* as a certain sort of *cognitive power*. Second, unlike more familiar sorts of constitutivism in the philosophy of action, in doing so it treats as fundamental, not our *distinctively practical* powers as *agents*, but rather reason as the power for understanding of *both* a theoretical *and* a practical sort. And third, it characterizes the nature of this capacity or power, not in the "knowledge-first" terms that have come to dominate contemporary analytic epistemology, but rather in terms of the aim of *understanding* or *making sense of* things, both theoretically and practically. In motivating these claims, I hope to develop a reading of Kant's philosophy on which that philosophy is centered around reason as a *self-organizing power for understanding*, both theoretical and practical.

a. The "Unity of Reason" in Kant

In all these ways and more, it seems to me that Kant's account of these issues still has much to teach us. But while I hope that these comments give the reader a taste of some of what I take the contemporary payoffs of my discussion to be, my focus here will not generally be on the contemporary debate. Rather, in what follows, I will generally foreground interpretative questions about how we should understand Kant's explicit and (sometimes) implicit views. In considering these questions, I will often use the philosophical payoffs of Kant's views in a contemporary context to help illustrate my reading of Kant, but I make no claim to fully develop

---

[3] See (Parfit 2011; Scanlon 2014; Kiesewetter 2017; Lord 2018; Schroeder 2021). For some critical discussion of such views, see (Schafer 2018a, 2020). Another interesting point of comparison here are views that focus on "reason" as mass noun in the sense discussed in (Fogal 2016), which provide an alternative way to think about the idea of "respecting reason" I discuss below (p. 196).

these payoffs in a systematic manner here. That is a task that I must leave for another time.

More precisely, in what follows, my focus will be Kant's conception of the unity of reason and the role that this conception plays in giving structure to his philosophical project. Unfortunately, as is so often true with Kant, merely to utter the phrase "the unity of reason in Kant" is to invite confusion. For there are, in fact, a variety of issues in Kant's philosophy that might reasonably be taken to be the proper referent of this phrase, including questions about the unity of reason as a capacity, the unity of our various rational capacities more broadly, the relationship between the sensible and intelligible worlds, and the unity of philosophy itself.

As I've already indicated, in inquiring into the "unity of reason", my focus will be on reason as a *unified capacity* or *power* or *faculty*.[4] But questions about the unity of reason in this sense can be further broken down into at least two subquestions, for Kant uses "reason" both in a narrow and a broad sense. In its narrow sense, the term refers only to the faculty of reason *in particular*, whereas in its broad one it refers to the whole system of all our "higher" intellectual faculties, including (at least) reason, the understanding, and the power of judgment.

When read in the first, narrower fashion, to ask about the "unity of reason" is to inquire into what explains the unity of reason as one rational capacity among others. Here, the most pressing question with respect to reason's unity relates to the unity of reason as a capacity *across the theoretical and practical divide*. For, as Kant often stresses, the idea that a single capacity of reason is responsible for both theoretical and practical reasoning is fundamental to the critical project:

> I require that the critique of a pure practical reason, if it is to be carried through completely, be able at the same time to present the unity of practical with speculative reason in a common principle, since *there can, in the end, be only one and the same reason, which must be distinguished merely in its application.*
> (GMS 4:391)

But even if we focus on reason in the first, narrower sense, this is hardly the only question about the unity of reason that arises in a Kantian context. For on both the theoretical and practical sides of this divide, Kant provides a variety of different characterizations of the nature of reason as capacity, both in terms of its characteristic aim or function and in terms of its characteristic principle. The most famous instance of *this* dimension of the "unity of reason" involves the

[4] Kant uses a variety of terms to refer to mental capacities or faculties, including *Vermögen*, *Fähigkeit* (generally translated as "capacity" or "ability" and indicating a broader class of abilities than *Vermögen*), and *Kraft*. There is considerable scholarly debate about the exact relationship between these terms, but in what follows I will generally use "capacity", "power", and "faculty" interchangeably to refer to what Kant refers to by "*Vermögen*".

relationship between Kant's various formulations of the supreme principle of practical reason or the moral law. But, as we will see, this is hardly the only case in which Kant's claims about theoretical and practical reason challenge us to explain exactly how reason can be unified in the manner that Kant claims it is. Thus, even in this narrower sense, the status of the "unity of reason" is anything but unproblematic.

For much of what follows, it is the unity of reason in this first sense that will be my explicit focus. But it is important to stress that this issue is closely connected with questions about the "unity of reason" in the second, broader sense. After all, with respect to this second use of "reason", we can also inquire about the "unity of reason", not with an eye towards the unity of reason as a particular rational capacity, but instead with an eye towards the sense in which *all* our rational capacities, taken together, form a unified system. For example, on Kant's account, theoretical rationality involves essential contributions from the understanding (*Verstand*), the power of judgment (*Urteilskraft*), and (in some form) sensibility, in addition to reason proper (*Vernunft*). And much the same is also true of practical rationality. Thus, much as we can investigate the unity of reason as a particular faculty, we can also inquire about what unifies these various rational capacities. And this too can be referred to as a question about the "unity of reason" if we use "reason" in the second, broader sense of this term.

As will become clear in what follows, I believe these two questions are tightly connected. For in the end, what gives unity to the whole system of our rational capacities—i.e. reason in the broad sense—can only be the highest (and most autonomous) of these capacities—namely, reason in the narrow sense. In other words, to grasp the unity of all our various rational capacities, we must understand these capacities as forming a *teleological system* that is organized around the ends that are distinctive of reason in the narrow sense. For Kant, the full system of rational capacities (or "reason" in the broad sense) acquires its unity precisely through being the way creatures like us realize the distinctive aims of "reason" in the narrow sense as the highest of these capacities.[5] As this indicates, in order to understand the "unity of reason" in the second, broad sense, we must begin with an understanding of "reason's unity" in the first, narrow sense. To avoid confusion on this point, in what follows I'll generally reserve the term "reason" for the faculty of reason in the narrower sense and use "rational faculties" or "rational capacities" to refer to the broader system of rational faculties.

Unfortunately, this hardly exhausts the potential ambiguities here, for there is also a third, closely related, sense in which the "unity of reason" might be taken to pick out a topic of interest to Kant. This relates to the characteristically Kantian idea that the distinctive *aim or function* of reason is (at least in part) to *bring*

---

[5] See (Schafer 2022a).

systematic unity to our (theoretical and practical) cognitions.[6] Not surprisingly, this will be a central component of Kant's account of the unity of reason as a faculty. For, as we will see, it precisely reason's distinctive interest in systematic understanding (or "comprehension") that makes systematic unity in cognition so important for it. And it is in the service of this sort of systematic unity that reason organizes its own activities, and those of our other cognitive faculties, into a teleological system like the one just described. But this, of course, raises further questions about Kant's account. For example, it is only natural to ask what explains or justifies reason's special interest in this "project of unification"; or to wonder, with many of Kant's critics, whether Kant's tight association of reason with systematic unity might be better regarded as the expression of a sort of extreme intellectual neuroticism.[7]

As we will see, many of the most pressing objections to Kant's philosophy relate in some way to this question. And it, in turn, gives rise to a fourth sense in which the "unity of reason" is an issue of interest to Kant. It is this fourth sense of the "unity of reason" that Kant most often uses *Vernunfteinheit* to refer to in his critical works—namely, the "unity of reason" as that unity which reason seeks to discover and/or produce as a result of its unifying activity:

> If the understanding may be a faculty of unity of appearances by means of rules, then reason is the faculty of the unity of the rules of understanding under principles. Thus it never applies directly to experience to any object, but instead applies to the understanding, in order to give unity *a priori* through concepts to the understanding's manifold cognitions, which may be called the 'unity of reason'.... (A302/B358)[8]

Not surprisingly, this unity can also be either theoretical in character—a unity that characterizes the domain of nature under causal laws; or it can be practical—that is, a unity that characterizes the domain of freedom under the principles of autonomy; or, most importantly, it can refer to a unity that encompasses both these domains—that is, a unity of nature *and* freedom in a single system of principles.

---

[6] Compare: "Under the government of reason our cognitions cannot at all constitute a rhapsody but must constitute a system, in which alone they can support and advance its essential ends. I understand by a system, however, the unity of the manifold cognitions under one idea. This is the rational concept of the form of a whole, insofar as through this the domain of the manifold as well as the position of the parts with respect to each other is determined a priori" (A832–3/B860–1). For some of the extensive discussion of the relationship between reason and "systematic unity", see (Guyer 1987, 2000, 2005, 2006; Neiman 1994; Rauscher 2010; Willaschek 2018; Proops 2021).

[7] For a famous expression of this concern, see (Adorno and Horkheimer 1997).

[8] See also: "The unity of reason is therefore not the unity of a possible experience, but is essentially different from that, which is the unity of understanding" (A306/B363).

It is this dimension of the "unity of reason" that seemed most problematic to many of Kant's immediate successors. But, in the context of Kant's Copernican Turn in philosophy, it is important to stress that this unity is best thought of as the "objective face" of the unity of reason as a capacity (in the first and second senses just noted). More precisely, as we will see, in the context of Kant's critical philosophy, there is a systematic relationship between (i) the unity of the cognitive subject, (ii) the unity of the objects which that subject cognizes, and (iii) the unity of the forms of cognition that relate that subject to these objects. Thus, as we will see, any faculty for (theoretical or practical) cognition can, for Kant, be (at least partially) characterized in terms of *each* of these three aspects of the cognitive unity that it seeks. For example, while we can characterize reason's interest in systematic unity through characterizing the sort of unity it seeks to achieve with respect to a *subject's* cognitions or representations, we can also characterize its interest in systematic unity by focusing on what the *objects* of such unified cognition would necessarily be like. Or we can characterize it by focusing on the nature of the *relationship* between subject and object that it thereby seeks to establish. Given the relationship between these levels of explanation, the question of the "unity of reason" in this fourth sense can be understood as the objective face of the questions about the unity of reason as capacity raised above (p. 5–6). Thus, by better understanding the unity of reason as a capacity, we can also make progress in understanding Kant's prospects for developing a systematic account of the "unity of reason" in this fourth sense.

Finally, there is a fifth aspect of the "unity of reason" that will also be important for the discussion to follow. This dimension of the "unity question" involves the relationship between the unity of reason and the unity of philosophy itself as a systematic body of cognition (a science or *Wissenschaft*). Since we will begin with this question in the next chapter, I will postpone further discussion of it until then. But plainly it is closely related to the "unity of reason" in the fourth sense, for a genuinely systematic philosophy will only be possible, for Kant, insofar we can achieve a unified account of both nature and freedom within a single system.

b. Explaining the Unity of Reason—Primacy and Unity

As this should indicate, all these various dimensions of the "unity of reason" are closely connected. Nonetheless, my focus here will be on the unity of reason as a capacity, both across the theoretical and practical divide *and* on either side of this divide. This, of course, is a topic that has received considerable attention over the entire reception of Kant's philosophy. Indeed, it has been said that the fundamental complaint of the German Idealists about Kant's philosophy was precisely that:

> ... Kant lacks a common principle for the theoretical and practical uses of reason that is such that it allows [him] to bring theoretical philosophy (the domain of the theoretical use of reason) and practical philosophy (the domain of the practical use of reason) into a connection that is accounted for by reason's command to achieve systematic unity. (Horstmann 2012, 67)

To orient ourselves, it will be useful to begin by briefly discussing some of the main interpretative options with respect to this question, with an eye towards situating the account to follow. To do so, let's begin with a few points that are relatively uncontroversial. First, it is uncontroversial that there is some sense in which Kant takes the capacity of reason to be "unified" across the theoretical and practical divide. At the same time, it is also clear that Kant struggled throughout the critical period to develop a fully satisfying account of this "unity". Particularly important in this regard is Kant's view that there is some sense in which practical reason takes "primacy" over theoretical reason. For example, as Kant writes, although reason is fundamentally unified, it is also true that, "in the union of pure speculative with pure practical reason in one cognition, the latter has primacy, assuming that this union is not *contingent* and discretionary but based a priori on reason itself and therefore *necessary*" (KpV 5:121).

As this indicates, there are at least *two* questions to consider with respect to the relationship between the theoretical and practical reason in Kant—namely, (i) the sense in which they form a *unity* and (ii) the sense in which one takes *primacy* over the other. It is useful to consider these two issues in conjunction with one another because many of the most prominent accounts of the unity of theoretical and practical reason, both with respect to Kant and more generally, attempt to *explain* the sense in which reason is "unified" by appealing to an explanation of how either theoretical or practical reason takes "primacy" over the other. We might call such accounts "primacy-first" accounts of the unity of reason since they begin with a picture of how one of reason's manifestations is prior to the other, and then use *this* to explain the sense in which reason is nevertheless unified. The most obvious way of spelling out a primacy-first account is *via* a reduction of one of reason's manifestations to a special instance of the other, but there are other less reductive forms such an explanation might take. What is common to all such views is that they attempt to explain the unity of theoretical and practical reason by explaining one of the manifestations of reason in terms of a more fundamental understanding of the other. Thus, such accounts attempt to explain the unity of reason by assigning a deep and systematic priority to either reason in its theoretical or its practical form.

This general strategy should be familiar, both from the contemporary debate about these issues and from recent scholarship on Kant. For example, consider cognitivists about intention. Such views, which attempt to reduce intentions to a special class of theoretical beliefs, can be seen as attempting to reduce (at least some forms of) practical rationality to a special form of theoretical rationality.[9] This strategy can be seen, for example, in Velleman's account of practical rationality in terms of a special form of self-realizing psychological self-understanding, or in Setiya's attempts to derive the principles of instrumental rationality from a cognitivist conception of intention.[10] But it can also be seen in extreme forms of Platonism on which our grasp of facts about (say) the good is simply one form of theoretical knowledge about the world—that is, a form of knowledge that is distinguished from other forms of theoretical knowledge only by the special character of the facts that are thereby known.[11]

As we will see, this way of approaching these questions is not completely absent from the literature on Kant. For one way to understand Kant's focus on reason as a *cognitive* faculty (in both its theoretical and practical manifestations) is to see him as treating practical reason as, in some sense, a special case of theoretical reason.[12] But Kant's explicit commitment to the "primacy of practical reason" has made it much more natural to develop a primacy-first approach to Kant by treating theoretical reason, at least in certain respects, as a special manifestation of practical reason.

The most natural way of developing this idea is to focus on the idea that theoretical reasoning and inquiry are themselves activities we can intentionally engage in with various aims in mind. The general thought is then that we can treat the requirements of theoretical rationality as the result of applying the general principles of practical rationality to the special case of theoretical reasoning and inquiry. In the contemporary literature, such views are most often associated with the various forms of instrumentalism about theoretical rationality or perhaps with the recent wave of interest in various forms of "expected epistemic utility".[13] But this sort of instrumentalism has little plausibility in a Kantian context. Rather, in the Kant literature, the central idea behind such accounts has generally been

---

[9] To be clear, not all forms of "cognitivism" about intention should be viewed in this light. But insofar as a view reduces rationality of intentions to the rationality of *theoretical beliefs*, I think such descriptions are apt.

[10] (Velleman 2000, 2009; Setiya 2007).

[11] For contemporary defenses of something like this form of realism, see (Shafer-Landau 2003; Enoch 2013; Larmore 2021; Bengson et al forthcoming). Such views are often associated with the influence of (Murdoch 1970).

[12] Something like this view might be associated with (Engstrom 2009), but that would (I think) involve a misinterpretation of his views, although some of those influenced by Engstrom may go further in this direction than Engstrom himself. Similarly, consider (Merritt 2018)'s claim that, "moral virtue is a specification of general cognitive virtue, and that general cognitive virtue is nothing other than the notion of healthy understanding" (8–9). Now, I think there is a sense in which what Merritt here says is quite right, but, as we will discuss below, I don't think her precise way of developing this idea fully captures the sense in which Kant does treat practical reason as having "primacy" over theoretical reason. For a clearer example of this tendency, see (Elizondo 2013), which goes further in this direction.

[13] See (Kelly 2003) for an important critical discussion of such views; see (Rinard 2017) for a prominent recent defense of them; see (Worsnip forthcoming) for further discussion.

that the requirements of theoretical reason can be derived from the supreme principle of practical reason—namely, some form of the categorical imperative.

The *locus classicus* for this reading is O'Neill's ground-breaking account of how the categorical imperative applies to theoretical reasoning.[14] In her discussion, O'Neill argues that for Kant, reason's proper functioning in both the practical and the theoretical cases is fundamentally a matter *not* of a special sort of cognition but rather of a particular sort of autonomous activity. Particularly important in this regard, for O'Neill's Kant, are the activities of communication, argument, and negotiation that occur between different rational individuals, activities that aim at securing the free agreement of all parties. Thus, for O'Neill, not only is Kant's conception of reason fundamentally *practical* as opposed to cognitive at its core, it is also *social and political* throughout. Indeed, this is *so* true for O'Neill that, according to her, Kant's conception of reason establishes "nothing... about principles of cognitive order for solitary beings."[15]

As we will see, I am sympathetic to a version of the idea that reason is, for Kant, essentially intersubjective in some sense. But I am skeptical of the quasi-Habermasian way O'Neill understands such claims. In any case, what is important for present purposes is less O'Neill's particular proposal than her general strategy: O'Neill begins with a certain conception of the nature of practical reasoning and then attempts to account for theoretical reasoning in terms of this more fundamental conception of reason as practical *rather than* theoretical. On this point, many other Kant scholars are in fundamental agreement with O'Neill. For example, in her classic study *The Unity of Reason*, Neiman argues that Kant secures the unity of reason by overturning a fundamentally cognitive conception of reason and *replacing* this with a practical conception of the same.[16] Thus, for Neiman's Kant, "Reason's nature is thoroughly practical; its problems cannot be secured by attaining knowledge."[17] And although things are more complex in this case, there are also significant elements of this approach within Korsgaard's hugely influential

---

[14] See (O'Neill 1989). For more recent developments of this line of interpretation, see (Cohen 2013, 2014) and (Mudd 2016, 2017). Mudd is especially clear on the interpretative point here, stating that, on her reading, "reason is a 'unity' because all our reasoning, including our theoretical reasoning, functions practically" (1).

[15] (O'Neill 1989, 27). Compare (Habermas 1981). Such claims capture something very important about Kant's conception of reason—namely, that this conception of reason is essentially intersubjective in *some* sense. But they secure this result only by presenting a misleading and rather one-sided reading of it. For while a conception of "communicative reason" does *follow* from Kant's understanding of reason, it does not provide us with the most fundamental characterization of reason as Kant understands it. Rather, for Kant, the rational significance of communication is something that is explained by deeper features of reason, such as the connection between what Kant calls "comprehension" (roughly speaking, understanding) and intersubjectivity. Thus, while O'Neill is right to stress that Kant's conception of reason constrains the forms rational communication and negotiation can take, and while they are also correct to think that reason's abstract demands can often only be *made determinate* through an actual process of communication and political negotiation between real agents in the world, they are wrong to think that the idea of such communication is what drives Kant's account of reason or serves as its foundation.

[16] (Neiman 1994, 7).   [17] (Neiman 1994, 7).

treatment of Kant on the "sources of normativity",[18] for Korsgaard's account of those sources takes them to be rooted in our nature as *agents*. Thus, albeit in a somewhat different fashion than O'Neill and Neiman, Korsgaard's account of the nature of reasons and rationality also tends to privilege practical rationality or agency over theoretical rationality in its attempt to reconstruct Kant's views.[19]

As we will see, there are many genuine insights in all these interpretations.[20] But contrary to them all, I believe that we cannot do justice to Kant's views by adopting any view on which the "primacy of practical reason" is prior to the "unity" of theoretical and practical reason as two manifestations of a single capacity.[21] Indeed, it seems to me that Kant's account functions in exactly the opposite fashion: For Kant, I will argue, it is only possible to understand the sense in which practical reason has primacy over theoretical reason by drawing on a prior, and more fundamental, understanding of the unity of theoretical and practical reason. Instead of a view that treats either theoretical or practical reason as more fundamental than the other, I believe that we can only do justice to Kant's views by developing a view of reason on which the unity of reason as a capacity is truly fundamental. Indeed, I believe that one of the main philosophical attractions of Kant's philosophy is precisely that it presents us with a powerful model for developing this sort of "unity-first" account of the relationship between theoretical and practical reason—an account, that is, that allows us to understand this unity without giving systematic priority to either form of reason over the other.

c. The Primacy of the Practical and Reason's Ends and Interests

In this way, all of the views discussed above, their many insights notwithstanding, seem to me to mischaracterize Kant's attempt to revolutionize how we think about reason. For the point of this revolution is not to *replace* a fundamentally cognitive model of reason *with* a practical one; rather, it is to show us that these two models, once properly understood, are not just compatible but *mutually*

---

[18] (Korsgaard 1996a, 2008, 2009).
[19] For some concerns about this approach, see (James 2007) and (Schafer 2018b, 2019a, 2019b). I think similar concerns arise with respect to Michael Smith's less explicitly Kantian form of constitutivism as well. See (Smith 2012, 2015, 2017).
[20] Also worth mentioning here are (K. L. Sylvan 2020), which begins to develop a Kantian epistemology that is founded on the value of respect for the truth. I think this is a much more promising way of extending Kant's treatment of practical reason to the theoretical domain, and will return to it below, but I think it does distort Kant's own views to some degree insofar as it treats something other than reason (or rational nature) as the fundamental object of respect in both the theoretical and practical spheres.
[21] This is also stressed by (Guyer 2019). For further discussion see (Guyer 1987; Wood 1999; Gardner 2007; Timmermann 2010; Piper 2012, 2013; Mudd 2016).

entailing.²² In other words, to understand Kant's conception of the unity of reason, we must first grasp that he aims to explain reason's unity, not by privileging one of these models of reason over the other, but by showing how they naturally converge on a single model of reason as *both cognitive and practical to its core*.

If this is right, then to understand Kant's account of the unity of reason, we must look beyond the idea that, as Neiman says, "it is practical reason which replaces speculative reason," in order to grasp the deeper unity behind both reason's speculative and practical manifestations.²³ On a purely textual level, the basis for this reading of Kant seems to me strong. For example, while Kant does insist that practical reason has "primacy" over theoretical reason, in doing so, he makes clear that this "primacy" involves "the prerogative of the interest of one [practical reason] insofar as the interest of the others [e.g. theoretical reason] is subordinated to it." Thus, the central claim of Kant's priority thesis relates specifically to the relationship between the *interests* of practical reason and the *interests* of theoretical reason: The thesis holds that the *interests* of practical reason must take priority over the *interests* of theoretical reason. And when we go on in this passage, we find that Kant explicitly commits himself to the view that it is the underlying unity of reason as a faculty that *explains* why practical reason's interests have primacy in this way. For he emphasizes that the primacy of the interests of practical reason rests on the fact that "it is still only one and the same reason which, whether from a theoretical or a practical perspective, judges according to a priori principles" (KpV 5:121). Thus, for Kant, it would be a mistake to take the primacy of practical reason to be what *explains* reason's unity; rather, he is quite explicit that the relationship between these ideas is the opposite.²⁴ It is the idea of theoretical and practical reason as two expressions of the single capacity that *explains* why practical reason takes "primacy" over theoretical reason.

To begin to understand why this is true, it will be helpful to pause here to briefly discuss how Kant conceives of the sort of internal teleology that is characteristic of rational capacities like reason. In considering this, it is important to stress that

---

[22] This idea has been stressed by (Engstrom 2002, 2009), although he does not develop it in the manner I do. For other versions of this idea, see (Kern 2006; Reath 2010, 2013; Rödl 2010; Merritt 2018). Of course, the idea of reason as both cognitive and practical is not unique to Kant. Rather, it extends through much of the vaguely Aristotelian tradition. But I think it is fair to say that (for Kant at least) none of these figures do full justice to both sides of reason. For example, someone like Aquinas would, by Kant's lights, have failed to fully capture the practical dimension of reason precisely insofar as he failed to develop a conception of reason as truly autonomous. Still, it is fair to note that Kant's revolution on these points—like at all revolutions—to some degree involves an attempt to recover a tradition for thinking about reason that had (at the time Kant was writing) fallen into disrepute.

[23] (Neiman 1994, 4).

[24] On this point, I agree with (Timmermann 2010) when he writes that, "the legitimacy of practical reason's filling in the gaps left open by theoretical reason is philosophically respectable only because there is only one faculty of reason" (195).

throughout the critical period Kant is consistent in describing the activities of such capacities in teleological terms, speaking, for example, of the "ends" and "interests" they possess. Indeed, as we will see, a teleological conception of our cognitive powers is implicit in Kant's basic conception of cognition itself, which sees cognition (and so our cognitive capacities) as striving to perfect their relationship with their objects. In keeping with this, Kant's conception of reason is always the conception of a certain sort of self-organizing cognitive power. The concept of such a power does not first appear in his philosophy with the third *Critique*; rather, the project of the third *Critique* is to extend Kant's prior understanding of the internal teleology of rational powers so that teleological concepts can *also* be used to think (in some sense) about things in nature. It would thus be a mistake to imagine that teleological concepts first enter into Kant's philosophy with the discussion of (say) natural teleology in the third *Critique*. Kant's conception of reason is deeply teleological from the start.[25]

But why does Kant associate "ends" or "interests" with faculties such as reason in the manner he does? And why does this association give rise to a "primacy of practical reason" with respect to those interests? A full answer to these questions will have to wait until Chapter 4, but we can begin to introduce some of the important aspects of Kant's answer to them by briefly considering Kant's official definitions of "end" and "interests". The first of these reads as follows:

[An end is] the concept of an object insofar as it at the same time contains the ground of the reality of this object.   (KU 5:180, compare MM 6:381)[26]

In passages like this one, Kant provides an abstract definition of an "end". So defined, an end is just the concept (or representation) of an object insofar as that representation is a potential ground of the existence of what it represents. As this makes clear, Kant's conception of what an end is ties this notion closely together with the sort of "practical representations" that function to bring into existence what they represent. We'll return to this notion of "practical representation" in Chapter 2. But for the moment the most important implication of this definition is the following: For Kant, to literally ascribe an end to some system or faculty is to think of that system or faculty as *governed by a representation of that end*, a representation that functions as a potential *ground* of what it represents.

Sometimes these governing representations (of a system's ends) will be external to the system in question—as is true, according to Kant, with artifacts, whose ends

---

[25] For the important of this point, see Longuenesse's foundational work on these topics, to which I will return below, and in particular (Longuenesse 1998, 2005).

[26] See also Kant's definition of a "purpose" in the third *Critique*: "in so far as the concept of an object also contains the ground for the object's actuality, the concept is called the thing's *purpose* and a thing's conformity with that character of things which is possible only through purposes is called the *purposiveness* of its form" (KU 5:180).

are fixed by the intentions of those who make or use them. But this is not the case with reason and its ends. Rather, like the ends of living things, the ends of our rational capacities are internal to those capacities. Rational powers like reason are thus characterized for Kant by a certain sort of *self-organizing cognitive activity*, a cognitive activity through which they strive to realize themselves by bringing form or structure to the "matter" that they operate upon. Indeed, as we will see, the ends of such faculties are internal to them in a much *stronger* sense than anything that is true of non-rational animals, at least according to Kant. For in the case of our rational faculties, a faculty has the ends it does precisely because its activities are governed by a representation of those ends *which is itself internal to that very faculty*.[27] In ascribing such ends to our rational faculties, Kant is treating the activities of these faculties as governed by a representation of those very ends, and he is treating these governing representations as internal to the faculties themselves. Thus, the idea of such faculties as having such ends is closely connected, for Kant, with the idea of them as guided by some sort of (implicit or explicit) *awareness or representation of these very ends*.[28] It is this, as we will see, that explains the tight connection that Kant sees between, on the one hand, the self-organizing activities characteristic of rationality and, on the other, the self-conscious or "apperceptive" character of rational thought and action.

Naturally enough, Kant's definition of "interests" builds upon his conception of an "end" by (effectively) adding a further element to it:

> The satisfaction that we combine with the representation of the existence of an object is called interest. Hence such a satisfaction always has at the same time a relation to the faculty of desire, either as its determining ground or else as necessarily interconnected with its determining ground. (KU 5:204)

According to this definition, to speak of someone or something as "interested" in something is to speak of them as *taking satisfaction in its existence*. Such "satisfaction" can be either intellectual or sensible for Kant.[29] But Kant generally reserves talk of "interests" for creatures who are finite and so subject to *needs*:

---

[27] Once again, in the third *Critique*, Kant *extends* this account of the concept of an end to allow for an "analogical" use of this concept in cognizing living things in nature. But even there, Kant continues to maintain that *insofar* as we treat natural things as governed by certain ends, we treat them as governed by some representation of those ends. This connection remains in force even when we make a merely analogical or regulative use of such ascriptions.

[28] Of course, the precise nature of this awareness is the subject of much debate. But lest this seem too arcane, note that some version of this idea is fundamental to even behavioristic attempts to rehabilitate the notion of teleology. See, for example, (Rosenblueth, Wiener, and Bigelow 1943, 19): "All purposeful behavior may be considered to require negative feedback. If a goal is to be attained, some signals from the goal are necessary at some time to direct the behavior."

[29] For example, Kant speaks of God taking satisfaction in his own works (V-Phil-Th/Pölitz 28:1065). But whatever satisfaction God is capable of cannot be a matter of sensible feelings or the like since God is free of the forms of sensibility or receptivity associated with such feelings.

"All interest presupposes a need [end] or produces one" (KU 5:210). As a result, the kind of satisfaction that Kant associates with *having interests* requires the possibility of a *need* that one would have an "interest" in fulfilling. So, for example, although Kant is willing to speak of God as taking "satisfaction" in creation, he generally avoids speaking of God as having "interests". Rather, for Kant, talk of "interests" is really only appropriate with respect to finite or "needy" creatures— creatures who take satisfaction in achieving their ends, without having any guarantee that this will occur.

For this reason, talk of interests (as opposed to ends) is appropriate for Kant only with respect to creatures that are *both* rational *and* sensibly conditioned. And when such creatures are moved to action by the ends they have set, this motivation must "appear" on the level of sensible feeling in their empirical psychology in some way. In other words, in order to make a difference to such a subject's "motivational set" on the empirical level, even purely intellectual sources of motivation—like the moral law—must make a difference to how that subject *feels* on the level of empirical psychology.[30] For this reason, even purely intellectual representations like our representation of the moral law can move a sensibly conditioned creature to action only insofar as they are accompanied by some *feeling* of pleasure or displeasure.

Thus, when Kant attributes an "interest" to our faculties, he means to characterize these faculties as having certain ends but also to stress that these ends are associated with corresponding feelings of pleasure and displeasure.[31] It is this package of the faculty's end, the satisfaction grounded in it, and the corresponding feelings of pleasure and displeasure, that constitutes the "interest" of a faculty for Kant. Kant's talk of a faculty's "interest" refers to the way in which a faculty's "ends" necessarily manifest themselves in finite, sensibly conditioned creatures like us.[32]

As we will see, it is this that explains why Kant insists so strongly that "all interest is ultimately practical" and that (as a result) the interest "even...of speculative reason is only conditional and is complete in practical use alone" (KpV 5:121). This is true, in essence, because in attributing ends and interests to our power of reason, we are also attributing those ends and interests to ourselves;

---

[30] It is for this reason, among others, that Kant insists that the moral law can only be motivationally efficacious for creatures like us insofar as it is a potential ground of moral feelings such as the feeling of respect. For more discussion of these sorts of "rational feelings" in Kant, see (Wood 2007; DeWitt 2014; Cohen 2020).

[31] Passages like A797/B825, where Kant speaks of the striving of reason as "grounded in" its various interests, might suggest a view on which these interests are "pathological". But Kant's discussion of the activities of pure practical reason makes it clear that many of these interests are not always "pathological" in this sense.

[32] As this indicates, if one finds it more natural to translate Kant's ascriptions of ends and interests to reason as a capacity into ascriptions of those ends and interests to the *rational individuals who possess this capacity*, that will generally not cause too many problems. *But*, as I discuss in the next chapter, there are principled reasons for Kant to focus on faculties and capacities in the manner he does.

and so, in doing so, we are making judgments that fall under the governance of practical reason as the ultimate court of appeals for all questions concerning our ultimate ends.[33] More precisely, while Kant believes that all of our faculties (both theoretical and practical) have ends and interests in this sense, he also takes *our understanding* of such ends to rest on our familiarity with representations that have a practical or productive relationship to their objects. And the canonical instance of such representations for us are the "practical representations" (maxims or choices) that characterize of our will (*Wille*) and our power of choice (*Willkür*)—representations whose function is to relate to their objects by making those objects actual. For this reason, according to Kant, our concept of an end (and by extension the concept of an interest) is rooted in our ability to form such "practical representations", and so, ultimately, in our power of practical reason.[34]

Since we are drawing on the capacity for practical representation whenever we represent a faculty in terms of its ends, the nature of even our theoretical faculties is something that can only be fully appreciated by drawing on conceptual resources that are provided to us by practical reason. For it is only by drawing on representations (like the concept of an end) that we possess in virtue of our power of practical reason that we can represent *any* faculty in teleological terms. A full grasp of the nature of *any* rational faculty—either theoretical or practical—will accordingly (at least for creatures like us) *only* be possible insofar as we draw upon representations that are fundamentally practical in origin.[35]

Of course, this does not mean that, whenever we represent X as the end of some system Y, we necessarily thereby make X one of *our own* ends. Rather, it means that, in representing X in this way, we treat X as playing the role for Y that our practical representations or ends play for us as practical agents. But when we turn to the first-personal case, this distinction begins to collapse. For, at least according to Kant, the activities and ends of my own rational powers are always also *my own activities and ends*. And so, when I attribute some end to (say) my faculty of reason, I effectively treat this end as one of *my own ends* as a rational being.

For this reason, I can only treat one of my rational powers as having some end insofar as I can bring this end into the system of ends that governs *what I do*. In doing so, I face the task of integrating that end into the system of ends that characterizes my own first-personal point of view on the question of what to do. Because of this, the correctness or incorrectness of our teleological representations of our own rational powers is ultimately, at least in part, a *practical matter* for

---

[33] Note that this does not mean that the manner these faculties represent themselves is necessarily best conceived of as involving a practical representation in this sense. Rather, as Kant stresses, this is best conceived as involving what Kant calls a merely "formal" representation of the faculty. I return to this below.

[34] Compare, again, (Rosenblueth, Wiener, and Bigelow 1943, 19): "The basis of the concept of purpose is the awareness of 'voluntary activity'."

[35] Compare (O'Neill 1989; Cohen 2013, 2014; Mudd 2016, 2017), although each of them take this point further than I think is justified here. See below (p. 146).

Kant. For insofar as they commit us to acceptance of certain ends as our own, the appropriateness of such representations must ultimately answer to the standards laid down by practical reason for all my practical representations or ends. In short, by conceiving of our own faculties in teleological terms, we are (for Kant) conceiving of them in ways whose correctness is ultimately, at least in part, a practical question—a question, that is, that must ultimately answer to practical reason as the final court of appeals for all questions concerning my final ends.

d. The Unity of Reason and the Unity of Comprehension (and Autonomy)

We will return to this story in the chapters to follow, but I hope that these remarks have given us an initial grip on why the interests of practical reason take "primacy" over those theoretical reason for Kant and why such claims of "primacy" are themselves an expression of the deeper unity of theoretical and practical reason as two manifestations of a unified power.[36] The question that this raises, of course, is how we ought to understand the unity of theoretical and practical reason *if* it is not to explained by privileging one of these manifestations of reason over the other. Here there is a variety of options in the literature. But these options, as they stand, are not terribly inspiring. For example, in his insightful discussion of these issues, Timmerman agrees that it is the unity of reason as a

---

[36] Much the same is also true of the famous "keystone" passage of the second *Critique*, in which Kant stresses that the idea of freedom plays a special role in completing the project of the critical system:

...the concept of freedom, insofar as its reality is proved by an apodictic law of practical reason, constitutes the *keystone* of the whole structure of a system of pure reason, even of speculative reason; and all other concepts (those of God and immortality), which as mere ideas remain without support in the latter, now attach themselves to this concept and with it and by means of it get stability and objective reality, that is, their *possibility* is *proved* by this: that freedom is real, for this idea reveals itself through the moral law. (KpV 5:4–5)

In reading this passage, it is crucial to keep in mind that the notion of freedom that plays this role is not something external to reason as a capacity; rather, as Kant stresses here, it is a concept that we can only arrive at through an understanding of reason's own internal ends and principles. Thus, the idea that freedom forms the "keystone" (*Schlußstein*) of the critical system should not be confused with the idea that it is freedom (or freedom alone) that provides this system with its foundations or starting points. After all, a keystone is not that which provides a structure with its foundations, but rather the *final part* of a structure, which secures its overall structural stability. In keeping with this thought, as we will discuss below, in order to understand the notions of freedom or autonomy that are at issue in passages such as this one, we need to understand them in the context of the other ways in which Kant characterizes the capacity of reason—e.g. as the capacity for cognition from principles or the capacity for comprehension. For example, as we will see, to understand what it means to speak of reason as autonomous in *Kant's* sense, we need to understand the internal relationship between Kant's conception of reason as autonomous and his conception of reason as the capacity for a certain sort of cognition or comprehension. Thus, Kant's emphasis here and elsewhere on the central role of freedom for the critical philosophy in no way calls into question the foundational role of a conception of reason as fundamentally *both* theoretical and practical.

capacity that is fundamental, but argues that Kant does not have very much of interest to say by way of an account of this unity.[37] Similarly, Rescher treats the unity of reason as simply a matter of the fundamental "identity" of reason in these two forms but does not really explain why or how this is true.[38] Unfortunately, as Kant's successors quickly realized, such accounts leave Kant's philosophy in a deeply dissatisfying position—one on which the unity of reason is fundamental to Kant's philosophical project, but where Kant has relatively little of interest to say about how and why we should regard reason as unified.[39]

Fortunately, it seems to me that Kant can do considerably better on this score. Despite the extensive literature on these issues, the story of the "unity of reason" in this sense seems to me to have been told very incompletely. Strikingly, and here Timmerman surely has a point, Kant himself was generally quite reticent about the degree to which he had provided us with a genuinely satisfying account of reason's unity. For example, in the passage we quoted at the beginning of this chapter, he writes that the second *Critique*:

> ...rightly occasion[s] *the expectation of perhaps being able some day to attain insight into the unity of the whole pure rational faculty* (theoretical as well as practical) *and to derive everything from one principle*—the undeniable need of human reason, which finds complete satisfaction only in a complete systematic unity of its cognitions. (KpV 5:91)

Here Kant is clear that an understanding of "unity of the whole pure rational faculty (theoretical as well as practical)" is a necessary condition on a rationally satisfactory form of philosophy. But he also describes the task of achieving "insight" into this unity as something that we "perhaps might some day" be able to fulfill, not as one that the critical philosophy has already completed. It is thus difficult to escape the sense, shared by most of Kant's successors, that Kant's critical philosophy was essentially incomplete.

Whether or not it is possible to *fully* complete this task within a Kantian framework is a complicated question. For, as we will see, one of the main lessons of that framework is that there are fundamental limits on our ability to achieve a *fully systematic* body of philosophical cognition in the manner such "insight" would require. But, as I will argue below, I believe that Kant was in position to say much more than passages like this suggest about the fundamental

---

[37] (Timmermann 2010). Compare here (Timmermann 2018) on the Canon in the first *Critique*: "Here as in the second *Critique*—where he asserts that it is after all 'only one and the same reason that, be it for theoretical or practical purposes, judges according to a priori principles'—it is just an assumption."

[38] (Rescher 2000).

[39] For other important accounts of the "unity of reason" that nonetheless seem to me less than fully satisfying on this issue, see (Kleingeld 1998; Nuzzo 2005; Guyer 2006).

unity of reason in its theoretical and practical forms. Thus, I believe that we can go much further within the confines of Kant's philosophy towards a systematic account of the unity of reason than has been appreciated. It is precisely this picture—sometimes explicit, sometimes implicit—of the unity of theoretical and practical reason that I will attempt to extract from Kant's thought here.

Unfortunately, despite the existence of a great deal of excellent recent work on theoretical and practical reason in Kant, rather little work has tackled this unity question head on. On the one hand, much of the recent work on Kant's conception of *theoretical reason* has focused on the negative side of that account—that is, on how theoretical reason, according to Kant, naturally gives rise to the illusions of dogmatic metaphysics.[40] But while this is obviously an important topic, it is ultimately incidental to the *unity* of theoretical and practical reason as a single unified power. Rather, as we will see, in order to understand this unity, it is much more important to grasp how Kant thinks of the *positive* role of theoretical reason and his conception of reason as the capacity for the sort of understanding that he calls "comprehension".[41] On the other hand, while there is obviously a vast body of work on the positive role of *practical reason* in Kant, most of this literature treats the topic in relative isolation from Kant's claims about theoretical reason. For example, this literature tends to focus on Kant's claims about practical reason and autonomy without much consideration of the more cognitive characterizations of reason that Kant also provides.[42] As a result, despite its insights, the literature on Kant's practical philosophy very often obscures the true foundations of his account of reason's unity.

One of my main hopes in what follows is to develop an account of the unity of reason in Kant that does better on this score. I will be developing a view on which the unity of theoretical and practical reason can be explained through reference to an abstract conception of the ends and activities of reason as a faculty, where this abstract conception of reason and its aims can be made more determinate in at least two interdependent ways, corresponding to theoretical and practical reason,

---

[40] For important recent studies of this topic, see (Grier 2001, 2008; Proops 2010, 2014, 2015; Willaschek 2018; De Boer 2020, Proops 2021; Watkins n.d.). My views about these issues are in some ways closest to (Proops 2021) and (especially) Watkins's work in progress on these topics. But De Boer's work has also been very important in returning our focus to the more metaphysical aspects of Kant's discussion here.

[41] Here my thought has been especially influenced by conversations with Tolley about these issues. For important recent work on the positive role of reason, see (Allison 2004; Guyer 2005; Rauscher 2010; Breitenbach 2013, 2014; Tolley 2017b; Mudd 2017). But a good deal of this work tends to focus especially on the role of reason in natural science, as opposed to the broader topics I am interested in here.

[42] Notable exceptions in this regard are (Engstrom 2002, 2009; Reath 2010, 2012, 2019; Elizondo 2013; Merritt 2018). My account of practical reason below is deeply influenced by this work, although I develop this style of account quite differently than they do. For example, as I discuss below, while I am sympathetic at this level of abstraction to Engstrom's approach, I disagree with many details of his reading of Kant.

respectively.[43] Thus, my hope is to develop a genuine *explanation* of reason's unity, one that does not privilege either theoretical or practical reason in the manner many more familiar accounts do but instead treats them as *coequal* manifestations of reason's fundamental form of activity.

To emphasize the fundamental unity of reason as *equally* theoretical and practical, I will approach Kant's conception of reason as a faculty by beginning with his "more cognitive" characterizations of reason and its function, before exploring these questions in a manner that emphasizes his "more practical or agentive" characterizations of reason. As we will see, at the heart of the first way of thinking about reason are two (ultimately equivalent) characterizations of reason's proper function: (i) the idea of reason as the capacity for "cognition from principles" and (ii) the idea of reason as the capacity for what Kant calls "comprehension" or systematic understanding. Each of these characterizations might seem more apt with respect to theoretical as opposed to practical reason, but, as we will see, Kant believes that "cognition from principles" and "comprehension" both come in a theoretical *and* a practical form.[44] Thus, by working through these ideas, we can begin to see how Kant is able to provide a unified account of both theoretical and practical reason, beginning with the idea of reason as our highest *cognitive power*.

But this is only one half of Kant's unifying project. For Kant also aims to show that we can provide a unified conception of reason when we begin with what might seem to be a "more practical or agentive" conception of reason. At the heart of this conception of reason is the idea of reason as a genuinely autonomous faculty—that is, as a faculty whose activities ought to be genuinely self-determining or self-organizing in ways that go beyond what is true of *even* other rational powers. This idea of reason is, of course, most prominent in Kant's discussion of practical reason. But, as O'Neill has stressed, albeit in a somewhat different manner, both theoretical and practical reasoning can be understood as manifestations of reason when it is characterized in this fashion. Thus, beginning with the idea of reason as autonomous, we can also develop a parallel account of the unity of reason as a capacity. In the end, we will see that these two ways of providing a unified conception of reason are, at root, one and the same for Kant. In particular, we will show that the capacity for comprehension (in Kant's sense) must also be autonomous and that a capacity can be genuinely autonomous (for Kant) only insofar as it is a capacity for certain forms of comprehension. In this

---

[43] Structurally, my account of the relationship between theoretical and practical reason is quite similar on this score to what (Merritt 2018) calls the "specification thesis". Moreover, as will become clear, at least at a certain level of abstraction, I agree with much of what she says about how this idea plays out with respect to the idea of reason as a cognitive faculty. But, as noted above Merritt sometimes seems to me to overemphasize Kant's "more cognitive" characterizations of reason at the expense of his "more agential or practical" characterizations thereof.

[44] As I discuss below, Kant often follows the tradition by using "wisdom" (*Weisheit* or *sapientia*) to speak about the practical form that this can take.

way, we will arrive at a conception of reason's unity that truly does justice to both the theoretical and the practical aspects of reason without privileging either over the other.

e. Summary of the Chapters to Follow

With that overview in mind, I want to give the reader a sense of the chapters to follow. Once again, the primary line of argument in these chapters will be interpretative. But there is a more systematic subtext to our historical work, and at various points this subtext will become the primary focus of our discussion.

Part I: Kant's Rational Constitutivism

Chapter 1: As just noted, our discussion of the unity of reason will begin with a general discussion of Kant's philosophical methodology during the critical period. I begin in this way because in order to understand Kant's conception of reason, we need to keep in mind the role that reason is meant to play within Kant's broader philosophical system.[45] I will begin with a discussion of what I call Kant's "powers-first" or "capacities-first" approach to philosophy, an approach that treats our basic rational or cognitive capacities or powers as both epistemically and explanatorily fundamental, albeit in somewhat different ways.[46] As I'll sketch in this chapter, this framework for thinking about Kant's philosophical methodology sheds light on many familiar debates about his philosophy and also provides important context for thinking about Kant's conception of reason and its unity. Finally, I suggest that this approach remains attractive today insofar as it aims to capture precisely the aspects of rationality we must treat as foundational in philosophy *without* committing us to further metaphysical claims that are inessential in this context.

Chapter 2: With this background in mind, in Chapters 2 and 3, I will develop this reading of Kant's conception of our rational powers, focusing on the nature of spontaneous, self-conscious powers like reason or the understanding. To do so, in Chapter 2, I will develop our understanding of the connections Kant draws between rationality and self-consciousness by focusing on the fact that the rational powers at issue here are all, in some sense, capacities for cognition (*Erkenntnis*). Since Kant's conception of cognition will be central to much of the discussion to

---

[45] On this point, compare (Guyer 2006; Gardner 2007; Fugate 2014).
[46] In my past work, I tended to follow current convention in using "capacities" to refer to these cognitive powers, but I've come to often prefer "powers" in some contexts.

follow, I will discuss it in some detail here, taking care to distinguish it from the conception of knowledge that has dominated the contemporary epistemological debate. Then I will turn to the connections between this notion and the idea that rational powers are essentially self-conscious. As we will see, it follows from Kant's conception of cognition that cognition always involves a kind of (often implicit) consciousness or representation of its own standard of correctness. Thus, any faculty for cognition is also a capacity for a consciousness of the standards of correctness that apply to the form of cognition in question. This conclusion will provide us with one important way of understanding why Kant takes rational or cognitive powers to be self-conscious. And, as we will see, it will establish interesting connections between Kant's philosophy and the recent debate in epistemology about whether rational inference is governed by a "taking condition".

Chapter 3: In our third chapter, I will continue exploring the sort of self-consciousness that Kant takes to characterize reason (and other rational powers), focusing on his willingness to use both normative and descriptive terminology to describe the principles at work in rational powers. This will lead into the broadly metaethical dimension of Kant's philosophy—to his account, that is, of the "sources of normativity". Here I will argue that, for Kant, any rational power, be it practical *or* theoretical, is governed by an internal principle that can be characterized in either descriptive or normative terms. As we will see, this supports a version of the (now familiar) reading of Kant as a "meta-normative constitutivist". But the version of this view it supports is, once again, quite different, focusing, as it does, not on our nature as agents, but rather on the nature of reason as a unified faculty for *both* theoretical and practical understanding. In spelling out this view, I argue that in viewing Kant's "constitutivism" through the lens of his general commitment to a powers-first approach, we better understand the sense in which Kant both is and is not a constitutivist—and see why Kant's form of "constitutivism" remains attractive today.

Part II: Reason and Its Unity

In the second half of the book, we will build on this discussion of the nature of rational faculties *in general* to focus more on the nature of reason *in particular*. In doing so, our focus will be on how Kant conceives of reason as a *single unified capacity* with both a theoretical and a practical use. We will approach this question from several directions. First, we will focus on Kant's "more cognitive" characterizations of reason in order to see how they provide us with a picture of reason that covers both its theoretical and its practical activities. Then, in later chapters, we will do the same by focusing (i) on the *principle(s)* that govern reason's activity in both the theoretical and practical domains and (ii) on Kant's conception of reason as *autonomous*.

Chapter 4: In this chapter, we will approach the problem of reason's unity by focusing on the form of cognition that reason aims to achieve. In doing so, we will begin with the (relatively familiar) characterizations of reason as the capacity for inference and the capacity for cognition from principles, before turning to a third, more neglected conception of reason—namely, the idea of reason as the capacity for "comprehension" (*Begreifen*), a cognitive achievement that is *roughly* equivalent to what contemporary epistemologists have in mind when they speak of "understanding".[47] As we will see, comprehension in this sense is closely linked to both Kant's conception of cognition from principles and his conception of rational "insight" (*Einsehen*). For Kant conceives of comprehension in terms of a form of insight or cognition from principles that is sufficient to our purposes.

In the remainder of the chapter, we'll discuss the philosophical significance of this conception of reason, focusing on two issues. First, we will discuss the significance of the fact that, unlike his rationalist predecessors, Kant conceives of reason as the capacity, not for rational insight *full stop*, but rather for comprehension. As we will see, this way of conceiving of reason's aims is closely associated with Kant's critical modesty about the potential reach of reason. But Kant's characterization of reason as the capacity for comprehension is also significant for our understanding of the *unity* of theoretical and practical reason. For, as the highest perfection of cognition, comprehension comes in both a theoretical and a practical form. Thus, we can make use of the idea of reason as the capacity for comprehension to better understand the unity of reason across the theoretical-practical divide, while also using Kant's end- or purpose-relative conception of comprehension to more fully understand Kant's claims about the primacy of practical reason's interests.

Chapter 5: With this in mind, in our fifth and sixth chapters, I will turn to the various characterizations that Kant provides of reason's governing *principle*, focusing first on his discussion of this principle in the theoretical domain. In doing so, I will argue that reason's most fundamental principle (in both a theoretical and a practical context) can be thought of as *a version* of the Principle of Sufficient Reason (PSR), albeit one that is reinterpreted so as to make it acceptable within the confines of Kant's critical philosophy.

In a theoretical context, my discussion will be focused on Kant's two main characterizations of the fundamental principle of theoretical reason—what Kant calls theoretical reason's "logical maxim" and "supreme principle". I will argue that Kant's discussion of these formulas indicates a more positive appraisal of the PSR than most readers of Kant have assumed.[48] In particular, while Kant of course

---

[47] For a contemporary defense of this view of rationality, see (Schafer 2018b, 2019b, forthcoming a). For some discussion of the connection between reason and comprehension, see (Breitenbach 2013; Tolley 2017b). See also (Zinkin 2017, 2022).

[48] My thought about these issues has been especially influenced by conversations with Eric Watkins, whose work in progress on the "supreme principle" has been very important for my thinking about that

rejects the characteristic rationalist claim that the PSR can serve as a potential source of *cognition of the unconditioned*, I will argue that he nonetheless believes that we are rationally committed to a form of "doctrinal belief" in the bare existence of something unconditioned, and that this commitment holds *even* from a theoretical point of view.[49] That is, even with respect to the theoretical use of reason, Kant takes theoretical reason's interest in systematic comprehension to commit us, albeit only on "subjectively sufficient" grounds, to the proposition that every finite, conditioned thing is ultimately grounded in something unconditioned. I will go to explain why this commitment is compatible with Kant's critique of more traditional forms of rationalist metaphysics.

Chapter 6: In the next chapter, I will turn to the implications of these ideas for our understanding of the relationship between the PSR and the supreme principle of pure *practical reason*—that is, the *moral law*. In doing so, I will mostly focus on the two formulations of the moral law that correspond most closely to the "logical maxim" and the "supreme principle", namely, the Formula of Universal Law (FUL) and the Formula of Humanity (FH). I will conclude by sketching how this discussion lays the groundwork for a more systematic picture of the relationship between all of the characterizations Kant provides of reason's fundamental principle *and* the relationship between this and Kant's conception of highest good.

Chapter 7: As this shows, the idea of reason as the faculty for comprehension provides us with one central characterization of reason's function, one that captures, in one way, the underlying unity of theoretical and practical reason. But, as discussed above we can also characterize reason's unity by approaching this question from a "more agentive" direction, by focusing on the idea of reason as the capacity for a sort of genuinely autonomous activity or self-organization. In this chapter, I will develop the claims of the last three chapters by arguing that these various ways of characterizing reason are ultimately one and the

---

topic. For more on his (in some ways quite similar) interpretation of Kant and the PSR, see (Watkins 2010, 2016, 2017, n.d., n.d.; Watkins and Stratmann 2021). I'm also very indebted to conversations with Nick Stang, Andrew Chignell, Clinton Tolley, Colin McLear, Dai Heide, Rosalind Chaplin, and Ian Proops about related issues. In work in progress, Jim Kreines also develops a reading of the "supreme principle" that, while weaker than mine in some ways, is structurally quite similar to it. Much of this work can be seen as developing Chignell's suggestion that "Kant does not materially abandon rationalist metaphysics in the critical period: he simply thinks that the form or status of its results must be reconceived" (Chignell 2007a, 350). For more traditional views of the place of the PSR in Kant's philosophy, see for example (Franks 2005; Boehm 2014, 2016; Proops 2014; Kreines 2015; Lu-Adler, n.d.). Non-Kantians are often even more blunt about this issue. See, for example, Della Rocca's comment that "Hume and Kant...made it their mission to articulate and argue for a worldview structured around the claim that the PSR is simply false" (Della Rocca 2010, 1–2). As we will see below (p. 169), comments like Della Rocca's give a misleading impression of Kant's actual attitudes towards the PSR.

[49] (Proops 2021) independently defends the same basic line of interpretation on this question, although he does not push this idea as far as I do here. Nonetheless, Proops develops the implications of these ideas for Kant's critique of rationalist metaphysics *much* more fully than I do here.

same. In particular, I will argue that the idea of reason as autonomous ultimately expresses the same fundamental conception of reason discussed previously in the context of the idea of reason as the capacity for comprehension or cognition from principles. I thus claim that comprehension and autonomy are simply two (equally important) ways of capturing what is valuable about the distinctive activity of reason as Kant understands it. As we will discuss, each of these ways of thinking about reason's activity is useful for certain purposes, but both are required if we are to fully understand Kant's conception of reason and its unity. In other words, for Kant, the unity of theoretical and practical reason can only be fully understood if we understand the *unity of comprehension and autonomy*.[50]

Conclusion: I conclude our discussion by discussing four issues. First, I will return to the implications of this conception of reason for our understanding of the entire system of rational capacities, arguing that what results from my account is a sort of radicalization of Longuenesse's groundbreaking work on the teleological structure of these capacities and their activities. Then I will return to the potential advantages of the resulting "reason-first" approach to meta-normative questions by comparing this approach to some of the forms of "reasons fundamentalism" in the recent literature. Next, I will argue that the connections we've established between reason, understanding, and autonomy provide a powerful framework for critiquing many social and political institutions as implicitly irrational. This will point towards one way of further developing the ideas we have been discussing. But then I will end our discussion on a less optimistic note, by briefly considering whether Kant *really* provides us with a satisfying framework for thinking about how reason is realized in finite, sensibly conditioned creatures. In doing so, I will suggest that Kant's conception of the unity of theoretical and practical reason, while powerful, remains insufficient in some ways to do justice to their deep interdependence. A more satisfying picture of this relationship, I will suggest, points us towards the attempts of Kant's idealist successors to better integrate these concerns into the foundations of the critical system.

---

[50] For example, given this dual characterization of reason in terms of comprehension *and* autonomy, the basic task facing reason in *both* its theoretical and practical forms is to reconcile the various aspects of what comprehension and autonomy require. Two of these aspects are particularly important for Kant. First, there is the need to do justice to the *determinacy of particulars*—either, on the theoretical side, by capturing this determinacy in our theoretical cognitions, or, on the practical side, by translating our general ends into particular, determinate actions in the world. But this demand for determinacy in our theoretical and practical cognition must be balanced against the need to place these determinate things or actions in a more *systematic context* which allows us to *make sense* of them in the manner that both comprehension and autonomy requires. Thus, both practical and theoretical reasoning involve an attempt to reconcile a need for determinacy with a need for systematicity, although, as we will see, the challenges facing each in this effort are rather different, with practical reason able to do far better on this score than theoretical reason can. It is Kant's sensitivity to both these demands that separates him from some of his immediate followers, such as Reinhold and Fichte. For an excellent recent treatment of the *two-sided* character of this interaction between particular and universal in both the theoretical *and the practical* spheres, see (Bremner forthcoming).

f. A Note about the Historical Development of Kant's Thought

Before moving on, I want to conclude this introduction with a note about the historical development of Kant's ideas about these questions. In recent years, here has been a lively debate about the degree to which the fundamental elements within Kant's philosophy shift during the critical period. To put my interpretative cards on the table, I am generally inclined to emphasize the continuities in Kant's thought during this period as opposed to the discontinuities. But there is no doubt that there are significant additions to the critical system during it.

At least three potential shifts of this sort might be thought relevant to the discussion to follow. First, there is the idea, made famous by Paul Guyer's work on this subject, that Kant "relocated" many of the functions of theoretical reason to the power of judgment in the third *Critique*.[51] We will return to this below but, as already noted, I tend to read the significance of the third *Critique* on this score rather differently than Guyer does. There is no doubt that Kant comes to view the power of judgment as a much more robust faculty in the third *Critique* than he had previously thought. But I do not read this addition to the critical system as *removing* anything from Kant's conception of reason as a unified theoretical and practical faculty. Rather, I read Kant's increased emphasis on the interest of the power of judgment in systematic unity as an expression of his deepening appreciation of the manner in which *all* of our intellectual powers form a teleological system which is organized around the ends and interests that are characteristic of both theoretical and practical reason. Thus, far from "demoting" theoretical reason from the important place it holds in the first *Critique*, the third *Critique's* discussion of the power of judgment should be read as an expression of a richer appreciation of the manner in which the activities of our "lower" intellectual faculties are guided by the ends of reason.

Similarly, as noted above, although the third *Critique* obviously presents a new model for how teleological concepts can be *applied to* living things in the natural world, I do not think it should be seen as the heart of Kant's account of such concepts more generally. Rather, the foundations of Kant's account of "teleological thought in general" lie in his practical philosophy. In this context, the third *Critique*'s discussion of teleology *in nature* is best seen as an account of how the use of these (already characterized) forms of thought can be *extended* to think about things in nature. Thus, while the third *Critique* represents a significant shift in Kant's views about teleology, it does not represent a fundamental shift in his views about the forms of teleological thinking that will be most relevant to our discussion here—namely, the forms of teleological thinking that Kant uses to

---

[51] See e.g. (Guyer 1990, 2005).

think, not about biological forms of life, but rather the basic structure of our rational capacities like reason.[52]

Finally, due in large part to Pauline Kleingeld's important recent work on these issues, there has been much recent debate about whether Kant's basic account of autonomy shifts from (say) the second *Critique* to the later practical works like the *Metaphysics of Morals*.[53] Much of this debate will not be relevant to my discussion here, since I will focus mostly on elements of Kant's conception of autonomy that Kleingeld herself takes to be constant during this period. But in my discussion of the Formula of Autonomy, I will argue that this principle (in some form) is more essential to Kant's basic conception of autonomy than Kleingeld suggests, so there remains *some* difference of opinion between us on this score, to which I will return below.

In any case, since the historical development of Kant's ideas is not the primary focus of this essay, I will not be able to give these debates the attention they really require. If one is more inclined to read Kant's views as undergoing dramatic shifts during this period, some of my claims may be best read as claims about Kant's critical philosophy during the period around the publication of the second *Critique* and the second edition of the first *Critique*.[54] I leave it up to the reader to decide when such a restriction is appropriate, although (as should be obvious) I believe that most of the main claims I will be making apply to the critical philosophy throughout this period.

---

[52] Compare the insightful treatment of these issues in (Ypi 2021). I agree with good deal of what Ypi has to say about the structure of Kant's arguments in the first *Critique*, but I disagree with her that that structure changes dramatically when we turn to the third *Critique*. Instead, I see Kant's basic framework for thinking about teleology as much more continuous throughout the critical period. Unfortunately Ypi's important work on these topics appeared too late in the writing of this book for me to engage with it in detail here.

[53] See e.g. (Kleingeld 2018).

[54] I put things in this way, in part, to set aside the question of whether Kant's views about the foundations of practical philosophy shift dramatically between the *Groundwork* and the second *Critique*. Once again, I think the best reading of these passages yields the result that they do not undergo a dramatic change then. But I will not argue for this in detail here. For a nice presentation of the case for continuity on this score, see (Tenenbaum 2012).

PART I
KANT'S RATIONAL CONSTITUTIVISM

1
Transcendental Philosophy and the Self-Consciousness of Reason

Contemporary philosophy is full of pleas for the primacy of this or that concept or property.[1] There is, for example, the "knowledge-first" program which dominates large swaths of contemporary epistemology and beyond. And there are the many contemporary "reasons-first" approaches to meta-ethics, ethics, and epistemology, which attempt to understand the normative domain by explaining all normative or evaluative claims in terms of claims about reasons for and against actions and attitudes.[2] But the sorts of priority that seem most attractive to us from a contemporary perspective may not have seemed so obvious to figures in the past. My goal in this chapter is to begin to explore how this is true of Kant (and many of those influenced by him). In doing so, I will argue that Kant's philosophical methodology can indeed be understood as falling into the "X-first" framework for thinking about philosophical positions in *some* sense. But the "X" that comes first for Kant is certain basic rational or cognitive capacities or powers and their constitutive forms of cognitive activity. In this sense, I will argue that Kant is best understood as a "rational-powers" or "capacities-first" philosopher—as a philosopher, that is, who treats *reason* as a rational power (and not "reasons" as the considerations to which this power is responsive) as "coming first" in the order of philosophical understanding.[3]

As we will see, such capacities or powers are defined in terms of what they are powers *to do*, and the capacities at issue here are all (in some sense) capacities for forms of cognition. Thus, we might also characterize Kant as treating the relevant forms of *cognition* as fundamental. In particular, as we will see, Kant conceives of

---

[1] This chapter draws heavily upon (Schafer 2019a, 2021b, forthcoming b).
[2] For further discussion of the relationship of such views to the sort of view discussed below, see (Schafer 2018b, 2020, 2015b, 2015c). For some doubts about the utility of these debates, see (Wodak 2020). As will become clear, the conception of rational powers or capacities I am interested in here is one on which such skepticism is justified, at least up to a point. For contemporary work in a broadly Kantian vein that gives capacities or powers a fundamental role, see (Kern 2006; Engstrom 2009; McDowell 2011; Newton 2015; Rödl 2018; Land 2018; Schellenberg 2018; Marcus 2021; Gomes et al. 2022; Pendlebury 2022; Stephenson 2021, forthcoming; Fix forthcoming) among others.
[3] As noted above, I will generally use both "capacity" and "power" to translate Kant's use of "*Vermögen*". Each translation is current in the contemporary Anglophone literature, and both have certain advantages and disadvantages. But "capacity" has a connotation of passivity or mere potentiality that has increasingly led me to prefer the more active terminology of "powers" to refer to what is at issue here. Thanks to Sasha Newton in particular for discussion of this issue.

reason as the capacity for the highest form of (human) cognition—namely, what he calls "comprehension".[4] In this sense, Kant is perhaps best thought of as a "reason-first" philosopher. For, as we will see, the critical philosophy is ultimately just the attempt to bring reason's implicit consciousness of its own nature, principles, and ends to the level of explicit and systematic self-consciousness—a self-consciousness that (Kant hopes) will provide philosophy with the foundations it requires to count as a genuine form of comprehension or systematic understanding. In this way, Kant's conception of philosophy begins with the nature of reason as the capacity for comprehension and ends with the actualization of this capacity, insofar as this is possible for us.

a. A Look Ahead: Kant on the Aims of Philosophical Inquiry

To explore these ideas and set the stage for the discussion to follow, let's begin by jumping ahead in our narrative to briefly consider how Kant conceives of the goals of human inquiry in general. As we will discuss below, three cognitive achievements are particularly important for understanding Kant's conception of rational inquiry—namely, what he calls "cognition" (*Erkenntnis*), "knowledge" (*Wissen*), and "comprehension" (*Begreifen*).[5] In what follows, we will have the occasion to discuss each of these in more detail, but I want to begin by briefly sketching how Kant conceives of them, since this will be crucial below.

In the first instance, Kant conceives of rational inquiry as aiming at what he calls "cognition" (*Erkenntnis*).[6] As we will discuss, to cognize something (in the sense relevant here) is to form an "objective representation" of it "with consciousness" (B376-7; cf. Log 9:65, V-Lo/Blomberg 24:133-4). Cognition, in this sense, is the cognitive achievement through which we become *conscious of objective features* of reality, as opposed to merely being conscious of our own subjective states. To have cognition is thus to be conscious of something that imposes a real or "material" standard of correctness on our representations of it—a standard of correctness, that is, which goes beyond the merely "formal" or logical standards of correctness that are internal to any representation as such.[7]

---

[4] For more on this, see (Schafer forthcoming).

[5] None of these translations is perfect. For example, while I will follow most contemporary scholars in reserving "knowledge" to translate "*Wissen*", all three of these can be regarded as forms of "knowledge" in the everyday sense of this word.

[6] Beginning with Smit's important work (Smit 1999, 2000, 2009, 2019), there has been an explosion of recent work on Kant's conception of cognition. For my views on this, see Chapter 2, and see (Chignell 2014; Tolley 2017b; Watkins and Willaschek 2017) and the other references there for other important discussions of it.

[7] For more on this, see Chapter 2.

As we will see, such cognition may be either *theoretical*—that is, cognition of *what is*—or *practical*—that is, cognition of *what ought to be*.[8] As Kant understands this distinction, theoretical cognition aims to accurately represent an independently existing object or state of affairs, while practical cognition aims to make it the case that the objects it represents exist. Thus, theoretical cognition is fundamentally receptive, while practical cognition is fundamentally productive or active. But, in both cases, we can achieve cognition only insofar we have conscious access to (i) an object (either as what is *or* as what ought to be), (ii) a representation of that object, and (iii) a non-accidental relationship between that object and that representation, which will be receptive in the case of theoretical cognition and productive or active in the case of practical cognition.[9]

Thus, for Kant, genuine inquiry is distinguished from the mere subjective play of our faculties insofar as it aims to get at *something objective* over and above the subject's fleeting subjective states. More precisely, in aiming at cognition, inquiry aims to bring this "object" (be it theoretical or practical) *to consciousness*. But inquiry does not merely aim at *bare* cognition for Kant. For the ultimate aim of inquiry is not mere *cognition* (*Erkenntnis*), but rather the further perfections of cognition that Kant associates with what he calls "insight" (*Einsehen*) and "comprehension" (*Begreifen*). In essence, these "higher" forms of cognition go beyond mere cognition insofar as they satisfy, not just the understanding's need for determinate cognition of objects, but also reason's need for a systematic grasp of *how* and *why* things are (or ought to be) as one cognizes them to be (or ought to be).[10] Thus, for example, insight and comprehension go beyond mere cognition insofar as they require not merely the "coordination" of marks, which is required to distinguish one thing from another, but also the "subordination" of them that is required in order to grasp explanatory relationships.[11] In this way, they go beyond piecemeal cognition of particular objects (be it theoretical or practical) because they place this cognition into a more general *system*—a system that allows us to explain and justify what we cognize and so *make sense* of it (either theoretically or practically) (A645/B673; cf. A680/B708, A738–9/B765–6).

Once again, it is important to stress that "comprehension" in this broad sense comes in both a theoretical and a practical form, though Kant often prefers to use the traditional term "*wisdom*" (*Weisheit*) to refer to its practical variant. As we will

---

[8] Here my account draws on the important work of (Engstrom 2002, 2006, 2009). See (Merritt 2018) for a similar account. For related but distinct views of these issues, see (O'Neill 1989; Neiman 1994; Cohen 2014; Mudd 2017; Guyer 2006, 2019).

[9] See (Tolley 2017b) for this in the case of empirical cognition. Lest this requirement seem too demanding, it is important to stress that having conscious access to these aspects of cognition does not require one to possess the concepts needed to form discursive thoughts about them—although it will put me in a position to form such concepts through reflection upon my relationship to the objects I cognize.

[10] In claiming that these further perfections of cognition go beyond "mere cognition", I don't mean to deny that there is a sense in which all cognition, for Kant, aims at this sort of systematic cognition.

[11] See BL 24:134–5.

see, this is crucial for understanding the unity of reason.[12] For, given this, we can characterize the aims of reason *in general* in terms of a drive for insight and comprehension and then subsequently distinguish *theoretical* from *practical reason* in terms of whether the comprehension in question is theoretical or practical. But what matters at present is that Kant, drawing on the traditional notion of *scientia*, conceives of this sort of *systematic understanding* as what distinguishes genuinely "scientific" or "rational" cognition from ordinary "popular" cognition: "systematic unity is that which first makes ordinary cognition into a science, i.e. makes a system out of a mere aggregate of it" (A832/B860). Thus, given that reason aims at this sort of comprehension, a body of cognition will only be fully rationally satisfactory for Kant insofar as it possesses the sort of systematic unity that makes comprehension possible. In this sense, reason will be fully satisfied by a body of cognitions only insofar as it takes the form of a systematic "science" (*Wissenschaft*).[13]

As the term "*Wissenschaft*" suggests, the sort of systematic unity that is characteristic of comprehension is also closely associated with what Kant calls "knowledge" (*Wissen*). As Kant uses these terms, knowledge is the highest perfection of the *modality* of cognition—roughly, how cognition involves a "taking to be true" or assent (*Fürwahrhalten*)—while comprehension is the highest perfection of the relationship of cognition to its "objective content". These two perfections of cognition are thus logically distinct from one another; nonetheless, to seek one of them is also necessarily to seek the other, at least to some degree. For example, for Kant, a "taking to be true" can count as an instance of knowledge (*Wissen*) just in case it is based on grounds that are both "subjectively and objectively sufficient".[14] And, in order to have such grounds, at least two things are required. First, we must connect our representations together in a systematic manner that makes one representation available as a potential ground for others. And second, at least some of those representations must provide us with the consciousness *of objects* that is characteristic of cognition, for only this will allow these objects to serve as grounds for assent that are sufficient in both a subjective *and* an objective sense. Thus, the availability of such grounds to the conscious subject's acts of "taking to be true" is constrained by the degree to which that subject has achieved cognition (*Erkenntnis*) of the objects those "takings to be true" concern. And such cognition will only be relevant to these "takings to be true" insofar as the cognition in question has the systematic structure that is

---

[12] For related ideas, see (Merritt 2018; Guyer 2019). It is useful to contrast this approach to the "unity of reason" with the more "pragmatic" line taken by (O'Neill 1989; Neiman 1994; Cohen 2014; Mudd 2017).

[13] Of course, this sets a very high standard, which is beyond the cognitive capacities of human beings in many domains.

[14] For more on Kant's conception of "taking to be true", see (Chignell 2007a, 2007b, 2014). I return to this in Chapter 2. For a contemporary variant on Kant's views about knowledge in this sense, see (Schroeder 2015a, 2015b).

characteristic of comprehension (*Begreifen*). Thus, although comprehension and knowledge (*Wissen*) are perfections of cognition along two distinct axes for Kant, they remain very closely connected. And it remains true in general that our ability to achieve either of these two perfections is constrained by our ability to achieve the other, even though there are special cases in which we may possess one in the absence of the other.[15]

b. Philosophical Principles and Rational Powers

These points apply in some form to any area of human inquiry, but what is important at present is their application to philosophy itself. Given that reason aims at systematic comprehension, philosophy will only be rationally satisfactory insofar as it takes on a systematic form:

> Philosophy in *sensu scholastico* involves two things, (1.) A sufficient supply of cognitions of reason. (2.) A correct connection of these, or a system. For a system is the connection of many cognitions in accordance with an idea.
> (V-Lo/Wiener 24:799)

> The two must be united; for without cognitions one will never become a philosopher, but cognitions alone will never constitute the philosopher either, unless there is in addition a purposive combination of all cognitions and skills in a unity, and an insight into their agreement with the highest ends of human reason. (Log 9:25)

As we will explore below, this sort of systematic unity is only possible insofar as a body of cognitions is grounded in a unified system of philosophical first principles or explanatory grounds.[16] Indeed, there are several senses of "principle" in which this is true for Kant. First, there is the most general sense of "principle" (or *Prinzip*) on which this term refers to anything that can serve as the ground or explanatory basis for something else. Importantly, "principles" in this most general sense can have propositional form, but they need not. So, in this most general sense of "principle", a fundamental logical or metaphysical law or principle may serve as a "principle", but so too may a power like reason or a substance like God. In this sense of "principle", the need for philosophical "principles" follows immediately from the idea of philosophy as a system of comprehension

---

[15] For more detailed discussion of the significance of this for Kant's philosophical methodology, see (Schafer forthcoming b).
[16] For further of discussion of the sense in which philosophy should form such a system, see (Wood 1999; Grier 2001; Amerikss 2003, 2012; Franks 2005; Guyer 2005; Nisenbaum 2017; Willaschek 2018; Watkins 2019; De Boer 2020).

from such explanatory grounds. But in addition to "principles" in this broad sense, when Kant speaks "principles" (*Prinzipien* or *Grundsätze*) he has in mind something closer to what we today would generally call a principle: something like a general fact or proposition, from which other facts or propositions can be derived. Principles in this sense can be either *real*, metaphysical principles, which serve to ground other real facts or existences, or *representations* of such principles, which serve to ground other such representations. Although Kant is not always terribly rigorous in his use of these terms, the first notion of principle is generally more closely associated with his use of "*Prinzipien*", while the second is more closely associated with "*Grundsätze*".

Although distinct, all these notions of "principle" are closely related for Kant. For example, in keeping with Kant's metaphysics of causal powers, any genuine capacity or power will be governed for Kant by an internal principle of activity that (when free of external interference) determines how that capacity functions.[17] For example, reason's inferential activities can be thought of as governed by the principle that reason should seek comprehension or understanding. But this (real, metaphysical) principle of activity can also be represented by a cognitive subject and, when so represented, can serve as the basis for further judgments *about* the capacity in question. For example, as philosophers, we may form explicit representations of reason's characteristic principle, and we may try to use these representations for our own cognitive purposes. Moreover, in the case of *self-conscious* rational capacities like reason, these two forms that a "principle" can take will be especially closely connected. For, as we will see, in the case of such capacities there is a constitutive connection between the real internal principle that governs the activities of the capacity and the manner in which any rational subject with that capacity must represent this principle (at least implicitly).[18] To say, for example, that reason is governed by a principle like the one just noted is to say that reason's activities are guided by a representation of that principle—that is, a representation of the sort of ideal understanding reason seeks. In this sense, as we will see, Kant conceives of reason as a sort of *self-organizing* or *self-regulating power* for comprehension or understanding.

As such, self-conscious rational powers like reason involve "principles" in all three of these senses. First, as we are about to discuss in more detail, such powers are themselves "principles" insofar as they serve as a basis for the explanation of

---

[17] At least in their pure form, such principles are "internal" both in the sense of being essential to the capacities in question and in the sense of being "intrinsic" to them. But it is also crucial to Kant's discussion of, say, the relationship between sensibility and the understanding, that these pure principles can be made more determinate through the relationship between a capacity and other capacities.
[18] I return to the question of the sense in which this is true below. For some recent discussion of this question, see (Smit 1999; Boyle 2009, 2011; Longuenesse 2017; Merritt 2018; McLear 2019; Newton 2019; Smit 2019; Kraus 2020).

other things (*Prinzipien* in the most general sense). Second, they are also governed by metaphysically real internal principles of activity (*Prinzipien* in the narrower, but still real sense). And third, these principles of activity are constitutively connected with the possibility of their own representation (as cognitive *Grundsätze*). That is, they enable us to become conscious of these principles as governing these basic rational powers and so provide us with potential *Grundsätze* from which other cognitions can be derived in the manner that systematic philosophy requires.

We'll return to this below. But some of the implications of these claims for philosophical methodology should already be clear. First, philosophy will only be rationally satisfactory, according to Kant, insofar as it forms a *unified system* of judgments or cognitions. And second, philosophy can only be systematic in this sense insofar as it is grounded in a system of fundamental principles—or, alternatively, in a unifying idea or ideas—that provide it with the structure that is characteristic of a genuine rational system. To say this, it is important to stress, is not to say that "systematic unity" in this sense requires us to reduce all our cognitions to a single first principle in the manner often associated with (say) a "Parmenidean" reading of Spinoza.[19] But it is to say that a body of cognitions will have this sort of unity only insofar as those cognitions are grounded in principles that *themselves* embody the sort of unity in question. And, of course, these grounding principles must not be merely "subjective" general representations. Rather, to play this role, they must also correspond to real, explanatory features of reality.

This raises what is, in some ways, the fundamental question about the possibility of philosophy for Kant and the German idealists—namely, how we can locate the principles that can play this foundational role, and, in particular, how we can do so in a non-arbitrary and rationally satisfying fashion.[20] It is Kant's response to this challenge that brings us to the aspects of his philosophy that most clearly display his "rational-capacities" or "rational powers-first" methodology in action. For when it comes to the foundations of the critical project, Kant insists that human insight or understanding reaches its limit in certain basic faculties or powers, faculties that cannot, at least by us, be explained in more fundamental terms, but which nonetheless provide a non-arbitrary basis for further theorizing:

---

[19] For contemporary defense of such a view, see (Della Rocca 2020).

[20] For an overview of this history, see, for example, (Franks 2005; Förster 2011; Horstmann 2012; Nisenbaum 2017). In setting up the "problem space" for Kant's philosophical project, I've focused here on how systematic philosophy is possible, as opposed to more familiar questions about synthetic a priori cognition. This should not be taken as neglect of the latter question but rather an intensification of it. After all, the principles that systematic philosophy requires must, according to Kant, be both a priori and synthetic in character. So, in showing how systematic philosophy is possible, we are also showing how synthetic a priori cognition is possible as well. The problem of how philosophy can be systematic is thus, in a sense, the most challenging version of the more familiar problem of synthetic a priori cognition.

But all human *insight* is at an end as soon as we have arrived at *basic powers or basic faculties; for there is nothing through which their possibility can be conceived, and yet it may not be invented and assumed at one's discretion.*

(KpV 5:46–7, my emphasis)[21]

As such passages make clear, for the critical Kant, our insight (*Einsehen*) and comprehension (*Begreifen*) reaches its endpoint once we have arrived at certain basic powers or faculties—in particular, certain basic cognitive powers such as reason or sensibility.[22]

In interpreting such claims, it is important to remember that they have implications both for the order of human cognition (the *ratio cognoscendi* of things) and the order of metaphysical explanation (their *ratio essendi*), at least insofar as such explanations are accessible to human beings. On the one hand, Kant believes that, at least within the limits of human cognition, our ability to grasp the fundamental explanation of things (our grasp of their *ratio essendi*) bottoms out in our grasp of certain basic faculties like reason, the understanding, or sensibility. Thus, these faculties must take priority in the order of *metaphysical or philosophical explanation*, at least insofar as we are able to grasp these explanations. According to Kant, this is as deep as creatures with our cognitive limitations can penetrate into the nature of things, even if we also recognize that a creature without these limitations (such as God) might be able to go deeper by (say) cognizing the essential nature of the substances that realize these powers.

But, on the other hand, while creatures with our cognitive limitations reach explanatory bedrock with such certain capacities or powers, at least some of these capacities, in virtue of their self-conscious character, also provide us with a set of cognitive fixed points—that is, with something that may not invented or dismissed in a discretionary fashion. Thus, the self-consciousness of such basic faculties, or, more precisely, the self-conscious character of their activities, also provides us with something that takes priority in the order of human cognition (*ratio cognoscendi*).

In saying this, it is important to stress that the cognitive or epistemic role of this form of self-consciousness is not necessarily to serve as a starting point for philosophical inquiry. That is, the point here is not necessarily that philosophical inquiry should begin with a conscious of these capacities and their acts and principles. After all, Kant is clear that achieving this sort of consciousness often

---

[21] Note that Kant goes on here to say, "Therefore in the theoretical use of reason only experience can justify us in assuming them." This might seem to count against the point I am making here, but as Kant goes on to make clear, what he has in mind when he refers to "the theoretical use of reason" is the use of reason in *the empirical sciences* and *not* the critique of theoretical reason which provides those sciences with their foundation.

[22] See also the following passage from the *Religion*: "Now reason's ability to become master over all the inclinations striving against it through the mere idea of a law is absolutely inexplicable; hence it is also incomprehensible how the senses could have the ability to become master over a reason which commands with such authority on its side" (RGV 6:59). And compare: " . . . the chief question always remains, 'What and how much understanding and reason cognize free of all experience?' and not: 'How is the **faculty of thinking** itself possible?' " (Axvi–xvii).

requires hard philosophical and reflective work. So philosophical inquiry will often with something more robust—say with the ordinary forms of empirical and moral experience. The point here is rather that, once inquiry is complete, these capacities and their acts and principles will have been revealed to have a special cognitive or epistemic status such that they are in principle accessible to us via this sort of reflection. In this sense our most basic self-conscious capacities will be shown by Kant's philosophy to be cognitively or epistemically non-arbitrary—so, in that sense, they are also cognitively or epistemically fundamental for us.

Given this, there are at least two, closely related, senses in which the critical Kant may be regarded as developing a "capacities-first" or "powers-first" framework for philosophy.[23] First, the critical philosophy treats the nature of certain basic cognitive powers as providing it with its explanatory foundations—that is, as providing it with the fundamental explanatory principles it needs to take on a rationally satisfying form. But second, it also treats these cognitive powers and their activities, at least insofar as they are self-conscious, as non-negotiable cognitive or epistemic fixed points.[24]

In thinking about the foundational role of such capacities or powers, it is worth stressing that they are explanatorily fundamental for Kant in at least two related senses. First, such powers ground the *possibility* of the acts that are characteristic of them. In doing so, a capacity or power may be regarded as the *formal cause* of its acts: when a power acts, the form or general nature of these acts is explained by reference to the capacity in question. So, for example, Kant writes in a reflection, "The inner principle of the possibility of the act is the capacity" (Refl 17:73). But powers also play a crucial role in explaining the actuality of those acts as well–for a central part of the broadly Aristotelian conception of powers that Kant inherits from Leibniz is the idea that such powers must, in some sense, aim at their own actualization through their characteristic mode of activity.[25] As Reath nicely puts the point, any such capacity or power "is constitutively aimed at its own proper exercise" (Reath 2013, 577). Kant thus takes capacities or powers like reason to be organized around an internal teleology, one which leads them to strive to express

---

[23] For some similar thoughts about the foundational role of rational capacities in Kant's philosophy, see (Stephenson 2021, forthcoming). For the importance of faculties for Kant's philosophy, see also (Kern 2006; Engstrom 2009; McDowell 2011; Newton 2015; Rödl 2018; Nunez 2014; Land 2018, 2021; Pendelbury 2022).

[24] Note that, in cases like our capacity for sensibility, the capacities that come first in an explanatory sense may not be strictly speaking identical to the capacities that come first in a cognitive or epistemic sense.

[25] As Merritt has stressed to me, this conception of capacities is only "Aristotelian" in a very broad sense of this term. For example, as developed in Kant (and many other broadly Leibnizian thinkers) the idea of such capacities is often closer to what we find in the Stoics than it is to anything in Aristotle himself. Given Kant's personal interest in Stoic thought and ethics, this should come as no surprise. Nonetheless, there are certain central elements of Kant's views that are (at least by the standards of early modern philosophy) broadly Aristotelian in character. For discussion of this, see (Herman 2007; Engstrom 2009; Rödl 2010; Reath 2013). But see also (Merritt 2021a, 2021b).

themselves in a characteristic form of activity.[26] In a slogan, such capacities or powers are *self-organizing* in accordance with their own (often implicit) representation of their proper form of activity.

As we will return to below, this feature of rational powers is rooted in how their activities are guided by an awareness of their own proper form of exercise. In particular, as we will see in the next chapter, it is distinctive of Kant's conception of cognition that acts of cognition involve an (implicit) consciousness or representation of their own standards of correctness. In this way, cognition in Kant's sense necessarily carries within it its own form of internal teleology. So, as powers for certain forms of cognition, the capacities of interest to us here must strive to realize themselves through the sort of self-organization that cognition requires. Thus, at least in the cases of interest to us, the sort of self-actualizing activity that characterizes such powers is also a form of self-consciousness.

This brings us, once again, to the idea of these powers as playing a foundational role with respect to both the order of explanation and the order of cognition.[27] As I've argued elsewhere, we can see this basic methodology on display in many aspects of Kant's philosophical system. Indeed, a focus on this aspect of Kant's critical method can help us to develop a picture of transcendental idealism that identifies the metaphysical commitments that come with this view without thereby saddling Kant with a fully determinate picture of the metaphysical relationship between appearances and things in themselves.[28] But nowhere is this methodology more clearly on display than in Kant's discussion of the famous (or infamous) *Faktum der Vernunft*. This part of the second *Critique* has often been regarded as a regrettable retreat into a pre-critical form of moral dogmatism.[29] But when read carefully, Kant's appeal there to a basic consciousness of the moral law as foundational for practical philosophy appears in a very different light—as an instance of precisely the approach to philosophy that is central, for Kant, to the *difference* between transcendental philosophy and dogmatic rationalism. Indeed, as we will explore further in Chapter 3, far from being a retreat into rational intuitionism, the *Faktum der Vernunft* represents one of Kant's clearest applications of his alternative conception of philosophy: a form of philosophy that begins, not with reason's apprehension of fundamental metaphysical truths "out

---

[26] As noted above, this is one reason to prefer "power" to "capacity" in describing these powers. The *mere* capacity to perform an action (e.g. the capacity to play the trumpet) does not obviously carry with it this sort of internal teleology.

[27] Compare: "But it should not go unnoticed that the mere representation I in relation to all others (the collective unity of which it makes possible) is the transcendental consciousness. Now it does not matter here whether this representation be clear (empirical consciousness) or obscure, even whether it be actual; but the possibility of the logical form of all cognition necessarily rests on the relationship to this apperception **as a faculty**" (A117).

[28] For more on this, see (Schafer 2022b) See also (Allais 2015; Stang 2017; Stang 2018; Jauernig 2021).

[29] For some recent discussion of this issue, see (Timmermann 2010; Ware 2014, 2022).

there in the ether", but rather with *reason's own self-consciousness*—that is, with the consciousness it provides us of its fundamental principles and activities.[30]

Indeed, the *Faktum der Vernunft* is especially interesting here because it clearly displays the priority of our basic rational faculties in *both* the order of cognition *and* the order of explanation. On the one hand, in the *Faktum der Vernunft*, Kant treats our consciousness of ourselves as free as grounded in our consciousness of ourselves as subject to the moral law (as its *ratio cognoscendi*). And this latter consciousness is, in turn, analyzed in terms of our consciousness of ourselves as creatures who are both rational and sensibly conditioned—creatures, that is, who are conscious of the principles of pure practical reason, but merely as *imperatives* that characterize what we *ought* to do and not as necessary descriptive laws that characterize what we *will* do. Thus, Kant presents us here with a model of our understanding of ourselves as free on which the order of cognition begins with the way in which finite, sensibly conditioned creatures like us are necessarily conscious of practical reason as a capacity—and how practical reason's consciousness of its own internal principles manifests itself in us. This, of course, is just what we would expect, if Kant's picture of the order of cognition followed a capacities-first model and began with the self-consciousness of rational capacities like reason. But, on the other hand, in these passages Kant also treats the nature of practical reason as fundamental with respect to the order of philosophical explanation. For, as we will discuss below, in claiming that autonomy is the *ratio essendi* of morality, Kant is claiming that it is the nature of practical reason as a power—and, in particular, its character as autonomous—that explains why we are subject to the moral law in the first place. Thus, in this passage the capacity of reason plays both a cognitively fundamental role (by providing us with *consciousness* of its own fundamental principle) and a metaphysically fundamental role as well (by *being* autonomous and so explaining why the moral law applies to us).

c. The Project of the Critical Philosophy and the Autonomy of Reason

As this should indicate, Kant's attraction to a methodology that begins with reason's self-consciousness is closely tied to his conception of reason as autonomous or free from external constraint. As is familiar, this notion—of a reason that should be subject *only* to laws which it has given itself—is fundamental to Kant's

---

[30] Of course, one might wonder how much this really matters. After all, for both the "dogmatic rationalist" and the critical philosopher, there is a place where philosophical explanations and justifications must come to end (at least for human beings). So why does it matter that this stopping point is provided by the self-consciousness of our own rational capacities as opposed to a rational intuition of some "external moral fact". Unlike some, I don't think there is a simple answer to this question, but for some potential advantages of the Kantian response, see (Schafer 2015b, 2015c).

conception of what distinguishes the philosophy of the Enlightenment from what has come before it:[31] "If reason will not subject itself to the laws it gives itself, it has to bow under the yoke of laws given by another; for without any law, nothing—not even nonsense—can play its game for long" (O 8:145).

Kant concludes from this that "freedom in thinking signifies the subjection of reason to no laws except those which it gives itself" (O 8:145). Thus, "...the original right of human reason...recognizes no other judge than universal human reason itself" (A753/B781). This provides Kant with an additional motivation to conceive of his philosophical project as one that treats the capacity of reason (and *only* that) as truly fundamental. After all, if the proper exercise of reason consists in reason operating in accordance with a "law" that it "gives to itself", in settling foundational philosophical questions, we can only look to reason and its own internal principles for the fundamental criteria that distinguish correct answers to these questions from incorrect.[32] And if only the capacity of reason can sit in judgment *of* reason, then in asking questions about reason and its status, we can properly appeal *only* to the nature of reason itself to settle them. Thus, this conception of "Enlightenment philosophy" naturally suggests a view on which reason must play a fundamental role in settling these questions and (by doing so) establishing a foundation for further philosophical reflection.

More precisely, Kant conceives of the critical philosophy as involving two basic stages: a first, "critical" stage and a second "doctrinal" or "metaphysical" one:

> Now the philosophy of pure reason is either propaedeutic (preparation), which investigates the faculty of reason in regard to all pure *a priori* cognition, and is called **critique**, or, second, the system of pure reason (science), the whole (true as well as apparent) philosophical cognition from pure reason in systematic interconnection, and is called **metaphysics**.... Metaphysics is divided into the metaphysics of the **speculative** and the **practical** use of pure reason, and is therefore either **metaphysics of nature** or **metaphysics of morals**.
> (A841/B869, compare KU 5:176, EEKU 20:195)

The role of philosophy's first, "critical" stage is both negative *and* positive for Kant. Of these, it is the negative aspect that will be most familiar. For of course, critique in Kant's sense is meant to provide our cognitive faculties with a source of "discipline" by determining their boundaries in a principled fashion. This is an aim that Kant shares with many other early modern philosophers. But Kant takes himself to go beyond these philosophers by providing us with a genuine "critique of pure reason" as opposed to a mere "censorship" of it. That is, he claims that his philosophy "subjects to evaluation not the *facta* of reason but reason itself, as concerns the entire capacity and its suitability for pure *a priori* cognitions" (A761/B789). Thus,

---

[31] See (O'Neill 1989).   [32] I discuss the autonomy of reason in much more detail in Chapter 7.

according to Kant, a genuine *critique* of pure reason is possible only insofar as it is concerned with reason as a capacity or power—just as we have been suggesting here.

Critique in this sense is crucial, Kant writes, because it would establish, "not merely limits but rather the determinate boundaries" for reason—boundaries that are "not merely suspected but are proved from principles" (A761/B789). As this makes clear, even in its negative role, a genuine *critique* of reason is possible for Kant only insofar as it is grounded in a principled understanding of the nature of reason and our other rational powers. Critique differs from mere censorship insofar as it is grounded in *reason's own self-understanding*—a self-understanding that provides critique with the first principles it needs to have the systematic form that reason seeks. In this way, as Kant writes, critique operates by "revealing the deceptions of a reason that misjudges its own boundaries and of bringing the self-conceit of speculation back to modest but thorough self-cognition [*Selbsterkenntnis*] by means of sufficient illumination of our concepts" (A735/B763).

As this indicates, a genuine *critique* of pure reason in Kant's sense is only possible insofar as that critique *provides itself* with the a priori principles that a systematic account of the nature of our cognitive powers requires. But it is important to stress that the significance of philosophy's initial "critical" stage is always, for Kant, a matter of how it makes possible a second "doctrinal" or "metaphysical" stage in which we *use* these principles to construct a systematic account of the objects of theoretical and practical cognition—or, in other words, of the natural and moral world. It is here that the positive role of philosophy's first, critical phase finds its full expression, for the essence of Kant's "Copernican revolution" in philosophy lies precisely in the idea that the same principles that explain the activity of our cognitive faculties can also serve as a foundation for philosophy's second, "metaphysical" or "doctrinal" phase.

Thus, for Kant, we arrive at the foundational principles required by a "metaphysics of nature" and a "metaphysics of morals" precisely through a principled critique of our rational faculties:

> In this way the a priori principles of two faculties of the mind, the faculty of cognition and that of desire, would be found and determined as to the conditions, extent, and boundaries of their use, and *a firm basis would thereby be laid for a scientific system of philosophy, both theoretical and practical.*
> (KpV 5:12, my emphasis, compare KU 5:169)

> The concepts of nature, which contain the ground for all theoretical cognition *a priori*, rested on the legislation of the understanding.... The concept of freedom, which contains the ground for all sensibly unconditioned practical precepts *a priori*, rested on the legislation of reason. (KU 5:176)

The most important role of critique is thus not to give us a systematic understanding of the *boundaries* of our faculties but rather to give us the *principles* that philosophy requires in order to construct a systematic picture of nature and morality. As Kant writes, looking back on the first two *Critiques* from the third, just as the "critique of pure theoretical reason... yielded the laws of nature", the "critique of practical reason [yielded] the law of freedom," thereby securing the foundational principles for both (EEKU 20:202).

d. The Critical Project and the Foundational Role of Self-Consciousness

If this is right, then Kant's critical project may be thought of as an attempt to bring reason's implicit self-consciousness to the level of explicit, systematic understanding, and then to use that understanding as a foundation for a systematic form of philosophy.[33] This, as any reader knows very well, means that Kant's conception of the nature of reason (and our other rational capacities) must bear a great deal of weight in the critical system, so it is only fair to wonder whether Kant's conception of reason is up to this task.

In particular, we can ask what establishes the legitimacy of the critical philosophy's foundational claims about the rational powers or capacities it takes for granted. (See again Axvi–xvii.) In Kant and the broader Kantian literature, one can find at least two basic strategies for answering such questions. First, it might be that we are able to take certain rational faculties for granted in philosophical theorizing simply in virtue of their *self-conscious* character. Or, second, it might be that in order to introduce such faculties into our philosophical system, we must provide some sort of "transcendental argument" or "regressive argument" that shows them to be necessary conditions on even more basic features of human consciousness.

I would be the last to deny that both these strategies have an important role to play in Kant's philosophical methodology.[34] Nonetheless, it seems to me that the *ultimate* foundations for Kant's philosophical project must be arrived at *via* the first of them. The importance of the self-conscious character of these powers can be seen from the fact that, unlike (say) Reinhold or Fichte, Kant begins his "transcendental reflections" in all three *Critiques* with quite robust cognitive achievements. For example, the starting point of Kant's "transcendental reflections" in the first *Critique* is not the bare fact of self-consciousness, but rather the fact that we are creatures with a capacity (at least in principle) for *empirical cognition* of a non-trivial sort. Similarly, Kant's reflections in the second *Critique* begin with our consciousness of ourselves as beings with a robust

---

[33] Compare (Nunez 2014)'s comment that, "Kant's use of the synthetic method begins with our cognitive faculty as its first principle, not a series of definitions." My discussion of these ideas is much indebted to discussions with Nunez.

[34] See (Schafer 2021c for a discussion of the continuing relevance of these ideas for epistemology of a broadly Kantian variety. There is, of course, a great deal of literature on the precise sense in which Kant is interested in providing us with something like a "transcendental argument". Since such arguments will not be at the forefront of my account here, I will mostly leave such debates to the side. For some of the relevant literature, see (Stroud 1968; P. Strawson 1990; Brueckner 1996; Cassam 1997).

power of pure practical reason, where this involves the capacity for practical cognition and action from absolute (moral) principles. In both cases, Kant's procedure is to begin with our capacity for entirely non-trivial forms of synthetic a priori cognition and then to investigate what else must be true of us, and the objects of our cognition, in order for such cognition to be possible.[35]

At least in the context of Kant's philosophy, then, there does not seem to be any real alternative to the existence and nature of *some* basic rational faculties being something that can be established in virtue of their self-conscious character. In other words, for Kant at least, the order of philosophical cognition begins with conscious rational activities and the awareness of our rational capacities this provides us with.[36] Thus, while Kant is of course interested in what are often called "transcendental" or "regressive arguments", which attempt to establish the legitimacy of some philosophical principle by showing that it (or its acceptance) is a necessary condition on more basic features of human consciousness, such arguments acquire their significance for him in the context of these foundational forms of self-consciousness. Beginning from the forms of self-consciousness characteristic of our form of rationality, the critical philosopher can proceed to make this implicit consciousness explicit, and can then use this "principle" as a foundation for further philosophical theorizing. In many cases, this will involve appeals to regressive or "transcendental" arguments of various sorts. But the starting point of these reflections is the consciousness of our own rational activities and forms of cognition that is characteristic of rationality itself.[37]

As we will explore in the next chapter, this is not at all an ad hoc feature of Kant's account of rationality. Rather, it follows from the connection between rationality and cognition, together with the fact that all cognition, for Kant, requires a sort of active, first-personal consciousness of the standards of correctness that apply to it. Kant's conception of cognition involves an essential moment of (at least implicit) self-consciousness—one that provides us with what Schapiro has recently called "a 'guiding conception' of the activities that we undertake" (Schapiro 2021). But this is true, for Kant, because such a "guiding conception" is *already* implicit in the nature of the cognitive activities we are engaged in as the

---

[35] Of course, many have tried to interpret the Transcendental Deduction as involving a much more ambitious transcendental argument than this. Particularly notable in this regard is Guyer's important work on this question. But even Guyer admits that Kant's arguments cannot succeed if they are read in the very ambitious manner Guyer advocates. And, since the textual evidence that Guyer gives for this interpretation can also be read as implying a less ambitious project in the Deduction, the most charitable reading of the Deduction's project seems to me to be one on which this project is considerably less ambitious than Guyer takes it to be. For relevant discussion, see (Guyer 2006).

[36] Compare (Boyle 2009; Longuenesse, 2017; Smit 2019) for related discussion. And see (Allison 2004). Note that this means that we should be careful not to overstate the difficulties in achieving certain forms of self-consciousness for Kant. Contrast O'Neill's comment that, "Reason may be (in whole or in part) 'in' each participant, but it cannot be discovered by introspection: Kant insists that we are opaque, not transparent to ourselves" (O'Neill 1989, 7).

[37] Of course, this leaves unexplained why this consciousness provides us with a consciousness, not only of the actuality of these principles, but also of their necessity in some sense. I return to this in Chapter 3.

cognitive activities they are. Thus, for Kant at least, to achieve a "guiding conception" of these rational activities, we need only to better understand *what* those activities and capacities *already are*, albeit (and here I agree with Shapiro) from a first-personal perspective.

It is precisely this sort of conscious reflection, on the "guiding conception" that is implicit in our cognitive activities, which provides Kant's philosophy with its most basic philosophical foundations. For example, as Kant writes in the second *Critique*:

> [w]e can become aware of practical laws just as we are aware of pure theoretical principles, by attending to the necessity with which reason prescribes them to us and to the setting aside of all empirical conditions to which reason directs us. The concept of a pure will arises from the first, as a consciousness of a pure understanding arises from the latter. (KpV 5:30, compare A108)

As such passages indicate, in order to become conscious of the principles that are constitutive of practical reason or the will and the understanding, we need only to reflect on the activity of these faculties, abstracting away from the ways in which our empirical, sensible nature conditions this activity.[38] In this way, as Kant says in an important reflection, "All philosophy has as its object reason: maxims, limits, and the end" (Refl 18:52). Or, as Kant writes at the beginning of the first *Critique*:

> [n]othing here can escape us, because what reason brings forth entirely out of itself cannot be hidden, but is brought to light by reason itself as soon as reason's common principle has been discovered.
> (Axx, compare V-Phil-Th/Pölitz 28:1051)[39]

---

[38] Note that to say that philosophy rests on our capacity for reason is *not* to say that it rests on the mere *concept* of this capacity, which, on its own, is inadequate (for Kant) to play the role required here (RGV 6:26). An important question here is whether this model also applies to the case of sensibility. I discuss this issue in more detail in (Schafer 2022a), which offers a sympathetic but critical discussion of (Boyle 2016; Conant 2016). See also (McLear 2022).

[39] Here it may be worth comparing Kant's method with the post-Kantian methodology recently advocated by Sebastian Rödl. Rödl (somewhat notoriously) describes this methodology as follows:

> This explains what may appear a curious character of the present essay: it propounds no theses, advances no hypotheses, does not recommend a view or position; it does not give arguments that are to support a view, it does not defend a position against competing ones, it does nothing to rule out contrary theses. It does nothing of the sort because it is—it brings to explicit consciousness—the self-consciousness of judgment. (Rödl 2018, 12–13)

On the most fundamental point, Rödl agrees with my reading of Kant here, for we both see the task of foundational philosophy as one of bringing reason to full and explicit self-consciousness. Nonetheless, Rödl's insistence that this task should not involve "giving arguments" or "defending positions against competing ones" is removed from Kant's understanding of what bringing reason to self-consciousness involves. After all, as we will discuss below, reason is, among other things, the faculty for mediate inference. Thus, we should expect that one of the characteristic forms that bringing reason to full and explicit self-consciousness will take is precisely that of giving arguments for or against certain views. To ignore this is to forget that the self-consciousness at issue here is the self-

From such passages, we can see that there is an important sense in which Kant's conception of the foundations of philosophy involves an attempt to develop a form of philosophy in which, as Hegel claims about his own conception of logic: "the usual subject matter, the kinds of concepts, judgments, and syllogisms, would no longer simply be taken up from observation and thus gathered up merely empirically, but...derived from thinking itself" (EL 42A). As I've tried to indicate, there is a sense in which this would also be a very apt way of describing what Kant is up to in the critical philosophy. For, as we have just seen, it is ultimately the *self-conscious activity* of our basic rational powers (of thinking, judging, reasoning, and so on) that forms the starting point of Kant's philosophical reflections.

For Kant at least, this starting-point must be clearly distinguished from any attempt to arrive at the truth about logic merely through abstraction from the results of the various empirical sciences or other forms of "experience". Of course, this does not mean that *Hegel* would be satisfied with Kant's conception of philosophical methodology here. For Hegel would, of course, maintain that this sort of self-consciousness must either be empty, and so incapable of playing a real foundational role, or somehow implicitly "dogmatic" in taking something merely subjective and elevating it to a foundational principle for philosophy.[40] This is indeed a natural worry. From a historical perspective, though, it is important to stress that Hegel's desire to develop a truly "presuppositionless philosophy" was not fully shared by Kant. Rather, Kant's aim is to develop a philosophy that, in a certain sense, *presupposes only reason itself* as the self-conscious power it is. This, Kant would insist, is the highest point to which our critical reflections can aspire: "a system that takes no foundation as given except reason itself, and that therefore tries to develop cognition out of its original seeds without relying on any fact whatever" (Prol 4:274).

Thus, Kant's claims about these capacities—and the faculty of reason in particular—are not meant to be *mere assumptions* in anything like the ordinary sense of this term.[41] Rather, Kant takes these claims to be implicit in the self-consciousness that is characteristic of our form of rationality. What Kant's philosophy presupposes is not so much some set of assumptions or claims *about* the faculty of reason, but rather simply *this faculty itself* as the self-conscious rational capacity it is. So, if "assumptions" are meant to be propositional claims that Kant's philosophy takes for granted, I think there is a reasonable case to be made that Kant's philosophy does not begin with any "assumptions" at all. Rather, for Kant, our entitlement to such foundational propositions or principles is always rooted in

---

consciousness *of reason*. Interestingly, despite Rödl's avowed Hegelianism, this point appeals equally well (if not better) to Hegel. Indeed, on this point, Rödl seems to me closer to (say) Reinhold or early Fichte than he is to either Kant or Hegel.

[40] See (McNulty 2022; Stang forthcoming).
[41] The next paragraph draws on work for a forthcoming volume on *Kant's Fundamental Assumptions*.

something more basic—namely, the self-consciousness of reason as an active cognitive faculty. In this sense, as Fichte recognized, the starting point of Kant's philosophy is simply reason's active self-consciousness of its own nature—or, more simply, *reason's self-positing*.[42]

e. The Limits of Self-Consciousness: Capacities, Acts, and Substances

In any case, putting Fichte and Hegel aside for the moment, it is important to stress that many of the issues that drive Kant's view that *traditional metaphysics* requires critique do not apply to reason's own self-consciousness, at least in the same way. For example, insofar as such terms can even be applied here, with respect to the consciousness reason provides of its own activities, the relationship between "representation" and "object" is an especially tight one. Thus, the sorts of concerns that drive Kant to ask how synthetic a priori representations are possible do not obviously arise here in the manner they do with respect to our a priori knowledge of the world, so Kant is not being obviously inconsistent in maintaining that reason's self-critique can rest content with a form of philosophy that is not wholly presuppositionless, but rather only presupposes the capacity of reason itself.

Nonetheless, this raises a question that goes straight to the coherence of Kant's philosophical project—namely, whether this sort of self-conscious access to the acts of our own rational capacities is compatible with the limits that Kant himself places on our cognitive powers. A full answer to this question will have to wait until our discussion of Kant's conception of cognition in the next chapter. But we can give a preliminary answer to it now by noting that while, for Kant, reason does possess a *consciousness* of its own acts, principles, and ends, this consciousness does not rise to the level of genuine *cognition* (*Erkenntnis*) of our rational capacities, or of the "soul" or any other substance underlying them. Thus, in attributing this sort of consciousness to us, Kant is not obviously trespassing against his official restrictions on the scope of our cognitive powers.

More precisely, while Kant does insist that we have a grasp of reason's fundamental principle of activity and its associated ends simply in virtue of being rational, this grasp is far too indeterminate to count as *cognition of an object* in anything like Kant's sense of this phrase. For example, as Kant stresses in the Paralogisms, our conscious of ourselves as thinkers and reasoners provides us with no basis for determining whether such capacities are capacities of (say) a single spiritual substance *or* a network of cooperating substances *or* something else

---

[42] Indeed, to assume that "assumptions" must be propositional in nature is to raise these questions in a manner that leaves no room for the sort of "assumption" that Kant is *actually* beginning with.

entirely. As a result, as Kant sometimes puts the point, our consciousness of the acts and principles of reason remains merely "formal"; it does not provide us with the "material" consciousness of real *objects* that is characteristic of *cognition* in a strict sense:[43]

> All rational cognition is either material and concerned with some object, or formal and occupied only with the form of the understanding and of reason itself and with the universal rules of thinking in general, without distinction of objects. Formal philosophy is called logic, whereas material philosophy, which has to do with determinate objects and the laws to which they are subject, is in turn divided into two. For these laws are either laws of nature or laws of freedom. The science of the first is called physics, that of the other is ethics; the former is also called the doctrine of nature, the latter the doctrine of morals. (GMS 4:387)

We therefore need not worry that these forms of rational self-consciousness trespass against Kant's ban on *theoretical cognition of things in themselves*. For this consciousness is neither *genuine cognition* (of a "material" sort) nor, strictly speaking, *theoretical* in character. Rather, like all "merely formal" forms of self-consciousness, it involves a form of consciousness that is prior to the very distinction between theoretical and practical cognition, a distinction that concerns the proper relationship between a cognition and *its object* and so only really arises for *material* cognition.

Since the sort of formal self-consciousness that is at issue here is not a form of material cognition, it is, a fortiori, not a form of *theoretical* material cognition. To see the importance of this, it may be useful to briefly compare the "capacities-" or "powers-first" approach with the reading of Kant that Colin McLear is developing in his work in progress on this topic.[44] There, McLear reads Kant as a sort of "substance-first" philosopher. In developing this reading, McLear begins with observations very much like those above. But he attempts to extend them by noting that, for Kant, the *ultimate* explanation of the activity or nature of a capacity must be grounded in the nature of the *being* whose capacity it is. Thus, McLear concludes, it cannot be capacities or powers that take explanatory priority for Kant; rather, it must be the *substances that realize these capacities*.[45]

---

[43] See (Engstrom 2016).   [44] See (McLear 2020, 2022, forthcoming-a, forthcoming-b).
[45] McLear also attempts to argue against views like mine by noting that "humans are possessed of a kind of duality in light of which they are, e.g., assessable in terms of deontic norms of permission and requirement. It is precisely the duality of our rational animal nature that makes this possible, a normativity that cannot reside either in a capacity for rationality or animality alone." As we will see in Chapter 3, I very much agree with this basic point, but it presents no objection to the capacities-first model, once that model is properly understood. For the point of the model is not that such facts could be grounded in any particular capacity considered in isolation from the others, but rather that they are grounded in the full system of such capacities as realized in us.

The fundamental problem with this interpretative line is not that McLear is mistaken about Kant's basic metaphysical commitments. It is rather that McLear's interpretation is insufficiently sensitive to Kant's claims about where *exactly* philosophical explanations must come to an end for creatures like us. For example, even in the second *Critique*, where Kant goes furthest towards endorsing something like a practical cognition of our nature as noumenal agents, he still insists that "human insight is at an end as soon as we have arrived at basic powers or basic faculties" (KpV 5:46–7). Thus, at least for human beings like us, philosophical explanations come to an end, not with a cognition of ourselves as (say) spiritual substances, but rather with a consciousness of basic rational capacities like reason and their acts. Of course, as McLear notes, these capacities and powers must be realized by one or more underlying substances.[46] But again, all *we* can know of these substances is that they (somehow) realize these capacities. So, in the context of a *human* form of philosophy, it is these capacities or powers, and their various cognitive acts, which provide philosophy with its first principles, and not the (otherwise unknowable) substances that realize them. Thus, as Kant says in one important remark, for subjects like us, "I exist as an intelligence that is merely conscious of its faculty for combination" (B158–9).

In this way, it seems to me that McLear's alleged alternative to my account either collapses into a notational variant of it or reverts to a form of metaphysical theorizing that could fairly be criticized as "pre-critical" or "dogmatic". And this is not merely an interpretative point: it matters for the philosophical attractiveness of Kant's account. For one of the attractions of a reason-first approach to these issues is its fundamental *metaphysical flexibility*. After all, powers like reason can be potentially realized by a wide variety of different things, including individual subjects, organized collectives, and even larger natural systems.[47] Thus, the general powers-first approach is compatible with a wide range of views about the metaphysics underlying the existence of these powers. In this way, the powers-first approach allows us to work with a conception of reason on which reason is conceived as the power for a certain sort of cognition, while also insisting that this power that may be multiply realizable, and that this is true along several dimensions. This metaphysical flexibility seems to me one of the real virtues of a capacities- or powers-first approach like Kant's.

For similar reasons, even if one is tempted to take Kant's talk of reason's ends and interests to be an elliptical way of making claims about the ends and interests of various rational individuals, this does not mean that such references are entirely

---

[46] It is useful to compare Kant's views on this point to Wolff's. See, in particular, paragraphs 114–20 of the *German Metaphysics*.

[47] This is especially important in the context of comments like the following (from the Idea for a Universal History from a Cosmopolitan Perspective):

"In the human being (as the only rational creature on earth), those predispositions whose goal is the use of his reason were to develop completely only in the species, but not in the individual." (IAG 8:18–19)

dispensable here. Rather, in the present context, Kant's tendency to attribute ends and interests to our faculties can be understood, not as a regrettable tendency to *personify* such faculties, but as a further dimension of the metaphysical modesty at work in his philosophy. That is, it seems to me that Kant tends to speak of the interests and ends of reason itself, as opposed to the ends and interests of the various individuals who possess reason, precisely because he takes our access to the nature of the individuals or substances who possess reason to be limited in many ways. In this context, a focus on *reason as such*, as opposed to this or that individual rational subject, can be seen as another way of remaining as neutral as possible about how powers like reason are realized in us.[48]

Kant's modesty about whether the self-consciousness of reason amounts to genuine *self-cognition* in this sense is surely one of the most distinctive features of his philosophy, one that distinguishes him from both his rationalist predecessors *and* many of those who followed in his wake. Consider, for example, the difference between Kant and Fichte on this point. For Fichte, like many who followed Kant, "Reason necessarily cognizes itself completely, and an analysis of its entire procedure, or a system of reason, is possible" (GA I, 5:68–9). But, for Kant, to speak of reason's "cognizing itself completely" would be to attribute powers to human reason that lie beyond its purview. In a sense, it is here that we can locate the fundamental divide between Kant and the more ambitious idealists who followed in his wake. For Kant, while the self-consciousness of reason is the foundation of all genuine philosophy, this self-consciousness (at least in its human form) is limited in how far it can penetrate. For Fichte or Hegel, on the other hand, the idea that reason's self-consciousness might be, in this sense, *essentially incomplete* is incompatible with reason's own demand for systematic comprehension.[49] As we will see in our discussion of Kant's conception of comprehension below, this difference runs to the very heart of Kant's conception of human reason and why this stops short of the sort of absolute idealism that Schelling or Hegel endorses.

Nonetheless, it remains true that the capacities-first approach represents a form of idealism in a more modest sense. For it does attempt to explain many very basic features of the world, both natural and normative, in terms of certain basic cognitive or rational faculties. In this way, there is undoubtedly an element of idealism in how it explains (at least the "form" of) the objects of theoretical and

---

[48] Thanks to an anonymous referee here. Nonetheless, if one wishes to treat claims about reason's ends and interests as claims about the ends or interests of the individuals who have reason, that would generally be acceptable. Note that our ability to form at least rationally justified beliefs about such matters is extended considerably by the access to the moral law that practical reason provides us with. My focus here is on the limits on theoretical cognition of the self for Kant, and not the practical extension of this. For further discussion of the latter, see Chapter 3 and (Schafer forthcoming a). I return to the place of rational individuals into Kant's system in Chapter 6.

[49] As Daniel Smyth notes, Kant does sometimes use the term "*Selbsterkenntnis*" to characterize the sort of formal self-consciousness at issue here. But the basic distinction between merely formal self-consciousness (or cognition) and material cognition that I am drawing here remains.

practical cognition. At the same time, it is important to stress again that what Kant treats as explanatorily fundamental in this regard are not the cognitive faculties of any *particular* subject or subjects. Instead, as we will see, Kant's starting point here is a conception of reason as something potentially universal and so essentially intersubjective.[50] For Kant, the principles of reason are in no way "*up to us*", nor are they local to our particular cognitive constitution.[51] If there is a sort of idealism at work within Kant's capacities-first framework, then, it is one that (at least with respect to reason) begins from a starting point that aims to provide philosophy within a genuinely "objective" or "intersubjective" foundation. In short, while Kant is a powers-first theorist, he treats the powers that "come first" on this view in an objective manner.[52] What really comes first for Kant is the general capacity or power for certain forms of cognition as such, however this is actually realized.

f. The Plausibility of a Capacities-First or Powers-First Approach Today

The task of this chapter has been to sketch a picture of Kant's general critical methodology. The core of this approach has consisted in the idea of a philosophical method that treats our basic rational capacities (and reason in particular) as fundamental in two senses. First, epistemologically or cognitively, it treats some of these capacities—or, perhaps better, their activities and principles—as potentially available to reflection simply in virtue of their self-conscious character. And second, in a more explanatory vein, it treats these capacities or powers as providing us with a principled foundation for a genuinely systematic account of both theoretical and practical philosophy, at least insofar as such a systematic account is possible for human beings. Thus, on this account of his philosophical method, Kant's critical philosophy is one that adopts a "capacities-first" approach in both an epistemological and an explanatory sense.

Given the complexity of Kant's conception of such capacities, the relationship between such a reading of Kant and other competing interpretations will often itself be complex. For example, consider the foundations of Kant's practical philosophy. According to the capacities-first approach, these foundations lie in Kant's conception of practical reason as this is realized in finite, sensibly conditioned beings. Such a reading *might* be contrasted with readings that take treat as

---

[50] Or at least potentially universal with respect to all finite rational beings.
[51] Compare (Sensen 2012; Pollok 2017). In this respect, Kant's form of capacities-first philosophy differs from more radical forms of idealism that treat, say, the properties of the objects of perception as dependent upon the *particular* constitution of our faculties for sensible perception, or more existentialist views, which take as fundamental choices or values that are truly *up to us*.
[52] Here it is interesting to compare (Bommarito 2020)'s discussion of the foundations of certain forms of Buddhism.

fundamental, say, what is most fundamentally *valuable* (as suggested by Allen Wood), or a certain conception of *reflective agency* (as suggested by Korsgaard and others), or certain *practical feelings* (in the manner associated with the sort of sentimentalism that Kant was attracted to prior to his critical phase).[53] But the contrast between these views will often be less clear than it might seem since many of these elements are part of the package that is constitutive of Kant's conception of practical reason. For example, as noted above, for Kant every rational capacity is associated with certain ends or interests that characterize its proper functioning, so it is not as if the values that Wood takes to be fundamental to Kant's account are absent from the capacities-first interpretation—though on the capacities-first approach, in order to understand the nature of these ends, we must consider them in relation to our fundamental capacity of practical reason and its characteristic forms of activity. Similarly, as we have already begun to explore, the sort of reflective agency that forms Korsgaard's focus is very closely associated with the proper functioning of practical reason. Indeed, in many ways, the present reading might be regarded as developing certain central ideas within Korsgaard's account—only focusing, as Kant himself does, on the nature of reason as a capacity, as opposed to, say, agency per se.

We'll return to these connections in Chapter 3. But before moving on, it may be useful to pause briefly to consider the attractiveness of a capacities-first approach to philosophy in the contemporary context. Such an approach is likely to seem unattractive today for a variety of reasons. For one, it may seem to rest on an outdated, "facultistic" understanding of human psychology. Or talk of capacities and their activities might seem to be a relic of a mysterious, premodern teleological metaphysics that is best left in the past. Finally, one might question whether such talk of "reason" or "rational capacities" should be regarded as anything other than an attempt to reify, and so rationalize, a parochial set of culturally specific values or norms.

The contemporary appeal of Kant's conception of reason is not the primary topic of this chapter. But it is, just as surely, part of its subtext, so it would be disingenuous to plead the privilege of the historian in response to such questions. Nonetheless, it is far too earlier in our story to offer anything like a detailed response to them. But we can say something in response by noting some reasons for thinking that the idea of a philosophy that appeals, at a deep level, to a notion of our rational capacities or powers is not completely outdated. In doing so, it is worth noting that there are really two questions here. First, there is the question of whether *any* appeal to capacities or faculties within philosophy is an outdated relic of the past. And second, there is the question of whether it is plausible to give such capacities the *very* fundamental role (either epistemologically or explanatorily) in

---

[53] (Korsgaard 1996, 2009; Wood 1999, 2007).

philosophy that Kant assigns to them. That is, in considering these questions, it will be useful to distinguish the question of whether capacities and faculties might have some important role to play in contemporary philosophy from the question of whether this role should be to give philosophy its ultimate foundations in the manner I have suggested is true for Kant.

With respect to the first question, my view is that there is little reason today to dismiss capacity-theoretic notions out of hand. For instance, although it was once common to speak of psychology as having moved beyond an appeal to mental capacities or faculties, I think few psychologists would make such claims today. In recent years, the psychological respectability of capacity-theoretic notions has steadily been on the rise with the growing influence of the notion of the mind as modular (massively or otherwise). Thus, it is no surprise to find that the psychological cutting-edge with respect to the study of rationality focuses precisely on the notion of reason as capacity and reasoning as the characteristic activity of that capacity.[54] In this respect, Kant's way of thinking of reason and rationality is actually *more* in tune with the contemporary discussion of these topics in psychology than much of the contemporary philosophical discussion is.

Similar developments are also easy to recognize within philosophy, where capacity-theoretical notions have become much more prominent in recent years in areas such as virtue ethics, virtue epistemology, and neo-Aristotelian metaphysics. As a result, it is hard to dismiss the appeal to such notions as simply outdated in the manner that once was possible. Of course, these developments leave open the difficult philosophical question of how talk of capacities is best squared with (much of) contemporary philosophy's focus on a naturalistic picture of reality. This is a very complicated question. But for the moment, we can simply note that the capacity-theoretical philosopher has a variety of responses to such concerns available to them. On the one hand, someone who is very naturalistically inclined, but also attracted to capacity-theoretic notions, might turn to the attempts in contemporary philosophy of biology to make teleologically structured faculties naturalistically acceptable—say, by appeal to an etiological or a systems-theoretical understanding of this teleology. But someone less naturalistically inclined might see the philosophical important of capacity-theoretic notions as evidence that the whole truth about reality cannot be captured in purely "naturalistic" terms, although, of course, there is much room for dispute about how the idea of the "natural world" is to be understood in this context.

I think it is fair to say that Kant's own views represent a version of this second option. But this does not mean that a contemporary Kantian *must* follow Kant on this point. After all, at least one of Kant's primary motivations for such claims

---

[54] Compare (Mercier and Sperber 2017) and (Schellenberg 2018), for example. But such notions go back to the very beginning of cognitive science. See, for example, the defense of teleology in (Rosenblueth, Wiener, and Bigelow 1943). See also (Nagel 2012).

about the limits of a naturalistic perspective on reality were his (broadly incompatibilist) intuitions about the nature of freedom. If we do not share those intuitions, we may find it possible to develop a Kantian account of reason as cognitive power that is more fully integrated into a naturalistic picture of reality. Of course, doing so may lead us to reconsider the nature of a naturalistic picture of things in quite fundamental ways. For example, even if we remain compatibilists, Kant's views about these issues may push us away from more "Humean" conceptions of nature towards one, like Kant's, that sees the natural world as itself populated by active powers of some sort.[55] But this should not necessarily be seen as a turn away from "naturalism" in a broader sense of the term.

In short, then, both naturalists and those skeptical of naturalism are well positioned to appeal to capacity-theoretical notions in a philosophical and a psychological context. But, of course, this is only to defend the relevance of Kant's discussion of these issues with respect to our first question. That is, it gives us good reason to take seriously views on which capacity-theoretic notions do serious epistemic or explanatory work; this, of course, is hardly to defend the claim that philosophy should take certain capacities as truly fundamental in the manner that is characteristic of a global capacities-first strategy like Kant's. On this score, relatively few philosophers today will be willing to follow Kant all the way to a *generalized* capacity-first approach. For such a path naturally leads to a form of transcendental idealism (or formal idealism) that most contemporary philosophers would find unacceptable. Personally, I think such views deserve to be taken more seriously than they often are today. But even if we are not tempted towards them in general, they remain attractive in many areas of philosophy such as meta-ethics. Indeed, as we will see below one way to think about the contemporary wave of interest in "constructivist" or "constitutivist" accounts of normativity is in terms of the adoption of a form of a capacities-first approach to meta-normative questions. So, even if we are not tempted by a *global* version of the capacities-first approach, we may still be attracted to a view of the normative domain that treats the capacity of reason as fundamental in much the manner that Kant does. This would provide us with an account of the values and norms that apply to us as rational beings that sees these values and norms as rooted in our own cognitive or rational capacities. Thus, such an approach provides a promising strategy for explaining the objectivity of values and norms in a manner that neither alienates us from these values nor characterizes the relationship between the normative and the non-normative in terms of a series of unexplained, brute facts. Once again, we will return to this in Chapter 3 below.

---

[55] Whether this is really possible depends a great deal on whether the nature of such powers is compatible with the sort of explanation characteristic of natural science. For an insightful discussion of why Kant took mechanical causation to be incompatible with genuine teleology, see (Brink forthcoming). But of course we might not follow Kant in giving priority to mechanistic explanations within a natural scientific context.

2
Self-Consciousness, Cognition, and the Taking Condition

In the last chapter, I laid out the core elements of Kant's powers- or capacities-first methodology during the critical period. In next two chapters, I want to deepen our understanding of the conception of rational powers that sits at the heart of that methodology by focusing on two aspects of Kant's account that will be crucial for our discussion of reason to follow: First, Kant's conception of "cognition" (*Erkenntnis*) in its various forms; and second, the relationship between the normative and the descriptive aspects of capacities like reason.

Our focus in this chapter will be the first of these topics. As we will see, this is vital for understanding Kant's conception of reason. For to understand reason as a capacity or power, we need to understand what reason is a capacity *to do*. And to understand this, we need to understand the sort of cognition that reason makes possible and strives to achieve. Kant's powers-first philosophical method is thus equally a "cognition-first" one. Indeed, as we will see below on Kant's conception of cognition, cognition itself possesses a sort of internal teleology, one that makes it appropriate to view cognition as striving to organize itself in accordance with certain aims that are internal to it as a form of "objective representation with consciousness".[1] In this sense, on my reading, Kant's conception of cognition itself anticipates Hegel's famous claim that, properly understood, "consciousness [or cognition] in its own self provides its own standard" (PS 84). The reading of Kant on cognition I will develop here might therefore reasonably be regarded as a proto-Hegelian one.

To explore this, in the next section, I will provide a more detailed account of Kant's conception of cognition, focusing on the ways in which this notion is different from what contemporary epistemologists generally have in mind when they speak of "knowledge". Then, I will show how Kant's conception of cognition *in general* allows for a distinction between two basic ways cognition can relate to

---

[1] If the idea of forms of cognition striving to develop themselves in this manner seems mysterious, just think of an ordinary instance of understanding. Part of understanding something is a propensity to understand other things through that understanding and (at least in many cases) to search for further pieces of understanding that will aid one in that activity. In this way, as the contemporary literature on understanding has stressed, understanding is generally constituted by a complex set of propensities and capacities – propensities and capacities for (in part) the further development of the understanding in question. See (Hills 2015; Bengson 2017; Hannon 2021) for some recent discussion of this.

its object, generating a basic distinction between theoretical and practical cognition. Finally, I will conclude this chapter by drawing on this account of cognition to deepen our understanding of why and how rational capacities must be self-conscious for Kant. In doing so, I will connect Kant's discussion of these issues with the contemporary debate about whether rational activities like inference must be governed by some version of a "taking condition", suggesting that Kant anticipates that debate in potentially illuminating ways.

a. Kant's Conception of Cognition

The main topic of this chapter will be the connections between rationality, cognition, and self-consciousness as Kant understands them.[2] In particular, as we will see, "cognition" (*Erkenntnis*) in Kant's sense essentially involves a basic form of self-consciousness. Thus, one way of understanding Kant's claims about the relationship between rationality and self-consciousness is through Kant conception of "cognition" (*Erkenntnis*).

To understand this, though, we must first understand what Kant means by "cognition" (*Erkenntnis*). It is important to discuss this topic carefully because Kant's use of this term has often been the subject of confusion in the scholarly literature. For instance, Kant's references to "cognition" (*Erkenntnis*) have often been translated into English by rendering *Erkenntnis* as "knowledge". This rendering, quite naturally, has encouraged the identification of "cognition" in Kant's sense with the contemporary notion of "knowledge" as something like *non-accidental justified true belief*. But while cognition in Kant's sense is indeed a form of "knowledge" in the broad, ordinary sense of the term, the assimilation of Kant's notion of cognition to "knowledge" in this technical sense invites a misleading picture of Kant's main concerns. We must be careful to reconstruct Kant's way of thinking about cognition and knowledge on its own terms, before attempting to connect it together with the contemporary epistemological debate.

To do so, let's begin with what is probably Kant's most familiar definition of cognition—namely, the idea of cognition as "objective representation with consciousness". This definition is prominent, for example, in the famous *Stufenleiter* passage of the first *Critique*:[3]

---

[2] This section draws heavily upon (Schafer 2022b, forthcoming a). My understanding of these issues is heavily indebted to discussions with Houston Smit, Clinton Tolley, and Eric Watkins. For other important work on Kant's conception of cognition, see (Smit 2000, 2009; Chignell 2012; Tolley 2017b; Watkins and Willaschek 2017) among others. Also compare here (Ginsborg 2014)'s distinction between discrimination (*Kenntnis*) and consciousness of difference (*Erkenntnis*). In an appendix, I consider the relationship between my reading of "cognition" and several other recent interpretations in more detail, but I will focus on my positive account here.

[3] Beginning with the *Stufenleiter* may seem unwise given the extensive debate about how it is best interpreted. In particular, one might wonder whether the notion of "cognition" at issue in *Stufenleiter*

The genus is *representation* as such (repraesentatio). Under this stands representation with consciousness (perceptio). A *perception* that is related merely to the subject as a modification of its state is *sensation* (sensatio), an objective perception is *cognition* (cognitio). This is either intuition or concept (intuitus vel conceptus). (B376-7)

According to this passage, "cognition" is "objective perception", and since "perception" is defined as "representation with consciousness", Kant here defines cognition as "objective representation with consciousness". As we will see, this definition also appears elsewhere in the Kantian corpus. But what does "objective representation with consciousness" consist in for Kant?

As Kant uses these terms, an objective representation with consciousness is a representation that represents something *to* one's consciousness in a manner that makes one *conscious of it as something objective* in at least the minimal sense that one is conscious of it as something more than a mere episode in one's subjective experience. When Kant speaks of cognition qua "objective representation with consciousness", what he has in mind is the sort of representation that makes one *conscious of objects* as opposed to merely providing one with a consciousness of one's own subjective state.[4] Beginning with the first of these characteristics, the claim that a cognition is a representation *with consciousness* might be taken simply to mean that it is a representation we are conscious of. But this is only part of what Kant has in mind here. For, when we are dealing with an *objective* representation—that is, a representation that has a relation to both the subject and some object or objects—this representation will only count as an objective representation *with consciousness* in Kant's sense if it also provides us with consciousness of the object(s) that it is a representation of. Otherwise, the representation would present itself to consciousness merely as a modification of the subject's subjective state, and not as having a relation to an object that is independent of this state. Thus, for a representation to count as a cognition for

---

can possibly be the same as the one at issue in the *Logic* passages below, given that the *Stufenleiter* includes both intuitions and ideas of reason under the heading of "cognition" *qua* "objective representations with consciousness". In the end, nothing here hinges on this passage in particular, but in fact it is not difficult to read the *Stufenleiter* as referring to cognition in the same sense as the *Logic*. For instance, so long as we read Kant's reference to "intuition" in *Stufenleiter* to refer to intuitions which have been synthesized in accordance with the categories as rules for sensible synthesis, there is nothing very surprising about the inclusion of intuitions under the heading of cognitions *qua* "objective representations with consciousness". And, similarly, while the ideas of reason may not provide *us* with theoretical cognition of their objects, one of them is central to our *practical* cognition of ourselves as free. Moreover, these ideas (or something akin to them) presumably provide less limited beings with cognition of certain objects. So, given their potential to play this role, it is not surprising to find them included here under the heading of "cognitions", even though they do not rise to the level of genuine cognitions *for beings like us*. For a somewhat different reading of the *Stufenleiter*, which supports the same basic point, see (Tolley 2017b).

[4] Compare (Rödl 2007). For more on this distinction, see (Longuenesse 2005; Sethi 2020).

Kant, it must provide its subject with (at least implicit) consciousness of its object(s) *as objective* in this sense:

Consciousness of the Object: In order to cognize X we must be able to become *conscious* of X as an object, i.e. as something that is independent of the subjective state of mind involved our particular representations of X.[5]

As a result, for Kant, what is distinctive of cognition is not merely that it stands in a certain relationship to its object, but also that it makes us *conscious* (at least implicitly) *of this relationship*. Thus, cognition for Kant always involves an (at least implicit) consciousness of three things: (i) our representation of something, (ii) the thing represented as something distinct from our representation of it, and (iii) an appropriate relationship between these two.[6]

As this indicates, what is at issue in Kant's discussion of cognition is first and foremost our *conscious grasp of objects*—a grasp of objects that brings them to consciousness. It is this very basic cognitive achievement, or relationship between "mind" and "world", that Kant's discussion of cognition is meant to explore. Thus, while we once again might think of cognition in this sense as a sort of "knowledge" in the everyday sense of this term, what is at issue here is first and foremost a knowledge *of objects*.[7] Moreover, unlike the sort of binary knowledge-relations that are generally the focus of contemporary epistemology, the sort of "knowledge" involved in Kantian cognition comes in different degrees of perfection— degrees of perfection that correspond to various forms this sort of relation to an object can take for us. As we will see, some of these forms of "knowledge" are much more basic than "knowledge" in the contemporary sense while others are more complex. But to understand *any* of them, we need to be careful to distinguish "cognition" in Kant's sense from the conceptions of "knowledge" that dominate much of contemporary epistemology.

What, then, is the relationship between a representation and its object that is characteristic of cognition for Kant? In keeping with Kant's discursive conception of human cognition, I take the most fundamental feature of the object of a cognition to be the connection between it and the "material truth or falsity" of judgments involving the cognitions to which it is related.[8] For example, a judgment whose subject is a singular cognition will be true just in case this judgment attaches a predicate to this cognition that agrees with the cognition's object. And a

---

[5] Here my view is quite close to that developed by Tolley, although we develop this basic thought in different ways.

[6] This is nicely stressed by (Tolley 2017b).

[7] Of course, Kant believes that our knowledge of objects is essentially discursive, and so structured by concepts, judgments, and inferences. But this does not mean that we should forget that Kant's conception of cognition is first and foremost a conception of our cognitive relation to objects (and not to propositions or facts).

[8] Compare (Heis 2014) here.

judgment whose subject is a general concept will be true just in case it attaches a predicate to this concept that agrees with all the possible objects that fall under the subject concept.[9] Thus, in being related to an object (or objects), a cognition (or its associated judgments) acquires a standard of correctness—of "material truth or falsity"—that extends beyond anything internal to the judgment itself, considered as a state of the subject.[10]

A representation has a "material" standard of correctness in this sense, just in case it is answerable to something that goes beyond the nature of the subject's concepts (or other representations) for its correctness or success.[11] As an "*objective* representation", any genuine cognition *has* a material standard of correctness in this sense. But, as an "objective representation *with consciousness*", it also makes the subject *conscious* (at least implicitly or potentially) of the fact that this is the case. For, according to Kant, to be conscious of *this* is just what it is to be conscious of a representation as representing something objective.[12] For example, suppose that I have a conscious representation of some object O as having the property P. Then, through reflection, I will be in a position to become conscious of myself as representing O in this way. And *this* will enable me to recognize that this representation (or judgments involving it) is correct just in case O in fact has P. In this way, according to Kant, if we are conscious of some representation as representing an object, we will also (at least implicitly) be conscious of it as falling under a material standard of correctness. Thus, as Kant writes in the first *Critique*, "our thought of the relation of all cognition to its object carries something of necessity with it, since namely the latter is regarded as that which is opposed to our cognitions being determined at pleasure or arbitrarily" (A104).

In saying this, it is important to remember that it is *not* the case that only cognitions (in this sense) can be true or false. For instance, it is perfectly possible

---

[9] Here I restrict myself to judgments with the simplest subject-predicate form.

[10] I want to remain neutral on the vexed question of whether these standards *only* apply to judgments involving the cognition or whether they may be extended in some sense to the cognition *itself*. Obviously, there is a sense in which standards for the correctness of judgments involving some cognition might be translated into standards of accuracy for that cognition itself. But dealing with those connections would take us beyond the focus of this chapter.

[11] It should be stressed that this does not mean that the object that accounts for this material standard of correctness must be *wholly* independent of the representations in question. The important point is simply that the correctness of the representation in question cannot be wholly captured in terms of the logical relations between the concepts involved in it. In addition, it should also be noted that this distinction between "formal or logical" standards of correctness and "material" standards of correctness does not apply to an intuitive intellect like God, who does not use discursive concepts. In this way, the nature of divine cognition remains something we can grasp (for Kant) only *via* an analogy with our own form thereof. Compare (Matherne 2021).

[12] As we will see, this relates to Kant's views about the nature of our rational capacities and the manner in which such capacities must be conscious of their own internal "standards of proper use". For part of what is at issue in Kant's discussion of cognition of objects is that such cognition should not just refer to some object, but also make us conscious of its object as something that imposes a real standard of correctness upon our representations of it. As we will discuss below, this has interesting connections with the contemporary discussion about whether rational attitudes and activities are governed by some sort of "taking condition".

for a representation to acquire a merely "formal" standard of correctness without thereby qualifying as a cognition in Kant's sense of the term. After all, on Kant's view, a judgment is subject to such "formal standards" simply in virtue of the nature of the concepts involved in it, without consideration of its relationship to any object or objects. Indeed, a representation can even acquire a *material* standard of truth or falsity (in some sense) without counting as a cognition for Kant. For there is of course a gap between a representation (i) merely *referring* some object in the sense required in order to be subject to a material standard of truth or falsity, and (ii) presenting this object *to consciousness* in the manner required for cognition in Kant's sense. For example, as Kant discusses in the *Jäsche Logic*, mere animals possess many representations that do not rise to the level of cognitions.[13] But while these representations do not give the creatures that possess them the sort of consciousness of their objects that is required for cognition, they are used by these creatures to (unconsciously) differentiate between different things.[14] Thus, although these animal representations will not count as full-fledged cognitions, it nonetheless makes sense to evaluate their "material" accuracy or inaccuracy, so it is possible for us to think of these sorts of representations as subject to material standards of correctness (in some sense) even when they do not rise to the level of genuine cognition.[15]

As this indicates once again, what genuine cognition in Kant's sense requires is not simply that a representation has a material standard of correctness, but also that it makes us (at least potentially) conscious of this standard. It is this that separates the view of cognition being developed here from a purely "semantic" interpretation of Kant's conception of cognition.[16] For what is at issue here is not merely the ability of a cognition to achieve genuine "reference" to an object in the sense familiar from contemporary semantics, but also its ability to make the cognizer *conscious* of the object it refers to and the standards that this object places on our representations of it. This is something that is neither purely epistemic nor purely semantic in character, although it involves elements of both.

Summing this up, genuine cognition of an object, for Kant, involves *both* of the following features:

1. The cognition must be subject to material standards of correctness that extend beyond the requirements of logic alone.

---

[13] For a helpful discussion of animal cognition in Kant, see (McLear 2011). Compare again the discussion of this in (Ginsborg 2014).

[14] This is especially true of representations that fall into Kant's third class in this progression: those (instances of *Kenntnis*) that allow one to represent something in comparison with other things as to identity and diversity *without* consciousness.

[15] Again, the nature of these standards, and the sort of normativity that attaches to them, is something I want to remain neutral on here.

[16] Such as (Hanna 2006).

2. The subject must, at least implicitly, be conscious of these material standards of correctness as they apply to this representation. That is, through reflecting on their cognitions, they must be able to form explicit representations of what these standards are.

Importantly, this does not mean that these elements of cognition must be something the cognitive subject *explicitly attends to* in forming a cognition of an object. It only means that they must be in a position to bring these features to explicit consciousness *via* reflection, provided that nothing else interferes with this process. In this sense, the consciousness of these elements that is involved in cognition is generally merely implicit for Kant—though it is crucial that it can become the target of explicit consciousness through philosophical reflection.

Similarly, these claims do not mean that the subject must always be able to be conscious of *whether* their representation *meets* these standards through reflection alone. After all, in ordinary empirical cases, becoming conscious of *this* will normally require a good deal more than mere reflection on my representations. What is important is rather whether the subject can, through reflection, become conscious of what must be the case *if* their representation is to meet these standards. What must be accessible to the subject is not *whether* their representations are correct, but what would have to the case in order for them to be correct. For this reason, these claims should not be taken to conflict with the fact that things that lie beyond our consciousness often contribute to the material standards of correctness that apply to our representation. Rather, the claim is only that *insofar* as the material standards of correctness have this status, they are not relevant to our ability to become *conscious of objects* in the manner involved in cognition. Thus, nothing in Kant's conception of cognition conflicts with the semantic externalist idea that unknown (and sometimes unknowable) facts often partially determine the material standards of correctness that apply to our representations. Indeed, much of what Kant has to say about our ignorance of things of themselves would be unintelligible if this were not the case. Kant's point here is only the more modest one that, insofar as such "externalist" standards remain outside our consciousness, they do not contribute to our consciousness of the objects of our representations.

In essence, then, Kant's idea here is that a representation can only make us conscious of what it represents insofar as it also makes us (at least implicitly or potentially) conscious of the standards of material correctness that apply to it. This element in Kant's understanding of cognition is crucial for understanding many of the features he ascribes to cognition as such. For Kant goes on to argue that, in order to provide a standard of material correctness in the sense at issue here, the object of a cognition must have two further features. First, the object in question must be something that *could actually exist*—or, as Kant puts it, it must be something that is "really possible."[17] And second, it must be relatively *determinate* what the object (or objects) of the cognition is and what they are like. Thus, for a representation to provide us with objective representation *with consciousness*, it must possess an object with both these features *and* it must make us (at least implicitly) conscious of this object as possessing them:

Real Possibility: In order to cognize X we must be able to become conscious of X as a real possibility.[18]

Determinate Content: We can only cognize X to the degree that we are able to become conscious of X's determinate identity (both numerical and qualitative).

Both these constraints follow from the idea of cognitions as involving a consciousness of their material standards of correctness. To see why, let's begin with the Real Possibility Constraint. According to this constraint, a representation will make us conscious of a material standard of correctness only insofar as it makes us conscious of its object as not just logically possible, but really possible as well. The distinction between real and merely logical possibility at work in such claims has been the subject of much recent debate, but the important point for present purposes is that the standards of logical possibility are wholly determined by the nature of our concepts and other representations.[19] Thus, these standards are not in any meaningful sense determined by features of the objects of these representations as such; talk of "merely logically possible things" is simply a way of *reifying* the logical constraints on our representations that are already internal to those representations themselves. For this reason, a representation that makes us conscious of something as a *mere logical possibility* does not really make us conscious of anything objective *over and above* the standards of correctness that are already implicit in our concepts and other representations. As such, it does not provide us with the sort of consciousness *of objects* that cognition involves.

Rather, for us to be conscious of an object as placing *material* standards of correctness on our representations of it, we must be conscious of it as a *real possibility*. In this way, genuine cognition of objects requires an (often implicit) consciousness of those objects as really possible. But it is also true that a representation will make us conscious of a (non-trivial) material standard of correctness only insofar as it makes us consciousness of its object as a determinate thing

---

[17] This constraint has been stressed by Chignell in much of his recent work on these issues. See (Chignell 2012, 2017) for more discussion.

[18] It's worth stressing that some interpreters take something stronger than this to follow here—namely, that cognition requires not just the real possibility of its object, but its actual existence. I mean to remain neutral on this question here, but for some discussion, see (Schafer 2017). One might take the Determinate Content Constraint to also push us in this direction, insofar as one viewed merely possible objects as essentially indeterminate in some sense, but I'll leave that to the side here.

[19] See (Stang 2016) for a detailed treatment of Kant's theory of modality. And compare (Abaci 2019).

with certain determinate properties as opposed to others. Kant stresses this feature of cognitions again and again. For example, in the B Deduction, he writes that:

> Understanding is, generally speaking, the faculty of cognitions. These consist in the *determinate* relation of a given representation to an object. An object, however, is that in the concept of which the manifold of a given intuition is united. (B137; my emphasis)

And a bit further on, we have the following:

> ... the categories are not restricted in thinking by the conditions of our sensible intuition, but have an unbounded field, and only the cognition of objects that we think, the *determination* of the object, requires intuition. (B166; my emphasis)

Finally, later on in the *Critique*, he writes that:

> If we separate [intuitions from concepts], then we have representations that we cannot relate to any *determinate* object. (A258/B314; my emphasis)

In these passages, Kant puts the point in different ways, focusing, in turn, on the determinacy of the "relation" of a cognition to its object, on its "determination" of its object, and on its relation to a "determinate object". But all these passages express the same basic thought—namely, that a representation is a cognition of an object only insofar as it is determinate what the "object of that representation" is and is like.

But why must the object of a cognition be determinate in this sense? For Kant, this requirement is a direct consequence of the idea that a cognition's object provides it with a material standard of correctness. After all, as Kant puts it: "Material truth must consist in this agreement of a cognition with just that determinate object to which it is related" (Log 9:51). More precisely, an object will be capable of playing this role only if two things are true of it. First, it must be determinate which object (or class of possible objects) is relevant to the truth or falsity of judgments involving the cognition in question:

> If truth consists in the agreement of a cognition with its object, then this object must thereby be distinguished from others; for a cognition is false if it does not agree with the object to which it is related even if it contains something that could well be valid of other objects. (A58/B83)

But for an object to provide the cognition associated with it with a material standard of correctness, something more than this is required. For an object will only be able to play this role to the degree that the following is also true of it: for any quality, it is determinate whether the object in question possesses this quality. Thus, the object of a cognition can play this role only to the degree that it is determinate in two senses. It must be determinate *which thing* this object (or class of possible objects) *is*, and it must be determinate *what* this object (or class of possible objects) *is like*.

Thus, there are at least two respects in which cognition of an object must represent that object in a reasonably determinate fashion: (i) with respect to its identity and difference with other things (its "numerical identity") and (ii) with respect to the qualities it possesses (its "qualitative identity"). Of course, such determinacy is a matter of degree. But, as we will see, this is very much in keeping with Kant's approach to understanding our cognitive powers, which sees these powers as possessing an internal teleology that pushes them to realize themselves through ever more perfect forms of cognition, insofar as this is required by our proper ends as finite rational creatures.[20]

It is this dimension of cognition that is the focus of the definitions of cognition that Kant provides in his logic lectures—e.g. in the *Jäsche* and *Blomberg Logics*. In the first of these, Kant defines "cognition" as the fourth degree (*Grad*) of a more complicated hierarchy of forms of representation in terms of their various relationships with their objects:

> In regard to the objective content of our cognition in general, we may think the following *degrees*, in accordance with which cognition can, in this respect, be graded:
>
> The *first* degree of cognition is: *to represent* something;
>
> The *second*: to represent something with consciousness, or *to perceive* (*percipere*);

---

[20] Confirmation that cognition is a matter of degree in this sense can be found in many passages. For example, consider the following: "in order to cognize a thing completely one has to cognize everything possible and determine the thing through it, whether affirmatively or negatively. Thoroughgoing determination is consequently a concept that we can never exhibit *in concreto* in its totality" (A573/B601). As this passage indicates, there is a sense in which we never achieve complete cognition of any empirical object for Kant.

The idea that cognition requires the representation of a determinate object has deep roots in the Leibnizian philosophy of mind that was dominant in Germany during Kant's lifetime. But the history of a connection between these two notions is much older than this. In fact, both the idea that cognition requires the representation of a determinate object *and* the idea that this is only possible (in human beings) through the cooperation of an individual's sensible and intellectual faculties is fundamental to a great deal of scholastic philosophy of mind. For instance, compare the following comment of Aquinas in the *Summa contra Gentiles*:

> ...the substance of the human soul is immaterial and consequently, as we saw, is of intellectual nature: all immaterial substances are. But this doesn't yet make it a mind representing this or that thing, which it must be if it is to know determinately this or that thing.... So the mind is still potential in regard to determinate representation of the sort of things we can know, namely, the natures of things sensed. Now it is exactly these determinate natures of things that are presented to us in our images.... so the images are understandable potentially and determinate representations of things actually.... (2.77)

The *third*: *to be acquainted* with something (*noscere*), or to represent something in comparison with other things, both as to sameness and as to difference.

The *fourth*: to be acquainted with something *with consciousness*, i.e. to *cognize* it (*cognoscere*). Animals are *acquainted* with objects too, but they do not *cognize* them.

The *fifth*: *to understand* something (*intelligere*), i.e. to cognize something *through the understanding by means of concepts*, or to *conceive*. One can conceive much, although one cannot comprehend it, e.g. a *perpetuum mobile*, whose impossibility is shown in mechanics.

The *sixth*: to cognize something through reason, or *to have insight* into it (*perspicere*). With few things do we get this far, and our cognitions become fewer and fewer in number the more that we seek to perfect them as to content.

The *seventh, finally*: *to comprehend* something (*comprehendere*), i.e. to cognize something through reason or *a priori* to the degree that is sufficient for our purpose. For all our comprehension is only *relative*, i.e. sufficient for a certain purpose; we do not comprehend anything without qualification. Nothing can be comprehended more than what the mathematician demonstrates, e.g. that all lines in the circle are proportional. And yet he does not comprehend how it happens that such a simple figure has these properties. The field of understanding or of the understanding is thus in general much greater than the field of comprehension or of reason.[21]

In presenting us with a hierarchy of more or less perfect or ideal forms of cognition, Kant is operating with something like a form of what (Pasnau 2018) calls "idealized epistemology": an epistemology interested less in locating necessary and sufficient conditions on (say) knowledge and more in characterizing our ordinary cognitive states in relation to certain epistemological or cognitive ideals. We will return to the later stages of this hierarchy in Chapter 4, but for present purposes, the most important parts of it are the first four stages leading up to a

---

[21] Log 9:65, compare V-Lo/Blomberg 24:133–4. A similar, although interestingly distinct progression appears in Refl 15:171:

Etwas vorstellen [*repraesentatio*]; etwas warnehmen [*perceptio*] (mit Bewustseyn); erkennen [*cognitio*] (von anderem unterscheiden); wissen [*scientia*] (unterschieden von annehmen [*glauben*]); verstehen [*intellectio*] (durch den Verstand erkennen); *perspicientia* Einsehen (durch Vernunft); *comprehensio*: Begreifen (der Größe [dem Grad] Nach hinreichend).

Despite the differences between this passage and the *Logic* passages, both support the line of interpretation above. In Chapter 4, we will return to this passage to discuss the final three stages of this progression.

definition of cognition. For it is this part of the hierarchy that locates "cognition" as a distinctive sort of conscious relation between a representation and its object.

In doing so, the hierarchy begins with the bare notion of a "representation of something", where this minimal notion of representation implies neither that the representation in question is available to consciousness nor that it involves a grasp of the nature of the thing represented. This can be thought of as expressing the most minimal conception of a "representation" as involving an, at this stage wholly indeterminate, relation between itself and something that it represents in some sense.

At the second stage of the progression, we begin to make the relation between representation and represented at issue here more determinate. For here we encounter the notion of "perception"—that is, of a representation insofar as that representation is "with consciousness". Representations with consciousness are themselves present to consciousness. Thus, Kant will sometimes gloss consciousness in terms of the "representation of a representation" in us (Log 9:33, V-Met/Mron 29:889). But this should not necessarily be taken as an endorsement of a "higher-order representation" view of consciousness in the contemporary sense of this phrase. For a "representation of a representation" in this sense need not require two numerically distinct representations, one of which represents the other. Rather, Kant's considered view seems to be that conscious representations are sometimes partially constituted by how those very representations *represent themselves*. So, far from involving an infinite hierarchy of "representations of representations", Kant's conception of conscious representation is one on which a conscious representation often just is a representation that has a distinctive form: a form that enables that representation to represent both itself and its object to the subject.

At this second stage, our representations make us *conscious of something*—for example, themselves. But they do not necessarily make us conscious of anything *as an object*—that is, as something objective over and above our representations of it. It is at the third stage of the hierarchy that this notion of objectivity begins to enter the picture. For here we encounter the further form of representation that Kant calls "acquaintance" (*Kenntnis*). For Kant, to be acquainted with something in this sense involves representing this thing "in comparison with other things, both as to sameness and as to difference". This is crucial here, because this sort of comparison is required in order to represent something in a manner that allows one to discriminate it from other things. Thus, at this stage we begin to encounter representations that have the determinacy of content required by "objective representation", but only on a level that does not involve the *consciousness* of this content required by the Determinate Content Constraint. That is, at this stage, we have representations that allow the representing creature to discriminate between things, but only on a level that does not require *consciousness* either of the discriminations in question or of the differences between things that ground them.[22] It is this sort of representation that is distinctive, for Kant, of many animals, whose representations allow them to make systematic discriminations between objects, but not in a manner that makes them conscious of these objects as such. Thus, for Kant, animals grasp objects in the world, but they do not do so in a manner that allows them to be conscious of these objects as distinct from their representations of them.

With these three preliminary steps in mind, Kant then goes on to define cognition (*Erkenntnis*) by bringing together this definition of *acquaintance* with his prior distinction between representation and representation *with consciousness*.[23] Thus, Kant claims, we can think of cognition in terms of being "acquainted with something with consciousness". Once again, this fits very well with our discussion of cognition since acquaintance with consciousness is just what is required if representation of something is to provide us with a *consciousness* of that thing as a *determinate* object distinct from other objects. In this way, this passage helps to bring out the central significance of the Determinate Content Constraint for Kant's account of cognition. But it is crucial to remember that *both* this constraint and the Real Possibility Constraint must be satisfied if we are to achieve genuine cognition of an object in Kant's sense.

To understand why both constraints are essential, note that, on their own, neither fully explains why Kant holds that theoretical cognition of things-in-themselves is impossible for us. After all, even from a theoretical point of view, Kant is perfectly happy to acknowledge that we can form representations of things-in-themselves that satisfy one of these constraints in isolation from the other at least to some degree. In the end, it is the *interaction* of the Real Possibility Constraint *and* the Determinate Content Constraint that lies at the root of Kant's claims about the limits of theoretical cognition.[24] For instance, according to Kant, we can know that appearances are really possible in virtue of their presence in intuition. And Kant believes that we also know that any appearance must be grounded in some thing- or things-in-themselves.[25] Thus, by forming the definite

---

[22] For the relationship between mere discrimination and discrimination with a consciousness of differences that ground these discriminations, see FS 2:59 and B414–15n. In (McLear forthcoming-b), McLear constructs a theory of cognition in Kant which treats this distinction as definitional of cognition in Kant's sense. But while I agree that cognition requires a consciousness of both discriminations between objects and the differences between objects that ground these discriminations, I see this feature of cognition as downstream from Kant's definition of what cognition *is*. In this sense, like the views of cognition in Kant discussed below, McLear's reading seems to me to fail to get to the real heart of Kant's discussion of these issues.

[23] Note that, in requiring that all acquaintance require consciousness, (Tolley 2017b) doesn't fully do justice to this point.

[24] On this point, see (Jauernig 2008; Smit 2009; Stang 2016; Stang 2017). Smit's work has been particularly important for the contemporary debate about this point, and an early conversation with him, Nick Stang, and Andrew Chignell was particularly influential for my thought about it.

[25] Although this is subject to dispute, Kant appears to take this to be an analytic truth which follows from the concept of an "appearance". See, for example, (Beizaei forthcoming).

description "the thing- or things-in-themselves that ground my present appearances", I can form an *indeterminate representation* of things-in-themselves that assures me of their real possibility (indeed their *actuality*) and does so even from a theoretical point of view.

As this indicates, what prevents this representation from being a cognition is not the Real Possibility Constraint but rather its lack of Determinate Content. On the other hand, even given the limitations that Kant places on our ability to think about things in themselves, I could certainly form a *richer* conception of the things-in-themselves underlying the appearances I have direct experience of. For example, even using only the unschematized categories, I could think of all my current appearances as grounded in a single thing-in-itself in the manner that would be true if these appearances were the phenomena of a single Leibnizian monad. But while this would give my representation of this thing-in-itself a greater determinacy of content, it would thereby sacrifice the justification I had for asserting that such things in themselves are actual and so really possible—since I have no theoretical reason to think that *this particular sort* of thing in itself is really, as opposed to merely logically, possible.

Thus, in the end, it is the *combination* of these two constraints that explains Kant's insistence that cognition of things in themselves is impossible from a theoretical point of view. In this context, intuition is especially significant for Kant because it provides us with a way of giving determinate content to a concept, while also demonstrating its real possibility. Indeed, the ability to perform these two tasks *simultaneously* is distinctive, for Kant, of a representation that is both *singular* and *immediate* in its relationship to its object. Thus, it is not just that intuition can play both these roles—it is in a sense *the* theoretical representation that is capable of doing so, at least for creatures like us.

b. Cognition, Knowledge, and Belief in Kant

Hopefully, this gives one an initial sense of the distinctive conception of "cognition" that sits at the core of Kant's philosophy. As noted above, it is important not to confuse this conception of cognition with "knowledge" in the sense that has come to dominate contemporary epistemology. But it is also important to distinguish "cognition" (*Erkenntnis*) in Kant's sense from Kant's conception of *Wissen*, which is generally translated as "knowledge" today. This is not at all unnatural, since it is this element of Kant's system that is, in many ways, closest to the sense of "knowledge" that dominates the contemporary epistemological debate. In particular, unlike cognition, which Kant conceives primarily as a form of conscious representation, knowledge (*Wissen*) is a way of "taking" or "holding" some representation "to be true" (*Fürwharhalten*). Thus, while they are connected, Kant's conception of knowledge (*Wissen*) needs to be carefully distinguished from his conception of cognition. As we have just seen, cognition is defined by the place of cognition in a hierarchy of different forms of *representation* in terms of the relationship of those representations to their "objective content". Knowledge (*Wissen*), on the other hand, is defined by its place in a different hierarchy: a hierarchy of different forms of "taking to be true", which are distinguished from one another in terms of the *grounds* on which one takes something to be true.[26] Thus, as Kant uses these terms, "knowledge" (*Wissen*) can be thought of as the highest perfection of cognition with respect to the manner in which it involves a "taking to be true" (*Fürwahrhalten*), while "cognition" (*Erkenntnis*) involves a perfection of representation relating to the degree to which a representation makes us conscious of that representation's object.

In his discussion of the former, Kant distinguishes three basic forms of "taking to be true". First, there is what Kant calls mere "opinion" (*Meinung*), which is a taking to be true that is based on grounds that are sufficient in *neither* a subjective *nor* an objective sense. Second, there is "belief" or "faith" (*Glauben*), which is a taking to be true that is based on grounds that are subjectively sufficient, but not objectively sufficient. And third, there is knowledge (*Wissen*), which is a taking to be true that is based on grounds that are both subjectively and objectively sufficient. There is a large and growing literature on how best to think about these distinctions in Kant, but for our purposes here what is most important is to understand the notion of grounds that are both "subjectively and objectively sufficient", which Kant uses to distinguish knowledge (*Wissen*) from both opinion and belief. For it is here that Kant's discussion of "knowledge" connects up directly with the discussion of "cognition" we have been focusing on.

Kant provides us with two basic ways of thinking about the distinction between "objectively sufficient" and "merely subjectively sufficient grounds". First, he writes that objectively sufficient grounds go beyond merely subjectively sufficient grounds insofar as they hold equally for any possible rational subject, no matter their particular subjective constitution. But he takes this criterion to be a merely external mark, or touchstone, of a deeper sense in which a ground for assent can be said to be "objectively sufficient". In this deeper sense, such grounds are objectively sufficient only insofar as they are themselves grounded in the object known. For example, immediately prior to his definition of knowledge (*Wissen*), Kant writes that:

---

[26] See (Chignell 2007a, 2007b). Like Chignell, I take Kant's discussion towards the end of the first *Critique* to represent his considered views, at least in broad outlines. That said, I think that Chignell is wrong to draw the distinction between objective and subjective grounds in terms of a freestanding distinction between epistemic and non-epistemic merit. Rather, insofar as something like this is at work here, it seems to me to be captured by the fact that objectively sufficient grounds must be grounded in the features of the object known. Thus, as we will see, it is possible to acquire objectively sufficient grounds for assent on a distinctively practical basis. In addition, *pace* Chignell, I am doubtful that there are merely subjective rational grounds that hold for all rational subjects. For example, as I discuss elsewhere, it is not strictly speaking true that the grounds Kant cites for practical faith in God and immortality hold for *all* possible rational subjects (as Chignell claims). See Schafer(forthcoming a) for more discussion.

> Truth, however, rests upon agreement with the object, with regard to which, consequently, the judgments of every understanding must agree (*consentientia uni tertio, consentiunt inter se*). The touchstone of whether taking something to be true is conviction or mere persuasion is therefore, externally, the possibility of communicating it and finding it to be valid for the reason of every human being to take it to be true; for in that case there is at least a presumption that the ground of the agreement of all judgments, regardless of the difference among the subjects, rests on the common ground, namely the object, with which they therefore agree and through which the truth of the judgment is proved. (A821/B849)

Such passages indicate that we can have objectively sufficient grounds for assent just in case these are located in the object or objects this assent concerns. In thinking about such claims, it is crucial to remember that the notion of object that is at issue here is the one discussed above—namely, something that places objective, material conditions on the correctness of our cognition—so we should not imagine that the object at issue in this passage is wholly independent of our cognition of it. For, of course, it is essential to Kant's critical method that one of the most important sources of objective constraints on cognition are the necessary conditions on the possibility of cognition itself. Thus, when considering the formal features of objects, the *ultimate* source of objectively sufficient grounds will often be the nature of our cognitive capacities. The important point is that, when they are objectively sufficient, these grounds are *also* connected to the objects cognized, insofar as these objects have the form they do in virtue of facts about our cognitive faculties.

We should thus be careful not to read *too* much into Kant's insistence that objectively sufficient grounds must be grounded in the object of cognition. Rather, this is best understood as establishing a *formal* connection between the objects of cognition and the manner in which our cognition can ground acts of "taking to be true", as opposed to as providing us with a robust theory of such grounds. Nonetheless, these claims are sufficient to establish a close relationship between cognition (*Erkenntnis*) and knowledge (*Wissen*) as Kant understands them. For, given Kant's account of such grounds, taking a judgment to be true can be based on subjectively and objectively sufficient grounds only insofar as we are *conscious of these grounds as objectively sufficient*. After all, without such consciousness of objective sufficiency, even if our grounds are (unbeknownst to us) appropriately related to the object, our acts of assent will not be *based* on this connection, and so *our assent* cannot be said to be based on these grounds *as* objectively sufficient.[27]

---

[27] In making these claims I mean to mostly be neutral with respect to the lively debate about whether knowledge (in this sense) is fallible for Kant, although text seems to me to speak in favor of an infallibilist reading over all. For a recent defense of that reading, see (Benzenberg forthcoming b). For a recent defense of the fallibilist interpretation, see (Chignell 2021).

Thus, our grounds for assent will be subjectively and objectively sufficient only if we are conscious of these grounds as rooted in the object or objects at issue. And given this, our ability to achieve cognition (*Erkenntnis*) of some object will normally constrain our ability to achieve knowledge (*Wissen*) about it. For we can have objectively sufficient grounds for assenting to a judgment only if our assent is based in a consciousness of the features of its objects that make it correct. And, of course, it is just this sort of consciousness of objects that is characteristic of cognition (*Erkenntnis*) of an object. So, in general, the limits that Kant places on our ability to achieve of cognition of objects will also translate into limitations on our ability to make claims about those objects in the manner that is characteristic of genuine knowledge (*Wissen*).

Nonetheless, it is important to stress that there are special cases, such as very abstract claims about things-in-themselves, in which it is possible to take some claim to be true on objectively sufficient grounds even though we do not have cognition of the objects this claim concerns. For example, as just discussed, Kant believes that we can know that appearances actually exist through their presence in intuition. And he also appears to believe that it is a basic conceptual truth about appearances that any appearance must be the appearance "of something".[28] Thus, we infer the existence of "things in themselves" in this very abstract sense from the existence of "appearances", which appears to give us grounds for assenting to the existence of things in themselves that are both subjectively and objectively sufficient in the sense defined above. After all, these grounds apply equally to all rational beings, and they are appropriately related to the objects they concern. With respect to certain abstract claims about things in themselves, then, we seem to be able to assent to those claims in the manner that is characteristic of knowledge (*Wissen*) for Kant.

This is important, of course, to the coherence of Kant's critical project, given Kant's insistence that "[i]n philosophy [proper] there is no belief" (24:30) is fortunate that our ability to achieve knowledge (*Wissen*) of such abstract claim. In this context, its about things in themselves is wholly consistent with Kant's insistence that we cannot cognize them, at least from a theoretical point of view. The reason for this, once again, is that while we can achieve knowledge (*Wissen*) of the mere existence of "the thing or things in themselves that ground my present appearances", our grasp of the nature of these "things or things in themselves" remains so indeterminate that it cannot count as cognition of an object in Kant's sense of these terms.[29] Moreover, it remains true that when our judgments about things in themselves go beyond a few very abstract claims, these judgments can only be

---

[28] Compare again (Beizaei forthcoming).

[29] As noted above, my treatment of these issues is inspired by conversations with Houston Smit, Nicholas Stang, and Andrew Chignell. I learned of Smit's views on this distinction and its potential relevance to the proper interpretation of Kant's transcendental idealism during a very illuminating conversation at the 2005 Kant Congress in Brazil. In many ways, the interpretation of Kant I offer below may be thought of as an attempt to build upon Smit's views about these matters—although I am

based on objectively sufficient grounds insofar as we can cognize the things they concern. So, for the most part, judgments can only be candidates for knowledge (*Wissen*) insofar as they provide us with cognition (*Erkenntnis*) of their objects, and it will follow from Kant's insistence that theoretical cognition of things-in-themselves is impossible that we also cannot have objectively sufficient *theoretical* grounds for any but a few very abstract claims about such things.

c. Cognition: Theoretical and Practical

We have just seen that cognition of an object (in Kant's sense) requires a consciousness of that object as placing objective, material constraints on the correctness of one's representation of it. Thus, cognition always involves at least an implicit consciousness of one's representation as subject to a material standard of correctness. In this sense, we can say that cognition represents itself under the "guise of the (materially) correct".

Crucially, this sort of "correctness" can take *both* a theoretical *and* a practical form, depending on how the representation in question is related to its object.[30] In the theoretical case, as we will see, cognition proceeds under a form of the "guise of the true"; in the practical case, it proceeds under a version of the "guise of the good". But in the context of Kant's account, both of these are best understood as ways of making determinate the general idea that any cognition must involve an implicit consciousness of the standards of correctness that apply to it.

Kant often traces these two basic forms of cognition back to the fact that there are two basic ways a representation can acquire the relationship to an object cognition requires.[31] For example, right at the beginning of the first *Critique*, he writes that:

---

sure he would not agree with everything I say here. (I gather from conversation with Smit that he has also for many years been working on an unpublished paper on this topic, which is entitled "Cognition, Understanding, and Determination: A Reply to Jacobi.")

[30] It is worth stressing that much of what I say about "practical cognition" and "practical cognition from principles" could also be expressed in terms of claims about the determination of the will or action from principles if one finds the notion of "practical cognition" unattractive.

[31] In this context, it is worth noting that Kant also regularly uses "cognition" in a more restricted manner than he does in these passages, such that "cognition" refers *only* to theoretical cognition in the sense above. It is against this background that we should understand claims like the following: Practical reason "does not have to do with objects for the sake of [theoretically] *cognizing* them but with its own ability to *make them real*..." (KpV 5:89). Here Kant is making use of "cognition" in the narrow sense. But this should not be taken to mean that practical reason is not concerned with "cognition" in the broader sense we have just been discussing.

Something similar might be thought to apply when Kant opposes the "faculty of cognition" to the "faculty of desire" in the "First Introduction" to the third *Critique* (EEKU 20:206). But Kant's use of the term "cognition" there is best understood in the broader sense. After all, Kant continues to claim in this passage that the a priori principles for the faculty of desire are provided by pure reason (EEKU 20:207–8). And, as we'll discuss, he has just identified reason with one part of the faculty of cognition (EEKU 20:201). So it is implicit is his discussion that, when reason does determine the faculty of desire, the result will be practical cognition.

Insofar as there is to be reason in these sciences, something in them must be cognized *a priori*, and this cognition can relate to its object in either of two ways, either merely determining the object and its concept (which must be given from elsewhere), or else also making the object actual. The former is theoretical, the latter practical cognition of reason. (Bix–x)[32]

In such passages, Kant distinguishes theoretical and practical cognition in terms of their characteristic relationship with their objects. According to this way of drawing this distinction, in the canonical case, theoretical cognitions depend upon an object that is "given" to the cognizer. Thus, theoretical cognitions can be thought of as cognitions where (when all goes well) the existence of our representation of an object is dependent upon the existence of this object in some way. In this sense, the fundamental function of theoretical cognition is to be responsive to objects whose existence is not dependent upon our representation of them.

Of course, in saying this, it is important to stress that this does not mean that the object's *form* must be independent of our cognitive capacities. For the core claim of Kant's transcendental idealism is precisely that the form of the objects of theoretical cognition (at least for us) is grounded in the form of our cognitive faculties. Rather, Kant's claims about the dependence of theoretical cognitions on their objects are specifically related to the existence and matter of these representation as opposed to their form.

This means that the existence of a theoretical representation of an object will depend either on that object's existence *or* on the existence of some object appropriately related to the object in question. So, for example, we might form a theoretical representation of an object in direct response to outer sensible experience of it—an experience that embodies the receptivity of our form of sensibility. But we might also form a theoretical representation of an object on the basis of scientific reasoning that extends our more direct forms of theoretical cognition to include cognition of objects insofar as these are *causally related* to objects we have direct experience of. Both of these would, for Kant, count as forms of theoretical cognition in the sense at issue here.

In practical cognition, on the other hand, this relation of existential dependence is reversed. In other words, practical cognition functions so that the existence of a representation of an object grounds the existence of that very object. Thus, while the canonical role of theoretical cognition is to be receptive to independently existing things, the function of practical cognition is to bring into existence the things it represents. In this broad sense, practical cognition involves a kind of

---

[32] Cf. KpV 5:10, KpV 5:20, KpV 5:46, KpV 5:57, KU 5:171, KU 5:177–8, EEKU 20:197, EEKU 20:199, EEKU 20:230.

"maker's knowledge" or "practical knowledge" in the sense familiar from Aquinas and made famous in the twentieth century by Anscombe.

The canonical instance of this sort of practical representation, for Kant, are thus the maxims of our will, for these are the canonical instance in us of representations whose function is to make their objects actual through action. That having been said, much as was true in the theoretical case, many instances of practical cognition in the sense will be not function as the *direct* ground of their object's existence.[33] In the theoretical case, such possibilities arose because we can form a theoretical representation of some object on (say) the basis of scientific reasoning that extends our more direct forms of theoretical cognition to include cognition of objects insofar as these are *related* to objects we have direct experience of. Thus, while theoretical cognition in general acquires its relationship to its objects *via* being responsive to their existence, this should not be taken to imply that every instance of theoretical cognition is directly responsive to the existence of the particular object it represents. Not surprisingly, the same basic point applies to practical representations as well. For example, when planning what to do, I may form plans that concern all sorts of situations, including situations I could never personally find myself in.[34] In forming such representations, I will be forming practical representations in the sense at issue here even though I may know that these representations will never be the ground of the existence of their particular objects. Similarly, for Kant, although practical cognition in general relates to its objects by serving as a potential ground of their existence, this should not be taken to imply that the function of every individual practical cognition is to make its particular object actual. Rather, many practical representations acquire a "practical relationship to their objects" *via* their place in a larger system of representations that functions in this way.

This, then, is one way in which Kant draws the distinction between theoretical and practical cognition. But, given our discussion of cognition above, it should come as no surprise that he treats this distinction as closely related to a second, at least nominally distinct, way of drawing the distinction. According to this second distinction, theoretical cognitions may be thought of as cognitions that represent *what is*, while practical cognitions may be thought of as representing *what ought to be*. For example:

> Here I content myself with defining theoretical cognition as that through which I cognize what exists, and practical cognition as that through which I represent what ought to exist. According to this, theoretical use of reason is through which

---

[33] See here, for example, (Engstrom 2009)'s discussion of Kant on mere wishes.
[34] Compare (Gibbard 2003). For an application of this idea in a contemporary epistemological context, see (Schafer 2014b).

I cognize *a priori* (as necessary) that something is; but the practical use is that which it is cognized *a priori* what ought to happen. (A633/B661)[35]

This way of distinguishing theoretical and practical cognition focuses, then, not on the proper relationship between a cognition and the object it represents, but rather on the standards of correctness that apply to representations that have this relationship with their objects.

For example, because the function of theoretical cognitions is to represent independently existing objects, theoretical representations are correct only insofar as they are accurate in how they represent these objects. Moreover, as we just discussed, this standard of correctness does not merely *apply* to theoretical cognitions, it is also something that any theoretical cognizer is implicitly *conscious of* in forming theoretical cognitions of objects. In this way, for Kant, all theoretical cognition proceeds under the "guise of the true".[36]

And a similar story applies in the practical case, although things are somewhat more complicated there. In particular, because the function of practical cognitions is to bring about the existence of the objects they represent, practical cognitions are correct only insofar as their objects are things that *ought to be*. Just as in the theoretical case, Kant understands this as a claim not just about the standards of correctness that apply to such representations, but also about how any practical cognizer must represent the objects of practical cognition to themselves. Just as all theoretical cognition proceeds under the "guise of the true", practical cognition proceeds under the "guise of the ought to be" or, more simply, the "guise of the good".

This aspect of Kant's views can be seen from his willingness to treat these two accounts of the distinction between theoretical and practical cognition as equivalent. After all, to identify these two notions of (say) practical cognition is to treat as equivalent: (i) the idea of representations that represent their objects as things that ought to be and (ii) the idea of representations whose function is to bring about their objects. Once again, this should not be interpreted as claim about the relationship between my practical representations and their objects on an individual level, for, of course, we represent many things as good in full knowledge that we will never be in a position to make those goods actual through our own actions. Such representations cannot function to directly bring about their objects; nevertheless, they can still be part of a system of representations that stands in this relationship to what we do and so to the world around us. Thus, it remains

---

[35] Cf. A802/B830, A840/B868, GMS 4:387, KpV 5:5, KpV 5:109, KU 5:176, EEKU 20:246–7. This way of drawing this distinction is, of course, closely related to the traditional notion that truth is the "formal object" of theoretical cognition, while the good is the "formal object" of practical cognition. Compare (Reath 2013; Tenenbaum 2007, 2019).

[36] Or, for forms of theoretical thought that are probabilistic, the "guise of the likely true" or "the guise of the possible".

plausible that there is a systematic connection between a representation representing something as "good" or something that "ought to be" and that representation being of a sort that generally functions to bring about the existence of its objects.

As this should indicate, practical cognition is not just a kind of "practical knowledge" in something like Anscombe's sense of this term—that is, a knowledge of what one does or brings into existence through one's actions. It is also a kind of "practical knowledge" in a second (and in some ways more traditional) sense.[37] That is, not only is it cognition that is the "cause of what it represents", it is also a way of cognizing *what ought to be*. For Kant, like Anscombe or Aquinas, these two forms of practical cognition are closely connected, although it is important to keep in mind that they pick out two different dimensions of what Kant calls "practical cognition". In particular, while a theoretical cognition is correct just in case it accurately represents its object, in the case of practical cognitions, we need to distinguish at least two standards that apply to a cognition in virtue of its function, *both* of which extend beyond the constraints of logic alone. First, there are the standards of correctness that apply to a practical cognition as a representation of something that ought to be. In this sense, a practical representation can be said to be correct, just in case its object is indeed something that ought to exist. The ultimate basis of such standards, for Kant, are the principles of practical reason as such. But even if a practical representation *does* represent something that ought to be, this does not guarantee that that representation will be *successful* at bringing about the existence of what it represents. Thus, a practical representation can be correct in this first sense without being fully successful in the sense of bringing about the existence of its object. Given this, in addition to the standards of correctness that apply to a practical representation in virtue of how it represents what ought to be, there are also standards of success that apply to this representation in virtue of its function of bringing about the existence of what it represents.[38]

Crucially for what follows, this two-fold "formal" distinction between theoretical and practical cognition also generates a further distinction between two *uses of reason*. More precisely, while Kant conceives of reason as a unified faculty, he also contrasts two uses of this faculty. In keeping with our discussion above, these uses are distinguished by the interest or aim that guides the activity of reason— interests that are defined in terms of the "formal" distinction between theoretical and practical representation we have been discussing:

---

[37] As stressed by (Engstrom 2009).
[38] One might see these standards as analogous to the "non-accidentality" requirement on theoretical cognition. See (Setiya 2012; Schafer 2014c). Compare (Frost 2014). Note that, in addition to these two "formal" distinctions between theoretical and practical cognition, Kant also sometimes distinguishes them from one another in terms of their characteristic content. Cf. A800/B828, GMS 4:387, GMS 4:420, KpV 5:57, KU 5:171, EEKU 20:199, 20:246-7.

> The interest of its [reason's] speculative use consists in the cognition of the object up to the highest a priori principles; that of its practical use consists in the determination of the will with respect to the final and complete end.
>
> (KpV 5:120)

As this indicates, the interest of theoretical reason, according to Kant, consists in theoretical cognition of *cognition of what is*—in particular, in theoretical cognition from what Kant calls "absolute principles". Conversely, the interest of practical reason consists in the *determination of the will* or *cognition of what ought to be*, again from absolute or unconditioned principles of pure practical reason.[39]

We will return to such claims in Chapter 4. But in reading them, it is important to remember that these interests do not merely relate to the "internal" activities of reason considered in isolation from the world. Rather, because both theoretical and practical reason are interested in genuine cognition, these interests extend beyond the "internal structure" of their own activities to include the relationship between them and their objects. For example, to achieve genuine theoretical cognition requires accurately cognizing the objects one forms judgments about and, indeed, doing so on the right sorts of grounds. Similarly, fully successful or fully realized practical cognition requires not just that one wills the right actions, but that these maxims be effectively translated into action in the world. Just as the interests of theoretical reason can only be fully realized insofar as sensibility provides us with the right sort of receptivity, the interests of practical reason can only be fully realized insofar as the lower practical capacities, such as the power of choice (*Willkür*) and the various forms of practical feeling, are appropriately responsive to the will (*Wille*). In this way, both theoretical and practical reason's interests demand a certain sort of systematic relationship between mind and world, one that can only come about insofar as all of our rational capacities form a teleological system under the governance of reason's ends.

Finally, Kant makes use of this distinction between two uses of reason to draw a further distinction that will be relevant here—namely, a distinction between theoretical and practical *grounds* for assent or taking to be true.[40] A ground for assent is theoretical, according to Kant, when it is based in activities that are guided by reason's interest in cognition of what is, while a ground is practical when it is generated by reason's interest in determining the will in accordance

---

[39] This distinction between the interests and corresponding uses of theoretical and practical reason provides the basis for the three famous questions that Kant raises towards the end of the first *Critique*. The first of these—*what can I know?*—corresponds to the interest of theoretical reason in achieving systematic theoretical cognition of what is (or theoretical comprehension). The second—*what should I do?*—corresponds to the interest of practical reason in determining the will to action through its cognition of what ought to be. And, as we will see, the third—*what should I hope?*—combines these two uses of reason together, by considering what I am entitled to assume about what is on both theoretical *and* practical grounds.

[40] Cf. A823–4/B851–2, KpV 5:4–5, 5:134–5.

with principles.[41] Thus, Kant's basic distinction between theoretical and practical forms of cognition generates both a distinction between two uses or manifestations of reason *and* a distinction between two kinds of grounds that reason can generate for assenting to some judgment.

In saying this, it is important to remember that the relationship between these distinctions is often quite complex. For example, for Kant, our practical commitment to the highest good generates distinctively practical grounds for assenting to God's existence since God is a necessary condition on the realizability of the highest good. But, of course, when we claim that God exists, this is a theoretical as opposed to a practical representation in the first and second "formal" senses noted above; after all, the existence of God in no way depends upon our representation of his existence, and when we claim that God exists, we are not asserting something about what *ought* to be, we are asserting something about what *is*. Thus, our belief in God is plainly a theoretical representation as opposed to a practical one, even though it is based on distinctively practical grounds. In cases like this, as Kant stresses, the practical *use* of reason can lead to an extension of our *cognition of what is*, even though the *interest* that lies behind this use lies in something practical.

d. Cognition, Self-Consciousness, and the "Taking Condition"

We will return to these distinctions in the next chapter; what is most important at present is just the basic distinction between theoretical and practical cognition as two ways of becoming *conscious of an object* in the manner that cognition in the general sense requires. For this allows us to approach the connections between rationality and self-consciousness we began to explore in the last chapter from a new direction. After all, rational capacities are all, directly or indirectly, capacities for cognition for Kant. So, given that cognition requires a basic (if implicit) consciousness of the standards of correctness that apply to one's representations, the exercise of these capacities can be a source of cognition only insofar as it is also a potential source of this sort of consciousness. In this sense, it follows from Kant's general conception of cognition that *any* capacity for cognition must be (in part) a capacity for a consciousness of the standards of correctness that apply to that capacity's acts and representations.

In this way, by beginning with Kant's account of cognition, we see why any cognitive capacity must provide its subject with an implicit consciousness of the

---

[41] "Now yet another experiment remains open to us: namely, whether pure reason is also to be found in practical use, whether in that use it leads us to the ideas that attain the highest ends of pure reason which we have just adduced, and thus whether from the point of view of its practical interest reason may not be able to guarantee that which in regard to its speculative interest it entirely refuses to us" (A804/B832).

conditions under which its representations and acts are correct or incorrect.[42] In his discussion of cognition, Kant's focus is (naturally) on this implicit consciousness of correctness as applied to our (theoretical and practical) representations of objects. But the same point also applies to the other representations and activities of these capacities, at least insofar as their functional role is to contribute to cognition in this sense. For example, just as cognition of an object requires an implicit consciousness of how that object imposes material standards of correctness on our representations of it, something similar is also true of acts of inference and judgment insofar as these acts are a potential source of cognition. For instance, as we will discuss below, inferences are cognitively significant for Kant because of how they contribute to our consciousness of the (logical and real) connections between our various representations (and their associated objects). But acts of inference can play this role only insofar as they make us conscious of these connections *as relevant* to the material standards of correctness that apply to these representations.[43] For it is only through doing *this* that such inferences will be able to enrich our cognition of objects in the sense defined above.

As this example indicates, the connections established above between cognition and consciousness of the standards of correctness that apply to our representations extend to all the activities of a rational capacity—or at least to all these activities *insofar* as they are meant to contribute to (theoretical or practical) cognition. For such activities can contribute to cognition in this way only insofar as they contribute to our (implicit or explicit) consciousness of the standards of correctness that apply to our representations of objects. And these activities can play this role only insofar as they are associated with a consciousness of their own standards of correctness as potential sources of cognition in this sense.

This provides us with another reason why any cognitive capacity must, for Kant, involve a basic consciousness of its own proper mode of activity.[44] For it is just this consciousness that transforms unconsciousness representations (instances of "mere acquaintance" in Kant's sense) into representations that provide the subject with a consciousness of their own standards of correctness in the manner *cognition* requires. In other words, according to Kant, for a rational activity like inference to be a potential source of cognition, this activity must (at least implicitly) *make sense* to the subject as potentially contributing to their cognition of objects. In this sense, as noted above, any cognitive capacity must

---

[42] Compare the discussion in (Ginsborg 2014), which emphasis the importance of a consciousness of "primitive normativity" to cognition. In this regard, it is perhaps worth noting that I agree with Ginsborg that, in the case or reflective (as opposed to determinative) judgment, this consciousness does not rise to the level of a consciousness of standards for correctness. Rather we only achieve that consciousness (even on an implicit level) once we have actually formed the relevant empirical concept.

[43] Compare (Hlobil 2019).

[44] Note here that sensibility only becomes a genuine capacity for cognition in *this* sense insofar as its activities are integrated with the activities of the understanding—a process through which our form of sensibility becomes self-conscious in the manner at issue here.

for Kant be governed by what Schapiro has recently called a "guiding conception" of its activities (Schapiro 2021).

As we noted above, this feature of cognition is closely connected with Kant's conception of rational capacities as governed by an internal teleology of ends and interests. According to Kant, capacities like reason strive to realize themselves through their own characteristic mode of activity *precisely because* they (at least implicitly) represent doing so as their own end. In this way, for Kant, our rational capacities strive to realize themselves in certain forms of activity because of how they represent that form of activity to themselves.

What we have just seen is that this is no accidental feature of Kant's account. Rather, such capacities *must* represent their activity in this way in order to count as capacities for cognition at all. Thus, Kant's conception of cognition as governed by a consciousness of its object is also a conception of our cognitive faculties as striving to realize themselves in such cognition. In other words, to think of cognition as directed at an object in the sense outlined above is also to think of it as striving to realize itself through bringing this object more fully to consciousness. In this way, all cognition carries with it a certain sort of internal teleology, one that pushes *mere* representation or cognition towards the "more perfect" forms of cognition like insight and comprehension—forms of cognition that, as we will see, are characteristic of reason as the highest of our cognitive powers. It is this idea that Hegel will take up in the *Phenomenology of Spirit*'s narrative of consciousness's repeated dissatisfaction with its relationship to its object. But if I am right, the fundamental connection between consciousness, cognition, and teleological striving that is at work in Hegel's theory is already present in Kant. What is lacking in Kant is Hegel's grasp of the *diversity of forms* these relationships can take, but the essential framework is already in place.

Lest this seem too mysterious, I want to close this chapter by emphasizing the role that similar concepts have come to play in the contemporary debate about rational activities like inference. Such activities have been a source of puzzlement insofar as they seem to be subject to what Boghossian has called the "taking condition"—that is, the requirement that rational inference be accompanied by some sort of acceptance or awareness of the validity of the very inference in question.[45] Something like this principle seems to be required, for example, if we are to distinguish genuine inferences from (say) mere associations between ideas.[46] So, it is very hard to see how a plausible conception of inference might be developed that wholly dispenses with it. But, at the same time, it has proved difficult to give an account of *how* this condition could be true. For example, if we think of inference as satisfying this condition because every inference is governed

---

[45] See (Boghossian 2008, 2012, 2014). [46] See (Dogramaci 2017; Valaris 2017).

by a further belief in its own validity, we seem to arrive at a picture of inference on which even very ordinary inferences are only possible insofar as one possesses the ability to form explicit beliefs about validity. And not only is such a conception of inference highly intellectualized, it also seems likely to require an infinite regress of such "representations of validity" in even very ordinary cases.[47]

I believe that our discussion of the relationship between self-consciousness and rationality in Kant helps to lay the groundwork for a distinctively Kantian response to this puzzle. On the one hand, Kant believes that the internal teleology of our rational powers can only be understood insofar as we take the activities of these powers to be governed by how they represent their own standards of proper functioning. And, as we have just seen, in order for these capacities to function as capacities for cognition, they must provide us with an (at least implicit) awareness of the standards of correctness that apply to their activities. Taken together, these two ideas provide with a deep picture of why rational activities like inference must be governed by something like a "taking condition". But, on the other hand, it is characteristic of Kant's account of this basic form of "self-consciousness" that it neither (i) treats this (often implicit) consciousness as a *further judgment* sitting over and above the activities of our rational capacities, nor (ii) reduces it to something merely dispositional. Thus, when viewed through the lens of the contemporary debate, Kant's views about the self-conscious character of rational activities potentially provide us with a middle way between accounts of the "taking condition" on which inference always requires a further explicit judgment over and above any inference and accounts that attempt to treat the "taking condition" in merely dispositional terms.[48]

For example, while it is central to Kant's conception of our cognitive capacities that these capacities involve a "governing representation" of their own standards of proper functioning, this should not be understood to imply that this representation is anything like a further explicit discursive judgment over and above those activities.[49] Rather, as Kant's account of the acquisition of the categories makes clear, in this most fundamental form, this awareness involves something very basic, which does not require the formation of *any* discursive judgments at all. Indeed, as Kant stresses, without this awareness, "concepts [themselves], and with

---

[47] This point, of course, was famously made by (Carroll 1895), but it is much older.
[48] Also compare (Stephenson2021)'s remark that, "for Kant, I reflectively know what receptive knowledge is from my own case. Receptive knowledge is a product of a rational capacity, and the key claim here is that exercising such a capacity *constitutively* involves *reflective* knowledge of the nature of *what one is thereby doing*.... Hence my reflective knowledge of receptive knowledge, unlike my receptive knowledge itself, is not knowledge of something independent of or distinct from what is known" (18).
[49] This might be thought to conflict with Kant's claim that "the only use that the understanding can make of these concepts is to judge by means of them" (A68/B93). But following (Longuenesse 2005), I read such claims as expressing the fact that both uses of concepts (as rules for sensible synthesis and as rules for judgment) aim at the formation of discursive judgments.

them cognition of objects, would be entirely impossible" (A103-4).[50] Thus, we should not present Kant as operating with a highly intellectualized conception of this basic awareness of the acts of our rational capacities. Nor should we think of this awareness as requiring that we be constantly engaged in explicit, conscious reflection on these capacities and their activities. Rather, as we find Kant saying about the rules of logic, "every man observes the rules before he can reduce them to formulas. Gradually, however, he attends to what he does" (V-Lo/Wiener 24.791).

It is helpful, I think, to think about this in terms of Kant's hylomorphic model for thinking about the acts of our rational capacities.[51] On such a model, any such act involves both (i) a form, which is provided by the rational capacity in question, and (ii) some matter, which is what distinguishes one particular manifestation of the capacity from other possible manifestations of it. And, for Kant at least, it is a rational capacity's awareness of its own characteristic form of activity that provides its conscious representations and acts with their form. So, it follows from Kant's conception of such activities as form-matter hybrids that this awareness must be *partially constitutive* of these activities themselves, as the form that makes them the activities they are. Given this, the idea of these activities as essentially self-conscious in the sense that follows from Kant's conception of cognition should not be thought of as triggering an infinite regress of judgments or representations in the manner many have been concerned with in the contemporary debate.

Moreover, the appeal of such a conception of rational activities like inference is not difficult to locate in the contemporary literature on these issues. To choose only one such example, in a series of recent papers, Ram Neta has argued that what is distinctive of rational activities and attitudes is precisely that they involve a *de se* representation of their own correctness.[52] So, according to Neta's account of what it is to base one rational attitude on another, "the basing relation involves a disposition exercise that is individuated by the agent's object-involving *de se* representation of that very exercise *as justifying*."[53] It is this sort of *de se* representation of the exercise of one's own capacities as fitting or correct that, for Neta, captures the manner in which rational attitudes commit one to further actions or attitudes:

---

[50] For one reading of this distinction, see (Grüne 2009). These ideas are also closely related to Kant's distinction between rules considered *"in abstracto"* and *"in concreto"*. See A134/B173, A711/B739. See also: "Ordinary understanding is the faculty of judging according to laws of experience or from cognition *in concreto* to that *in abstracto* or to advance from the particular to the universal" (Refl 16.14). See the discussion of the cultivation of our rational capacities in (Merritt 2018), which contains a much more detailed discussion of this.

[51] Compare (Boyle 2009, 2011).

[52] See (Dogramaci 2013; Valaris 2014, 2017; Neta 2018, 2019; Hlobil 2019). Compare (Rödl 2007) for a more radical version of a similar thought. And see the discussion of the epistemic significance of consciousness in (Smithies 2019).

[53] (Neta 2019).

A series of events or states in the agent can amount to the agent's being committed to something only by virtue of the agent's representing those very same events or states *as* appropriately responsive to, or expressive of, that commitment. And in so constituting her own events or states as the events or states that they are, the agent makes herself answerable to assessment in terms of rationality, because she thereby makes herself capable (at least in principle) of understanding and answering to such assessments. This is why agents who are incapable of reflection on their own events and states might be assessable as functioning properly or improperly, but they cannot be assessable as proceeding rationally or irrationally.[54]

Thus, on Neta's account, the activity of any rational capacity is constituted in part by a consciousness of this very activity as appropriate. In this sense, for Neta, just as for Kant, the characteristic form of any rational activity involves a certain sort of consciousness of the activity in question. It is this that, for Neta, explains why such activities generate rational commitments when mere dispositions do not. And moreover, for Neta, as for Kant, the consciousness in question is not something over and above the activity in question. Rather, it partially constitutes the nature of this very activity by being its "formal cause" in a broadly Aristotelian sense of these terms.[55]

In any case, I mention Neta here simply to illustrate the contemporary resonance of Kant's approach to these issues—not because I wish to endorse everything that Neta says about them. Indeed, as we will see in the next chapter, Kant conceives of the nature of the self-consciousness involved in rationality as (in some sense) both descriptive and normative in character, and this does not map neatly onto any of the options in the contemporary debate.[56] Nonetheless, Kant shares with Neta the basic idea that, in engaging in a rational activity, we must have some sort of implicit consciousness of the appropriateness of what we are thereby doing—a consciousness that puts us in a position to develop an explicit consciousness of the principles governing such rational activities through reflecting upon them. As we have seen in this chapter and the last, this connection between rationality and self-consciousness is central to both Kant's conception of the manner in which capacities like reason are governed by an internal teleology and his conception of cognition of an object.

[54] (Neta 2018).
[55] Variations on these themes can also be found in the recent work on inference by (Valaris 2017; Hlobil 2019). In keeping with the discussion of (Schafer 2013), I find Hlobil's focus on a notion of "inferential force" in this context more promising than Neta's focus on the content of a certain sort of representation. But these details don't matter too much for the present comparison.
[56] To my mind, perhaps the most congenial contemporary account of these issues is provided by (Marcus 2021), which (helpfully to my mind) focuses on the relationship between rational activities like inference and understanding. For more on this connection, see Chapter 4.

Appendix: Alternative Accounts of Cognition in Kant

In this appendix to Chapter 2, I want to briefly discuss how my view of cognition in Kant relates to two other recent accounts of the same. As noted above, all of these accounts agree on a great deal, so any of them will be compatible with most of what I say above. But nonetheless it will be helpful to say a bit here about the differences between them, and about why I prefer my own account to the others.

The first alternative I want to discuss is due to Tolley's important recent work on these issues. Much as I have done here, in that work, Tolley emphasizes the manner in which Kant locates "cognition" within a progression of different forms of representation. And, in doing so, he similarly emphasizes the idea that cognition in Kant's sense is a matter of a certain sort of representation with consciousness—namely, the sort of representation that makes us conscious of an object as something distinct from our merely subjective state of mind. But Tolley objects to my account of cognition by arguing that my view cannot do justice to one crucial case in which Kant seems to allow that we can, even from a theoretical perspective, achieve a "highly determinate" conception of something supersensible—namely, the conception of God licensed by Kant's discussion of the *ens realissimum*. Here, Tolley writes the following:

> What is more, this particular thought <God exists> allows us to think of an object which Kant himself insists is 'determinable or even determined *as an individual thing* through an *idea* alone' (B596; my ital.)—hence, it would seem, determinable without any recourse to intuition.   (Tolley 2017b, 19)[57]

I have two responses to this objection. First, and more importantly, it seems to me to rest on a conflation of two senses in which we might be said to have a consciousness of something *as a determinate object*. In the case in question, we do (of course) represent God as wholly determined with regards to all possible predicates, for this is just what representing God as the *ens realissimum* involves. But that conception of God remains highly abstract and indeterminate in the sense relevant to Kant's account of cognition. In particular, in representing God in this way, we do not thereby have any grasp of which particular predicates God possesses. In other words, in conceiving of God in this way, we form a description of God that can only have one thing as its referent (namely, God as the ground of all real possibility), but in doing so, we do not achieve anything like the consciousness of God's determinate nature that cognition requires.[58] Thus, this manner of conceiving of God is very much akin to the conception of things in themselves as "whatever grounds appearances" that we discussed above. In such cases, we know that *some* thing (or things) in itself must satisfy an abstract description, and, in the case of God, we know that there can only be a single individual that can do so, but we do not thereby gain any real consciousness

---

[57] Note that Tolley does somewhat mischaracterize my view here as requiring only a form of "determinate reference". As discussed above, this is not the essential issue in these cases for Kant.

[58] One might miss this if one focuses only on the determinateness of this representation with respect to numerical identity and diversity, since this conception of God is wholly determinate in this sense. But, as stressed above, this is only one half of what the Determinate Content Constraint demands of us here.

of that thing as a determinate object in the sense relevant to, say, determining which material standards of correctness apply to judgments about it.

Second, in considering this objection, it is important to remember the importance of *both* of the two constraints on cognition noted above. In particular, while we can come up with a concept of God that represents him in the manner described above, this does not, on its own, mean that we can establish the real possibility of such a being in the manner that cognition would require. So, for example, in Kant's discussion of the *ens realissimum*, Kant acknowledges that such a concept would be sufficient to fully determine a particular individual as its referent, but at the same time insists that we are not necessary in a position to theoretically know (*Wissen*) that such a being is really possible, let alone actual. In order to achieve genuine theoretical cognition of God, we would not only need to achieve a real consciousness of God's determinate nature, as opposed to the highly abstract description of this nature that Kant here provides; we would also need to be able to prove (on theoretical grounds) that a thing with this nature is really possible.

As we will see in Chapter 5, my views about this second question are rather complicated since I do believe that theoretical reason provides us with *subjectively* sufficient grounds for *belief* in God in some sense. But nonetheless, I also maintain that these grounds do not extend to the sort of objectively sufficient grounds that are characteristic of knowledge (*Wissen*). So here we have located a second reason why our conception of the *ens realissimum* does not provide us with theoretical cognition of God in my sense. Indeed, taking these two points together, the discussion of the Transcendental Ideal actually provides us with a particularly elegant illustration of the importance of the interaction of these two constraints for Kant's account of the limits of cognition.

For these reasons, I do not think that Tolley's objection on this point draws blood against my view. But what does Tolley say about the nature of cognition? Unlike me, Tolley does not make very much of either the Determinate Content Constraint or the Real Possibility constraint, nor does he attempt to derive these from a more basic notion of "objective representation with consciousness" in the manner I have done here. Instead, Tolley's discussion of cognition focuses on the following conception of cognition:

> More specifically, I have argued that Kant conceives of cognition as a species of representation which involves four features: it is a representation (i) of a real object, which it represents (ii) mediately, by means of representing other representations, and which involves (iii) 'consciousness [Bewußtsein]' of the real relation between these other mediating representations and their object, a consciousness enabled by (iv) sensations which arise in the mind due to affection by the object in question.
> (Tolley 2017b, 28)

As should be clear, there is much in this characterization of cognition that I agree with. In particular, I agree that cognition always involves a consciousness of at least three elements: (i) a "real object", which it represents, (ii) a representation by means of which this representation occurs, and (iii) some relationship between the two. Moreover, in the theoretical case, the nature of this relationship generally takes much the form that Tolley here describes. In particular, as we have already explained, in theoretical cognition, we generally become conscious of objects as really possible determinate things by conceiving of these objects as standing in "real relations" to our own representations *via* the dependence of our intuitions on these objects.

The fundamental problem with Tolley's account, to my mind, is that it does not provide us with a unified account of *why* these various constraints on cognition follow from Kant's definitions of cognition as "acquaintance with consciousness" or "objective representation with consciousness". For instance, while it does follow from the latter definition that cognition must involve some sort of consciousness of a relation between our representations and the objects it represents, in order to understand why this consciousness must involve a consciousness of "real relations" between the representations and objects of the sort that sensibility provides, we need to consider the manner in which sensibility makes it possible to simultaneously satisfy the two constraints noted above. In this way, it seems to me that my account of cognition takes these matters deeper than Tolley's does.

This issue also shows up in a variety of ways when we consider cases other than the standard case of theoretical cognition of empirical objects. For in these cases, Tolley's lack of a deeper explanation of his claims sometimes leads his account to generate the wrong results. For example, consider again the case of the things in themselves that ground the appearances we cognize. On Tolley's account, we can cognize these appearances because we can represent them as standing in real relations to our sensations. But we also know that these appearances themselves stand in a metaphysically real relation of dependence with the things in themselves (whatever they are) that ground them. So, whenever we cognize some appearance, we are also in a position to represent certain things in themselves as standing in a metaphysically real relation to our sensations, since we know that our sensations stand in real relations to certain appearances and that these appearances stand in real relations to certain (indeterminately conceived) things in themselves. Thus, in such cases, Tolley's account would seem to imply that we *can* in fact cognize things in themselves, even from a theoretical point of view. Or, perhaps better, it can only avoid this result by placing what seems like an arbitrary and philosophically unmotivated constraint on Kant's conception of "cognition".

As discussed above, I think we can avoid this result if we attend to the importance of the Determinate Content Constraint. So insofar as it neglects this aspect of Kant's conception of cognition, Tolley's account seems to me to struggle to properly account for basic cases like this one. Moreover, similar issues with Tolley's account also arise when we consider forms of practically grounded cognition such as our ability to cognize our own nature as free beings from a practical point of view.[59] For in this case, we encounter a form of cognition that is grounded, not in the receptivity of sensibility, but rather in our own self-activity as practically rational beings. In other words, by treating an appeal to the receptivity of sensibility as part of the *definition* of Kant's general conception of cognition, Tolley's account seems to me doomed to generate the wrong results when we turn from the more familiar case of empirical forms of theoretical cognition to the forms of cognition that arise in a distinctively practical context.

---

[59] Although this claim is somewhat controversial, it really should not be, given Kant's consistent willingness to use the term "cognition" to refer to this sort of practically grounded grasp of our own freedom. For more discussion, see (Kain 2010; Schafer forthcominga).

Once again, this is an indication I think that Tolley has not taken his discussion of "cognition" as deep as it needs to go to cover all the cases of interest to Kant. And something very similar seems to me to be true of Watkins and Willaschek's insightful recent discussion of these issues. Once again, there is much in their discussion that I am sympathetic to. But I also have a number of issues with it. Some of these I will not dwell on here—such as the manner in which they unnecessarily multiply senses of "cognition" in Kant. For my fundamental disagreement with their account is in some ways similar to my complaints against Tolley's—namely, that Watkins and Willaschek take Kant's account of one canonical form of cognition—empirical cognition—and treat this as providing us with a definition of what cognition in general consists in. As a result, Watkins and Willaschek seem to me to fail to take Kant's account of empirical cognition all the way to its foundations, while also arriving at an overly narrow conception of the scope of cognition in Kant's sense of this term.

Much as I have been doing here, Watkins and Willaschek take cognition in Kant's sense to be governed by two basic constraints. But they understand these two constraints rather differently than I do. In particular, they write:

> That is, cognition in this sense must satisfy two conditions: (i) a *givenness*-condition, according to which an object must be given to the mind and (ii) a *thought*-condition, according to which the given object must be conceptually determined (cf. A50/B74; A92/B125; B137; B146). Although Kant never explicitly defines givenness as such, in its most general sense it seems to mean that an object is made available to the mind so that one can be aware of the existence of the object and (at least some of) its features. Kant claims that in human beings givenness involves passivity insofar as the object must act on our sensibility to be given to us (cf. A19/B33).... Thus it is only for finite beings like ourselves that objects are given in sensible intuition, which for Kant means that the object is represented not as exhibiting general features, but in its particularity. Similarly, only in finite beings does the thought-condition require the use of general concepts (which represent an object not in its entirety, but only partially, through marks it shares with other objects; cf. A68/B93; A320/B377; Log 9:58)....
>
> (Watkins and Willaschek 2017, 6)

Now, there is no doubt that Watkins and Willaschek are right to insist that human theoretical cognition requires both the satisfaction of some sort of "givenness-condition" and some sort of "thought-condition". That, of course, is one of the primary lessons of Kant's insistence that human theoretical cognition always requires the cooperation of intuitions and concepts. And it is a result that follows, as we have seen, from the conception of cognition proposed above as well. So the difference between my view and Watkins and Willaschek's view does not relate to whether human theoretical cognition is governed by these two constraints in some form. That is common currency (to a very large extent) between both views, even if we do have some disagreements about how these conditions are best understood. What separates my view from Watkins and Willaschek is that I believe that these constraints are explained by deeper features of Kant's conception of what cognition is. Thus, what Watkins and Willaschek take to be a primitive assumption at work in Kant's account, I take to be something that Kant explains in terms of a deeper and more general conception of what cognition is.

One issue that this raises for Watkins and Willasheck revolves around the way in which their conception of cognition forces them to read Kant as uses "cognition" in a variety of different senses even when discussing cognition of a theoretical sort. Of course, it is not implausible that Kant sometimes does this, but it seems to me that Watkins and Willasheck must attribute more such shifts in usage to Kant than a view like mine needs to. But more important for present purposes is the relationship of Watkins and Willasheck's account to Kant's fundamental conception of cognition as something that comes in both a theoretical and a practical form. In particular, as Watkins and Willasheck explicitly acknowledge, their account of cognition is at best only suited to a treatment of what Kant calls "theoretical cognition" or "cognition of what is" and is wholly unsuited to a treatment of "practical cognition" or "cognition of what ought to be". Thus, Watkins and Willasheck's account of cognition is at most suitable to only half of Kant's discussion of "cognition" in this most general sense. Much as was true of Tolley's account, this seems to me a symptom of a failure on Watkins and Willasheck's part to really get to the bottom of Kant's conception of cognition. In short, the narrowness of Watkins and Willasheck's conception of cognition (in comparison with Kant's own general conception thereof) seems to me to be a sign that Watkins and Willasheck have not really identified the conception of cognition that is most fundamental for Kant's discussion of both theoretical and practical cognition.[60] I believe that the conception of cognition laid out above does better on this score.

This can be seen, I think, even if we set "practical cognition" to the side, as Watkins and Willasheck do, to focus on cognition in its theoretical forms. For even there, I think we can see that Watkins and Willasheck do not take the matter nearly as deep as Kant himself does in his account of the nature of our form of cognition. For suppose we ask why it is that theoretical cognition must satisfy the two constraints laid out by Watkins and Willasheck. On their account, these constraints define what it is to be an instance of "theoretical cognition" for Kant, so there is rather little we can say in response to this question. But this would have been deeply dissatisfying, even within the historical context in which Kant was operating. For of course, one of the main opponents of the Kantian account of cognition are broadly Leibnizian accounts of cognition that would deny that theoretical cognition requires that any sort of object be "given" to us *via* something like affection by objects. Thus, at least if not supplemented with further arguments, Watkins and Willaschek's reading of "cognition" threatens to make Kant's discussion of the nature of cognition question-begging from the start, not just with respect to the contemporary debate about these issues, but also with respect to the historical context in which Kant himself was writing.

Of course, Watkins and Willaschek might offer further arguments for the "givenness condition" they impose here. But such arguments would have to appeal to some other *more fundamental* conception of cognition (or some related cognitive achievement) that does not simply take a "givenness-condition" on cognition to be written into Kant's definition of what cognition is. Similarly, Kant certainly has a number of different arguments against the Leibnizian account of cognition. But, again, these arguments can only be fully understood against the background of a conception of cognition that does not take a "givenness"

---

[60] Of course, one might try to extend the "givenness condition" so that it is satisfied by the Fact of Reason in the practical case. Once again, I am not completely unsympathetic to such moves, but I think they are best carried out in the context of a deeper understanding of why cognition might have a connection to "givenness" in the first place.

condition on cognition for granted. In other words, we can only fully appreciate why Kant thinks we should reject conceptions of cognition that do not require either the "givenness-condition" or the "thought-condition" by going deeper into Kant's own thought about these issues to uncover a more fundamental conception of cognition at work in it—a conception of cognition, that is, that does not merely assume that human theoretical cognition is subject to these constraints, but rather explains why it is subject to these constraints in terms of even more basic features of the nature of cognition as a cognitive achievement. It is precisely this sort of account of cognition I have tried to develop above. Thus, while I agree with much of what Watkins and Willasheck and Tolley say about the nature of cognition for Kant, none of them seem to me to capture the most fundamental conception of cognition at work in Kant's thought about these issues, as it appears both in the theoretical and in the practical domain.

3
Kant's Rational Constitutivism

In the last chapter, we explored the basic elements of Kant's conception of cognition, with a focus on the connection between cognizing something and (at least implicitly) being conscious of one's representation of that thing as subject to certain (theoretical or practical) standards of correctness. In this chapter, I want to develop that discussion while fleshing out some of the implications of the "reason-first" approach to philosophy we outlined in Chapter 1. In doing so, I will focus on questions that would today be considered part of "meta-ethics", although this term is not always apt when applied to Kant. Nonetheless, as we will see, one result of viewing Kant's implicit "meta-ethics" in the light of the previous two chapters will be a reading of Kant that agrees with many Kantians in seeing Kant as a sort of *constitutivist* about the "sources of normativity".[1]

More precisely, I will interpret Kant as claiming that the most fundamental norms that apply to finite rational beings like us are grounded in the sort of rational beings we are. But, on my reading, unlike most recent forms of meta-ethical constitutivism, Kant's constitutivism attempts to ground the fundamental norms that apply to us not just in facts about (say) our form of practical agency, but rather in our form of finite rationality, where rationality is conceived of as *equally* theoretical and practical. Thus, for my Kant, the norms that apply to us are grounded in how our form of rationality involves a system of rational capacities or powers, *both* theoretical *and* practical, under the governance of reason. Kant, I will argue, is best thought of as what I will call a *rational constitutivist*: a constitutivist who grounds the basic norms that apply to all rational beings in the forms of self-consciousness constitutive of reason itself.

a. Practical Reason's Self-Consciousness and the Categorical Imperative

To explore these ideas, I want to begin by returning to the connections between cognition and self-consciousness discussed in the last chapter. There, we saw that Kant's conception of cognition implies that any cognitive power must be a capacity for a certain sort of self-consciousness. In particular, we saw that any

---

[1] This chapter draws heavily on (Schafer 2019a, forthcoming a).

such capacity must provide the cognizing subject with an (implicit) consciousness of how its acts of cognition are subject to "material" standards of correctness. In this way, every cognitive power must be governed (at least implicitly) by a representation of what it would be for that power to function correctly as the cognitive capacity it is.

This representation may be thought of as capturing the inner principle of activity that is distinctive of the cognitive capacity in question. For this reason, Kant treats cognitive powers like reason as having the "formal aim" of actualizing themselves in their characteristic form of activity.[2] Thus, he writes that, "To every faculty of the mind one can attribute an *interest*, that is *a principle that contains the condition under which alone its exercise is promoted*" (KpV 5:120, my emphasis). As this indicates, for Kant, every mental faculty is *interested* in its own actualization in its proper form of exercise. And so, as we discussed above, any rational being will experience a sense of "satisfaction" in the proper exercise of its own rational powers—a satisfaction that Kant associates with what he sometimes calls the "higher faculty of pleasure and displeasure" (KU 5:204, EEKU 28:228–9).[3]

For present purposes, the important point is that Kant attributes such ends and interests to our rational powers (in part) because they are capacities for various forms of cognition and, as such, must be governed by an (implicit) consciousness of their own standards of proper exercise.[4] It is because these powers are governed by such a representation that we can treat them as literally having ends and interests that are internal to them, and, in particular, that we can attribute to them an interest in functioning in this fashion. Kant thus sees a tight connection between (i) the fact that rational capacities are capacities for cognition, (ii) the manner in which such capacities are self-conscious, and (iii) how they are governed by an internal teleology of ends and interests. In this chapter, I want to deepen our understanding of the consciousness that governs the activities of rational capacities like reason by turning to an aspect of that account we have neglected thus far: Kant's attempt to ground imperatives or ought-claims in the nature of these capacities.

Kant expresses the core of this part of his account in passages like this one:

A practical rule is always a product of reason because it prescribes action as a means to an effect, which is its purpose. But for a being in whom reason quite alone is not the determining ground of the will, this rule is an imperative, that is, *a rule indicated by an 'ought', which...signifies that if reason completely*

---

[2] For the importance of this, see (Engstrom 2002, 2009; Reath 2010, 2012, 2013).
[3] For more discussion of this, see (DeWitt 2014, 2018; Elizondo 2014).
[4] Whether and how these points extend to non-cognitive capacities or powers is a complicated question, which I discuss in detail in (Schafer 2022a). Here, I mean to be considering only genuine capacities *for cognition* in the sense defined above.

determined the will the action would without fail take place in accordance with this rule. (KpV 5:20, my emphasis, compare GMS 4:449, KpV 5:159)

As this makes clear, for Kant, an imperative X applies to some agent A just in case the content of that imperative X accurately characterizes what that agent A would do if their rational faculties (or reason in the broad sense) were free of any extra-rational forms of "external hindrance".[5] In this way, for Kant, imperatives apply to beings who possess reason, but in a finite or limited form—beings, that is, in whom reason's proper operation may be hindered by various extra-rational influences, including aspects of our system of rational capacities insofar as they have not been brought under reason's governance. Thus, for Kant, imperatives apply only to *imperfectly rational beings*: beings who possess the power of reason, and so *should* be governed by its internal principles, but who are also subject to extra-rational influences that can lead them to act contrary to reason's demands.[6] As a result, to be conscious of such an imperative ("a law that is also an incentive") is to be conscious of "a power *ruling over sensibility*"—namely, reason as realized in imperfect creatures like us (KpV 5:159). With respect to imperfectly rational creatures, the principles of reason serve as "laws", but these laws are not "purely necessary" in the way ordinary causal laws are, since they do not invariably determine what we do. Rather, in such cases, these laws merely "necessitate" us to act in certain ways (V-MS/Vigil 27:481, V-Met/Mron II 29:611).

The classic example of such "necessitation" is Kant's account of the moral law as expressed by the categorical imperative. As Kant conceives of it, the moral law may be thought of in two basic ways. First, it may be thought of as a principle that characterizes how practical reason must function *insofar as* it is free of any extra-rational influence.[7] In this sense, it is "descriptive" or "constitutive" of practical reason as such.[8] But, with respect to creatures in whom reason *can* be interfered with by various extra-rational factors, it is better represented as an imperative or ought-claim—namely, by the categorical imperative in its various formulations.

---

[5] Compare (Schönecker and Horn 2006; Sensen 2017; Rosefeldt 2019; Marshall 2022).

[6] For an illuminating discussion of this aspect of Kantian views, see (Lavin 2004).

[7] Compare Kant's remark that "all errors of subreption [errors of dialectical inference] are always to be ascribed to a defect in judgment, never to understanding or to reason" (A643/B671). As Kant stresses in the *Religion*, exactly how this sort of "hindrance" occurs is (in some cases) "inscrutable" for us, given that it must leave evil actions imputable to us and so traceable to our spontaneous power of choice (RGV 6:21). Nonetheless, even in the *Religion*, where Kant accounts for moral evil as involving a "deed" of the free power of choice that subordinates the incentive of the moral law to the incentive of the "law of self-love", he continues to stress (i) that this deviation from the moral law cannot be regarded as internal to practical reason, and (ii) that it only occurs insofar as our sensible nature provides the power of choice with an incentive that conflicts with the moral law. So, even on this model of "radical moral evil", it remains true that such evil is always the product of some "external hindrance" to the proper functioning of reason (in the broad sense of the term).

[8] Compare and contrast (Marshall 2022), who generally reads Kant as engaging in a more reductive project, although he sets aside the question of whether the reduction in question might take teleological facts as its basis.

For, once again, this way of representing the moral law captures how it "merely necessitates" action in creatures like us, as opposed to determining what we do with "pure necessity":

> ...this "ought" is strictly speaking a "will" that holds for every rational being under the condition that reason in him is practical without hindrance; but for beings like us—who are also affected by sensibility, by incentives of a different kind, and in whose case that which reason by itself would do is not always done—that necessity of action is called only an "ought," and the subjective necessity is distinguished from the objective. (GMS 4:449)

Given this, when we consider reason in the context of error-prone, finite creatures like us, reason's principle will always be *both* constitutive (of reason's exercise insofar as this is free of illicit extra-rational influences) *and* normative (for the subject's thoughts and actions given that they are subject to such influences).[9]

As this indicates, for Kant, the very possibility of a distinctively practical form of representation—a representation of X as something that *merely ought to be*, as opposed to as something that *simply is*—is grounded in the existence of reason in an imperfectly realized form.[10] A perfect form of reason, like God's, would not allow for any potential gap between its representations and reality, and so would have no need for representations that capture a distinction between what ought to be and what is. Rather, for God, representing something as good is one and the same as representing it as real. Unfortunately, for creatures like us, in whom the realization of reason's ends requires struggle and effort, things are quite different. For us, there is always the possibility of a gap between reason's principles and ends and reality, and in the context of that potential gap, it becomes appropriate to characterize reason's principles and ends as imperatives: as principles that characterize how things ought to be as opposed to merely how they are. In this sense, as many have stressed, for Kant, the use of imperatives to characterize the operations of some capacity is only appropriate insofar as that capacity is subject to the possibility of error.[11] But this in turn is only because the very distinction

---

[9] In his helpful discussion of these issues, (Pollok 2017) also claims that such principles are both constitutive and normative, but he does not explain this in the manner I do. I note some issues with Pollock's reading below, although much of what he says is compatible with my account.

[10] See also passages like (MS 5:403–4), which make clear the connection between this idea and the distinction between phenomena and noumena.

[11] For contemporary discussion of this idea, see (Lavin 2004; Fix 2020). As we will discuss below, this is one reason why we should be cautious about treating Kant's account of the nature of *imperatives* as exhausting his account of the nature of "normativity" in the broad sense familiar from contemporary meta-ethics. For example, while Kant of course denies that God would represent reality in imperatival terms, he does not deny that God takes a certain form of "satisfaction" in his creation, or that God would in some sense find that creation *good* (V-Phil-Th/Pölitz 28:1065). So, Kant's account of imperatives does not exhaust his account of evaluative thought or goodness in general since the former, but not the latter, is limited to imperfectly rational creatures like you or me.

between practical and theoretical representations would not even arise in the first place for a creature that was incapable of error.[12]

b. Principles, Imperatives, and the *Faktum der Vernunft*

As a result, in creatures like us, the principle of practical reason, or the moral law, is *both* constitutive of reason's proper form of activity, when it is free of illicit extra-rational influences, *and* normative for our thoughts and actions, when they are subject to such influences. It is thus fundamental to Kant's account of such principles that they can be expressed in *both* a descriptive *and* a normative fashion (although it is important to always remember that the need to draw such a distinction in the first place is itself a product of our own cognitive imperfections). Nowhere is the duality better expressed than in Kant's discussion of the *Faktum der Vernunft*, which provides his mature practical philosophy with its foundation. That discussion begins with Kant stressing something that should be familiar— namely, that possession of practical reason necessarily involves an (often implicit) consciousness of the principles at work in that faculty, a consciousness that makes it possible for us to become explicitly conscious of these principles. More precisely, according to Kant, we can grasp these laws or principles through reflecting on practical reason and attending to how it "directs us" to set aside "all empirical conditions":

> We can become aware of practical laws just as we are aware of pure theoretical principles, by attending to the necessity with which reason prescribes them to us and to the setting aside of all empirical conditions to which reason directs us.
>
> (KpV 5:30)

We will return to the nature of this consciousness in a moment. But fundamentally, I take this sort of reflection to be relevant here insofar as it helps us make explicit to ourselves how reason imposes standards of correctness upon our practical representations—standards that hold simply in virtue of the nature of reason itself and not because of some further empirical condition.

---

[12] Note that this means that sensibility *considered in isolation from* our other faculties is not subject to imperatives in *this* sense. Rather, sensibility is only subject to such imperatives insofar as it has been integrated into the operations of our higher cognitive powers in the manner to be discussed in (Schafer 2022a). Of course, once sensibility is so integrated, its proper operation can be interfered with by external factors, including, crucially, the operations of those higher, spontaneous faculties insofar as they are not themselves operating properly. (See Kant's discussion of mental illnesses like hypochondria for an example of just this phenomenon.) But, even in such cases, the ultimate root of the "hindrance" to the *system* of cognitive faculties must, for Kant, lie in sensibility and not in the nature of rational capacities as such.

It is just this consciousness that Kant's famous gallows thought experiment is meant to provide us with an example of:

> Suppose someone asserts of his lustful inclination that, when the desired object and the opportunity are present, it is quite irresistible to him; ask him whether, if a gallows were erected in front of the house where he finds this opportunity and he would be hanged on it immediately after gratifying his lust, he would not then control his inclination. One need not conjecture very long what he would reply. But ask him whether, if his prince demanded, on pain of the same immediate execution, that he give false testimony against an honorable man whom the prince would like to destroy under a plausible pretext, he would consider it possible to overcome his love of life, however great it may be. He would perhaps not venture to assert whether he would do it or not, but he must admit without hesitation that it would be possible for him. He judges, therefore, that he can do something because he is aware that he ought to do it and cognizes freedom within him, which, without the moral law, would have remained unknown to him.   (KpV 5:30)

Through considering such cases, Kant believes, we can clarify our already implicit consciousness of the sort of power that reason is in us, thereby coming to a better understanding of how this capacity is practical. In particular, through reflecting on such cases, we can bring to explicit consciousness the existence of a practical principle in us that can move us to act as morality demands, even when the ordinary empirical sources of motivation speak against that action. In this way, according to Kant, to become fully conscious of the principles at work in practical reason, we need only reflect on the potential acts of that faculty, and, in particular, on how it can determine us to action independently of any empirical or sensible condition.

On my reading, it is this consciousness of the activity and principles of reason *as such* that provides us with what Kant calls a "fact of reason" (*Faktum der Vernunft*)—namely, a consciousness of the moral law *as the principle of practical reason* in the form of the categorical imperative:

> Consciousness of this fundamental law may be called a fact of reason because one cannot reason it out from antecedent data of reason, for example, from consciousness of freedom (since this is not antecedently given to us) and because it instead forces itself upon us as a synthetic a priori proposition that is not based on any intuition, either pure or empirical....   (KpV 5:31)

Thus, on my reading, this "fact" is just our consciousness of our power of practical reason as governed by such a law. More precisely, in the first instance, what this consciousness involves is a consciousness of the moral law as a practical principle in the form of the categorical imperative—a principle, that is, that characterizes how we ought to act.

But this, of course, is not the end of Kant's story. For Kant also insists that the *Faktum der Vernunft* provides us with practical, but nonetheless rational, grounds for assenting to the proposition that we are noumenally free and so *can* always act in accordance with the demands of the moral law.[13] For this reason, through his consciousness of the moral law, a rational being can judge "that he can do something because he is aware that he ought to do it and cognizes freedom within which, without the moral law, would have remained unknown to him" (KpV 5:30). Such claims express Kant's conviction that the moral law is the *ratio cognoscendi* of freedom—his conviction, that is, that our consciousness of the moral law provides us with a cognitive basis for taking ourselves to be noumenally free. According to Kant, the ability of the moral law to play this role is ultimately a product of the fact that the concepts of "freedom and unconditional practical law reciprocally imply each other" (KpV 5:29). Thus, Kant argues, to conceive of a power that ought to function in accordance with an unconditional practical law like the moral law just is to conceive of a power that is genuinely autonomous and so capable of acting in a transcendentally free manner.

In this way, according to the second *Critique*, it is our consciousness of ourselves as subject to the moral law (as an imperative) that grounds our consciousness of ourselves as free. There is a transition here of some sort between, on the one hand, a representation of ourselves as subject to the moral law and, on the other, a representation of ourselves as free. Nonetheless, contrary to the way it is often presented in the literature, we should be careful not to think of this transition as necessarily involving anything as complex as a multi-premise, syllogistic inference from one of these to the other.[14] For the relationship at issue here between the representation of ourselves as subject to the moral law and the representation of ourselves as free is, I believe, more immediate than this. Indeed, as Kant suggests just prior to this example, our consciousness of ourselves as subject to the categorical imperative seems closer to simply being the self-consciousness of a being who is sensibly conditioned, but also noumenally free:

> Now I do not ask here whether they are in fact different or whether it is not much rather the case that an unconditional law is merely the self-consciousness

---

[13] The literature on the *Faktum der Vernunft* is extensive. See, for example, (Allison 1990; Ameriks 2000; Proops 2003; Sussman 2008; Tenenbaum 2012; Schönecker 2013; Ware 2014). As noted above, I will mostly abstract away from the scholarly debates about the precise sense of "*Faktum*" at issue in this passage, since I suspect that Kant means to use this term in a manner that reflects a number of different uses of it during the period in which he was writing.

[14] To be clear, this does not mean that it would be *impossible* to make this transition by means of such a syllogism, only that this is not the most basic form the transition takes.

of a pure practical reason, this being identical with the positive concept of - freedom.... (KpV 5:29)

Thus, as Kant goes on to say, "the moral law expresses nothing other than the autonomy of pure practical reason, that is, freedom" (KpV 5:33). Such passages suggest that we should not place *too much* space between our consciousness of our capacity for freedom and our consciousness of ourselves as subject to the moral law.[15] After all, as Kant repeatedly stresses, these are reciprocal representations that *immediately imply* one another; if there is an inference from one representation *to* another here, it does not seem to be a multi-premise syllogistic inference.

To do justice to everything that Kant says in these passages, then, we need to find a way of understanding the relationship between (i) the "what ought to be" representation of ourselves as subject to the categorical imperative and (ii) the "what is" representation of ourselves as free, on which there is an *immediate inferential connection* between these two representations. This is especially challenging because the transition involves (in some sense) moving from a *practical* mode of representation (what ought to be) to a *theoretical* one (what is) and thus seems impossible to model using the resources of Kant's general "concept-containment" model of immediate inference.[16] And, in any case, any attempt to treat this transition between an "ought" and an "is" as an immediate inference would seem to invite Hume's famous complaint:

> In every system of morality, which I have hitherto met with...I am surpriz'd to find, that instead of the usual copulations of propositions, is, and is not, I meet with no proposition that is not connected with an ought, or an ought not. This change is imperceptible; but is, however, of the last consequence. For as this ought, or ought not, expresses some new relation or affirmation, it is necessary that it should be observed and explained; and at the same time that a reason should be given, for what seems altogether inconceivable, how this new relation can be a deduction from others, which are entirely different from it. (T 3.1.1.27)

And even today, it is easy to find Kantians who claim that this feature of Kant's account represents a deep, and perhaps fatal, problem: a failure by Kant, as Guyer puts it, to recognize "the clear distinction between is and ought, between the descriptive and the normative" (Guyer 2006, 33).

But is this right? Or do complaints like Guyer's miss the real force of the view Kant is developing? To defend Kant against these charges, we need to make sense

---

[15] There is a sense, as we have already seen, in which the same point applies to our theoretical self-consciousness as well. But there the scope and determinateness of this consciousness is much more modest than it is in the practical case.

[16] For a detailed discussion of this model, see (Anderson 2015).

of the tight connection he seems to draw between our consciousness of ourselves as subject to the moral law and our consciousness of ourselves as free. And to do this, what we need is the idea that two representations of oneself—one practical, the other theoretical—might *both* express a single underlying aspect of one's rational nature. That is, what we need is a view on which these two representations differ from one another *primarily in their form*—that is, insofar as one of them is theoretical and the other practical.

On such a view, both representations would (in some sense) make us conscious of a single reality: our underlying finite capacity for rationality. The difference between them would be that one does so in a practical, "what ought to be" guise, and the other in a theoretical, "what is" guise. Thus, on such a view, each of these representations would immediately imply the other, not because one of them is contained in the *content* of the other, but rather because of a special relationship between their respective *forms*. In this case, the transition from a consciousness of the categorical imperative to a consciousness of our capacity for freedom would simply be a matter of making explicit something that was implicit all along in our consciousness of ourselves as subject to the categorical imperative.

I hope it is already clear that such a view fits well with Kant's claims about *what it is* for an agent to be subject to an ought claim in the first place. After all, as we have seen, what it is for someone to be subject to the categorical imperative (*as an imperative*) is just for them to be a creature who possesses the capacity of practical reason, but in a form that is also subject to various extra-rational influences, and so to be a creature who is *merely necessitated* to act in the manner reason demands. The fact that we *ought* to comply with the moral law simply reflects the fact that we are creatures who are both sensible and rational—or, in other words, that we are capable of rational self-determination but also prone to deviate from the demands of rationality.[17] And it is just this package of capacities that we attribute to ourselves when we regard ourselves as noumenally free but also susceptible to sensible inclination. Kant's account of imperatives thus makes it easy to see how the difference between our consciousness of ourselves as free and our consciousness of ourselves as subject to the moral law is primarily due to a *formal* difference between two representations of ourselves—one theoretical and the other practical—both of which are made valid by the same underlying features of our finite form of rationality.[18]

---

[17] Compare again (Schönecker and Horn 2006; Marshall 2022).

[18] Of course, this formal difference will, in some sense, correspond to a difference in the content of these claims. For what we represent, in one case, as something that is—namely, *our imperfect power to act rationally or autonomously*—is different from what we represent, in the other, as something that ought to be—namely, that *we ought to act in a rational or autonomous fashion*. But there is a deeper sense in which both representations simply make us conscious of a single underlying reality, on this account.

If this is right, then for Kant there are two basic ways for finite rational creatures like us to become conscious of our imperfect capacity for freedom—one theoretical and the other practical—with the latter serving as the *ratio cognoscendi* of the former.[19] In many ways, as we will see, this idea comprises the core of Kant's account of the "sources of normativity". Indeed, one might read such passages as providing the core of a Kantian *reduction* of the normative to the non-normative of just the sort that many contemporary meta-ethicists have sought.[20] But, as I discuss below, we should be cautious about interpreting these claims in a reductive fashion. After all, while such passages do develop an account of the nature of imperatives in terms of features of (imperfectly realized) practical reason, the conception of practical reason at work in them itself involves teleological notions. And these teleological notions would normally be placed on the "normative" side of the "normative/non-normative" divide within contemporary meta-ethics. Thus, while Kant might be read as attempting to explain the validity of imperatives in broadly non-imperatival terms, we should not rush to interpret this project in terms of a general attempt to reduce the "normative" to the "non-normative". Rather, if we are to associate Kant with a view within the contemporary debate, it would be better to understand his view as a form of *non-reductive constitutivism*, on which certain normative principles (like imperatives) that apply to us are explained in terms of our human form of reason, but where this is itself understood in teleological terms.[21]

It is also important to stress that this formal difference would *not* exist (at least in the same way) for a purely rational being. For such beings are not subject to ought claims for Kant and would not understand the moral law in such terms. Thus, for such a being, there would be no formal difference between the representation of itself as free and the representation of itself as subject to the moral law. Indeed, in such creatures, the very distinction we observe in us between theoretical and practical modes of representation would break down in a sense. For related discussion, see (Stern 2011).

[19] As noted above, both of these should be distinguished from the "merely formal" self-consciousness of reason as such, which is prior to any distinction between the theoretical and practical as two forms of "material cognition". In particular, as I argue in (Schafer forthcoming a), our consciousness of ourself as noumenally free possesses many of the central marks of cognition for Kant, albeit on distinctively practical grounds. For through our consciousness of the moral law, we not only gain a consciousness of ourselves as possessing a capacity for noumenal freedom, but (i) we are also able to show that this capacity is actual, and so really possible (as the necessary condition on the validity of the categorical imperative), and (ii) we are able to enrich our understanding of the nature of this capacity (through the consciousness the categorical imperative provides of its essential principle). In particular, our consciousness of the moral law allows us to make claims about the relations of identity and difference that obtain with respect to noumenally free beings in ways that our consciousness of our other rational capacities does not. For it is only through this consciousness of identity and diversity that we are capable of assigning moral responsibility for phenomenal actions to noumenal agents in the manner the application of the categorical imperative requires. Thus, our consciousness of the moral law not only provides us with a genuine form of practical cognition, it also allows to achieve something very like cognition of our own nature as free, rational beings, albeit only on distinctively practical grounds. For another presentation of a similar line of thought, see (Abaci 2022).

[20] See (Marshall 2022), although again Marshall largely sets to the side the role of teleology in Kant's conception of reason in his discussion of these issues, and has moved towards a position like the one I am defending here since writing that paper.

[21] Compare again (Mensch 2013)'s discussion of the centrality of teleological notions to Kant's conception of reason and our faculties. It is possible to read Kant as giving a further reduction of the

Similarly, although Kant's account of imperatives does establish a kind of equivalence between certain theoretical claims about the nature of our rational capacities and certain practical claims about how those faculties ought to function, this equivalence should not be seen in terms of an attempt to reduce the latter to the former. Rather, Kant's view seems to be that, while finite rational beings like us must relate to reality in the two basic ways that generate a distinction between theoretical and practical cognition, *this distinction itself* is a product of our limited access to reality. Thus, the very distinction between the theoretical and practical perspectives is itself, for Kant, a symptom of our cognitive imperfection. It would be misleading, then, to present Kant as trying to reduce *either* the practical to the theoretical *or* the theoretical to practical. Rather, his view is that the theoretical and practical perspectives on reality are systematically related to one in another in the manner they are because they are both (in some sense) grounded in something more fundamental, which transcends the very distinction between them.

c. Interlude: Imperatives and the Normativity of Logic

This story is most familiar as applied to the faculty of practical reason and its characteristic principle, the moral law, so it is there that I have been focusing. But I believe that it is not unique to that case, at least according to Kant. Rather, for Kant, something very like this applies in some sense to any rational faculty whatsoever. So, according to Kant, the principle of *any* finite rational capacity, be it theoretical or practical, can be expressed as either a theoretical claim about how this faculty will function (when "left to function by its own devices") or a normative claim about how it *ought* to function (when it is realized in rationally imperfect creatures like ourselves).[22]

This fact is, I believe, what lies at the root of the ongoing debate about whether Kant conceives of logic as normative or constitutive for thought. Such debates

---

teleological nature of our faculties to facts about how these faculties represent their own activities, but I think that it is difficult to read Kant's account of the relationship between teleology and self-consciousness in a fully reductive fashion.

[22] Although I cannot develop this point here, it is worth noting that this story about deontic modals such as ought lays the groundwork for a systematic picture of the relationship between Kant's views about the modal categories in both a theoretical and a practical context, building upon the account of modality in Kant provided by the agenda-setting (Stang 2016, 2019, forthcoming). On that account, for Kant, "Modalities describe the relation of contents of representation to the capacity by which we represent them," with modals of necessity expressing (at first pass) "the relation of a capacity to an object whose opposite does not agree with the form of that capacity, i.e. is not possible" (Stang forthcoming, 7). This fits well with the form of constitutivism about ought claims I am attributing to Kant here, since that account takes such claims to be made valid by the relationship of a potential object of practical cognition to our capacity for practical cognition (practical reason). For more on this and the (surprisingly neglected) table of the categories of freedom, see (Bader 2009).

have proved intractable, in part, because Kant often refers to the principles of logic using both descriptive and normative language. For example, we can find many passages in Kant's logic lectures that appear to claim that logic is essentially normative as opposed to descriptive:[23]

> Logic does not really contain the rules in accordance with which man actually thinks but the rules for how man ought to think. For man often uses his understanding and thinks otherwise than he ought to think and use his understanding. (V-Lo/Blomberg 25)

But at the same time, in those same lectures, Kant also stresses that the normative character of logical principles is closely associated with their character as *necessary principles of thought*—as principles that (as he says here) describe what must be true if the understanding is to "agree with itself":

> In logic, however, the question is not about *contingent* but about *necessary* rules; not how we do think, but how we ought to think. The rules of logic must thus be derived not from the *contingent* but from the *necessary* use of the understanding, which one finds in oneself apart from all psychology. In logic we do not want to know how the understanding is and does think and how it has previously proceeded in thought, but rather how it ought to proceed in thought. Logic is to teach us the correct use of the understanding, i.e., that in which it agrees with itself. (Log 9:14)

> As a science of the necessary laws of thought, without which no use of the understanding or of reason takes place at all, laws which consequently are conditions under which the understanding can and ought to agree with itself alone—the necessary laws and conditions of its correct use—logic is, however, a canon. (Log 9:13)

The juxtaposition of these two characterizations of logic—as, on the one hand, giving a *normative* characterization of how we ought to think, and, on the other, characterizing the *necessary* principles of thought itself—has fueled an extensive

---

[23] (Tolley 2006) claims that the idea that Kant takes logic to be a "normative" discipline is based almost entirely on certain passages from the *Jäsche Logic* whose standing is dubious at best. But, as this passage indicates, there are many places outside the *Jäsche Logic* where Kant appears to describe logical principles in broadly normative terms. (Compare BL 19, BL 39, BL 119, A135/B174, A133/B172, A671/B699.) Of course, none of these passages is decisive. But once we see how Kant reconciles the "constitutive" and "normative" dimensions of the moral law with one another, they make it very natural to extend this basic model to the case of logic. Thus, while I agree with much of what Tolley has to say about the "constitutive" dimension of logical principles, I take this to be compatible with these principles *also* being normative for imperfectly rational beings.

debate about whether logic, according to Kant, is normative for thought or (instead) constitutive of its very possibility.[24]

Fortunately, if we keep the model of imperatives just described in mind, we can see that much of this debate rests on something of a false dichotomy.[25] After all, if we apply the model just developed, not to practical reason and its principle, but rather to the understanding and its laws, then we reach the result that the principles of logic are both constitutive (of the "unhindered" activities of the understanding) *and* normative (for those activities insofar as they are subject to extra-rational hindrances).[26] Thus, if Kant is thinking about the laws of logic using the same basic framework he used to think about the moral law, the answer to the question, "Are the laws of logic normative or constitutive for Kant?", must be that they are *both*.

In this way, the best explanation of Kant's willingness to describe logical principles in both these ways seems to me to be that he is simply applying the same basic model of the source of normative principles or imperatives to the logical case that we have just been exploring in the case of the moral law. Strikingly, this is just what we find when we turn to passages in which Kant describes how it is possible for the understanding to function incorrectly. For in those passages, much as in his discussion of practical reason, Kant stresses that errors of *the understanding* are always the product, not of the understanding itself, but rather of the "unnoticed influence of sensibility" upon us.[27] This way of thinking about the normativity of logic in Kant bears important similarities to a number of recent accounts of this issue, including notably (Tolley 2006, 2012; Lu-Adler 2018; Merritt 2018; Nunez 2019). But it differs from each of these in important respects. For example, while my discussion here is inspired by certain aspects of Tolley's, it gives much greater weight to the normative dimension of logical principles. Thus, contrary to what Tolley suggests, it seems to me a mistake to think that we must choose between a "constitutivist" and a "normativist"

---

[24] See (MacFarlane 2002; Tolley 2006, 2012; Anderson 2015; Nunez 2019) for further discussion of these issues.

[25] (Nunez 2019) helpfully argues for a version of this point and discusses the implications of it for Kant's account of what "thought" is in much more detail than I do here. But he does not trace it to its roots in Kant's general account of the nature of imperatives in the manner I do. On this, though, compare (Haase 2009) for an insightful discussion.

[26] As this indicates, the basic model Kant is operating with here applies equally to synthetic and analytic principles (insofar as these are constitutive of a rational faculty). Thus, there is no reason to treat (say) the principles of logic as purely constitutive as opposed to normative as (Pollok 2017) does. Again, the widespread focus in this debate on extreme cases like the case of explicitly self-contradictory judgments seems to me to be misleading here. For while the constitutivist line on such cases may be correct, this does not rule out a more general reconciliation of the constitutivist and normativist positions.

[27] A294/B350-1. As (Kern 2006; Engstrom 2009; McDowell 2009, 2011) have noted, this again represents a distinctively Aristotelian aspect of Kant's views. For here the "privative" cases in which the capacity malfunctions are always explained not by the nature of the relevant capacity itself, but rather by something external to the capacity, which hinders its proper functioning.

reading of Kant's conception of logic. Rather, Kant's account is one on which logical laws have a normative significance for us because of the imperfect manner in which we realize the capacities they are constitutive of. Nonetheless, it is important to stress that I agree with Tolley that there will be limiting cases, such as the case of *explicitly self-contradictory judgments*, in which the formation of some alleged "thought" may simply be impossible for any rational being, imperfect or otherwise. On the present account that is no surprise. After all, there may be cases in which the deviation from the laws of logic involved in some "alleged thought" is so obvious than it is impossible for this "alleged thought" to come about through the "unnoticed influence" of extra-rational factors on the understanding. In such cases, it may be impossible not to "notice" this influence simply in virtue of the structure of the alleged thought we are trying to think. In such cases, I agree that there may be little room for the laws of logic to function in a normative as opposed to constitutive fashion. But these are only extreme cases at the very limit of the thinkable. The vast majority of illogical thought is far less self-evidentially incoherent, and so much easier for imperfectly rational beings to entertain.[28]

In a similar vein, (Merritt 2018) argues that the principles of pure logic are always constitutive, while the principles of applied logic are always normative. She makes this claim for reasons that sit well with my discussion here—namely, that only with the move from pure to applied logic does the possibly of imperfection and error that makes these principles *normative* as opposed to constitutive come into view. But while we agree that these principles are only normative insofar as we consider their realization in imperfectly rational beings, I believe it is misleading to say that this means that the principles of *pure logic* are always constitutive as opposed to normative for Kant. Rather, it seems to me that when we consider their realization in imperfectly rational beings, *the principles of pure logic* become normative for such beings as well—in just the way the moral law, as the practical principle that is constitutive of pure practical reason, becomes normative for imperfectly rational beings in the practical domain. Thus, while pure logic is not concerned with the nature of imperfectly rational beings *as such*, the principles that pure logic arrives at continue to play *both* a constitutive and a normative role for Kant.

Moreover, similar remarks apply to the power of judgment as well.[29] If this is right, then a very general view of the "source" of imperatives or normative

---

[28] Compare (Worsnip 2021)'s recent treatment of incoherence in terms of sets of attitudes of which it is constitutively true that anyone who has them would be disposed to revise them under conditions of full transparency.

[29] See (EEKU 20:225, EEKU 20:239, KU 5:181). There too it seems clear that the sort of legislation that is characteristic of the power of judgment can also be accurately represented in imperatival terms—something that is (once again) easily intelligible if we take Kant here to be applying a general account of the nature of imperatives to the power of judgment.

principles follows from Kant's conception of our rational capacities. On this account, the normative principles that apply to the activities of *any* rational faculty will be grounded in the nature of that faculty and its characteristic form of activity. Or, more precisely, these principles will be grounded in the nature of the relevant rational capacity, while their status *as normative* (as opposed to simply constitutive) will be grounded in the fact that this rational capacity is imperfect and so not free of extra-rational hindrances. In this way, on this account, the normative character of such principles is rooted in the imperfect manner in which such capacities are realized in creatures like us.

One important implication of this is that the nature of any rational capacity, either theoretical or practical, will ground claims about how that faculty ought to function. For this reason, it is misleading to follow Kitcher in denying that, for Kant, "there is a special sort of accountability involved in cognition" (Kitcher 2011, 247). In particular, the present account casts doubt on Kitcher's claim that, for Kant, "it is not errors of theoretical reasoning *per se* that are imputable, but [moral or practical] failures to *develop* reasoning skills and to *take up* controversial topics that can be faulted" (158, my emphasis). Rather, as we have just seen, the nature of any rational faculty, simply considered as such, makes it apt for representation in normative or imperatival terms.[30] Thus, contrary to what Kitcher suggests, we can *directly* apply normative categories to the errors of any spontaneous rational faculty, simply in virtue of Kant's account of the nature of imperatives. Given this, in order to think of us as responsible for our theoretical errors, we do not need to *trace* these errors *back* to some *practical failing* on our part in the manner Kitcher describes. Rather, quite on the contrary, there is a basic sense in which we can be said to have not done what we *ought* whenever one of our rational capacities does not function as it should.[31]

At the same time, there is another sense in which Kitcher is right to stress the primacy of the practical point of view with respect to these sorts of claims. For imperatives are always themselves, for Kant, practical representations. Thus, as noted above, whenever I represent the principle of any faculty in imperatival terms, I am always making use of the resources of practical reason to think about this faculty. In this way, whenever we *represent* the principle of a theoretical faculty *as an imperative*, we are indeed conceiving of that faculty *in relation to our will*.[32] And, at least when the faculties are my own, this means that the correctness or incorrectness of such representations will always be answerable to

---

[30] On this point, also contrast (O'Neill 1989; Cohen 2013, 2014; Mudd 2016, 2017), all of who in some sense attempt to treat epistemic norms to a special case of moral norms. Mudd is especially clear on this point, writing that, the principle of systematicity at work in theoretical reason is, "usefully be interpreted as a species of practical principle".
[31] See (McLear forthcoming-b), who argues in detail that Kant's conception of "imputability" applies equally to our higher theoretical and practical faculties.
[32] Compare (Mudd 2017)'s discussion of a broad sense of "practical" at work in Kant's writings.

the standards that practical reason sets for all my practical representation as such. In this sense, Kitcher is completely correct to emphasize the importance of the moral law to the evaluation of how our theoretical faculties ought to function. But this fact about *the sort of representation* involved in representing a principle as an imperative does not undermine the more fundamental point here—namely, that the principles of any rational faculty (be it theoretical or practical) are *apt for* this sort of representation simply in virtue of being the principles of a rational faculty. Thus, while we need to bring our practical faculties to bear on our theoretical faculties in order to represent their principles *as imperatives*, in doing so, we are not "adding" anything extra to these faculties themselves. Rather, we are simply bringing out a dimension of these principles that only appears to us when we consider them from a practical point of view.[33]

d. Rational Constitutivism

If this is right, then Kant's account of imperatives provides us with the basis for a quite general "meta-normative" account of the nature of ought-claims, one that grounds the validity of such claims in more fundamental facts about our basic rational powers. On this account, the principle of any sensibly conditioned rational faculty can be expressed *both* as a descriptive claim about how that faculty will function, when it is free of external interference, *and* in terms of an imperative expressing how it should function, when such interference is possible.[34] As I've noted above, the resulting view can be seen as a form of meta-normative constitutivism, at least if we define "constitutivism" in a broad sense on which this label applies to any view that attempts to make sense of the basic norms that apply to something through an appeal to what that thing is or takes itself to be:

---

[33] Again, contrast (Cohen 2013, 2014)'s attempt to treat epistemic norms as a special case of practical norms here. Once again, although I agree with Cohen that both epistemic norms and practical norms have a common root in the general nature of reason as a faculty, and so agree that they are structurally isomorphic in many ways, I disagree that this idea is best captured through the attempt to derive the norms that characterize good epistemic functioning from the norms that characterize good practical functioning. On this point, again, I am closer to (Merritt 2018), although I think she sometimes goes too far in the other direction. This is also relevant to my differences with (Rosefeldt 2019), which provides a useful point of comparison here because he agrees with much of the picture I have been sketching here. But Rosefeldt disagrees with me in taking this account to apply *only* to practical reason or the will. On Rosefeldt's "normative voluntarist" reading, talk of imperatives is only appropriate insofar as we are speaking about the will as opposed to other rational faculties. For discussion of why Rosefeldt's restriction on the scope of Kant's account of imperatives is under-motivated, see (McLear forthcoming).

[34] Again, this would not be true of creatures who were not subject to the "hindrances" of sensibility. But this is because, in such creatures, "there would be no distinction between what should be done and what is done, between a practical law concerning that which is possible through us and the theoretical law concerning that which is actual through us" (MS 5:404).

Core Constitutivist Claim: The fundamental norms that apply to X are explained by what X is (or what X takes itself to be).

More precisely, the view I am attributing to Kant might be regarded as a form of what (Fix 2021) calls a "nature-first" constitutivism.[35] But, as we will see, if there is a "nature" in play in Kant's account, it is the nature of reason itself. And, as we have already seen, if reason has a "nature" or "essence", this "nature" is defined in terms of how reason implicitly represents its own proper form of activity. Thus, the "nature" at issue here is not given *to* reason (or any rational creature) from an external source. Nor is it a "brute fact" that is simply imposed upon us. Rather, the nature of reason is contained within reason's own essential form of implicit self-consciousness.

As is often noted, something like the Core Constitutivist Claim is almost unavoidable with respect to the norms that apply to "functional kinds" such as artifacts or life-forms—that is, with respect to things whose nature seems to be defined in terms of their capacity to play a certain sort of functional role in a larger whole.[36] For example, artifacts like knives are defined in terms of the functions they "ought to perform", and this functional essence seems to ground various norms that apply to them as the sorts of thing they are—norms, say, that characterize what it is to be a "good knife". And something similar is, of course, true in the case of living things as well, although there the details of the story are the subject of much greater debate. But while the availability of this mode of explanation in some cases is relatively uncontroversial, constitutivism as a meta-normative view goes well beyond such claims to ground all norms (directly or indirectly) in this manner.

So defined, constitutivism, in some sense, might be taken to be a kind of "reduction" of norms to the natures of things. But, as noted above, whether this counts as a full "meta-normative reduction" depends on how we conceive of the natures that do the explanatory work in this story. For example, as we have seen, Kant explains the applicability of imperatives or ought-claims to us in terms of our nature as finite rational beings. Thus, there is a sense in which Kant is attempting to understand how ought-claims become valid against the background of a fundamental characterization of reality in which such claims do not necessarily figure as such. *But* Kant does not take this more fundamental description of reality to be exhausted by the terms of natural science. Nor does he take reality (say) to be fundamentally best characterized in theoretical or descriptive as opposed to practical or normative terms. Rather, his view seems to be that reality on the most fundamental level somehow transcends the very distinction between the theoretical and the practical points of view.

---

[35] See also the important discussion in (Fix forthcoming) here.
[36] Compare (Thomson 2008) and (Ferrero 2019).

Moreover, as we have seen, what Kant treats as fundamental here is our rational powers, where these are understood in broadly teleological terms that cannot be captured (for Kant at least) within a purely naturalistic framework. If there is any sort of reduction here, the set of facts that forms the "reduction basis" of Kant's account of imperatives involves elements that would, for most contemporary meta-ethicists, sit on the normative side of the normative/non-normative divide. Thus, in contemporary terms, it is probably best to view Kant as developing a *non-reductive form of meta-ethical constitutivism*. For, while Kant does establish a systematic equivalence between "ought" claims and certain "is" claims, the "is" in question involves teleologically structured rational capacities that many meta-ethicists would place on the normative side of the "normative/non-normative" divide. The "reduction" at play here is thus probably best understood as an *intra-normative reduction* as opposed to a reduction of the normative to something else.[37]

As this indicates, one important feature of my general definition of constitutivism is that it is silent about the sort of *philosophical work* constitutivism is meant to accomplish. This is worth stressing here because "constitutivism" is often defined so that quite dramatic claims about what it can accomplish are built into the very definition of the view. For example, one might define constitutivism as a program for answering, in a decisive fashion, what Korsgaard has dubbed "the normative question".[38] Or one might define constitutivism so that it is committed to closing the alleged gap between is and ought in a systematic fashion.[39] But while these are some of the most prominent ways of *motivating* constitutivism, it would be a mistake to treat such claims as part of the definition of what constitutivism *is*. For many constitutivists disagree about what exactly constitutivism can accomplish, and it is far from clear that the appeal of constitutivism stands or falls with its ability to perform any task in particular.[40] So, in considering its merits, it is important to keep the *mode of philosophical explanation* that is essential to constitutivism separate from the philosophical work it can accomplish.[41]

---

[37] It is important to stress that these claims about how philosophical explanations must come to an end are, for Kant, only claims about how such explanations come to an end from a human perspective, and not claims about how they would come to an end from (say) a God's-eye point of view.

[38] (Korsgaard 1996b) is often read this way, although the precise sense in which this is true of her work is open to some dispute.

[39] Compare here (Lindeman 2017).

[40] For more modest conceptions of constitutivism, see (Smith 2012, 2015; Schafer 2015b, 2015c, 2018b; K. Sylvan and Lord forthcoming). This is especially significant because some of the most prominent objections to constitutivism are best understood not as objections to constitutivism as such, but rather as objections to further claims about what constitutivism can accomplish. See the discussion of "shmagency" below. For the canonical statement of this worry, see (Enoch 2006, 2011). For further discussion, see (Ferrero 2009; Tiffany 2012; Silverstein 2015), and compare (Schafer 2015b, 2015c). For a more detailed defense of this point, see (Paakkunainen 2018).

[41] In a Kantian context, for example, the truth of the Core Constitutivist Claim would license both arguments in an analytic and a synthetic form. Thus, Kantian constitutivism should not be associated with either of these in particular

This is one sense in which my definition of constitutivism is purposely broad. But there is a second issue on which my definition is intentionally silent—namely, exactly *which* X's it applies to and why. For example, the Core Constitutivist Claim says nothing about which description of me it is that grounds the fundamental norms that apply to me. It is here, of course, that constitutivism breaks into a wide range of subgenres. For example, neo-Aristotelian constitutivists will focus here on my nature as a *human being*, arguing that the fundamental norms that govern my activities are grounded in the standards of proper functioning implicit in the human life-form.[42] Neo-Humean constitutivists, on the other hand, will tend to focus on my nature as a rational being or agent in some quite minimal sense of "rational" or "agent", on which this requires certain forms of internal coherence. But our interest here is in forms of constitutivism with a Kantian pedigree. Following Korsgaard's lead, Kantian constitutivism is often also thought of as beginning with a conception of our nature as *agents*. On this way of thinking of things, both Kantian and Humean forms of constitutivism are conceived of as forms what we might call Agential Constitutivism:

Agential Constitutivism: The fundamental norms that apply to us are grounded in our nature as *agents*.[43]

Despite its popularity, it should already be clear that I believe that this way of presenting Kant's form of constitutivism is potentially misleading. After all, if what we have been arguing is correct, what is most fundamental to Kant's account of the "sources of normativity" is not something specific to us as *agents*, or even something specific to reason in a distinctively practical form, but rather a quite general account of how reason and our rational faculties, both theoretical and practical, give rise to normative principles concerning how they ought to function. On such an account, the normative principles that apply to the activities of any cognitive faculty will be grounded in that faculty. Or, better, the principles in question will be grounded in the relevant capacity, while the status of these principles *as normative* (as opposed to merely descriptive) will be grounded in the fact that this capacity is *not* free of external hindrance as realized in creature like us.[44]

---

[42] (Foot 2003; LeBar 2008; Thompson 2008). It is worth noting here that there is a reading of Aristotle on which his views come *very* close to the view I will be attributed to Kant here—namely, the reading on which the idea of a "human being" that is relevant here is just the idea of a "rational animal" in the abstract sense of a finite, sensibly conditioned rational being. This is not the reading of Aristotle that has dominated contemporary neo-Aristotelianism, but this would be a form of "Aristotelian constitutivism" that would agree in its essential elements with the view I attribute to Kant. See (Elizondo 2022) for more discussion of these connections.

[43] Again, this sort of view is most closely associated with the work of Korsgaard and Velleman. For related views, see (James 2007; Smith 2012; Katsafanas 2013; Bagnoli 2011, 2013, 2021; Smith 2015, 2017; Müller 2020; Tenenbaum 2021), among others.

[44] Compare the view of Kant presented in (Tenenbaum 2019). For more discussion of this point, see (Schafer 2018b, 2019a). Compare (Walden 2018). For discussion of Hegelian variants of this view, see (Gledhill and Stein 2020).

In this way, the form of constitutivism that emerges from Kant's discussion is best thought of not in terms of Agential Constitutivism, but rather in terms of what I will call Rational Constitutivism:

Rational Constitutivism: The most fundamental norms that apply to us are grounded in the fact that we are *finite rational beings* or *sensibly conditioned creatures with the power of reason*.

Now, so defined, Rational Constitutivism leaves the nature of the capacity of reason entirely open. Thus, on its own, it tells us very little about the norms which follow from this approach. The primary focus of the second half of this book will be better understanding the conception of reason that sits at the heart of this view. There, I will focus on three of Kant's main characterizations of reason's characteristic form of activity in particular:

(i) Reason's proper activity lies in (theoretical and practical) *cognition from principles*.
(ii) Reason's proper activity lies in (theoretical and practical) *comprehension*.
(iii) Reason's proper form of activity lies in *autonomous* self-determination.

The first of these characterizes reason in terms of its concern for cognition *from principles*. What this means is a complicated question, but the fundamental idea here is simple enough. One has cognition from principles insofar as one's cognitions are grounded in more fundamental and general cognitions. So, for example, one has theoretical cognition from principles insofar as one's theoretical cognitions are grounded in the cognition of other, more basic features of reality. This search for systematic (theoretical and practical) cognition is one of the distinctive aspects of reason for Kant. Crucially, cognition from principles in this sense involves a grasp not just of which properties something has (or ought to have), but also of how these *ground one another*. So, as we'll discuss in the next chapter, cognition from principles goes beyond mere cognition (*Erkenntnis*) to encompass the sort of understanding that Kant calls comprehension (*Begreifen*). This brings us to the second characterization of reason's function: the idea of reason as the faculty for comprehension, or, to put things in contemporary jargon, as the capacity for understanding. Once again, such comprehension or understanding may be either theoretical—an understanding of what is—or practical—an understanding of what ought to be. So, on this characterization, the ultimate task of reason is to achieve a *systematic understanding of what is and what ought to be*.[45] As we will see, one of Kant's insights is that these first two ways of characterizing reason are ultimately equivalent to the third—namely, the idea of reason as

---

[45] This focus on comprehension/understanding as the ultimate cognitive aim of reason marks one important difference between my interpretation and Engstrom's.

autonomous. Putting things very simply, on Kant's conception of autonomy, for reason to be autonomous is just for its activities to be determined only by reason's own internal a priori principles. So, as we will see, the activity of practical reason will be autonomous just in case this activity is an (absolute or unqualified) instance of *practical cognition from principles* or the sort of practical comprehension or determination of the will from principles that Kant often calls "wisdom". We will thus find a tight connection between the idea of reason as essentially autonomous and the idea of reason as the capacity for comprehension or cognition from principles.

By the end of Part Two, we will therefore be able to take the basic idea of Rational Constitutivism and see that it is equivalent, for Kant, to *both* of the following views:

Comprehension Constitutivism: The most fundamental norms that apply to us are grounded in the fact that we are *sensibly conditioned* creatures with the *capacity for (theoretical and practical) comprehension*.

Autonomy Constitutivism: The most fundamental norms that apply to us are grounded in the fact that we are *sensibly conditioned* creatures with the *capacity for autonomous self-determination*.

As this should indicate, Agential Constitutivism can also be thought of as a particular instance of Rational Constitutivism, since agency (in the sense intended by Korsgaard and others) is itself a rational power. But Rational Constitutivism is considerably more ecumenical about the "sources of normativity", for it views these as rooted, not merely in our nature as *practical agents*, but rather in all the aspects of our rationality, both theoretical and practical, both as directed at ourselves and at the broader world around us. This last point is especially important with respect to the comparison between this reading of Kant and Korsgaard's. Korsgaard famously introduces the "normative problem" that motivates her meta-normative views by arguing that the need for normative concepts arises because we are capable of self-conscious reflection—reflection, that is, which allows us to take a step back from our perceptions, desires, and other attitudes and ask questions about whether and why we should accept those attitudes (Korsgaard 1996b, 92–4). As Korsgaard describes it, in engaging in this sort of reflection, we normally take a step back from our perceptions and desires and make *those perceptions and desires* the object of reflection. Given this, it is no surprise that what becomes salient to us through such reflection are, first and foremost, the ways in which our own attitudes and activities conflict with one another, and that the problem that such reflection poses to us is primarily a problem of *self*-unification or *self*-constitution.[46] In this way, for Korsgaard, the "normative problem" arises through reflection on the status and relations of our

---

[46] See (Gibbard 1999).

own attitudes. And such reflection will naturally generate a consciousness of *our own* lack of unity. So, given this starting point, the primary task that reflection poses to us will be that of overcoming this *internal disunity*, and the fundamental aim of rational agency will be the demand to *unify oneself.*

To be clear, I think this is indeed an important dimension of the task of reason for Kant. But at the same time, it is hard to escape the thought that there is something egocentric, or even narcissistic, about Korsgaard's focus on our own *internal* unity or disunity. For surely reason is just as interested in understanding other things as it is in its own self-constitution.[47] Fortunately, the idea of reason as the capacity for *both* autonomous self-determination *and* comprehension can help us see why the Kantian account is not objectionably narcissistic in this way. For once we recognize the tight connection between these two aspects of reason, we can see that (for the Kantian) an interest in autonomy or internal unity is ultimately just the "subject-directed" side of its "object-directed" interest in comprehending or understanding the objects of theoretical and practical thought. In this way, as we will see, by developing a more balanced picture of reason's interests in both autonomy and comprehension, we can develop a form of constitutivism that does better justice to both the "subject-directed" and the "object-directed" dimensions of rationality.

e. Constitutivism, Shmagency, and Why Be Rational?

We return to these issues below. But it should already be clear that, like any form of constitutivism, Rational Constitutivism makes the conception of reason at its heart bear a great deal of meta-normative weight. And, given this, it is only fair to wonder whether Kant's conception of reason can really bear such a load. One way of making such worries vivid is through the most famous objection to contemporary forms of meta-normative constitutivism: Enoch's "shmagency objection".[48] Unfortunately, the nature of this objection has itself been the subject of much debate. Still, the fundamental idea behind it is simple enough. Suppose the constitutivist claims to have explained the basic norms that apply to us in terms of some conception of our nature as "rational beings" or "agents". Well, so what? That is, what significance should this explanation have for us from a first-

---

[47] Note that these objections apply most clearly to (Korsgaard 1996b). Whether they apply to Korsgaard's more recent defense of her views in (Korsgaard 2009) is a complicated question that I cannot consider here. See also the recent discussion of "self-formation" in (Kraus 2020).

[48] For the canonical statement of the shmagency worry, see (Enoch 2006, 2011). For further discussion, see (Ferrero 2009; Tiffany 2012; Silverstein 2015; Arruda 2016, 2017; Rosati 2016), among others. See (Schafer 2015b, 2015c). For a more involved defense of this point, see (Paakkunainen 2018). That being said, the "shmagency point" might point to certain explanatory limitations of constitutivism—limitations that could have much broader significance for the constitutivist strategy.

person perspective? Suppose, for instance, I find the resulting norms implausible. If that is the case, won't the connection that the constitutivist establishes between these norms and the relevant conception of our nature as "agents" or "rational beings" simply lead me to doubt the normative significance of "agency" or "rationality" in that sense? In short, if the constitutivist insists that I can only deviate from some dubious norm on pain of failing to live up to the standards that are constitutive of "agency" or "rationality", aren't I likely to respond simply by saying, "So much the worse for 'agency' or 'rationality' in that sense. If that is what 'agency' is, then I prefer to be something else—a 'shmagent'!"

As a response to the idea that appealing to a conception of "agency" or "rationality" could decisively settle such first-personal normative questions, I think that the "shmagency objection" has considerable force. After all, even if the constitutivist is successful at extracting certain norms or standards of proper functioning from a certain conception of agency or rationality, this will only settle the status of those norms *for us* insofar as *we* regard the normative significance of that conception as itself settled. And it only takes the slightest acquaintance with the history of philosophy to see that very little about such questions is ever settled in this way.

Moreover, this remains true *even* if we follow Kant in accepting a view of rationality on which rational activities necessarily involve an implicit consciousness of the standards of proper functioning that apply to them. If this is true, then any deviation from these constitutive standards *will* involve some inconsistency or conflict between the implicit self-consciousness at work in these capacities and one's explicit choices and beliefs. But even *this* need not decisively settle the first-person normative questions we are considering for the most skeptical among us. After all, in such a case, the self-professed "shmagent" is likely to simply reply that this sort of inconsistency is preferable, if the alternative is a commitment to the norms in question. In this way, it seems to me naive to assume that *any* conception of rationality or agency, *even* one that is transparent to self-consciousness, could decisively settle these sorts of normative questions in the manner some Kantians have suggested.

I agree with its proponents, then, that the "shmagency point" indicates a real limit on what constitutivist strategies can accomplish. But note that if the "shmagency point" is correct, this it is a limitation that applies in some sense to any conceivable meta-ethical view whatsoever. So, while it removes one potential advantage of constitutivism, it does not thereby disadvantage it in comparison with other meta-ethical views.[49] And given this, these limitations need not be fatal to Kant's form of constitutivism once its ambitions are properly understood. For the essence of this form of constitutivism is a certain strategy for *explaining* the

---

[49] For a more forceful version of this response, see (Horst 2022).

basic norms that govern us as rational beings, and the success or failure of that strategy must be evaluated on *explanatory* grounds, not in terms of its ability to provide some sort of skeptic-proof response to *all* doubts about the norms it derives.

This is particularly important in the present context because Kant's own interest in broadly constitutivist ideas was not motivated primarily by the "anti-skeptical" use of these ideas the shmagency objection targets. After all, Kant did not intend his account of the relationship between moral requirements and practical reason to provide us with a dialectically effective response to *all* forms of moral skepticism. Rather, Kant's position is that our cognitive access to the nature of practical reason occurs *via* our consciousness of the moral law (as the fundamental principle of pure practical reason).[50] In this way, according to Kant, it is our consciousness of the moral law that comes first in the order of cognition, thereby providing a basis for reaching certain conclusions about our nature as free beings. Given this, the point of Kant's constitutivism could hardly be to provide us with a skeptic-proof answer to the question of why we should be moral. For, quite on the contrary to any such account, Kant believes that we can only know our nature as free, rational beings *through* our knowledge of the moral law.

As this makes plain, while Kant can be seen as a sort of constitutivist, the point of his constitutivism is, in the first instance, explanatory. That is, its significance lies in the idea that we explain a wide variety of quite robust normative principles (such as theoretical and practical versions of the Principle of Sufficient Reason) through an investigation of the nature of reason. At the same time, given the self-conscious character of these rational powers, it is also true that these principles can be thought of as characterizing standards of correctness we are already tacitly committed to simply in virtue of making use of these powers. More precisely, as we saw in the last chapter, every act of cognition involves an implicit consciousness of that act as subject to certain standards of correctness. Thus, in deviating from these standards, we are deviating from standards governing the functioning of our cognitive powers that we *already* implicitly accept. In this sense, we might say that Kant's response to the question, "Why be rational?", is that we ought to be rational because that is the sort of beings *we are and already take ourselves to be*.[51] Of course, this does not mean that there may not be certain cases in which

---

[50] Here I take the second *Critique* to provide Kant's canonical statement of his views on this issue. I don't believe this should be especially controversial. I concede that in the *Groundwork*, Kant does *flirt* with aims more like those that Enoch targets at times, but this flirtation is always uneasy, and disappears almost entirely by the time of the second *Critique*. See (Tenenbaum 2012).

[51] This, in turn, is crucial to remember if we wish to connect Kant's account of reason up to the contemporary debate about whether we have any "reason to be rational" in the sense made famous by the literature spawned by (Broome 1999; Kolodny 2005). We will return to this question below, but in answering it, it is crucial to keep in mind that while Kant's account does treat reason or rationality as having foundational normative significance, this is (in the first instance) a point about the form that valuable things must have as the proper objects of practical cognition, and not a straight-forward piece of "first-order axiology".

deviating from the standards of rationality is justified by further reasons we possess.[52] And in some radical cases, such reasons may be robust enough to justify us in trying to become an entirely different sort of being than we currently are. In that sense, it may be that the standards implicit in our conception of ourselves as rational beings are "self-effacing".[53] But in the end, for Kant, we can only reject these norms on pain of rejecting our own implicit consciousness of our own form of rationality—a consciousness that is "always already" at work in any act of our rational capacities, even one that aims at rejecting these norms.

For Kant, then, any attempt to systematically deviate from these norms must involve a quite basic form of *self-alienation*. Given how the self-consciousness of reason guides its acts, any attempt to reject these basic principles will involve a sort of implicit self-contradiction: not just a rejection of our own nature as rational beings but also a rejection of how we conceive of that nature. Moreover, one of the strengths of Kant's approach to constitutivism, and of the conception of reason that sits at its heart, is how it brings together a *variety* of attractive ways of characterizing what matters to us as rational beings from a first-person point of view. For instance, if Kant is correct, the nature of reason as a faculty establishes a necessary connection between *two* of our most basic needs as rational beings: (i) the need to *understand* what is and what to do and (ii) the need to manifest a basic form of *autonomy* or self-determination. If this is right, then the norms that Kant extracts from his conception of reason can be rejected only on pain of rejecting *both of these ends*. And this, even if it is not strictly speaking impossible, seems to be something that every few of us find attractive from a first-person point of view.[54]

---

[52] See (Parfit 1984) on "rational irrationality", for example. Kant does not need to take issue with such cases in order to make the point at issue here.

[53] Compare the discussion of "immodesty" in (Lewis 1971; Schafer 2016).

[54] For example, it seems to me that *fully* successful inquiry into any theoretical or practical question must conclude, not with mere belief, or even mere knowledge of the answer to this question, but rather only with an understanding of it (theoretical or practical, as the case may be). In this way, there seems to be an essential connection between the nature of inquiry itself and the aim of understanding—a connection that is transparent to us when we consider what it is for inquiry to succeed first-personally.

This, it is important to stress, is a point about the *form* of rational inquiry, and not, at least in the first instance, one about its objects. Whatever the objects of inquiry or concern may be, rational inquiry into those objects must (as such) be structured around an implicit concern to understand those very objects. Thus, this *formal* point is compatible with a wide-ranging pluralism about the objects of "first-order" rational concern, allowing that for most individuals, understanding as such does not rank very high in the hierarchy of first-order goods.

PART II
THE UNITY OF REASON

Ich ist in der Welt zu Hause, wenn es sie kennt,
noch mehr, wenn es sie begriffen hat.

(Hegel, PR 4)

4
Reason
The Capacity for Comprehension

In Part I, our focus was Kant's conception of cognitive or rational powers, and the significance of such powers for Kant's overall philosophical project. In Part II, our focus will shift to a discussion of reason in particular as the highest of these capacities or powers. As we have already begun to explore, Kant's conception of reason is foundational for many aspects of his philosophy. For instance, the idea that "one and the same" faculty of reason is responsible for both theoretical and practical reasoning provides Kant's theoretical and practical philosophy with their systematic unity.[1] And, as the highest of our rational faculties, it is reason that provides the larger system of rational faculties with its teleological structure and unity.[2] More locally, the nature of theoretical reason is central to Kant's diagnosis of the errors of rationalist metaphysics.[3] And, of course, as we've begun to discuss, the nature of practical reason as a faculty is central to Kant's account of the moral law.[4]

We'll return to each of these topics in the chapters to follow. But first, in this chapter, I hope to accomplish four main tasks.[5] First, I will briefly lay out two characterizations of the faculty of reason, which should be familiar to most readers of Kant: first, the idea of reason as the faculty for (mediate) inference and, second, the idea of reason as the faculty for cognition from principles. Then I will attempt to expand our understanding of Kant's conception of reason by adding to these a third characterization of reason that we can find in Kant—namely, the idea of reason as the faculty for the sort of cognition or understanding that Kant calls "comprehension" (*Begreifen*). Next, I will argue that this conception of reason, as aiming at comprehension as opposed to what Kant calls "insight" (*Einsehen*), illustrates a central difference between Kant's conception of reason and that of his rationalist predecessors. And finally, I will argue that this conception of reason

---

[1] For classic discussions of this issue see (Guyer 1987; O'Neill 1989; Henrich 1994; Neiman 1994; Wood 1999, 2007; Nuzzo 2005) and many others.
[2] For more on this see (Schafer forthcoming c). Compare the important discussion of this topic in (Fugate 2014).
[3] For recent work on Kant's critique of traditional metaphysics, see (Grier 2001; Willaschek 2018; Boer 2020; Heide 2021; Proops 2021a). As I discuss in the next chapter, my view of these issues is in some ways closest to Proops's excellent discussion.
[4] See (O'Neill 1989; Neiman 1994; Herman 1996, 2007; Korsgaard 1996a, 1996b, 2009; Wood 1999, 2007; Guyer 2019).
[5] This chapter draws heavily upon (Schafer forthcoming c).

provides us with a powerful lens for understanding the unity of theoretical and practical reason. In discussing this last issue, I will argue that attention to Kant's *end-relative* conception of comprehension (as opposed to cognition or knowledge in a more generic sense) allows us to develop an account of the unity of reason as a faculty that does full justice to how Kant assigns "primacy" to practical reason *over* theoretical reason, while also recognizing that this "primacy" is ultimately grounded in a *more basic* unity of theoretical and practical reason.

a. Reason: The Faculty for (Mediate) Inference

But what exactly is the faculty of reason, according to Kant? As noted above, Kant uses "reason" to refer *both* to the entire system of our rational capacities *and* to a particular faculty within that system. In this chapter, my focus will be on "reason" in the second, narrower sense, although many of its lessons extend to "reason" in the broader sense as well, since it is reason in the narrow sense that gives unity and structure to reason in the broad sense.[6] In this narrower sense, Kant uses "reason" to refer to a faculty of the mind (*Seelenvermögen*). As we've already discussed, faculties in this sense represent a special instance of capacities or powers more generally. This notion of a capacity or power (*Vermögen* or *Fähigkeit*) to do something is one of the fundamental elements within Kant's account of causality.[7] For example, even in the case of physical causes and effects, Kant treats causation in terms of the active powers or capacities of substances, as opposed to trying to reduce causal relations to necessary connections between events. Thus, for Kant, the basic framework for thinking about *all* forms of causality involves a network of closely connected concepts: substances, the capacities of those substances, the powers or forces which manifest themselves when these capacities are actualized, and the acts or activities that are the actualization of these capacities.[8]

But reason is not just any such capacity. It is, along with the understanding and the power of judgment, one of the intellectual powers of the mind. As such, reason has several features that distinguish it from the merely physical powers we encounter in nature or (in more complicated ways) the merely animal powers of living things. First, reason is a genuinely spontaneous capacity, which means, roughly, that it is capable of forms of activity that are explained solely by reference its own internal principles and aims.[9] Second, reason is a self-conscious capacity.

---

[6] For more discussion, see (Schafer 2022a).
[7] Again, here I will generally follow (Longuenesse 1998) in using "capacity" and "faculty" interchangeably to refer to what Kant refers to by "*Vermögen*". My discussion of these issues here builds on the very helpful discussion in (Willaschek 2018).
[8] See (Watkins 2005, 2019; Chignell and Pereboom 2010; Tolley 2017a).
[9] We will return to the sense in which this is true in Chapter 7. For recent discussion, see (Kohl 2015; McLear forthcoming). Note that there is some complexity concerning the degree to which all such capacities have a genuinely internal aim, see below and the discussions in (McLear 2022; Schafer 2022a; McLear forthcoming-b; Brink forthcoming.

That is, at the very least, its characteristic activities are accessible to consciousness, so that it is possible for a rational subject to reflect upon these activities and form further representations of them.[10] And third, reason's activities are structured by a distinctive form of internal teleology, so that these activities can be regarded as being performed for the sake of general ends or needs that are characteristic of the faculty of reason as such.

More precisely, as we've seen above, like all spontaneous rational powers, reason has the "formal aim" of actualizing itself in its characteristic form of activity.[11] And given this, to understand what reason is, we need to understand what this characteristic form of activity consists in. Once again, some of the features of this form of activity are shared, for Kant, with our other higher intellectual powers. For instance, reason is a cognitive faculty (*Erkenntnisvermögen*). Thus, its activities can be characterized in terms of how they contribute to (theoretical and practical) *cognition*.[12] More precisely, at least in us, reason is a faculty for *discursive* cognition, so its distinctive form of cognition is essentially connected with conceptual representations like those involved in judgment and inference. And it is (at least in principle) a faculty for a priori cognition. Indeed, as we will see, there is a sense in which reason can be thought of as *the* faculty for "absolutely" a priori cognition. Thus, according to Kant, reason is a faculty for a priori discursive cognition.

But again, these characteristics are shared by reason and several other rational faculties, including the understanding and the power of judgment. Thus, in order to understand what is *distinctive* about reason, we need to go beyond these characterizations to consider what Kant says about the differences between reason and these other discursive cognitive faculties. In drawing this distinction, Kant begins with the traditional idea that reason is the faculty for *mediate inference*.[13] In other words, as Kant explains, while the activities of the understanding (*Verstand*) aim at the *combination of concepts into judgments*, reason's activities aim at the *combination of judgments* that is involved in inferences or syllogisms:

> As in the case of the understanding, there is in the case of reason a merely formal, i.e., logical use, where reason abstracts from all content of cognition ... [this] first

---

[10] As noted above, the sense in which these activities are "self-conscious" is one of the most debated topics in Kant scholarship. For some relevant recent discussion see (Boyle 2009, 2011; Kitcher 2011; Longuenesse 2017; Merritt 2018; Smit 2019; Boyle forthcoming).
[11] For the importance of this passage, see (Engstrom 2002, 2009; Reath 2010, 2012, 2013).
[12] See (Engstrom 2009; Reath 2013; Merritt 2018).
[13] Compare the very insightful discussion of Kant's conception of reason in (Willaschek 2018), which I draw on here, and which discusses many of these issues in greater detail. As Willaschek notes, Kant's discussion can be seen, in part, as an attempt to provide a systematic way of connecting together two basic ways of thinking about reason: (i) the idea of reason as the faculty for inference, and (ii) reason as the faculty for a certain sort of intellectual "intuition". Of course, Kant does not believe that we are capable of anything like this sort of robust "intellectual intuition" (at least in the theoretical sphere), but his treatment of reason is meant to explain why it is so tempting to view reason as providing us with this sort of robust a priori cognition of things in themselves.

faculty has obviously long since been defined by the logicians as that of **drawing inferences mediately**. (A299/B355)

The "mediate inferences" that Kant refers to in this passage are inferences that connect two judgments together *via* a third. Thus, "mediate inferences" are distinguished from "immediate inferences" that connect two judgments together directly without any reliance on an intermediate judgment:[14]

> An **immediate** inference (*consequentia immediata*) is the derivation (*deductio*) of one judgment from the other without a mediating judgment (*judicium intermedium*). An inference is **mediate** if, besides the concept that a judgment contains in itself, one needs still others in order to derive a cognition from it.
> (Log 9:114)

Since Kant continues to think of logic within the framework provided by Aristotelian syllogistic logic, the canonical instances of mediate inferences for him are the various forms of Aristotelian syllogism.[15] Such inferences connect a premise (the minor premise) together with a conclusion *via* a second premise or rule (the major premise), which establishes a relation between the concepts involved in the minor premise and those involved in the conclusion. For example, consider the following classical inference form:

All As are Bs. [Major premise]

Socrates is A. [Minor premise]

Therefore, Socrates is a B. [Conclusion]

It is the activity of drawing such syllogistic inferences that Kant is thinking of, in the first instance, when he characterizes reason as the capacity for (mediate) inference.

In thinking about such claims, it is important to distinguish several different things one might associate with the term "inference". First, there is inference in the sense of an explicit, conscious act of drawing a conclusion from some premises. In this sense, inference is an *activity* that takes place during moments of *conscious deliberation*—that is, it is an activity that takes place in the context of an attempt to determine one's views about what is (in the theoretical case) or what ought to be (in the practical). Inference in this sense is, of course, a topic of interest

---

[14] See (Lu-Adler 2018) for a much more detailed discussion. In the early modern literature on inference and reasoning, "immediate judgments" often represent a sort of boundary case of "inference". Thus, some authors will classify them as inferences, while others will not do so. Compare the discussion of Locke and Hume in (Owen 1999).

[15] Compare the helpful discussion in (Rohlf 2010). Whether Kant believes that there are inferences that are mediate, but *not* syllogistic, is an interesting question I will not tackle here, although I assume that most of us today would accept the existence of such inferences in some form.

to Kant, but we should be careful not to limit inference in Kant's sense to these sorts of deliberate and fully conscious acts of inference. For the activity of drawing a conclusion from some premises is something that, for Kant, can also occur in a much less deliberate and fully explicit fashion. Indeed, for Kant, the vast majority of our "inferential activities" do not take the form of an explicit and fully deliberate attempt to see what follows from some set of premises. Rather, most of the inferential activity we engage in—as is true in general of the synthesizing activities of all our rational capacities—is not the focus of attention or conscious reflection. Rather, most of the time, when we connect judgments together *via* inferences, this activity is not the focus of our consciousness—although, of course, it is crucial for Kant that it be available to conscious reflection in some sense.[16]

As this indicates, the *activity of inference* is closely associated with a certain sort of *inferential form or structure* which we bring to bear on our judgments when we unify them *via* the activity of inference. Thus, another way to think about the activity of inference for Kant is in terms of the activity of *unifying* our judgments together into a larger system which is characterized by this sort of inferential structure. In contemporary terms, we might speak of this as a matter of placing our judgments into a system in which these judgments stand in various "basing relations" to one another as reasons for (assent to) one another.[17] But in saying this, it is important to stress that these "syllogistic basing relations" are not the only form that such basing relations can take for Kant. For example, as we already saw in our discussion of the *Faktum der Vernunft*, a judgment can also be based on another in virtue of an *immediate* inferential relationship between them. So, while the sort of "basing relation" that is characteristic of reason as the faculty for mediate inference is of central importance to Kant, it does not exhaust Kant's account of that relation in the contemporary sense of the term, nor (as we will see) are such "reasons for assent" really Kant's primary concern with respect to this inferential activity.

b. Reason: The Faculty of Principles

There is much more that could be said about inference in Kant. But, since this is a relatively familiar topic, and since Kant's account of inference is likely to seem outdated in many respects, I won't linger on the details of it here. Rather, what interests me are the systematic connections Kant establishes between (i) certain basic forms of inference, (ii) certain basic forms of explanation, and (iii) certain basic forms of "comprehension" or understanding. For these connections remain

---

[16] Again, this does *not* mean that these activities are *unconscious* for Kant. The important point (again) is that this sort of self-consciousness does not require us to form a further explicit reflective judgment about these activities.
[17] Compare (Neta 2019).

compelling, I believe, even in a contemporary context. Thus, as Kant himself stresses, if we want to understand the ultimate *point* of reason's inferential activity, and so the ultimate foundations of reason's unity, we need to look beyond such "merely logical" characterizations of reason to other, more fruitful ways of thinking about this capacity.

The first of these is the idea of reason as *the faculty of principles*:

> In the first part of our transcendental logic we defined the understanding as the faculty of rules; here we will distinguish reason from understanding by calling reason the **faculty of principles**. (A299/B356)[18]

According to Kant, this characterization is fruitful for our understanding of reason because it provides us with a "higher concept" of reason that emphasizes its role as a potential "source of cognition". But to understand why this is true, we need to first understand why Kant believes that the idea of reason as the faculty for inference carries with it the idea of reason as the faculty of principles.

To do so, we should remember first that, in Kant, "principle" can refer both to a metaphysically *real* law or explanatory principle and the *representation* of this law or principle in the form of a general judgment or representation. Since our focus here is on the possibility of "cognition from principles", it will generally be the second of these notions of "principle" that will be our focus. That is, we will generally be concerned with how some general representation or cognition can serve as a "principle" from which other cognitions can be derived. But, of course, these general representations can only ground genuine *cognition* from principles insofar as they represent some real explanatory feature of the objects they represent. Thus, in the end, the sort of "cognition from principles" that reason seeks will require that the "cognitive principles" which ground our cognitions of objects track the "real principles" that explain those objects and their features.[19]

Kant introduces the precise sense of "principle" that is relevant to his discussion of reason as follows:

> Thus the understanding cannot yield synthetic cognitions from concepts at all, and it is properly these that I call principles absolutely; nevertheless, all universal propositions in general can be called principles comparatively. (A301/B358)

---

[18] Compare: "The faculty of cognition from *a priori* principles can be called pure reason..." (KU 5:167). See also A405, V-Lo/Wiener 797.

[19] In Leibnizian authors like Wolff, this sort of cognition from explanatory grounds is always also cognition from (the analysis of) concepts. But, of course, given Kant's insistence on the existence of synthetic a priori cognitive principles, such an equation is no longer apt in a Kantian context. Still, as we are about to discuss, Kant sometimes speaks in a manner that suggests such a view, e.g. at A301/B358.

As this indicates, a principle in the strict or "absolute" sense of this term is something that provides us with synthetic cognition on grounds that is, not just a priori, but also purely "conceptual".

As is familiar, this is a very high bar for Kant—one that generally lies beyond the limits of our capacities for theoretical cognition. For these capacities (in their human form) can achieve cognition only through the cooperation of concepts and intuitions. Indeed, the very idea of *synthetic cognition from concepts* might seem to be something of any oxymoron for Kant, at least as applied to creatures with our form of discursive understanding. After all, how else can a cognition be "from concepts" other than being *analytically* derived from the relations between concepts? And if that is the only form that cognition from concepts can take for us, doesn't that make the very idea of "synthetic cognition from concepts" simply incoherent (at least in our case)?

The answers to these questions are, indeed, relatively clear with respect to the domain of theoretical cognition. For there Kant does deny that cognition from absolute principles is possible for us on very much these grounds. But, as is so often the case, things are considerably less clear when we turn from theoretical cognition to the practical domain. For there, as we will see, Kant ultimately accepts that it is possible for us to achieve a form of practical cognition from absolute principles—namely, cognition of what we ought to do that is based in our unconditioned grasp of the moral law. The question this raises is whether we can understand this form of practical cognition as an instance of "synthetic cognition from concepts" in the sense at issue in passages like this one. Or does the development of Kant's views about the nature of moral cognition require us to revise this definition of "absolute principles" if it is to apply to the theoretical and practical cases?

To answer these questions, we need to begin by noting that the idea of cognition from absolute principles at issue here does not require that our grasp of these principles be based in *something further* that is more fundamental than them. Rather, absolute principles are principles that can serve as the ultimate foundation for further forms of reasoning. Thus, in saying that absolute principles are forms of "synthetic cognition from concepts", Kant is not telling us that we should search for something *more fundamental* than these principles, which can serve as their basis—namely, certain "concepts" over and above them. Rather, he is telling us something about the nature of these principles themselves: that they provide us with a form of synthetic cognition that is independent of any contribution from sensibility, arising solely out of our intellectual faculties. In this sense, absolute practical principles are forms of "synthetic cognition from concepts" not because there are *some more basic concepts* on which these principles are grounded, but rather because such principles are due to practical reason operating independently of sensibility.

In this sense, the moral law plainly is an instance of synthetic cognition "from concepts". But there is another sense in which we might describe the moral law in this way as well. For, as we saw in the last chapter, in us the moral law is closely associated with the concept of unconditional obligation or duty. Thus, whenever we cognize some action as "to be done" on the basis of the moral law, we can be thought of as having arrived at practical cognition of that action from this concept (the concept of duty). But, once again, this concept should not be seen as more basic than the moral law; rather, like the logical forms of judgment and the categories, the moral law and the concept of unconditional obligation form a package that stands or falls together for Kant. The important point is that this package *is* a potential source of practical cognition that arises out of the self-consciousness of pure practical reason, independently of any contribution from sensibility. It is this, once again, that allows us to speak of our cognition of the moral law as a form of "synthetic cognition from concepts" in the sense at issue here.

For these reasons, as we will discuss below, in the practical sphere a form of practical cognition from absolute principles is possible for us according to Kant, and making sense of this does not require to modify the definition of "absolute principles" we are discussing. But, of course, this is not true in theoretical sphere. That is why, to do justice to the sense in which theoretical reason is *also* a faculty for cognition from principles, in this passage Kant quickly introduces a weaker, merely "comparative" sense of "principle", on which any universal proposition or judgment may be called a "principle" in a "comparative" sense. Such "comparative principles" do not provide us with synthetic cognitions *purely* from concepts, but they can *function as principles relative to* some further body of cognitions. This is possible because any universal proposition can be *used* as a potential ground for more particular cognitions.[20] It is this use of a universal proposition that allows us to regard them as "principles comparatively"—i.e. as principles "compared to" some further body of more particular cognitions.

Universal propositions can play this role because every universal proposition involves an assertion made under some condition (Log 9:121). The precise sense in which this is true will vary depending on the logical form of the judgment in question in accordance with the three forms of relational judgment: categorical, hypothetical, and disjunctive (B95/A70). In categorical universal judgments—that is, judgments of the form, "All As are Bs"—the predicate concept B is asserted of all things that satisfy the subject concept A. Thus, in such judgments, B is asserted of something on the condition that that thing is an A. In hypothetical judgments, on the other hand, the "assertion" is itself a judgment, which is asserted only under the condition that some other judgment holds. And finally, in the case of disjunctive judgments—which Kant understands as involving a partition of logical

---

[20] Compare EEKU 20:201 and V-Lo/Dohna 703–4.

space into mutually exclusive alternatives—some claim is asserted on the condition that the other alternatives within the disjunction *fail* to obtain.

The details of these logical forms of judgment are important for many aspects of Kant's philosophy, but they aren't crucial to the line of thought I am exploring here. Rather, what matters for us is the simple idea that all universal judgments establish a relation between two judgments—a relation in which one of these judgments appears, in at least a logical sense, as the condition of the other.[21] It is this that allows any such judgment to serve as a "comparative principle" from which further cognitions (judgments) may be derived. To achieve this sort of "comparative cognition from principles", we must *use* the universal judgment in question to move from a second judgment, involving the "condition" in the first judgment, to a third judgment, involving the "assertion" that is conditioned by this condition (in the first judgment). In this way, any universal judgment establishes a relation of "logical conditioning" between a variety of further judgments.

For example, consider the inference:

All As are Bs. [Major premise]

All Cs are As. [Minor premise]

Therefore, all Cs are Bs. [Conclusion]

Here the major premise establishes a relation between an assertion (something is a B) and a condition (that the thing is an A). Then in this inference we *use* this "general rule" to connect together two other judgments: first, the judgment that all Cs are As, and second, the judgment that all Cs are Bs. In doing so, we, in effect, move from the idea of C as a condition under which A can be asserted to the idea of C as a condition under which B can also be asserted *via* the idea of A as a condition under which B can be asserted.[22] In such cases, as Kant puts it, reason proceeds under the general principle that, "*What stands under the condition of a rule also stands under the rule itself*" (Log 9:120).

The important point at present is that, in making any such inference, we achieve a very modest instance of "cognition from principles" in a comparative sense. And conversely, at least for creatures with our cognitive powers, in order to achieve cognition from principles, even in a comparative sense, we must relate our judgments to one another through inferences of this sort—inferences that, in some sense, move from the more universal to the less. It is for this reason that

---

[21] It is important to note that these conditioning relations also apply at the limit, not just to acts of predicating a concept of something, but also to what Kant describes as "positing" some concept—that is, roughly speaking, the act of positing that something matching this concept exists.

[22] As this indicates, relations of "logical conditioning" can be asymmetrical for Kant. This point will become important when we consider the relationship between logical conditioning and real conditioning.

Kant also calls reason "the faculty for the determination of the particular through the general (for the derivation from principles)" (EEKU 20:201).

Such "cognition from principles" is significant to Kant for several reasons. First, such inferences establish logical relations between our judgments, thereby allowing us to grasp how one judgment may be "logically conditioned" by another. Second, by doing so, they provide us with new epistemic grounds for taking these judgments to be true in the manner that belief (*Glauben*) and knowledge (*Wissen*) in Kant's sense of these terms require. Thus, when our cognitions are embedded in a larger inferential network of cognitions, they come to be epistemically relevant to one another in a manner that allows assent to one to serve as a possible ground for assent to others.[23] In this way, there is a general connection between the possibility of cognition from principles and the possibility of knowledge (*Wissen*) in Kant's sense of this term. And, as we extend our network of cognition from principles, we will extend our knowledge (*Wissen*) as well.

But such logical and epistemic relations between representations are ultimately of cognitive significance for Kant only insofar as they allow us to extend our grasp of the *real* explanatory connections between real things.[24] In this way, a grasp of "logical conditioning relations" is ultimately significant for Kant because it partially constitutes our grasp of the "real conditioning relations" between the objects of our representations (V-Met/Herder 28:11). For it is only by grasping *these* relations of "real conditioning" that we come to grasp the real relations of dependence between objects and facts, thus placing those particulars into a unified network of real explanatory relations in the manner that (as we will see) genuine "comprehension" in Kant's sense requires.[25] As a result, for Kant, "An inference of reason is the cognition of the necessity of a proposition through the subsumption of its condition under a given general rule", not merely with respect to logical necessity, but also with respect to relations of real necessity as well (Log 9:120).

At the same time, we should not overstate the role of mediate inference in such cases. For Kant is clear that we can grasp many real conditioning relations, at least to some degree, without making any explicit *mediate inference*. For example, causal relations in the natural world are clearly real conditioning relations, and we can often cognize such relations simply by bringing the relevant categories

---

[23] This, of course, can happen several different ways, depending on the case. For example, in cases in which we come to assent to some more particular judgment on the basis of some more universal judgment, the direction of epistemic dependence will run from the universal to the particular. But in cases in which we come to assent to some universal judgment on the basis of a set of more particular judgments, the direction of epistemic dependence will be reversed.

[24] Compare (Stang 2016; Willaschek 2018; Watkins 2019; Stang n.d.). As (McLear 2018) argues, something similar seems to be true of Kant's argument in the Preface of the *Metaphysical Foundations of Natural Science*. For the classic discussion of this passage, see (Friedman 1992, 2013).

[25] Compare the distinctions in (Stang 2019). But note that Stang is perhaps a bit quick to assimilate epistemic and cognitive grounds to one another. See (Chignell 2007b) for Kant's concept of justification or epistemic grounds. For some discussion of how this plays out in the practical case, see (Schafer forthcoming a).

(cause and effect) to bear on our experience of objects—for example, by synthesizing experience in accordance with these categories and their associated schemata.[26] Nonetheless, even in this case, it remains true, for Kant, that in order to grasp such real conditioning relations, we require *both* the logical conditioning relations that are implicit in our concepts, and some further synthetic principle that grounds our grasp of the real conditioning relation in question. What the case of ordinary causal cognition shows is that this grasp of a "further synthetic principle" need not involve an *explicit* multistep inference in which this principle figures as a premise. Instead, we can grasp many real conditioning relations simply in virtue of allowing the relevant principles to inform our activities of synthesis and judgment in the right way. But nonetheless, if we want to *make explicit* how these forms of cognition depend upon this background synthetic principle, we need to do so *via* exhibiting this dependence in the form of a mediate inference in which this principle figures as a premise. So, while mediate inference is not required for all cognition of real conditioning relations, it is only through such inferences that we can bring the foundations of such cognition to explicit consciousness. Thus, we might say that while the cognition of real conditioning relations does not depend upon *actually* performing mediate inferences, it remains true that all cognition of real conditioning relations depends on the *possibility* of such inferences insofar as it is only through these inferences that we come to fully understand the nature of the cognition in question.[27]

We'll return to this in a moment. But before moving on, I want to return to the general idea of reason as "the faculty of principles". As we have just seen, in calling reason "the faculty of principles", Kant is saying *both* that only reason is a (potential) source of *absolute* principles, and that only reason is capable of *using* a universal proposition *as a principle* (be it *absolute or comparative*).[28] In both

---

[26] Something similar is also true of the sorts of conditioning relations involved in spatial cognition. To say this is not, of course, to say that it is at all obvious how exactly this is possible for Kant. In general, there are many questions about how exactly the relational categories allow us to grasp not just logical conditioning relations, but real conditioning relations as well. I will say a bit about these issues below. But I will not attempt to give anything like a complete treatment here.

[27] Interestingly, this means that if (say) Wolff or Baumgarten were correct in claiming that all real conditioning relations are identical to logical conditioning relations, the significance of mediate (as opposed to immediate) inferences would be significantly reduced, and reason (as distinct from the understanding) would be left without one of its main functions.

[28] See A299/B356. An important conceptual possibility for Kant is the idea of a faculty that is a faculty for mere cognition from comparative principles, but not for cognition from absolute principles. As should already be plain, there is a sense in which this is exactly how Kant would describe our own faculty of theoretical reason since this faculty, while it aims in some sense at cognition from absolute principles, can at best achieve cognition from comparative principles in the theoretical sphere. Nonetheless, it is important to stress that Kant believes there to be a constitutive connection between these two conceptions of reason—that is, he takes it that any faculty that aims at comparative cognition from principles must thereby be driven towards the goal of absolute cognition from principles, even if it cannot achieve this. A similar distinction also arises, for Kant, in the practical sphere. In particular, merely hypothetical forms of practical reasoning can be understood to involve practical cognition from merely comparative principles, while moral forms of reasoning represent forms of practical cognition

these senses, reason is the faculty of (theoretical and practical) cognition from principles:

> The faculty of cognition from *a priori* principles can be called pure reason.
> (KU 5:167)

But there is also a third sense in which reason deserves the label "faculty of principles". For, in keeping with the idea that every rational faculty seeks to extend its own proper exercise, reason is driven by its nature to *search for* propositions that can play the role of principles. For this is just one aspect of what is involved in reason seeking the "promotion of its own exercise". Thus, not only is reason *capable* of producing cognition from principles, it is also *interested* in the extension of this capability through the discovery of further universal propositions that can play this role. And any rational being will take satisfaction in the discovery of such principles. Once again, this is one central aspect of Kant's conception of reason as a self-actualizing power for cognition from principles, one that we will return to repeatedly in the chapters below.

c. Reason as the Capacity for Comprehension

Given these two definitions of reason—as the faculty of inferences and the faculty of principles—reason's search for cognition from principles may be described either in terms of how it extends our *network of inferences* or in terms of the nature of the *principles* or *explanations* reason searches for. As we will see in the next chapter, these give rise to the two basic principles that Kant associates with the activity of theoretical reason—what he calls reason's "logical maxim" and its "supreme principle". But before we consider those principles, and their relationship to the traditional Principle of Sufficient Reason, I want to turn our attention to a third characterization of reason—one that adds to these two characterizations by giving us a fuller understanding of the distinctive form of "cognition" (*Erkenntnis*) that reason aims to achieve through inferring cognitions from more general principles.

This is the notion of reason as the capacity for what Kant refers to as the highest form of cognition—namely, what he calls "comprehension" (*Begreifen*).[29] As we

---

from absolute principles. At various points, Kant indicates that he takes the possibility of a merely hypothetical form of practical reason to be a conceptual (although not a real or metaphysical) possibility. This indicates that there is nothing conceptually incoherent in the idea of a faculty merely for practical cognition from comparative principles. But, at the same time, Kant insists that to make real metaphysical sense of such a capacity, we must conceive of it as a faculty that aims at both forms of practical cognition.

[29] For the importance of comprehension in this sense, see (Breitenbach 2014, 2016; Tolley 2017a, 2017b; Zinkin 2017; Makkreel 2018). My discussion here is particularly indebted to conversations with Tolley about these issues.

will see, this way of characterizing reason is closely related to the more familiar characterizations of reason we have just discussed. But it helps to bring to the fore important aspects of Kant's conception of reason, thereby providing us with a new basis for thinking about both Kant's relationship to the rationalists and his conception of the unity of reason as a faculty.

Kant stresses the special relationship between reason and "comprehension" in several important passages. For example, right at the beginning of the Transcendental Dialectic, he distinguishes the "concepts of reason" (i.e. ideas) from those of the understanding as follows:

> Concepts of reason serve for **comprehension**, just as concepts of the understanding serve for **understanding** (of perceptions). (A311/B367)

Similarly, in an important passage later in the first *Critique*, Kant associates the "necessary problem of pure reason" with the need for "the complete comprehensibility of what is given in appearance" (A411/B438). And, in the same vein, when discussing the "special rules of reason", Kant claims that reason can never be satisfied with the results of "apagogic proofs", precisely because these can deliver "certainty", but never "comprehensibility" (A789/B817).

A similar theme is also stressed in the *Prolegomena*'s discussion of the nature of systematic cognition, where Kant emphasizes the equivalence between "a comprehending" of something and a "system", with both of these being opposed to a mere "aggregate" of cognitions (Prol 4:322). And, in the *Nachlass*, Kant also speaks of "the interest of reason" as lying in "complete comprehension" (Refl 18:155, compare 15:711, 17:708). But why does Kant associate reason with comprehension in this way? A first clue to this is given by the broader meaning of "*begreifen*", which (in its verb form) Kant uses to describe a range of cases in which a manifold has been "grasped" or "united" or "comprehended together" (depending on the translation) in a single consciousness. It is this sort of "*begreifen*", for example, that is at issue when Kant writes of the representations of inner sense that, "only because I can comprehend their manifold in a consciousness do I call them all together my representations" (B133, compare A103). As such passages indicate, Kant often uses "*begreifen*" to refer to the sort of "combination" or "unification" of intuitions in one consciousness that is characteristic of all conceptual thought. Indeed, it is this function of concepts that makes it appropriate, according to Kant, to refer to them with the term "*Begriff*" in the first place.[30] Such uses of "*begreifen*" might seem to raise a challenge to any attempt to

---

[30] Translators often also translate another German term in Kant, "*Zusammenfassung*", as "comprehension". For reasons that we are discussing, this is very natural, since both "*Zusammenfassung*" and "*Begreifen*" involve a sort of unification of many elements in one consciousness. So it is not too surprising that Kant sometimes moves rather quickly between them, as we can see, for example, at KU 5:185.

associate this term *too* closely with reason in the narrow sense. For, of course, it is the understanding, and *not* reason in the narrow sense, that is the faculty of concepts in the sense at issue in these passages. But there is in fact a progression that connects together (i) the more modest sort of unification (or "*begreifen*") that is characteristic of *all* conceptual thought and (ii) the more demanding form of comprehension (or "*Begreifen*") that is characteristic of the aims of reason *in particular*. For just as the understanding aims to unify the diverse elements it finds in intuition in a single consciousness by bringing these elements under concepts, reason aims to unify our concepts and judgments into a larger system by placing them within a larger, unified system of inferences—a system of such inferences that constitutes genuine "cognition from principles" or "comprehension" in the full sense of these terms.[31]

In other words, as Kant stresses, while the understanding's activities aim at the *combination of concepts into judgments*, reason's activities aim at the *combination of judgments* that is involved in an inference or syllogism. Both these forms of combination may be regarded as instances of combination or "*begreifen*" in the general sense that applies to all forms of discursive thought. But the ultimate endpoint of this process of unification (or "comprehending together") is not the combination of intuitions under concepts that is characteristic of the understanding, nor even the combination of concepts in judgment, but rather the combination of these judgments into a genuinely systematic form of cognition from principles or explanatory grounds. And it is just *this* that Kant means to refer to when he speaks of comprehension ("*Begreifen*") in the more demanding sense that is distinctive of reason as the highest of our rational capacities.[32] In this sense, genuine comprehension ("*Begreifen*") is what provides this more general process of unification (or "*begreifen*") with its ultimate endpoint or *telos*.[33]

As this should indicate, to understand why Kant associates reason with "*Begreifen*" or comprehension in this more demanding sense, we need to understand how Kant conceives of the relationship between comprehension and

---

[31] One might draw on the role that reason's interest in systematic unity plays in making the "coherent use of the understanding" possible here to strengthen these points in a variety of ways. For an excellent presentation of the case that the faculty of the understanding itself depends on the grasp of systematic unity that reason provides, see (Brink n.d.).

[32] It is this gap that is at issue in passages like the following: "We can conceive [*concipiren*] many things, though we cannot comprehend [*begreifen*] them", although there is also a gap here between mere conception and genuine cognition of objects through concepts (Log 9:65).

[33] A nice example of this progression from "lower" to "higher" senses of "comprehension" is provided by Kant's discussion of the sublime in sections 26–7 of the third *Critique*, although that text raises further complications about the relationship between what Kant calls "*Zusammenfassung*" and "*Begreifen*", both of which are often translated as "comprehension". Nonetheless, those sections nicely illustrate how, under the guidance of reason, we find ourselves dissatisfied with the sort of "aesthetic comprehension" (*Zusammenfassung*) that is possible within intuition alone and begin to search for a more systematic and complete form of "intellectual comprehension" (*Zusammenfassung*)—one that only our intellectual faculties, and ultimately reason as the source of ideas of the unconditioned, can provide. See KU 5:255, 5:260.

cognition more generally. And to do this, it will be helpful to return to the hierarchy of different forms of representation from the logic lectures that we discussed in Chapter 2.[34] As we saw there, in that hierarchy, Kant presents seven distinct grades of representation, distinguished "in regard to their objective content", ranging from mere representation to comprehension.[35] But while our focus in Chapter 2 was on the transition from step one of this hierarchy to step four, I want to turn our attention now to the latter stages of it, and, in particular, to the transition from grades three and four to grades six and seven:

> In regard to the objective content of our cognition in general, we may think the following *degrees*, in accordance with which cognition can, in this respect, be graded:
>
> *The first* degree of cognition is: *to represent* something;
>
> The *second*: to represent something with consciousness, or *to perceive (percipere)*;
>
> The *third*: *to be acquainted* with something *(noscere)*, or to represent something in comparison with other things, both as to sameness and as to difference.
>
> The *fourth*: to be acquainted with something *with consciousness*, i.e., to *cognize* it *(cognoscere)*. Animals are *acquainted* with objects too, but they do not *cognize* them.
>
> The *fifth*: *to understand* something *(intelligere)*, i.e., to cognize something *through the understanding by means of concepts*, or to *conceive*. One can conceive much, although one cannot comprehend it, e.g., a *perpetuum mobile*, whose impossibility is shown in mechanics.
>
> The *sixth*: to cognize something through reason, or *to have insight* into it *(perspicere)*. With few things do we get this far, and our cognitions become fewer and fewer in number the more that we seek to perfect them as to content.

---

[34] Of course, there are many questions about the reliability of the various transcriptions of Kant's logic lectures. But the hierarchy at issue here figures in more than one of these lecture notes and fits well with Kant's published discussion of these issues, so I see no reason to be skeptical of them with respect to the points I discuss here. For some of the complexities here, see (Sommerlatte 2018).

[35] It has been suggested to me that Kant only emphasizes "comprehension" in the manner he does in his logic lectures because it plays a prominent role within Meier's *Auszug aus der Vernunftlehre*, which Kant used as his text for these lectures. But this is hardly the only place where Kant associates reason with comprehension, and what Kant says about comprehension in his lectures is quite different from what Meier says in his text. For example, compare the following passage, in which Meier presents a view of these issues far more in line with the standard "Leibnizian-Wolffian" account than what we find in Kant:

> In so ferne wir von einer Sache eine deutliche Erkenntniss haben, in so ferne begreifen wir sie (concipere). Was deutlich erkannt werden kann, ist begreiflich (conceptibile). Was nicht deutlich erkannt werden kann, ist unbegreiflich (inconceptibile), entweder schlechterdings (absolute inconceptibile), wenn es schlechterdings nicht zergliedert werden kann; oder nur beziehungsweise (relative inconceptibile), wenn es beziehungsweise nicht zergliedert warden kann. (Meier 1752, 140)

The *seventh, finally*: *to comprehend* something (*comprehendere*), i.e., to cognize something through reason or *a priori* to the degree that is sufficient for our purpose. For all our comprehension is only *relative*, i.e., sufficient for a certain purpose; we do not comprehend anything without qualification. Nothing can be comprehended more than what the mathematician demonstrates, e.g., that all lines in the circle are proportional. And yet he does not comprehend how it happens that such a simple figure has these properties. The field of understanding or of the understanding is thus in general much greater than the field of comprehension or of reason.[36]

As noted above, in presenting us with a hierarchy of more or less perfect forms of cognition, Kant is expressing a version of what (Pasnau 2018) has called "idealized epistemology"—that is, an epistemology that attempts to characterize our ordinary cognitive states in relation to certain epistemological or cognitive ideals. In Chapter 2, we focused on the first part of this hierarchy, but the most important part of it for us here will be the transitions that move us from its fourth stage—"cognition" (*Erkenntnis*)—through the remaining three stages—labeled "understanding" (*Verstehen*), "having insight" (*Einsehen*), and "comprehension" (*Begreifen*).[37]

In making these transitions, Kant defines "comprehension" as a further perfection of "cognition". So, to understand what "comprehension" is, it will be helpful to quickly rehearse some of the main points of our previous discussion of "cognition".[38] As we discussed above, cognition is "objective representation with consciousness". As Kant uses these terms, an objective representation with consciousness is a representation that represents something *to* one's consciousness in a manner that makes one *conscious of it as something objective*—that is, as something more than a mere episode in one's subjective experience.[39] As discussed above, whenever we have such a representation, we are a position to recognize that it possesses not merely a formal or logical standard of correctness, but also what Kant calls a "material" standard of correctness. And a representation has a "material" standard of correctness in this sense just in case it is answerable for its correctness to something that goes beyond the nature of the subject's concepts and other representations. As an "*objective* representation", any genuine cognition has a material standard of correctness in this sense. But, as an "objective representation *with consciousness*", it also makes the subject *conscious* of the fact that this is the case, at least implicitly.

---

[36] Log 9:65. Compare V-Lo/Blomberg 24:133–4. A similar though interestingly distinct progression appears in a *Reflexion* (Refl 15:171).

[37] In his work, Sommerlatte argues that Jäsche switches the order of the fourth and fifth degrees of this progression from Kant's original intention. I'm not convinced of this, but this issue is independent of my claims here.

[38] See Chapter 2. For other important recent work on Kant's conception of cognition, see (Smit 2000, 2009, 2010; Chignell 2007a, 2007b, 2012; Tolley 2014, 2017b; Watkins and Willaschek 2017).

[39] Compare (Rödl 2007).

In this way, as we've discussed, cognition for Kant always involves a consciousness of at least three things: (i) our representation of something, (ii) the thing represented as something distinct from our representation of it, and (iii) a relationship between these two.[40] Once again, this has several implications for what genuine cognition of an object requires. For a representation can provide us with a consciousness of itself as having a material standard of correctness only if it possesses two further features. First, it can count as a cognition in this sense only to the degree that it represents its object to our consciousness in a relatively *determinate* fashion. And second, it can count as a cognition only if we are conscious of its object as something that is not merely logically, but also *really possible*. Thus, to cognize an object is, for Kant, a matter of being conscious of this object as a reasonably determinate thing that imposes material, as opposed to merely logical, standards of correctness on our representations of it.

Since comprehension (*Begreifen*) is a further perfection of cognition, the same requirements apply to it as well. So, in order to comprehend something, we must have a reasonably determinate grasp of its real properties. For this reason, comprehension of something, like cognition in general, will require us to "coordinate" its various marks or features. That is, to cognize something, my representation of it must bring together a sufficient variety of its properties to satisfy the requirements just noted.[41] But the two highest grades of cognition in Kant's hierarchy—insight and comprehension—require something more than this:

> To understand something is far easier than to have insight into something, for in the first case it is only necessary that I *coordinate* the marks of a thing, but in the other case I must *subordinate* them. To understand what gold is I need nothing more than to know the properties of this metal, that it is e.g. ductile, yellow, heavier than others, etc., that it does not rust. But to have *insight into what gold is I must investigate one of its marks in particular and abstract from it its ground. E.g., why it does not rust, why is it ductile, heavier than others.*
>
> (V-Lo/Blomberg 24:134–5, my emphasis)

As this makes clear, these two highest grades of cognition require not just the "coordination" of marks, but also the "subordination" of them. That is, to have insight into something, we must be conscious, not just of *which* properties something has, but also of *how* these properties *ground* one another.[42] For example, to cognize something as a nugget of gold requires a grasp of the various

---

[40] (Tolley 2017b).
[41] Once again, this "bringing together" is a form of *begreifen* or *zusammenfassen* in the more general sense.
[42] This is also implicit in the definition of insight at Log 9:65, which defines insight in terms of cognizing "something through reason". For reason, as we have seen, is the capacity for *cognition from principles*. And so, to cognize something *through reason* is just to cognize it from principles or

properties that gold possesses—one that is sufficient to distinguish gold from other metals. Some of these properties may themselves involve explanatory or causal relations—e.g. they may involve facts about gold's lack of a propensity to rust—but at least in general, in order to have this sort of grasp of the nature of gold, I do not need to understand how its various properties are related to one another. Rather, to coordinate the properties of gold in this way, I only need attribute to gold a sufficient number of properties (or "marks") to differentiate it from other substances. But in order to truly *have insight* into gold, I must go beyond this and organize gold's various properties in an explanatory system, which allows me to grasp how the superficial features of gold are grounded in its more basic features. So, for example, to have insight into the nature of gold, I must be able to explain how gold's lack of a propensity to rust is grounded in other more fundamental properties. In this way, to have insight into the nature of gold is to bring its various properties into a sort of unified explanatory *system*. And in order to do this, I will normally need to appeal to more general explanatory principles or laws that apply far beyond the case of gold in particular. Thus, to *comprehend* the nature of gold requires not just bringing the properties of gold into explanatory relations with one another, but also bringing these properties into a larger explanatory system that applies to other cases as well. In both ways, the sort of "explanatory understanding" of the nature of gold that insight, and by extension comprehension, involves requires placing the properties of gold into a broader explanatory context.

Insight and comprehension thus require the systematic interconnection of our concepts and judgments into a meaningful system.[43] Such a system will allow us to:

> ...discover in them an order that we can grasp (*eine faßliche Ordnung*), to divide its products into genera and species in order to use the principles for the explanation and the understanding (*der Erklärung und des Verständnisses*) of one for the explanation and comprehension (*zur Erklärung und Begreifung*) of the other as well. (KU 5:185)

As this indicates, insight and comprehension are generally possible only insofar as we achieve a corresponding degree of "cognition from principles"—that is, cognition of something from its explanatory grounds. And this, as we have seen, will generally require us to draw on the resources of reason as the capacity for mediate inference. More precisely, insight requires a grasp of real conditioning relations

---

explanatory grounds. As such, to cognize something "through reason" always requires a grasp not just of the determinate properties of the thing cognized, but also of how these properties are grounded in more basic grounds or "principles".

[43] There are also interesting connections between these ideas and (Bengson 2017)'s discussion of "noetic conceptions".

between things and properties. And while we can often grasp some such relations simply by applying the relational categories to objects in intuition, this will not take us very far on its own. To go beyond this and develop a deeper understanding of the explanations that underlie the objects of ordinary experience, we must make use of the resources provided by reason as the faculty for mediate inference. In short, to penetrate very far in our insight into things, we must go beyond the sorts of superficial causal judgments that the Kantian understanding can provide us with, to develop an explanatorily *rich* and *deep* conception of what we are trying to understand. And to do this, we must extend our grasp of such relations *via* drawing on the resources for syllogistic inference provided by reason as the faculty for inference.

Of course, in doing so, the relational categories will continue to guide our inferential activity.[44] But the important point for present purposes is that achieving more than the most superficial understanding of real conditioning relations requires us to place our cognitions within an inferential structure in which these cognitions figure as the "conclusions" of some further "prosyllogism"—a syllogism, that is, which extends our existing network of syllogistic inferences *upward* towards first principles. Indeed, putting things in this way undersells the connections that Kant establishes between insight (and comprehension), cognition from principles, and inference. For even if we focus on the sorts of simple conditioning relations that can be grasped in a single judgment using the relational categories, it remains the case that *these* judgments provide us with a way of grasping such dependence relations only insofar as they are capable of serving as what Kant calls "comparative principles"—that is, general representations from which other less general representations may be derived in inference.[45] Thus, even in the case of simple "one-step" conditioning relations of this sort, there continues to be a constitutive connection between our grasp of such relations and the possibility of making use of this grasp (as "comparative principles") in an inferential context.

d. Comprehension, "Understanding", and "Knowledge"

Given all this, when we move from mere cognition to insight or comprehension, what we gain is not just an expanded grasp of what is (or ought to be), but also a grasp of *why* and *how* things have this status. In this way, insight and comprehension are superior to mere cognition, in the first instance, because they allow us to answer *why*- or *how*-questions that mere cognition cannot. Kant's conception

---

[44] Thus, it is no surprise to find these categories at work in the "ideas of reason" that Kant sees as providing us with models of what this ideal comprehension would have to be like.
[45] This coheres nicely with Kant's view that any cognition of a causal relation in some sense presupposes the existence of a full system of causal laws.

of "insight" and "comprehension" is thus in many ways similar to the notion of "understanding" that has been a focus of recent debate within epistemology.[46] For, like "understanding" in the contemporary sense, theoretical insight and comprehension require not just a grasp of what is, but also a grasp of *why* and *how* things are as they are. And practical comprehension or wisdom requires not simply a grasp of what to do, but also a grasp of *how* and *why* it is to be done. Thus, much as is true of "understanding" in the contemporary sense, to have insight into something or to comprehend something is, for Kant, to be able to *make sense* of it (theoretically or practically).[47]

To illustrate how intuitive this conception of reason as seeking theoretical and practical comprehension is, let's briefly consider an everyday example of (mixed) theoretical and practical reasoning. Suppose, for example, that I'm considering how to best accommodate the needs of my elderly parents. This is, in the first instance, a practical question—a question of what to do. In considering it, I will of course need to weigh my own needs and desires against those of my parents. But any such "weighing of considerations" will itself need to take place against the background of a network of other commitments, which is informed by my love for my parents, as well as the various ways I am indebted to them. And, of course, in considering these questions, I will also need to consider the needs of my partner and her family. Indeed, the question I am considering is almost certainly not one for me to decide *on my own*. The practical reasoning at issue here will thus have to be one that proceeds *via* conversation with the other people involved in it.

Despite all this complexity, in order to understand how to care for my parents, I need to decide on a particular course of action, one that is appropriately responsive to all these factors (and many more). In one direction, this will require me to make my general plan to "care for my parents" *more determinate* in a variety of respects. For practical reasoning can only take us all the way to action by making our general ends more determinate.[48] But to do *this* in a manner that is appropriately responsive to all these various considerations, I need to understand how they *interact* with one another under my circumstances.[49] And this will almost certainly require me to answer other practical and theoretical questions in turn. For example, to navigate the competing needs of my partner and my parents, I may need to better understand (at least implicitly) how my obligations

---

[46] Compare (Moore 2012).

[47] For a contemporary argument for the unity of theoretical and practical understanding that focuses on practical understanding in the sense of skill or a (sort of) "know how", see (Bengson 2017). But note that my account of practical comprehension here may implicitly takes issues with some of Bengson's claims there, such as his claim that "Practical understanding is not, or at least not usually, explanatory . . ." (30).

[48] For this point, which goes back at least to Aristotle, see (Ford 2011; Lavin 2015; Ford 2018; Mylonaki 2018; Small 2019).

[49] Such interactions will often be quite complex. See, for example, (Maguire and Lord 2016; Dancy 2018).

to each are grounded in an even more basic set of moral values or obligations. And to understand how my obligations to others interact with my own personal desires, I need to better understand (on an intuitive level at least) how the personal and impersonal dimensions of value relate. Moreover, to understand what sort of care my parents really need, I will need to develop a better understanding of their medical and emotional condition, and this may force me to engage in various forms of theoretical reasoning as well. Thus, the sort of understanding I am seeking here is not merely practical; it involves an essential theoretical component as well.

Of course, in developing a deeper understanding of all these issues, I need not engage in anything like explicit moral or scientific theorizing. But nonetheless, in striving to understand the interactions between these aspects of my practical situation, I will have to form an (at least implicit) picture of what to do that places this question in a more general context and allows me to make sense of its elements in more general terms. Given this, the theoretical and practical understanding (or comprehension) I am seeking is only possible insofar as I have a grasp of how particular actions are justified by more general grounds *of some kind*. In this way, understanding (or comprehension) is only possible insofar as we can discover some sort of general basis or ground or context that allows us to answer such questions. As this indicates, much like Kant's conceptions of insight and comprehension, the everyday notion of "understanding" requires that our particular (theoretical and practical) cognitions be placed into a larger explanatory system that allows us to *make sense* of the theoretical and practical questions we are considering.

Moreover, as noted above, understanding or comprehension in this sense is also significant because, by placing our judgments into this sort of inferentially articulated system, we also make them *epistemically relevant* to one another, such that assent to one can serve as a potential epistemic ground for assent to the other. When judgments stand in these sorts of relations, they have the potential to serve as subjectively and/or objectively sufficient grounds for assent to one another in the manner relevant to Kant's discussion of belief (*Glaube*) and knowledge (*Wissen*) (A820/B848). So, by placing our cognitions into systematic order in the manner comprehension requires, we not only put ourselves in a position to grasp the *real* explanatory (or conditioning) relations between things, we also gain access to the sorts of *objective grounds for assent* that are distinctive of knowledge in the sense of *Wissen*.[50]

---

[50] Note, though, that while an increase in comprehension generally brings with it an increase in our knowledge (*Wissen*), not all instances of knowledge are instances of comprehension for Kant. For not every objective "proof" of a claim is sufficient to generate comprehension. The complex relationship between reason's need for comprehension and the particular sorts of inferences or "proofs" that can satisfy this demand is at work in passages where Kant distinguishes between what he calls "apagogic" and what he calls "ostensive" proofs.

Thus, there is tight connection between knowledge (*Wissen*), insight and comprehension, cognition from principles, and inference on Kant's account. Given what we have said here, these connections should come as no surprise. For, as we have just seen, to have insight into or comprehension of something is just to grasp that thing's real explanatory grounds in the manner that understanding it requires. For this reason, to have insight or comprehension of something requires placing our cognition of it within a larger system of cognitions which are connected by various inferences. These inferences are crucial here, in the first instance, because they constitute our grasp of the real explanatory grounds (conditions) that insight and comprehension (making sense of things) require. But by connecting our cognitions in this way, they also provide us with new grounds for assent. Thus, by searching for the sorts of *explanatory* or *sense-making* grounds that comprehension (*Begreifen*) requires, we are also searching for the sorts of *justificatory* grounds that can give our acts of assent the status of knowledge (*Wissen*). But, once again, for Kant at least, it is not the justificatory side of this story that has primacy here. Rather, for Kant, like most of his contemporaries, the justificatory side of this story is ultimately secondary to the search for comprehension or understanding.[51] In this sense, the justificatory payoffs of reason's inferential activity, although real, are ultimately less central for Kant than they are for many contemporary epistemologists. On Kant's way of thinking of these matters, reason aims first and foremost to make sense of things, and only secondarily at developing a view of things that is well justified.

As this indicates, it is certainly true that the faculty of reason is the "reasons business" for Kant. For reason, as we have seen, is a faculty that seeks out the sorts of grounds that allow us to fully make sense of the objects of (theoretical and practical) cognition. But reason is interested in such grounds, in the first instance, not because it seeks better "justifications" for its claims—as if these claims needed to be defended against this or that objection—but rather for the more general reason that the discovery of such grounds allows it to make better sense of things in the sense that (theoretical and practical) comprehension requires. This, as we have seen, will also give rise to better justificatory reasons as well, but the focus here (for Kant) is on reasons as contributing to cognition from principles or comprehension. In this sense, we might say that Kant's conception of reason gives priority to reasons in the explanatory sense over reasons in the justificatory sense. But this would only be apt insofar as we understood "explanation" to cover both theoretical and practical modes of comprehension or "sense making". So it is probably better to speak of Kant's conception of reason as one that gives priority

---

[51] Contrast here (Ware 2021)'s presentation of Kant as concerned primarily with developing a "justification of ethics". For more on my reservations on that approach to Kant, see my review of Ware in the *Philosophical Quarterly*, although as I note there, the differences between us on this score are probably partially terminological.

to reasons as "sense-makers"—as considerations that help us understand our theoretical and practical conclusions. But the important point here is that, for Kant, reason is primarily interested in reasons because they play this sense-making role, and only secondarily because the discovery of reasons in this sense also helps us to discover reasons *qua* justifications.

e. The Modesty of Reason as the Capacity for Comprehension

As this should indicate, if Kant conceived of reason as *the faculty for rational insight*, his conception of reason would be very close to that endorsed by canonical "rationalists" like Leibniz or Wolff. After all, for such figures, reason or the intellect is the capacity for precisely this sort of cognition of the nature of things from first principles—for "a priori cognition" in the traditional "from grounds" sense of the a priori.[52] Thus, it is significant that Kant characterizes reason *not* as the faculty for a rational insight *simpliciter*, but rather as the faculty for "comprehension".[53] Once again, as Kant defines these terms, to have comprehension of something is "to cognize something through reason or a priori to the degree that is sufficient for our purpose." So, for Kant, comprehension differs from insight insofar as comprehension is *relativized to our ends or purposes*. In other words, comprehension differs from insight precisely because it *only* requires us to have insight into things (to cognize them through reason) *to the degree that* is required by our ends and purposes. In this way, Kant's conception of comprehension is effectively the result of relativizing the conception of insight we find in the Leibnizian-Wolffian rationalists to these ends and purposes.[54]

As this indicates, the move from insight to comprehension is significant, in part, because it expresses the more modest conception of reason that Kant views as the upshot of the critical philosophy. After all, *complete* insight, or "complete, unrestricted comprehension", is something our capacities for theoretical cognition cannot generally achieve. Thus, as Kant says, "all our comprehension is only *relative*, i.e. sufficient for a certain purpose; we do not comprehend anything without qualification" (Log 9:65). Given this relatively modest conception of the cognitive reach of reason, Kant is forced to reject attempts to define reason as the capacity for insight *full stop*. Rather, in describing reason as a faculty, Kant turns

---

[52] Thanks to an anonymous referee for pushing me to make more of this. For the importance of this notion of the "a priori" in Kant, see (Smit 2009, 2010), which draws upon (Adams 1997).

[53] Indeed, Kant sometimes describes such views as wrongheaded precisely because they claim that human reason is capable of achieving "rational insight" (*Vernunfteinsicht*) into issues like the existence of God (O 8:140).

[54] This aspect of Kant's conception of reason is also on display in his end-relative conception of the sciences. See (Sturm 2020) for discussion of this.

to an emphasis on "comprehension" in a relativized sense.[55] This relativizes the traditional demand for insight to our ends and purposes, and so opens the door to the possibility that human reason may be able to achieve *comprehension*, despite the very significant limitations that Kant places on its ability to achieve insight.[56] For example, once we have discovered the limits on our theoretical faculties that Kant exposes in the Transcendental Dialectic, Kant believes that we should abandon any expectation that we will achieve *complete theoretical insight* into the nature of things, and reconceive the ends or purposes at work in theoretical reasoning in more modest terms—e.g. in terms of a properly systematic metaphysics of nature. But once we reconceive the ends of theoretical reason in this way, then *relative to those ends*, we may very well be able to achieve theoretical comprehension in an end- or purpose-relative sense.[57] In this way, as we will see, Kant's conception of reason as the capacity for comprehension expresses the essence of what Kant takes to be a "genuinely critical" conception of reason and its limits.[58]

At the same time, a focus on "comprehension" is useful here because it helps to explain the point of reason's search for "systematic unity" or "cognition from principles". As we have just seen, these forms of cognition are important here because they provide us with answers to why- and how-questions—answers that go beyond the limited ones we can achieve by non-inferential means.[59] Thus, one of the payoffs of reading Kant as conceiving of reason as the capacity for comprehension is that it allows us to see him as defending a version of the idea that genuine understanding of some topic is constituted, not just by some body of unrelated judgments or pieces of knowledge, but by the inferences one uses to connect those judgments or pieces of knowledge into an integrated whole. When read in this way, one of Kant's fundamental points about reason is precisely that only an inferentially structured system of cognitions can constitute the sort of comprehension that truly *makes sense* of things, either theoretically or practically.

As I've argued elsewhere and will discuss below, this provides us with a powerful way of explaining the rational significance of many of our inferential practices.[60] For it allows us to see a variety of forms of inference, not just as reliable means of extending our body of true beliefs (or correct maxims), but as partially

---

[55] Note here that Kant also associates both "cognition" and the degree of cognition he calls "understanding" with the understanding. It is thus not surprising to find him also associating more than one stage of this progression with reason.

[56] Interestingly, Kant often uses the language of comprehension, or making something comprehensible, when discussing the fundamental *philosophical* explanation for some phenomena; see, for example: Axvi, B41, A89/B121, A113, A128, A149/B189.

[57] An interesting question here is exactly how this end- or purpose-relativity is best made precise.

[58] At the same time, it is worth stressing that this aspect of Kant's approach is a continuation of a long early modern debate about the degree to which we can achieve "adequate" conceptions or ideas of the nature of reality. One could tell much of the history of modern philosophy through the lens of this question.

[59] Compare (Breitenbach 2014).   [60] See (Schafer 2019b, forthcoming a).

constitutive of the sort of "understanding" that allows us to make sense of things in the manner that rationality requires. As we will see in the next chapter, this pushes us away from the focus on requirements of mere logical or instrumental coherence that have been the focus of much of the analytic literature on these issues, and towards more robust forms of "explanatory coherence"—forms of coherence that, as we will see below Kant associates with the principle of sufficient reason and the moral law.

f. The Unity of Reason and the Unity of Comprehension

As should already be plain, the connection between reason and comprehension has considerable significance with respect to many aspects of Kant's philosophy. As we will see, it also provides us with a powerful lens to think about Kant's conception of autonomy by allowing us to think of the autonomy of practical reason as constitutive of genuine practical comprehension or wisdom—that is, of an understanding of what to do "from practical principles".[61] In the remainder of the present chapter, I want to show how this discussion helps to illuminate the sense in which Kant takes reason to be a unified faculty across the theoretical-practical divide.[62]

Given what we have said so far, to understand the unity of theoretical and practical reason, we need to pair the characterization of reason just given *with* Kant's general account of the relationship between theoretical and practical cognition. For by doing so, we can first characterize reason's unity in terms of an abstract aim of "cognition from principles" or "comprehension" that is common to reason in both its theoretical and practical form. And then we can *distinguish* theoretical and practical reason from one another in terms of the *kind* of cognition from principles or comprehension that is the proper province of each—namely, theoretical as opposed to practical cognition from principles or comprehension.[63] In this way, we can develop an account of the "real unity" of reason as faculty, which traces all of reason's activity back to a single explanatory principle that underlines all of what reason does, in both a theoretical and practical form.

To flesh out this line of thought, let's return briefly to our discussion of Kant's distinction between theoretical and practical cognition. As we noted there, Kant

---

[61] For this reason, the present focus does not conflict with the idea that the principle of practical reason lies in its own autonomy. For the full development of practical reason's autonomy is just the development of the body of genuine practical comprehension.

[62] For other prominent discussions of the unity of reason in Kant, see (Henrich 1994; Neiman 1994; Kleingeld 1998; Nuzzo 2005), although Henrich and Nuzzo focus largely on issues that lie beyond the scope of my discussion here.

[63] For an excellent discussion of this basic framework, see (Merritt 2018).

distinguishes theoretical and practical cognition in two closely related ways.[64] First, he draws this distinction in terms of how a cognition's representation relates to its object.[65] In this sense, theoretical cognitions involve cognitions that depend upon an object that is in some sense "given" to the cognizer. In this way, theoretical cognitions can be thought of as cognitions where the existence of our representation of an object is dependent (directly or indirectly) on that object's existence. In practical cognition, on the other hand, this relation of existential dependence is reversed. Practical cognition functions so that the existence of our representation of an object can ground the existence of that object. Thus, while the canonical role of theoretical cognition is to be receptive to independently existing things, the canonical role of practical cognition is to bring into existence the things it represents. In this sense, practical cognition involves a kind of "maker's knowledge" or "practical knowledge".

As we've discussed, Kant ties this first way of drawing the theoretical/practical distinction very closely to a second, according to which it is a distinction between cognitions that represent their object as something *that is* (theoretical cognitions) and cognitions that represent their objects as something *that ought to be* (practical cognitions).[66] Once again, in treating this second distinction as equivalent to the first, Kant is endorsing a "formal" version of the doctrine of the guise of the true and the good.[67] That is, he is thinking of theoretical cognition as presenting its objects under the guise of "what is", while practical cognition presents its objects under the guise of "what ought to be".

For present purposes, the important point is that, given these distinctions, both "cognition from principles" and "comprehension" can be made determinate in at least two ways. For example, given this distinction, the general category of cognition from principles will include within its scope *both* theoretical cognition from principles *and* practical cognition from principles. And, similarly, since comprehension is a further perfection of cognition, comprehension will come in both a theoretical and a practical form.[68] Thus, if we conceive of reason as (say)

---

[64] For related discussion of the relationship between theoretical and practical cognition, see (Engstrom 2002, 2009; Rödl 2010; Reath 2012; Elizondo 2013; Merritt 2018). My discussion here takes inspiration from all these views, but in focusing on reason as the faculty for comprehension, it develops this basic line of thought differently than they do.

[65] Cf. Bix–x, KpV 5:10, KpV 5:20, KpV 5:46, KpV 5:57, KU 5:171, KU 5:177–8, EEKU 20:197, EEKU 20:199, EEKU 20:230.

[66] Cf. A633/B661, A802/B830, A840/B868, GMS 4:387, KpV 5:5, KpV 5:109, KU 5:176, EEKU 20:246–7.

[67] Compare (Tenenbaum 2007; Schafer 2013).

[68] When it is this sort of distinctively practical comprehension or cognition from principles that is at issue, Kant often prefers to speak of "wisdom"—that is, the "perfection of [practical] cognition in the derivation of an end from the system of all ends" (V-Phil-Th/Pölitz 28:1065, compare KpV 5:108, Anth 7:200). As passages like this indicate, to have wisdom is, for Kant, a matter of having both (i) systematic cognition of the ends one ought to pursue from basic principles and (ii) a will and faculty of choice that are determined by this practical cognition in its choice of actions. Thus, wisdom in this sense just is practical comprehension as defined above.

the faculty for comprehension, we can see why these abstract characterizations of reason can be made more determinate in (at least) two basic ways: as the faculty for theoretical comprehension *or* as the faculty for practical comprehension or wisdom. When reason's characteristic form of activity is made precise in the first, we arrive at a characterization of theoretical reason *in particular*. And when it is made precise in the second way, we arrive at a characterization of practical reason *in particular*. But a general conception of reason as the capacity for comprehension grounds both of these more determinate manifestations of reason.[69]

Of course, one might develop this general conception of the unity of theoretical and practical reason by focusing not on reason as the capacity for *comprehension*, but, rather, on the more familiar conception of reason as the capacity for *cognition from principles* or the even more general notion of reason as a faculty for a sort of knowledge or cognition. It is only fair, then, to ask what characterizing reason as the capacity for *comprehension* adds to that picture. I hope my comments above about the relationship between insight, comprehension, and "understanding" (in the contemporary sense of this term) go some way towards answering such questions. But the conception of reason as the capacity for comprehension—as opposed to, say, insight—also has special significance in the context of Kant's discussion of the relationship between practical and theoretical reason. For comprehension (unlike, say, insight) is end- or purpose-relative, so if reason aims at comprehension, this will explicitly relativize the aims of *both* theoretical and practical reason to our ends and purposes as the rational creatures we are. As a result, even in its theoretical use, what reason seeks is not insight or cognition from principles *simpliciter* but rather *a* degree of insight *that is sufficient for our purposes*. And this is crucial for understanding how Kant conceives of the *primacy* of practical reason, against the background of the basic unity of reason as a faculty.

In saying this, it is important to begin by stressing that the purposes that are relevant here will be both theoretical and practical in character—including our interests in both theoretical and practical comprehension. But nonetheless, Kant is clear that the *ultimate* court of appeals for *all* questions concerning our proper ends is reason in its *practical* form. After all, it is precisely the function of practical reason to decide such questions through providing us with a comprehension of our ultimate ends as rational beings. Thus, as Kant stresses, "all interest is ultimately practical" in character, and the interest "even...of speculative reason is only conditional and is complete in [its] practical use alone" (KpV 5:121). In other words, as Kant stresses, with respect to questions of interest, practical reason takes "primacy" over theoretical reason insofar as the interests of the latter are "subordinated" to those of the former (KpV 5:121). This is true, on the present

---

[69] See: "practical reason has as its basis the same cognitive faculty as does speculative reason so far as both are *pure reason*" (KpV 5:89, compare KpV 5:121).

reading, because *even* the ends and interests of theoretical reason are themselves end- or purpose-relative, and so subject to the governance of practical reason as the faculty for setting final ends.

In this way, by relativizing the aims of both theoretical and practical reason to our ends or purposes, Kant is placing *both* practical *and* theoretical reason under the governance of practical reason as the faculty for setting final ends.[70] Thus, to conceive of theoretical reason as aiming at theoretical comprehension, while also conceiving of comprehension in end- or purpose-relative terms, is to allow that practical reason must play a central role in determining *the sort* of insight that reason ought to aim at *even* in its theoretical use. In some sense, then, by making the aims of theoretical reason end-relative, Kant is introducing an element of what is today called "pragmatic encroachment" (and, indeed, "moral encroachment") into his account of the characteristic aims of theoretical reason, although it is important to stress that the pragmatic element here is (at least in the first instance) limited to the role of practical reason in determining *what degree* of theoretical insight theoretical reason requires. Practical reason's role in governing theoretical reason here relates, not to what theoretical insight itself *is*, but rather to the degree of this insight that theoretical reason demands of us.[71]

Nonetheless, it is this package of views that ultimately explains why Kant insists that, "in the union of pure speculative with pure practical reason in one cognition, the latter has primacy" (KpV 5:121). As this makes clear, the fact that Kant conceives of reason as the capacity for *comprehension* (and not, say, as the capacity for rational insight) is important for understanding the precise sense in which Kant takes the interests of practical reason to have primacy over the interests of reason in its theoretical use. For if reason aims at comprehension, then there is an important sense in which *all* the operations of reason, both theoretical and practical, are under the governance of *practical* reason. But, and this is crucial here, we have arrived at this result without needing to treat theoretical reasoning as (say) a special manifestation of practical reason in the manner characteristic of (say) O'Neill's or Neiman's treatments of these issues.[72] Nor have we made practical considerations directly relevant to our theoretical insight into the nature of things.

As we have seen, this is important here because, contrary to what readings like O'Neill's or Neiman's suggest, Kant's view is *not* that the unity of reason is

---

[70] Compare again (Sturm 2020)'s treatment of the manner in which the ends of the various special sciences are organized under the practical reason's end (i.e. wisdom).

[71] Although Schroeder does not discuss this connection, this is another respect in which the form of "pragmatic intellectualism" he defends in (Schroeder 2021) might be taken to echo certain themes in Kant.

[72] See (O'Neill 1989; Neiman 1994). Compare (Cohen 2014; Mudd 2016, 2017) for more recent discussion of these ideas. Mudd is especially clear on this point, stating that, "reason is a 'unity' because all our reasoning, including our theoretical reasoning, functions practically" (1).

explained by the (more fundamental) primacy of practical reason. Rather, it is that the (more fundamental) unity of theoretical and practical reason is what explains the sense in which practical reason has primacy over theoretical reason with respect to their interests. For, as Kant emphasizes, the primacy of practical reason rests on the fact that "it is still only one and the same reason which, whether from a theoretical or a practical perspective, judges according to a priori principles" (KpV 5:121). Given such passages, it would be a mistake to take the primacy of practical reason to be what *explains* reason's unity for Kant.[73] Rather, for Kant at least, it is the idea of theoretical and practical reason as two expressions of a single capacity that *explains* why practical reason takes "primacy" over theoretical reason. By thinking of reason as the capacity for comprehension, we can improve on precisely this aspect of O'Neill's discussion, and those influenced by her, by capturing the precise sense in which Kant takes practical reason to have primacy over theoretical reason, without thereby treating reason as most fundamentally a practical *as opposed to* theoretical faculty. On the one hand, comprehension comes in both a theoretical and practical form, and so the conception of reason as a capacity for comprehension naturally gives rise to both theoretical and practical reason as two basic and *metaphysically co-equal* manifestations of the capacity for comprehension. But, at the same time, in aiming at comprehension, the aims and interests of *both* theoretical and practical reason are subject to the governance of practical reason as the faculty for setting fundamental ends. Thus, by thinking through what reason as the capacity for comprehension is, we arrive at a picture of reason's unity, on which practical reason takes primacy over theoretical reason in *precisely* the sense Kant claims is true, *and no further*.

This is also important with respect to the familiar charge that Kant's philosophy leaves us with an irresolvable conflict or tension between the principles and aims of theoretical and practical reason. For if reason in general aims at comprehension, then the overarching aim of reason, in both its theoretical and its practical uses, must be to arrive at a unified system of theoretical *and* practical comprehension, where this is understood in terms of a system of insight or cognition from principles *insofar* as this is required by our proper ends as human beings. It is this more modest task that Kant takes to be distinctive of a truly "cosmopolitan" or "wordly" form of philosophy—that is, a philosophy which strives to be a "science of the relation of all cognition to the essential ends of human reason (*teleologia rationis humanae*)" (A839/B867). As such formulations make clear, Kant's philosophy does *not* aim to achieve the sort of rational insight into all of reality that the rationalists (or later idealists) sought, but only a unified comprehension of reality *insofar as this is required by our ends*. So the question, for Kant at least, is

---

[73] Here again I agree with (Timmermann 2010).

always whether his philosophy can accomplish this—and not whether it can provide a grand "unified theory" of reality of the sort his immediate critics often sought. In the conclusion to this book, we will return to question of whether this is a reason to prefer Kant's views to the more ambitious forms of idealism that followed in his wake.

> ...we do not indeed comprehend the practical unconditional necessity of the moral imperative, but we nevertheless comprehend its incomprehensibility; and this is all that can fairly be required of a philosophy that strives in its principles to the very boundary of human reason.   (GMS 4:463)

We can speak of the "comprehension of incomprehensibility" in this case precisely because our grasp of the "incomprehensibility" of freedom is nonetheless sufficient for our proper ends as the finite rational beings we are. The question, for Kant at least, is always whether his philosophy can accomplish this—and not whether it can provide a grand "unified theory" of reality of the sort his immediate critics often sought. In the conclusion to this book, we will return to question of whether this is a reason to prefer Kant's views to the more ambitious forms of idealism that followed in his wake.

5
Theoretical Reason's Supreme Principle and the Principle of Sufficient Reason

> ... reason does not beg but commands, though without being able to determine the bounds of this unity.
>
> (A653/B682)

In the last chapter, we saw how conceiving of reason as the capacity for the highest degree of cognition in Kant's system—namely, comprehension—helps to make sense of both the fundamental *unity* of reason as a theoretical and practical capacity and the manner in which practical reason takes *priority* over theoretical reason for Kant. In this chapter and the next, I want to deepen our understanding of reason's unity by focusing on Kant's conception of the overarching *principle* that governs reason's activity in both its theoretical and its practical use. In both cases, I will argue that reason's most fundamental principle can be thought of as *a version* of the Principle of Sufficient Reason (PSR) in some sense, albeit one that reinterprets the principle to make it acceptable within the confines of Kant's critical philosophy. Thus, *via* thinking of reason as the capacity for comprehension we can arrive at a reading of Kant on which he is far more positive about the PSR than most readers have assumed.[1]

In this chapter, our focus will be on the principles that Kant associates with reason in its theoretical use. But before turning to this topic, I will begin by briefly reviewing how Kant's conception of cognition generates three basic perspectives on the proper exercise of any cognitive faculty, to lay out how this helps to

---

[1] My thought about these issues has been especially influenced by conversations with Eric Watkins, whose work in progress on the "supreme principle" has been very important for my thought about that topic. For more on his interpretation, see (Watkins 2010, 2016, 2017, forthcoming-a, forthcoming-b Watkins and Stratmann 2021). I'm also very indebted to conversations with Nick Stang, Andrew Chignell, Clinton Tolley, Colin McLear, Dai Heide, Jim Kreines, and Ian Proops about these issues. (Kreines 2022) also independently develops a reading of the "supreme principle" that, while weaker than mine in some ways, is structurally similar. And my views about these issues are also similar in many ways to those in (Proops 2021a), although (despite our current geographical proximity) we developed these views largely independently. In particular, Proops agrees with me on the crucial question of whether Kant accepts that there are forms of theoretically grounded "doctrinal belief" in the existence of the unconditioned. But, as we will see, he understands the relevance of this to Kant's discussion of the "supreme principle" quite differently. Much of this work can be seen as developing Chignell's suggestion that "Kant does not materially abandon rationalist metaphysics in the critical period: he simply thinks that the form or status of its results must be reconceived" (Chignell 2007a, 350).

organize Kant's various characterizations of reason. Then, with that in mind, I will turn to Kant's two main characterizations of the principle of theoretical reason: what Kant calls theoretical reason's "logical maxim" and what he calls its "supreme principle". I will argue that Kant's discussion of these formulas indicates a more positive appraisal of the PSR than most readers of Kant have assumed.[2] In particular, while Kant of course rejects the characteristic rationalist claim that the PSR can serve as a potential source of cognition of the unconditioned, I will argue that he nonetheless believes that we are rationally committed to a form of "doctrinal belief" in the bare existence of something unconditioned, and that this is true *even* from a theoretical point of view.[3] That is, even with respect to the theoretical use of reason, Kant takes theoretical reason's interest in systematic comprehension to commit us (albeit only on "subjectively sufficient" grounds) to the proposition that every finite, conditioned thing is ultimately grounded in something unconditioned.[4] I will then go to explain why this commitment is compatible with Kant's critique of more traditional forms of rationalist metaphysics. Then, in the next chapter, I will turn to consider how these ideas apply to reason in its practical use.

a. One Faculty, Many Guises

As just noted, I want to approach these questions by reviewing how Kant's conception of the nature of cognition helps us make systematic sense of the

---

[2] We will see, though, that the story here is more complicated in some ways than this would suggest. For more traditional views of the place of the PSR in Kant's philosophy, see for example (Franks 2005; Boehm 2014; Proops 2014; Kreines 2015; Boehm 2016; Lu-Adler 2021), although of course there are many differences between these readings, some of which I'll return to below. Non-Kantians are often even more blunt about this issue. See, for example, Della Rocca's comment that "Hume and Kant ... made it their mission to articulate and argue for a world-view structured around the claim that the PSR is simply false" (Della Rocca 2010, 1–2).

[3] Compare the discussions in (Beck 1963; Stang 2016; Stang 2017; Proops 2021a; Stratmann forthcoming) in addition to some of the other citations above. Despite the differences noted below, I agree with Proops that, "although he unequivocally rejects the dogmatic project of attempting to gain theoretically grounded knowledge of the supersensible, Kant nonetheless endorses certain theoretically grounded arguments concerning these matters, arguments that he sees as producing something less than knowledge.... These beliefs are instances of a phenomenon Kant terms 'doctrinal belief'..." (Proops 2021a, 4).

[4] As Kreines argues in his important work in progress on these issues, this may mean that we should not make unqualified assertions of this claim within a strictly philosophical context. For there are passages in which Kant appears to claim that there is no room for assertions based on "mere belief" in philosophy. For example: "We can also accept certain propositions of reason on belief (*auf Glauben annehmen*).... In philosophy one cannot do this, however..." (V-Lo/Wiener 24:895). And: "In philosophy there is no belief" (V-Lo/Blomberg 24:30). I think there is plainly a sense of "philosophy" in which Kreines is right about this. But even if he is, it remains possible, even in a strictly philosophical context, to assert that theoretical reason commits us (on "subjectively sufficient" grounds) to the proposition that every finite, conditioned thing is ultimately grounded in something unconditioned. For *this claim* about theoretical reason is no mere belief. So ultimately, if Kreines is right about this point, it does not affect the basic line of argument I will be presenting here.

various characterizations of reason that Kant provides. We have seen that it follows from Kant's basic conception of cognition that the activity of *any* cognitive faculty, be it theoretical *or* practical, can be characterized in three interrelated ways. These three ways of conceiving of any such faculty can be thought of as falling out of the idea of cognition as requiring a *consciousness* of a (i) *representation* in the subject that is (ii) *appropriately related* to (iii) some *object or objects*.[5] Since cognition involves these three elements, any cognitive capacity can also be characterized (at least in part) in terms of what it aims to achieve with respect to each of them. For example, since all cognition involves conscious representations in the subject, the activity of any cognitive faculty can be described (at least in part) in terms of what that faculty tries to accomplish with respect to those *representations* simply as considered as such—that is, in terms of their *internal* or "merely logical" relations to one another. But, since all cognition also makes us conscious of an object (either as something that is or that ought to be), the activity of any cognitive faculty can also be described in terms of the nature of its *proper object(s)* and their relations. And since cognition requires a consciousness of a certain sort of relationship between the subject's representations and their objects, any such faculty can be described in terms of the *relation between the subject and these objects* that obtains when this faculty functions properly.

Given this basic framework for thinking about the activity of *any* cognitive faculty, we can begin to organize Kant's various characterizations of reason by placing them under these three general headings:

(i) We might characterize reason formally—that is, in terms of the **rational subject** and their internal activities and representations—e.g. in terms of a *merely logical* conception of cognition from principles—or, in other words, in terms of the *inferential* relations between more general representations and the more particular representations which follow from them.

(ii) We might characterize reason materially—that is, in terms of the **proper objects of reason**—e.g. in terms of the three *ideas of reason* (God, the self, and the world-whole) as characterizations of the ideal objects of theoretical comprehension or of the *highest good* as a system that relates together both our practical ends *and* these three ideas. Thus, as we will see, it is the highest good which provides us with our fullest grasp of the ideal object of theoretical and practical comprehension *together*.

---

[5] Compare (Engstrom 2009; Tolley 2017b). My discussion here is closest to Tolley's, since it seems to me to track more closely Kant's distinctions between (i) features of cognition *in general* and (ii) features that are distinctive of the sort of systematic cognition or comprehension that is the proper province of reason *in particular*. Nonetheless, since all parties (I think) agree that all these forms of cognition form a unified system under reason's governance, I would not want to make too much of this point.

(iii) Finally, we might characterize reason as striving towards a union of this form and this matter—that is, in terms of the **relationship** it seeks between the subject and these objects—e.g. in terms of the idea of reason as the capacity for *real* (theoretical and practical) cognition from principles or comprehension or, as we will discuss in Chapter 7, as the capacity for autonomous action in the world.

b. The Logical Maxim

With this in mind, let's turn now to this chapter's main topic: the different ways that Kant characterizes the fundamental principle that governs the activity of reason in theoretical use. To do so, I want to begin with the first of the three headings distinguished above—that is, with characterizations of theoretical reason's activity that focus on what that activity aims to accomplish with respect to the subject's *representations* considered as such or "merely logically". Not surprisingly, given the discussion of the last chapter, the fundamental expression of this aspect of reason's activity in the theoretical sphere is described by Kant as follows:

> Second, *reason in its logical use seeks the universal condition of its judgment (its conclusion)*, syllogism is nothing but a judgment mediated by the subsumption of its condition under a universal rule (the major premise). Now since this rule is once again exposed to this same attempt of reason, and the condition of its condition thereby has to sought (by means of a prosyllogism) as far as we may, we can see very well that *the proper principle of reason in general (in its logical use) is to find the unconditioned for conditioned cognitions of the understanding, with which its unity will be completed.* (A307/B364, my emphasis)

Kant immediately goes on to describe this final principle as theoretical reason's "logical maxim". This fits well with the framework just laid out. In particular, while this "logical maxim" does express reason's demand for *systematic unity* among our theoretical cognitions or representations, it does so in a manner that focuses, not on the objects of these representations, nor on the relationship between these objects and the subject, but rather on these representations considered "merely logically"—that is, in abstraction from those objects. In this way, it expresses reason's demand for systematicity in a "merely logical" form, as if this demand were merely a demand for a certain sort of logical structure among our representations, and not a demand for systematic comprehension of their objects. Thus, while the logical maxim does demand that we search for the "unconditioned for conditioned cognitions of the understanding", it characterizes this search for the "unconditioned" as if it related merely to the system of *logical conditioning* relations between our representations, as opposed to relating to our grasp of the *real conditioning* relations that obtain between those representations' objects.

Nonetheless, despite this "merely logical" character, it is important to stress that the logical maxim is *already* a very demanding principle for Kant. For example, this maxim is not limited to the following:

Maxim of Conditional Thought$_{Seek}$:   Seek *the condition* for every conditioned cognition of the understanding.

But extends to include:

Logical Maxim$_{Seek}$:   Seek *the unconditioned* for every conditioned cognition of the understanding *with which reason's unity will be completed*.

That is, the logical maxim demands, not just that we seek the "logical condition" for any "conditioned cognition of the understanding", but also that we seek to *complete* this process in the manner "with which its [reason's] unity will be completed". In this way, even taken on its own, the logical maxim goes well beyond the *understanding's* interest in cognition of objects to include (in a merely logical form) the distinctive interest of *reason* in systematic unity in cognition.

Indeed, at least in its final formulation, the logical maxim is even stronger than this. For in this formulation it demands of reason not just that it *seek* the unconditioned, but also that it *find it*:

Logical Maxim$_{Find}$:   *Find* the *unconditioned* for every conditioned cognition of the understanding, *with which reason's unity will be completed*.

Kant's formulation of the "logical maxim", even considered on its own, thus raises quite forcefully the question of why Kant takes the "logical use" of reason to demand *so much*. In considering this, it is important to remember that, for Kant, reason, like any rational faculty, seeks to actualize itself through its own characteristic mode of activity. Thus, since theoretical reason's characteristic mode of activity involves cognizing things from more general principles, theoretical reason naturally seeks to form the sorts of representations that make this sort of "cognition from principles" possible. In virtue of seeking to actualize itself in its characteristic form of activity—namely, theoretical cognition from principles—theoretical reason thus naturally seeks to form ever more general representations from which our more particular theoretical cognitions may be derived.[6]

Moreover, this is true *even* if we restrict ourselves to a "merely logical" perspective on reason, where reason is conceived of as a faculty that merely aims at a certain sort of inferential structure among our representations. Even in its logical use, reason is

---

[6] This is connected with the fact that reason is committed to "the absolute totality of synthesis **on the side of conditions**", but *not* "**from the side of the conditioned**" (A336/B393). For it is by ascending *up* the series of conditions that reason can locate the sort of ever more basic principles that its full self-actualization requires.

driven by its nature to seek out the sort of systematic unity in cognition that is associated with its full actualization as the capacity for cognition from principles. Thus, not only does reason seek to find the condition for every conditioned cognition, it also continues to seek for further conditions of this sort until it reaches a cognition that does not call for further conditions in this sense. In this way, simply through striving to actualize itself as the inferential faculty it is, theoretical reason necessarily seeks the unconditioned for every conditioned cognition in (at least) the minimal (and negative) sense of "unconditioned", on which an unconditioned cognition *just is* a cognition that does not demand that reason continue searching for further conditions in this way. As a result, reason will only be fully satisfied in its search for such conditions once it locates something that is not subject to further conditions of this sort. Thus, there is a sense in which the ultimate end of reason, even in its logical use, just is to find the unconditioned for every conditioned cognition.[7]

c. The Supreme Principle of Reason in Its Theoretical Use

As we have just noted, all this is true of theoretical reason, even if we restrict ourselves to its merely logical use. But Kant's ultimate concern in the Transcendental Dialectic does not lie with the merely logical use of reason. Rather, his focus is on the possibility that reason might have a *real use* that goes beyond this—that is, on the idea of reason as a faculty that allows us to grasp, not merely the *logical conditions of our representations*, but also the *real conditions of their objects*. This transition from the "logical use" of theoretical reason to its potential "real use" occurs when Kant moves from the "logical maxim" to what he calls the "supreme principle" of reason in its theoretical use:

> But this logical maxim cannot become a principle of **pure reason** unless *we assume that when the conditioned is given, then so is the whole series of conditions subordinated one to the other, which is itself unconditioned, also given (i.e. contained in the object and its connection).* (A307–8/B364, my emphasis)

Unlike the "logical maxim", this "supreme principle" focuses on what we must assume about the *objects* of ideal theoretical comprehension. That is, it tells us, not merely to establish certain logical relations between our representations, but also to assume that the objects of these representations stand in certain real explanatory relations to one another—certain "real conditioning" relations, that is.[8]

---

[7] As argued by (Willaschek 2018, Benzenberg forthcoming a) this basic line of thought can also be extended to explain why Kant claims in the Appendix to the Dialectic that theoretical reason seeks a particular sort of systematic unity with respect to natural laws. For example, as Benzenberg argues, these two forms of systematicity converge at the limit.

[8] For the importance of "real conditioning" here, see (Watkins 2005; Smit 2009; Kreines 2015; Watkins 2019; Stratmann forthcoming among others. Our grasp of such relations is, of course,

In this way, the "supreme principle" provides us with an "object-directed" counterpart of the logical maxim by characterizing the sort of object that *would* satisfy reason's needs: the proper object of theoretical reason in general. In a moment, we will discuss one important respect in which this principle is ambiguous for Kant. But there is another important ambiguity in the supreme principle that is worth discussing first. The supreme principle is often read as meaning something like the following:

Single Sequence Supreme: When some X conditioned in respect R is given, then the whole series of R-conditions involving X, which is itself unconditioned, also is given.

On this reading, the supreme principle is focused on a *particular sequence* of conditioning relations and demands of *any such sequence* that, if any part of it is given, so too is *that whole sequence*. As we will see, when read in this way, there is little doubt that Kant would reject this principle, at least in an unrestricted form. For example, as we will discuss below, Kant argues in the Antinomies that there are sequences of conditioning relations among appearances that are *indefinitely extendable*, without the whole infinite sequence of conditions thereby existing at any moment. Such sequences provide a clear counterexample to Single Sequence Supreme, at least as applied to sequences of conditions within the worlds of appearances.[9]

But, in fact, I don't think it is Single Sequence Supreme which we should take to be the "supreme principle" of reason in its theoretical use, at least in the most basic form this principle can take. One way of seeing this is to note that Single Sequence Supreme is *not* the version of the supreme principle that corresponds to the full logical maxim as interpretated above. After all, what the logical maxim demands of us is that we find the "unconditioned" for any "conditioned cognition of the understanding" in the manner that will "complete reason's unity". In many cases,

---

provided by the three relational categories, and the forms of syllogistic inference they license. Thus, the "supreme principle" demands that we "assume" the existence of the unconditioned in at least three basic senses of "conditioned", corresponding to these three basic forms of real conditioning. (See A321/B378–A324/B380.) That having been said, Kant is clear that reason will only be fully satisfied insofar as these three aspects of the unconditioned are themselves unified in something "absolutely unconditioned": "Now a transcendental concept of reason always goes to the absolute totality in the synthesis of conditions, and never ends except with the absolutely unconditioned, i.e. with what is unconditioned in every relation" (A326/B383). As we will see, there is a sense in which both theoretical and practical reason demand of us that we "assume" something absolutely unconditioned in this sense, but only practical reason (in the guise of its conception of the highest good) allows us to begin to determine what this absolutely unconditioned condition is like.

[9] For an excellent presentation of this point, see (Chaplin forthcoming). But note that Chaplin follows the literature in taking the true "supreme principle" to be (roughly) Single Sequence Supreme. As I will explain now, this seems to me a mistake, and because of it, I think she mischaracterizes Kant's ultimate attitude towards what I would regard as the genuine Supreme Principle in some respects.

doing this will require that we find the "whole sequence of conditions" in just the manner Single Sequence Supreme demands. But in other cases, like the indefinitely extendable sequences of conditions we encounter in appearances, it may require something else—namely, that we locate some further condition that grounds *this full sequence of conditions* in a manner that allows reason to "complete its unity" without (*per impossibile*) cognizing every element within the indefinitely extendable sequence in question.

To my knowledge, this point is neglected in most of the literature which, if it recognizes this issue, generally seeks to deal with it by restricting the supreme principle only to apply to things in themselves and not appearances. But that leaves the relevance of the supreme principle to appearances unexplained and so hardly seems a version of the "supreme principle" worthy of that name. Rather, to deal with this possibility, it is better, I want to suggest, to recognize that the version of the supreme principle that corresponds to the full "logical maxim" is not Single Sequence Supreme, but rather something more flexible—namely, something like the following:[10]

Supreme Principle: When some X conditioned in respect R is given, then either (i) the whole series of R-conditions involving X, which is itself unconditioned, is given or (ii) some other (non-R) condition(s) of X is given, which is sufficient to complete reason's unity.

It is *this* principle that I will generally have in mind when I speak of "the supreme principle". For it is this more abstract and flexible principle that best corresponds to the logical maxim's demand that, for any conditioned cognition, we find *something unconditioned* that will complete reason's search for systematic unity. And, on my reading, it is reason's demand for comprehension, and so for systematic unity, that should come first in our attempts to understand these principles. So, for instance, we need to understand the supreme principle in light of our understanding of comprehension, using the logical maxim as our guide. Doing so focuses our attention on the crucial question of what is required to "complete reason's unity" in the sense the logical maxim demands. And once we focus on this question, as we've just seen, what we arrive at as the "true supreme principle" is *not* Single Sequence Supreme, but rather what I call Supreme Principle. So it is Supreme Principle that will serve as my focus here.

That having been said, I don't want to make too much of the textual question of how exactly we should understand the referent of the "supreme principle" in this particular passage. Rather, what interests me here is the more philosophical question of which "object-directed" principle of theoretical reason corresponds best to the *full* logical maxim. And one might raise more philosophical objections

---

[10] For an even more radical view of the supreme principle, see Christopher Benzenberg's outstanding work in progress on these issues.

to my claim that it is not Single Sequence Supreme, but Supreme Principle that fills this role. For example, one might push back here by arguing that my Supreme Principle does not do sufficient justice to Kant's background commitment to what we might call "the separateness of conditioning relations".[11] For example, suppose that I'm trying to explain something *via* a search for its conditioning relations along a certain axis (a search for its R-conditions). Then one might think that it doesn't help with *that task* to locate other non-R-conditions that help to explain *other aspects* of the thing in question. If this is right, it would provide us with a principled philosophical reason to focus on Single Sequence Supreme and not my more flexible Supreme Principle in this context.

This is an important worry about my statement of the supreme principle. But note first that this is not really an objection to my version of Supreme Principle, so much as it is an argument that my Supreme Principle collapses into Single Sequence Supreme. For what we have here is, in effect, an argument that switching from one sort of conditioning relation to another will not really help us explain things in the manner that is required to "complete reason's unity" in the relevant sense. And if that is true, then my version of Supreme Principle's second disjunct will always be inert, and my version of the Supreme Principle will simply collapse into Single Sequence Supreme.

Of course, our objector is likely to feel that *this* is bad enough for my Supreme Principle. For isn't this sufficient to show that we should indeed stick with Single Sequence Supreme in this context? Not necessarily, for while there are many contexts in which switching from one sort of conditioning relation to another in this way will not help us "complete reason's unity" in the manner the Supreme Principle calls for, there are some special contexts in which such a switch is appropriate for Kant. In particular, as we will discuss below, it seems to me that such a switch is exactly what is called for in cases in which our inability to complete some sequence of conditions is *itself* grounded in the fact that all of these conditions are themselves *transcendentally ideal*. For, in this case, to *really* understand the nature of things that stand in these conditioning relations, we need to switch from the (endless) project of regressing along the sequence of such (ideal) relations, and instead understand how this *entire indefinitely extendable sequence* is grounded in something that is not ideal in this sense.[12]

We'll return to this issue below, but I hope I've said enough to motivate a focus on Supreme Principle for the moment.[13] Unfortunately, to understand Supreme Principle, we also need to remove a *further* ambiguity that infects *all* these versions of the supreme principle. For both Single Sequence Supreme and Supreme Principle are claims about when certain things are "given". And there are at

---

[11] Thanks to Rosalind Chaplin for pressing me on this issue and suggesting this way of framing this objection.
[12] To see this, just consider how God would approach the task of understanding such sequences.
[13] If one still believes that this principle collapses into Single Sequence Supreme, that's fine with me for the time being.

least two basic ways in which Kant speaks of something as "given" in his critical works.[14] First, Kant sometimes refers to something as "given" simply to indicate that the thing *exists* or to indicate that he is *positing* its bare existence. But he also often uses "given" in a different and more demanding sense, according to which an object is given only insofar as that object is given to us *as a determinate object of cognition*.[15] It is in this second sense of "given" that only intuition can "give" us objects of theoretical cognition *or* that the ideas of reason "have in fact no relation to any object that could be given congruent to them" (A336/B393).[16]

As is familiar, drawing such a distinction between two senses of "given" is crucial for understanding the structure of Kant's views.[17] For example, as noted above, for Kant the existence of appearances plainly commits us to the existence of some corresponding thing or things in themselves "that appears". So, in being "given" appearances as objects of cognition in the second, more demanding sense of "given", we are forced to posit the existence of things in themselves that ground those appearances, without these thereby being "given" to us as objects of cognition. Thus, being "given" appearances in the second sense of "given" requires being "given" things in themselves in the first, weaker sense. Crucially, this is true *however* we conceive of the metaphysical relationship between appearances and things in themselves. So, for example, none of these claims rely on a potentially problematic "two worlds" reading of transcendental idealism. Rather, no matter how we interpret it, the coherence of Kant's philosophical project requires that the limits on what can be "given" to us *as a determinate object of cognition* are not identical with the limits on what we should take as "given" in the weaker sense of merely *positing its existence*.

---

[14] The importance of ambiguity in this context is unsurprising, given Kant's insistence that the phrase the "Principle of Sufficient Reason" is itself ambiguous, although his focus is generally on the ambiguity of "sufficient" in this context, which I will return to below. (See NE 1:393.)

[15] (Willaschek 2018) notes this distinction in senses of "given", but does not make the use of it I do. (Grier 2001) could also be read as claiming that this principle requires disambiguation, but her understanding of this ambiguity is different than mine, which leads her to read Kant on this score in a weaker fashion than I will be doing here. Many of the differences between us on this score may be traced to her reliance on (Allison 2004)'s epistemic account of transcendental idealism. This leads her to introduce a series of complications into her reading that are only necessary if we adopt the Allisonian view. To my mind, this illustrates one of the many interpretative costs of a non-metaphysical reading like Allison's, although much of what I say here could be adapted to that framework. (Watkins forthcoming-a, forthcoming-b) also notes something like the ambiguity I focus on here and adds to this a further layer of ambiguity involving the sense in which the "totality" of "all" the conditions can be taken to follow from the existence of the conditioned. I agree that this is an important issue for Kant's discussion, but its significance seems to me downstream of the issues I am focusing on. (For example, the nature of the relevant "totality" of conditions seems to me to matter largely because of how that interacts with Kant's claims about what it would be to *cognize* the unconditioned.)

[16] To be clear, intuition on its own only "gives" us appearances as undetermined objects of cognition.

[17] See again (Smit 2000, 2009, 2010; Chignell 2007a, 2012, 2014; Tolley 2014, 2017b; Watkins and Willaschek 2017; Schafer 2022b; forthcoming a). My work on this topic is especially indebted to Smit, who (I understand) has been developing a version of this general line of thought for many years.

As I understand it, the gap between these two forms of "givenness" is explained by the special requirements that Kant places on cognition of an object noted above, and, in particular, by the requirement that genuine cognition of an object involve a grasp of this object as both *determinate* and *really possible*. For example, in cases like our general commitment to the existence of things in themselves, we fail to have genuine (theoretical) cognition of such things precisely because it is impossible for us to achieve a (theoretical) representation of them that meets both these constraints in the manner that cognition requires. But these details aren't essential here. Rather, what matters is that, when reading the "supreme principle", we need to disambiguate its reference to the whole series of conditions being "given", to respect these two readings.[18]

By doing so, we can see that Supreme Principle is ambiguous between at least two such principles:

Supreme Principle-1: When some X conditioned in respect R *exists* (or is posited), then either (i) the whole series of R-conditions involving X, which is itself unconditioned, *exists* (or is posited) or (ii) some other (non-R) conditions of X, which is itself sufficient to complete reason's unity, *exists* (or is posited).

Supreme Principle-2: When some X conditioned in respect R is *given as an object of cognition*, then either (i) the whole series of R-conditions involving X, which is itself unconditioned, is *given as an object of cognition* or (ii) some other (non-R) conditions of X, which is itself sufficient to complete reason's unity, is *given as an object of cognition*.

In reading these two principles, it is important to be clear that both involve "real" as opposed to merely "logical" claims in *some* sense. For they both make claims about the existence of the unconditioned.[19] So, on most standard readings of the Dialectic, both would be ruled out by Kant's critique of rationalist metaphysics. But, importantly, only the second of these principles claims we can achieve cognition of the unconditioned. So only the second involves a real use of reason *to determine an object of cognition*. This is crucial in the present context because I believe that Kant is best interpreted as arguing that we should *accept* (in some sense) the first of these principles as a legitimate requirement of theoretical reason, while *rejecting* the second as involving the sort of confusion that is characteristic of dogmatic, rationalist metaphysics.

---

[18] A similar ambiguity is present in passages like the one at A331–2/B388. There are also two further possible principles here, which slide from one sense of "given" to the other within a single principle. The possibility of such "mixed" principles is of considerable importance to Kant, since it foreshadows his diagnosis of the fallacies that arise in the context of the Paralogisms. For detailed discussion of what is fallacious about these inferences, see (Rosefeldt 2000; Proops 2010; Kitcher 2011; Longuensesse 2017).

[19] That having been said, an important question in the background of my discussion here is how such "bare acts of positing" are best understood. Indeed, one way to push my claims in the direction of the traditional reading would be to adopt a deflationary understanding of what this involves.

d. The Relationship between the Logical Maxim and the Supreme Principle

In other words, I believe that Kant holds that the acceptance of a version of the supreme principle—namely, a version of Supreme Principle-1—is a necessary condition on the "logical maxim" functioning as a principle of reason in its theoretical use, just as he seems to claim on the most natural reading of the passage that introduces the "supreme principle". Thus, as the framework above should already indicate, my view is that these two formulas—the "logical maxim" and the "supreme principle" (in the form of Supreme Principle-1)—are best regarded as two expressions of a single underlying principle.

More precisely, on my interpretation, these are both (at least in some form) legitimate expressions of the principle that is characteristic of the proper functioning of reason as a faculty, a principle that can be expressed either (i) as an imperative governing how we ought to extend our network of theoretical representations considered as such (the "logical maxim"), or (ii) as a claim about what we must assume about the objects of such cognitions, given reason's aims (the "supreme principle").[20] In this way, the "supreme principle" provides us with an "object-directed" counterpart of the logical maxim by characterizing the sort of object that *would* satisfy reason's needs—the proper object of theoretical reason in general.[21]

As already noted, the way in which Kant's text connects together the logical maxim and the supreme principle makes it quite natural to relate them in this way. But doing so is *very* controversial. For Kant's critique of the dialectical illusions thrown up by theoretical reason is often thought to rest precisely on the idea that we should accept the first of these principles (the "logical maxim"), while *rejecting* the second (the "supreme principle"), or (at most) accepting it *only* in a very weak and merely regulative or heuristic sense. But if the "supreme principle" is something like the "object-directed face" of one and the same principle that the "logical maxim" expresses in a "subject-directed" form, these two principles would seem to stand or fall together in a stronger sense than this.

For an example of the more traditional line of interpretation, consider Willaschek's excellent recent treatment of the transition from the "logical

---

[20] In this way, I agree with Grier when she writes that "Kant's view seems to be that" these two principles "express the very same demand of reason, viewed in different ways" (Grier 2001, 124). But Grier's Allisonian interpretation of *why* this is true is quite different from my own. Also compare (Mudd 2017)'s argument that this principle must be regarded as having categorical normativity for theoretical reason, as opposed to merely hypothetical normativity. On this, I fundamentally agree, but what Mudd does not discuss are the implications the categorical status of the normative version of this principle has for how a fully rational subject will represent the world.

[21] Compare here (Kraus 2020)'s recent treatment of such ideas as marking out "contexts of intelligibility in which we can make sense of certain kinds of cognition", although Kraus's treatment of this is more modest than the reading I am giving here (Kraus 2020, 216).

maxim" to the "supreme principle".[22] Modulo some differences of emphasis, I am sympathetic to much of what Willaschek has to say about this issue. But I disagree with him on the crucial question of what Kant means when he claims that, in order for reason to function in accordance with the "logical maxim", we must also "assume" that things are as the "supreme principle" claims they are—and, in particular, that the unconditioned exists. For Willaschek, the sense in which the existence of the "unconditioned" is properly "assumed" in this context is ultimately very weak: on his interpretation, we should *only* assume that the unconditioned exists "problematically". Thus, for Willaschek, we should only accept the "supreme principle" insofar as we make use of it as a "heuristic device" within a purely "hypothetical use of reason", where this does not require any degree of assent to the existence of the unconditioned outside of such hypothetical contexts (Willaschek 2018, 118).

In this, Willaschek is (again) aligned with the general interpretative consensus. Indeed, many interpreters would go further than Willaschek on this score. For example, in his excellent recent book on the Transcendental Dialectic, Proops challenges the idea that there is *any* legitimate transition from the logical maxim to the supreme principle to be found in these passages. Rather, for Proops, the temptation to move from the logical maxim to the supreme principle is simply a "mistake" based on a "misunderstanding" of the logical maxim. So, for instance, for Proops, "the mistake of taking P [the logical maxim] for D [the supreme principle] is . . . one central *instance* of the error that can arise when we succumb to [transcendental] illusion . . . [a mistake in which] we mistake the prescription, P for the putative statement of fact, D. In Kant's jargon, we mistake a 'regulative' for a 'constitutive' principle" (Proops 2021a, 47).

In making these claims, Proops points to the fact that Kant concludes the section under discussion (the Introduction to the Transcendental Dialectic) as follows:

> But whether the principle that the series of conditions (in the synthesis of appearances, or even in the thinking of things in general) reaches to the unconditioned, has objective correctness or not; what consequences flow from it for the empirical use of the understanding, or whether it rather yields no such objectively valid propositions of it at all, but is only a logical prescription in the ascent to ever higher conditions to approach completeness in them and thus to bring the highest possible unity of reason in our cognition; whether, I say, this need of reason has, through a misunderstanding, been taken for a transcendental principle of reason, which overhastily postulates such an unlimited completeness in the objects themselves; but in this case what other kinds of misinterpretations and delusions may have crept into the inferences of reason whose major premise

---

[22] (Willaschek 2018). It is important to stress here that my understanding of the structure of this transition is close to Willaschek's in many ways. Where we differ is with respect to the question whether this transition provides us with (subjectively) sufficient grounds for belief in the unconditioned. These differences notwithstanding, Willaschek's discussion, like that of (Grier 2001), is very helpful.

is taken from pure reason and ascends from experience to its conditions: All this will be our concern in the transcendental dialectic.... (A308–9/B365–6)

Here again Proops is not far from the interpretative consensus. For although it is phrased as a series of questions to be investigated, this passage is often read as providing a summary of Kant's conclusions concerning the relationship between the logical maxim and the supreme principle. And taken in that spirit, it does suggest a reading on which all versions of the "supreme principle" should be rejected as "overhastily postulating" something that is *really* only a product of "misinterpretation" or "delusion".

Contrary to such a reading, though, I think it is better to take this passage (like the transition from the logical maxim to the supreme principle itself) at face value. To do so involves reading this passage not as an oblique summary of Kant's initial conclusions concerning the supreme principle, but rather as a preview of the investigations to come. Indeed, the list of different possibilities Kant provides here is significant, I think, because there is a sense in which Kant wants to defend *all* the alternatives on offer in it. For example, as we will see, Kant surely does want to deny that the supreme principle has "objective validity" with respect to the objects of human theoretical cognition—namely, with respect to appearances. But this does not mean that he thereby means to deny that there is *a version* of the supreme principle that remains legitimate for us in some sense, although we cannot make use of it as a source of theoretical cognition from principles in the manner we might have hoped. In the context of Proops's interpretation, it is worth stressing that there is a sense in which Proops himself *ultimately* agrees with this point. After all, Proops ultimately agrees that theoretical reason licenses a form of "doctrinal belief" in the existence of the unconditioned. And this, as already noted, is sufficient to legitimate a version of the supreme principle as characterized above. Thus, Proops's interpretation forces him into the position of reading Kant as (i) rejecting any move from the logical maxim to the supreme principle as illegitimate, while also (ii) ultimately accepting the legitimacy of doctrinal belief in the unconditioned, and so a version of something like the supreme principle.

To read Kant in this way would, I think, involve treating the Transcendental Dialectic as involving a rather dramatic bait and switch. And, as noted already, such a reading also fits poorly with how Kant introduces the supreme principle in the passages under consideration. After all, in doing so, Kant explicitly claims that the "logical maxim" can only *become* a "principle of pure reason" if "we assume" that the whole series of conditions, and so the unconditioned, is in some sense "given".[23] And he stresses that the "logical maxim" is "the proper principle of reason in general (in its logical use)". Thus, putting these two points together,

---

[23] Compare Kant's insistence that "the possibility of something conditioned presupposes the totality of its conditions" (A337/B394). See also: "The logical principle of genera therefore presupposes a transcendental one if it is to be applied to nature (by which I here understand only objects that are given to us)" (A654/B682).

the most straightforward reading of this passage is that acceptance of the "logical maxim" (as the *proper principle* of theoretical reason in general in its logical use) requires acceptance of the existence of the unconditioned in accordance with the "supreme principle".[24] In this way, taken at face value, this passage seems to claim that if theoretical reason draws the inferences the logical maxim commands of it, this commits reason to the assumption that whenever something conditioned is given, its condition is given, and so on to the unconditioned, which is required to complete reason's unity. *And* Kant also seems to claim that reason functions *properly* when we do just this. Moreover, Kant reiterates this point in the Appendix to the Dialectic, when he writes that "it cannot even be seen how there could be a logical principle of rational unity among rules unless a transcendental principle is presupposed, through which a systematic unity, as pertaining to the object itself, is assumed *a priori* as necessary" (A650–1/B678–9). In this way, it certainly *seems* as though Kant is claiming that we should accept that reality is ultimately as the "supreme principle" says it is, and that doing so is a necessary condition on reason's search for systematic unity in even a logical sense.[25]

If this is right, then the move from the logical maxim to the supreme principle is not itself the "mistake" that Proops suggests it is.[26] Rather, as will become clear, the real mistake here would be to treat *either* the "logical maxim" *or* the "supreme principle" as principles *for theoretical cognition*—that is, as principles that provide us with real *cognition of the unconditioned*. It is this, on my reading, that is the source of what Kant calls "transcendental illusion". For, in keeping with Kant's use of "transcendental", "transcendental illusion" is first and foremost an illusion, not about *what exists*, but rather about our ability to achieve a priori cognition of those objects.[27] It is this sort of illusion about the scope and sources of our capacity for a priori cognition that, on my reading, is the focus of the Transcendental Dialectic. But, as I read Kant, the diagnosis of this illusion does not mean that the "logical maxim" should not be treated as a logical principle for reason's theoretical use.

---

[24] Again compare (Grier 2001). See also (Kraus 2020)'s recent critique of "fictional" readings of the role of transcendental ideas in this context. But note that Kraus's positive interpretation of the role of the ideas as involving "regulative principles that direct the acts of the understanding towards attaining a systematic unity of all cognitions within this domain" is considerably weaker than my reading here. Nonetheless, as my focus on comprehension should make clear, I'm very sympathetic to Kraus's general thought that these ideas mark out "contexts of intelligibility in which we can make sense of certain kinds of cognition" (Kraus 2020, 216). This seems to me exactly right, but (as we are discussing) it seems to me that Kant takes the commitments that follow from this to be somewhat more robust than Kraus suggests.

[25] On my reading, then, the transition from the logical maxim to the supreme principle should be understood as playing the role in the Transcendental Dialectic that the Metaphysical Deduction plays in Kant's account of the categories of the understanding. Like that discussion, the Introduction to the Transcendental Dialectic is meant to establish an abstract equivalence between certain forms of judgment/inference and certain concepts/ideas. And in both cases, Kant takes this equivalence to be sufficient to legitimate these concepts/ideas *insofar* as we are merely considering their role in thought, and not considering them as potential sources of cognition. Thus, in both cases, the real difficulties arise only when we attempt to use these concepts/ideas to cognize objects.

[26] Here I also take issue with (Neiman 1994).

[27] See, for example, "I call all cognition transcendental that is occupied not so much with objects but rather with our a priori concepts of objects in general." (A11–12)

Nor does it mean that it is the transition from the "logical maxim" to the "supreme principle" that is the problem here. Rather, as we will see, this transition on its own is often unproblematic, so long as we understand the "supreme principle" correctly.

e. Two Arguments from the Logical Maxim to the Supreme Principle

On my reading, Kant's account of the relationship between the "logical maxim" and the "supreme principle" rests on there being a tight connection between the rationality of methods of inference and the rationality of certain basic beliefs about the objects these inferences are concerned with, albeit only on grounds that are "subjectively" as opposed to "objectively sufficient". But why would Kant believe that these two principles are so tightly linked in this way?[28] Kant's thought seems to be that it would only make sense for theoretical reason to engage in the inferential activity that the logical maxim prescribes, and to do so *with the aim* of achieving cognition from principles through that activity, insofar as it (at least implicitly) takes reality to have a certain structure—namely, the sort of structure required in order for the inferential activity in question to be a means of achieving reason's ends in engaging in it.[29] In this way, in making this move, Kant is (in effect) articulating a version of Hume's famous claim that causal inference is only rational insofar as we "proceed on the principle" that nature is uniform. For the same basic point is at issue here—namely, that the rationality of a certain pattern of inference, at least as a potential source of cognition, stands or falls together with certain assumptions about the nature of reality—i.e. that reality has whatever structure is required to make this pattern of inference (at least) a potential source of cognition of objects.[30]

We can now make this general thought, as applied to the logical maxim, more precise in two ways. First, we can consider what must be true if reasoning in

---

[28] Thanks to Nicholas Stang, Colin McLear, and Dai Heide for very helpful discussion of this point.

[29] See, for example, the argument at A331–2/B388, which presents acceptance of the "unconditioned" as a necessary condition on the possibility of cognition from a priori principles of the sort reason seeks. As we will discuss below, the role of the supreme principle in this regard is analogous to the role that the FH plays within Kant's practical philosophy.

[30] This is a *sort* of transcendental argument, albeit a fairly modest sort. For more on the role of such arguments in Kant, see (Schafer forthcoming b). For a similar line of thought, see (Amijee 2021). (Watkins forthcoming-a) criticizes attempts to derive the "supreme principle" from the "logical maxim", but he does not consider transcendental arguments like this one, which focus on what theoretical reason (as the cognitive faculty it is) must assume if it is to be governed by the "logical maxim". Much as is true below in the case of the relationship between the FUL and the FH, it seems to me that the relationship between the "logical maxim" and the "supreme principle" only becomes clear once we consider them as principles of a cognitive faculty. I agree with Watkins that we cannot simply derive one principle from the other directly; rather, the connection between them must involve the nature of reason and reason's aims. We'll return to this below with respect to the relationship between the FUL and the FH.

accordance with the logical maxim is to be a source of *theoretical cognition from principles*, and not just an increasingly tidy system of representations. There are, for Kant, three basic ways this could be true of some conditioned cognition X of an object Y:

(1) X represents some object Y that is part of a *finite sequence of conditions* which terminates in a first, unconditioned element.
(2) X represents some object Y that is part of an *infinite sequence of conditions* that itself exists in full (and which is thereby itself unconditioned along the relevant dimension).
(3) X represents some object Y that is part of an *indefinitely extendable sequence of conditions*, without the whole sequence of conditions thereby existing or being posited.

Of these three options, (1) and (2) deliver the truth of the supreme principle with respect to this sequence. On the other hand, as mentioned above, (3) does not. But (3) can, for Kant, *only* be true of appearances or other *transcendentally ideal* things. And such appearances must themselves be grounded (directly or indirectly) in something that is not so ideal, something of which (1) or (2) will be true. That is, for Kant, everything can't be "ideal" in this sense "all the way down". So, it cannot be the case that reality consists in an indefinitely extendable sequence of indefinitely extendable sequences of... and so on to infinity.[31]

Thus, there are only two basic ways in which reasoning in accordance with the logical maxim can be a potential source of theoretical cognition from principles for Kant:

(1) Either the sequence in question is *limited to appearances*, in which case the "supreme principle" will not hold, but only because we are not dealing with the fundamental level of reality.
(2) Or the sequence in question is *not limited to appearances*, in which case, the "supreme principle" does hold, although we may not know anything about how or why it does.

Thus, while the supreme principle (Supreme Principle-1) does fail to hold of many sequences of conditions insofar as these are limited to appearances, if we consider things in a manner that abstracts away from the conditions that sensibility places upon our representations of things, and so consider conditions that apply to both appearances and things in themselves, we can "say directly", albeit

---

[31] Compare again (Stratmann forthcoming), which I only become aware of too late in the composition of this text to respond to in detail. Stratmann in some ways takes this line of thought further than even I would, but the fundamental idea behind our reconstructions of this first argument for the supreme principle is, I believe, the same.

on "subjectively sufficient grounds", that those things must be as the supreme principle (Supreme Principle-1) claims.[32]

Strikingly, this is just what Kant claims in passages like the following:[33]

> *If one represents everything through mere pure concepts of the understanding, without the conditions of sensible intuition, then one can say directly that for a given conditioned the whole series of conditions subordinated one to another is given; for the former is given only through the latter.* But with appearances a special limitation is encountered in the way conditions are given, namely through the successive synthesis of the manifold of intuition, which is supposed to be complete in the regress. Now whether this completeness is sensibly possible is still a problem. (A417/B444, my emphasis)

I believe that such passages show that even theoretical reason is committed to the existence of the unconditioned in some sense. *But* they leave the nature of this commitment open to considerable debate. To consider this issue, let's first turn to another way of approaching the transition from the logical maxim to the supreme principle. If the logical maxim (in full form) is a valid principle of theoretical reason in general, then it instructs theoretical reason to *find the unconditioned* for every conditioned cognition of the understanding that will allow it to "complete reason's unity". But, of course, it is only possible to find something *if it exists*. Thus, it is only possible for theoretical reason to do what the logical maxim demands if the unconditioned for every conditioned cognition of the understanding exists in whatever manner is required to "complete reason's unity". Accordingly, the logical maxim can be valid for theoretical reason in general *only if* theoretical reason is also entitled to treat reality as having the structure the supreme principle claims it does.[34] For otherwise, by imposing such goals upon us, reason would in some sense be in contradiction with itself.

More precisely, we can argue here as follows:[35]

(1) If the logical maxim is a valid principle of theoretical reason in general, then theoretical reason in general ought to find the unconditioned for every conditioned cognition of the understanding in the manner required to "complete reason's unity".

---

[32] (Jauernig 2021) argues that the supreme principle should be understood to be analytic of things in themselves. Whether or not we would go this far, this argument can be viewed as capturing the best line of thought at work in her argument for that claim.

[33] Compare the discussion in (Adams 1997; Ameriks 2000; Cleve 2003) in addition to those noted above.

[34] Once again, this indicates why it is Supreme Principle, and not Single Sequence Supreme, that should be our focus here.

[35] As I go on to explain, at least from a theoretical point of view, this is argument is supported by merely subjectively sufficient grounds for assent.

(2) But (as we have seen in Chapter 3) such an imperative can be valid of some capacity only if that capacity is capable of doing what the imperative demands of it. Indeed, an imperative applies to some capacity just in case it characterizes what this capacity would do if it, and one's other rational faculties, functioned properly.
(3) Thus, if the logical maxim is a valid principle of theoretical reason in general, then theoretical reason in general must be capable of finding the unconditioned for every conditioned cognition of the understanding in the manner required to "complete reason's unity".
(4) Theoretical reason in general is capable of finding the unconditioned for every conditioned cognition of the understanding in the manner required to "complete reason's unity" only if that unconditioned exists in that manner.
(5) Thus, if the logical maxim is a valid principle of theoretical reason in general, then the unconditioned for every conditioned cognition of the understanding exists in the manner required to "complete reason's unity".
(6) The logical maxim is a valid principle of theoretical reason in general.
(7) Thus, the unconditioned for every conditioned cognition of the understanding exists in the manner required to "complete reason's unity".[36]

Of course, as we just noted, this argument can apply only to series of conditions that are not limited to appearances. Thus, it can only be valid as an argument about theoretical reason *in general*, and not theoretical reason as limited to appearances. But nonetheless, Kant's view is that the logical maxim is a valid principle of theoretical reason in general. And considered in this light, the argument appears to be valid.

Indeed, it is just this sort of argument that Kant appeals to in the Appendix to Dialectic when he attempts to defend his claim that "it cannot even be seen how there could be a logical principle of rational unity among rules unless a transcendental principle is presupposed, through which a systematic unity, as pertaining to the object itself, is assumed *a priori* as necessary" (A650–1/B678–9). There he writes:

> For by warrant can reason in its logical use claim to treat the manifoldness of the powers which nature gives to our cognition as merely a concealed unity, and to derive them as far as it is able from some fundamental power, when reason is free to admit that it is just as possible that all powers are different in kind, and that its

---

[36] Doesn't this imply, not just that the unconditioned exists, but also that it would be possible (at least in principle) for reason to cognize it? After all, isn't that what truly "completing reason's unity" would require? Plausibly yes, at least for some conceivable form of reason. That is, reason is committed in some sense, not merely to the bare existence of this unconditioned, but to the possibility that some form of reason might be able to grasp or cognize the unconditioned in whatever sense "completing reason's unity" requires. But this would only be possible for reason of a very different sort than the reason we possess—so different, in fact, that it may be difficult for us to grasp what cognition for it would even look like. So, while all this is true, all human reason is in a position to do is to posit the bare existence of something that would fill this role, without in anyway cognizing it or its nature.

derivation of them from a systematic unity is not in conformity with nature? *For then reason would proceed directly contrary to its vocation, since it would set as its goal an idea that entirely contradicts the arrangement of nature*.... For the law of reason to seek unity is necessary, since without it we would have no reason, and without that, no coherent use of the understanding, and, lacking that, no sufficient mark of empirical truth; thus in regard to the latter we simply have to presuppose the systematic unity of nature as objectively valid and necessary.

(A651/B679, my emphasis)

For my purposes, the crucial line of this passage is Kant's appeal in it to the idea that reason cannot "proceed directly contrary to its vocation" and that, in particular, reason cannot "set as its goal" an idea that contradicts the "arrangement" it itself imposes upon nature. For if reason imposed such a goal upon us, it would effectively be in *contradiction with itself*. And Kant takes the nature of our rational powers to be free of this sort of irreparable self-contradiction. Rather, as he says, "Everything grounded in the nature of our powers must be purposive and consistent with their correct use, if only we can guard against a certain misunderstanding and find out their proper direction" (A642–3/B670–1).

Once again, it is important to stress that this is an argument that concerns the logical maxim considered as "the proper principle of reason *in general*". What is at issue here is not whether it is possible for our specifically human form of theoretical reason to find the unconditioned in the manner the logical maxim demands, but rather whether *any* form of theoretical reason *whatsoever* would be capable of this. For this reason, the various specific limitations that apply to the human form of theoretical reason *in particular* are not relevant to the argument we are considering. My claim here is that the logical maxim can be the proper principle of reason *in general* only insofar as it is not simply *in principle* impossible for reason *in general* to accomplish this task. For, if this is right, then theoretical reason is indeed committed to a version of the supreme principle, namely, Supreme Principle-1. After all, as we have just seen, it is only possible to achieve theoretical reason's cognitive aims through reasoning in accordance with the logical maxim, if reality is as the supreme principle claims it is. Thus, if theoretical reason in general is entitled to reason in accordance with the logical maxim, it must also be entitled to believe that reality is as the supreme principle claims. For otherwise theoretical reason would demand of itself that it do something that it was impossible for it to accomplish, *even* if we remove all the limitations that our finite human capacities places on our form of reason. And this fact about reason in general is something that even reason in its limited human form is capable of recognizing. Thus, while human reason can never "find" the unconditioned in the manner that would truly "complete reason's unity", it is entitled to believe that that unconditioned "something" exists in a fashion that would make this possible for reason, at least in general and in principle.

f. The Status of the Supreme Principle and the Critique of Metaphysics

In this way, we can establish a sort of equivalence between the logical maxim and the supreme principle as principles of theoretical reason in general. But this equivalence, like that between the various formulas of the moral law we'll discuss in the next chapter, runs through the idea of these principles *as principles of a certain sort of cognitive faculty with certain cognitive aims*. Thus, we should not expect that the relationship between these principles will be at all obvious to us upon an inspection of them in isolation from Kant's conception of the nature of such a capacity. Still, given all this, why is such a reading of "supreme principle" not more widespread? The obvious reason is that such an interpretation is generally thought to be incompatible with Kant's diagnosis of the illusions cast up by the dialectical use of reason in traditional metaphysics. For example, in his recent discussion of these issues, Guyer writes:

> Kant rejected all such uses of the principle [of sufficient reason] in what he called "speculative" metaphysics as outstripping the limits of our sensibility and thus the possibility of confirmation, and confined the use of the principle in theoretical philosophy to causal explanation within the limits of experience.
>
> (Guyer 2019, 34)

As Guyer suggests, it is generally thought that Kant's critique of dogmatic metaphysics requires him to distance himself more fully than I have been suggesting from the picture of reality the "supreme principle" paints. Thus, to defend the "naïve" reading of the principle we have just outlined, we need to explain why this reading is compatible with the *negative* aims of the Transcendental Dialectic.

This is no trivial task. For, as has long been recognized, the "supreme principle" expresses *one* central dimension of what is commonly called the Principle of Sufficient Reason (PSR).[37] In saying this, we should acknowledge that Kant most often uses the label "principle of sufficient reason" to refer to the causal principle defended in the Second Analogy, a principle that is, of course, only valid of appearances. (A201/B246, A217/B264-5, A782-3/B810-11) And this is no accident, for there are important differences between the "supreme principle" and the version of the PSR we find in (say) Leibniz or Wolff. For example, for Kant, the supreme principle is plainly synthetic in character and so irreducible to conceptual containment relations.[38] Thus, as Proops has stressed to me, if we

---

[37] For recent discussion of this connection, see (Cicovacki 2006; Kreines 2008, 2009; Boehm2014; Anderson 2015; Nisenbaum 2018; Willaschek 2018; Proops 2021a; Chaplin forthcoming). To my knowledge, the first to point out this connection in the recent literature was Cicovacki. But the connection is obvious enough that I'm sure it has been noted by others.

[38] See (Anderson 2015).

understand the PSR to demand that we be able to provide a sufficient reason-why for any fact, the supreme principle is considerably broader and more abstract than the PSR. For while there is plainly a connection between conditioning relations and reasons-why, it is hardly true that every instance of a conditioning relation in Kant's sense is a reason why something is true. That having been said, I think it would be a mistake to take the PSR to be concerned only with the provision of *propositional reasons-why* in this sense. Rather, the most basic version of the PSR should be seen as a principle that governs all the ways in which one thing can contribute to the *intelligibility* or *comprehensibility* of another. And when the PSR is understood in this way, it is easier to see the "supreme principle" as a highly abstract version of the PSR. For all the Kantian conditioning relations do, in one way or another, seem to characterize ways in which one thing can help us to understand something else. In this sense, all these conditioning relations contribute to the sort of "comprehension" (*Begreifen*) that reason seeks.

As such, it would perhaps better to think of the supreme principle as capturing a more general version of the PSR—one that we might call the "Principle of Sufficient Condition", but the basic connection between the supreme principle and the PSR seems to me to remain intact here. More worrisome, to my mind, is the fact that Kant follows Crusius in rejecting Leibniz's account of both human and divine freedom as committing Leibniz to an unacceptable form of necessaritarianism.[39] Kant's positive account of freedom thus requires him to reconceive the sense in which the "supreme principle" commits us to the existence of the unconditioned, so that this does not involve such "Spinozistic" commitments. How to accomplish this is something that Kant struggles with throughout the development of his philosophical system. But as Hogan has argued, it is very plausible that part of Kant's answer to this question involves a rejection of the claim that everything that exists must have necessitating grounds that fully determine its state. Thus, it seems that Kant's conception of freedom requires that there be "unconditioned" things whose states are not determined by necessitating grounds in this sense. Thus, as Chaplin has recently argued, if we take "sufficient reasons" to be "necessitating grounds" of this sort (as Kant often does), Kant is in fact committed to *rejecting* the claim that everything has a "sufficient reason" *in this sense*.[40] Rather, Kant's view seems to be that something can be genuinely unconditioned just in case it lacks further necessitating grounds. So, as Chaplin shows, the supreme principle's demand that we posit the

---

[39] See (Hogan 2009, 2013). Kant also follows Crusius in rejecting the label "the Principle of Sufficient Reason", on the grounds that this phrase is "ambiguous" (BDG 1:393). For more on this issue, see the discussion in (Franks 2005; Proops 2014; Lu-Adler forthcoming)—although these authors tend to attribute to Kant a more negative view of the "supreme principle" than I do here.

[40] In particular, this follows from these claims, plus Kant's commitment to the claim that real grounding relations between things must be irreflexive. As a result, Kant rejects the idea that something could be a ground of itself in the sense that one might associate with Spinoza. See the excellent discussion of (Chaplin forthcoming).

"unconditioned" actually conflicts (for Kant) with the demand that everything have a "sufficient reason" in the sense of "necessitating ground".

As Chaplin shows very nicely, this means that we should *not* associate the supreme principle with the "Principle of Sufficient Reason" if the latter principle is understood to demand the existence of necessitating grounds for contingent things. But this does not mean that there is no connection between the supreme principle and the PSR. After all, one of Kant's most consistent claims about the PSR is that it is ambiguous, and that this is true because "the expression '*sufficient*' is ambiguous, for it is not immediately clear how much is sufficient" (NE 1:393). In the pre-critical works, Kant generally resolves this ambiguity in much the manner that Chaplin suggests, and this usage continues to color Kant's comments about the PSR throughout the critical period. But given our work above, we can see that there is another meaning of "sufficient" that is salient in this context—namely, the notion of *sufficiency with respect to reason's ends or purposes* that characterizes Kant's conception of comprehension (*Begreifen*).

To be clear, in saying this, I'm not saying that we should discard the notion of "sufficient grounds" on which such grounds are just necessitating grounds. For I agree with Chaplin that this notion continues to be important to Kant. I am only urging that we supplement this notion of sufficiency with another more critical notion thereof—namely, the notion of "sufficiency with respect to reason's purposes" that is relevant to Kant's conception of comprehension. This is crucial here, for if we use that notion of "sufficiency" to resolve the ambiguity in the phrase "sufficient reason", we will arrive at a version of the PSR that is much closer to the supreme principle's appeal to what is required in order to complete reason's unity, while also being fully compatible with Kant's anti-Spinozistic commitments concerning freedom.[41] For example, as we will see in the chapters to come, in the practical domain, our grasp of the unconditioned (e.g. the moral law) can often be "sufficient for practical reason's purposes" even though no *further* necessitating or explanatory ground for the unconditioned can be given. Indeed, as we will see in Chapter 7, even though Kant consistently rejects the idea of (say) reason as its own "sufficient ground" in the sense of "necessitating ground", his mature doctrine of the autonomy of reason allows us to see another (purpose-relative) sense in which practical reason can indeed be the "sufficient ground of itself"—a sense in which (say) practical reason can be a ground that is "sufficient" with respect to its own purposes.[42] Thus, once we turn to the notion of sufficiency

---

[41] The existence of multiple senses of "sufficiency" that are relevant in this context is also important for understanding the status of the highest good for Kant. See (Nisenbaum forthcoming) for more discussion of this.

[42] More precisely, as we will see, it is important in this context to distinguish at least three purpose-relative forms of sufficiency: (i) sufficiency relative to theoretical reason in general's purposes, (ii) sufficiency relative to practical reason's purposes, and (iii) sufficiency relative to theoretical reason's purposes in the finite human case, once these have been made more modest by the results of the critical philosophy. As we will see in Chapter 7, in many cases reason's self-consciousness is indeed sufficient

that is at work in Kant's conception of comprehension, we can see why Chaplin's arguments are compatible with the claim that Kant *in fact* accepts a version of the "principle of sufficient reason", albeit a version of this principle that understands "sufficiency" quite differently from how either Leibniz or Spinoza would have.[43]

Thus, while the "supreme principle" is not equivalent to Leibniz's or Wolff's *version* of the PSR, there is little doubt that the "supreme principle" expresses *one important aspect* of the PSR for Kant. Indeed, this is something that even those who attempt to pull these principles apart (like Chaplin) readily accept. So if my reading of the supreme principle is correct, then far from rejecting the PSR in the Transcendental Dialectic, Kant in fact begins his discussion there by arguing that *even from a theoretical point of view* reason requires us to accept that reality is as *one version* (albeit an abstract and indeterminate one) of the PSR claims it is. How, then, is this compatible with Kant's critique of rationalist metaphysics?

Once again, to understand why it is possible for Kant to make these claims, we need to begin by disambiguating the supreme principle's reference to the whole series of conditions being "given" as follows:

Supreme Principle-1: When some X conditioned in respect R *exists* (or is posited), then either (i) the whole series of R-conditions involving X, which is itself unconditioned, *exists* (or is posited) or (ii) some other (non-R) conditions of X, which is itself sufficient to complete reason's unity, *exists* (or is posited).

Supreme Principle-2: When some X conditioned in respect R is *given as an object of cognition*, then either (i) the whole series of R-conditions involving X, which is itself unconditioned, is *given as an object of cognition* or (ii) some other (non-R) conditions of X, which is itself sufficient to complete reason's unity, is *given as an object of cognition*.

As noted above, on most standard readings of the Dialectic, both principles would be ruled out by Kant's critique of rationalist metaphysics. But only the second claims we can achieve cognition of the unconditioned. So only the second involves a real use of reason *to determine an object of cognition*. Once again, this is crucial because I believe that Kant is best interpreted as arguing that we should *accept* the

---

for its own purposes by the second and third of these standards, even if it is not sufficient by the first. But, in cases in which we must choose between these standards, Kant is clear that it is practical reason's ends that must ultimately take "primacy", Although the need to choose between theoretical and practical reason's ends in this way is itself a symptom of the way in which human forms of reason are inevitably frustrated. So I agree that the very need to make this choice is something that still expresses a deeper sense in which human reason is frustrated with itself for Kant.

[43] Does this mean that we should also introduce a purpose-relative notion of the unconditioned here which corresponds to our purpose-relative conception of sufficiency. I can't see any clear reason why we shouldn't, although it is surely true that (as a textual matter) Kant generally uses "unconditioned" in a non-purpose-relative sense. (Thanks to Chaplin for pressing me on this point as well.)

first of these as a legitimate requirement of theoretical reason, while *rejecting* the second as involving the sort of confusion that is characteristic of dogmatic, rationalist metaphysics.

More precisely, I believe that Kant takes the considerations just laid out to be sufficient to license what he sometimes calls "doctrinal belief" *(Glaube)* in the bare existence of the unconditioned, even from a theoretical point of view.[44] On this reading, the rational status of Supreme Principle-1 is sufficient to provide us with theoretical grounds for assenting to the existence of the unconditioned. It is just that those grounds, while rationally mandatory for us, are nonetheless (in Kant's terminology) merely *subjectively* as opposed to *objectively* sufficient. In other words, the grounds for belief at issue here are grounded in the nature of reason itself and *its* needs, as opposed to the objects we are positing the existence of. Kant defines this sort of "doctrinal belief" as a "theoretical analogue" of the more familiar category of practical belief: "there is in merely theoretical judgments an **analogue** of practical judgments, where taking them to be true is aptly described by the word **belief**, and which we can call **doctrinal beliefs**" (A825/B854). This "theoretical analogue" of practical belief involves assent to the existence of something (the positing of something) because that assent (or existence) is necessary for theoretical reason to successfully engage in its essential activities. Thus, "doctrinal belief" involves an act of assent that is grounded the essential ends and needs of theoretical reason.

In this sense, the grounds for assent at issue would be similar in structure to those involved in Kant's more famous moral proof of God's existence. As in the case of the moral proof, these grounds have a means-ends structure that is recognizably practical in nature. But, at the same time, the ends or needs or interests that provide the basis for these grounds would be ends and needs and interests of *theoretical*, and not practical reason. This may explain why Kant seems uncertain about how to locate this sort of assent.[45] But the important thing for present purposes is not how we categorize it, but rather the general idea that theoretical reason's ends and interests are sufficient to ground a certain sort of commitment to the existence of the unconditioned and so to the truth of Supreme Principle-1.[46]

---

[44] Conversations with Nick Stang have been particularly important for my thoughts about this issue. For more on this sense of "belief", see (Chignell 2007a, 2007b, 2014). For Stang's work on these issues, see (Stang 2016, 2019). Similarly, (Proops 2021a) agrees that theoretically grounded doctrinal belief in (say) the unconditioned is possible for Kant on the basis of certain arguments, but he doesn't take the further step of claiming that this allows us to locate a defensible version of the "supreme principle" in Kant.

[45] For example, it is not difficult to find passages in Kant that seem to describe "belief" *(Glauben)* as a phenomenon that is only possible on practical as opposed to theoretical grounds, which would seem to rule the possibility of the sort of theoretically grounded "doctrinal belief" I am appealing to here (A823/B852, compare KpV 9:67).

[46] Once again, as Kreines has argued in his work in progress on these issues, this *may* mean that we should not make unqualified assertions concerning the *truth* of this claim within a strictly philosophical context. But even if this is so, it remains possible in a philosophical context to assert that theoretical

Once again, this is compatible with Kant's rejection of rationalist metaphysics precisely because this acceptance of Supreme Principle-1 does not commit us to the sort of *cognition* of the unconditioned the rationalist metaphysician claims to be able to attain through pure reason[47] (A329/B386). In other words, it is possible for Kant to claim that acceptance of Supreme Principle-1 is rationally required (on subjectively sufficient grounds), while also criticizing the pretensions of the rationalist metaphysician, precisely because Kant denies that acceptance of Supreme Principle-2 follows from the acceptance of Supreme Principle-1. Instead, Kant's view is that we should reject Supreme Principle-2, which he believes is tempting to us primarily because of a natural, but unlicensed, slide from Supreme Principle-1 to Supreme Principle-2.

We are tempted to move from Supreme Principle-1 to Supreme Principle-2 in this way, on Kant's account, not just because these principles are so similar, but also because if Supreme Principle-2 *were* true, this would allow theoretical reason to achieve its most fundamental cognitive aims.[48] In particular, if Supreme Principle-2 were true, it would be possible for us to achieve exactly the sort of purely rational cognition from absolute principles that theoretical reason seeks. But this, for Kant at least, ultimately lies beyond the limits of our theoretical powers. Rather, the best we can hope for in the theoretical sphere is a continual expansion of the scope and depth of our theoretical cognition of nature from mere "comparative principles". Thus, while the inferential activity of reason does commit us to the acceptance of Supreme Principle-1, and so to doctrinal belief (*Glaube*) in the bare existence of the unconditioned in a highly abstract form, we must not confuse this commitment with an ability to achieve cognition of the unconditioned in the sense claimed by Supreme Principle-2.

This gap between Supreme Principle-1 and Supreme Principle-2 arises, in large part, because the legitimate "supreme principle" (Supreme Principle-1) does so little to *determine* what that "whole series of conditions" is like, and so says almost nothing about the nature of the unconditioned whose bare existence it posits.[49] That is, as Kant puts it, "This rule of pure reason cannot say *what the object is*, but

---

reason commits us on "subjectively sufficient" grounds to the proposition that every finite, conditioned thing is ultimately grounded in something unconditioned. For this claim about theoretical reason is itself no mere belief.

[47] For similar readings on this point, see (Gardner 1999; Ameriks 2006; Watkins 2016, forthcoming-a, forthcoming-b) My account of these issues is especially indebted to Watkins on this score. It is important to stress here that this is not merely a claim about the word "cognition" or any other term in German, Latin, or English. Rather the claim at issue here is one concerning a broad family of basic epistemic achievements, including what I call "cognition", but also the forms of knowledge, insight, comprehension, and understanding that rest on cognition in this sense. So, as I read him, Kant's point against the rationalists is that we can't cognize/know/comprehend/have insight into the unconditioned, *even though* belief in it is rationally mandatory. That's no mere point of terminology: it's a fundamental blow to rationalist epistemology.

[48] Compare (Proops 2014; Willaschek 2018).

[49] Compare Hume's conception of "merely relative ideas" here. For more on this, see (G. Strawson 1989; Garrett 2008; Schafer 2015a) among others.

only how the empirical regress is to be *carried out*" (A510/B538). As we have just seen, in saying the latter, it *does* commit us to the bare existence of the "whole series of conditions" and so the unconditioned. But this commitment tells us nothing about what this "whole series of conditions" is like. In this way, Supreme Principle-1's commitment to the "whole series of conditions" is very much like the commitment to the bare existence of things in themselves that is fundamental to transcendental idealism. In both cases, we are committed to the existence of something, but that commitment leaves the nature of the thing or things we are committed to almost wholly indeterminate. In both cases, our ability so much as think of these things is limited to a highly abstract characterization of their general *relationship* to the appearances that we *can* cognize. Thus, as Kant says at one point, we are sometimes forced to posit the existence of "the object of a mere idea", but only "relative to the world of sense" and "not in itself" (A677/B705).[50]

In this way, as Kant stresses, the "supreme principle", and the other principles that may be derived from it, "have *objective but indeterminate* validity" (A664/B692). As this phrase indicates, it is this lack of determinacy in the representation of the unconditioned that theoretical reason licenses us to accept, which generally forms the primary obstacle to the "supreme principle" providing us with anything like genuine cognition of the unconditioned. Thus, as Kant writes with respect to the question of whether theoretical reason commits to the existence of God:

> But in this way (one will continue to ask) **can** we nevertheless assume a unique wise and all-powerful world author? **Without any doubt**; and not only that, but we **must** presuppose such a being. But then do we extend our cognition beyond the field of possible experience? **By no means**. For we have only presupposed a Something, of which we have no concept at all of what it is in itself (a merely transcendental object).... (A697/B725, compare A677–8/B705–6)

Moreover, not only is it impossible for us to cognize the nature of God (or the unconditioned more generally), this lack of cognition (*Erkenntnis*) prevents us from achieving knowledge (*Wissen*) of God as well. For we can only know something in this sense if we take it to be true on grounds that are both subjectively and objectively sufficient. And this can only be true if we are conscious of these grounds as appropriately related to the object our knowledge concerns, which (in turn) can be true only insofar as we can cognize this object. So, our lack of cognition of the unconditioned implies a corresponding lack of knowledge and objectively sufficient grounds for assent as well. For this reason, while theoretical reason does commit us in some sense to the existence of the unconditioned, the nature of this commitment is such that it must be one that is

---

[50] For an excellent discussion of the sense in which this is true, see (Walden 2019), which I am much indebted to.

based only on grounds that are subjectively, but not objectively sufficient. That is, while these grounds are rationally necessary, they must be grounded in the needs and interests of theoretical reason, as opposed to anything in the unconditioned object itself.

Still, this leaves open a variety of possible views about the strength of these grounds. For example, consider the following options here:

Belief-Supreme-1: Believe (*Glauben*) that when the conditioned exists (or is posited), then the whole series of conditions subordinated one to the other, which is itself unconditioned, also exists (or is posited) in the manner required to "complete reason's unity".

Hope-Supreme-1: Hope that when the conditioned exists (or is posited), then the whole series of conditions subordinated one to the other, which is itself unconditioned, also exists (or is posited) in the manner required to "complete reason's unity".

Heuristic-Supreme-1: Use as a heuristic or hypothesis that when the conditioned exists (or is posited), then the whole series of conditions subordinated one to the other, which is itself unconditioned, also exists (or is posited) in the manner required to "complete reason's unity".

Fictionalist-Supreme-1: Posit as a useful fiction that when the conditioned exists (or is posited), the whole series of conditions subordinated one to the other, which is itself unconditioned, also exists (or is posited) in the manner required to "complete reason's unity". (See Jauernig 2021).

As this makes clear, even a traditional reading of these passages can be seen as endorsing a weak version of this line of thought in the form of an endorsement of something like Heuristic-Supreme-1.[51] Once again, I think Kant wants us to go further than this, at least insofar as we are thinking about the application of these principles to noumena or things in themselves. For I believe that Kant takes this connection to be sufficient to license what Kant calls "doctrinal belief" (*Glaube*) in the bare existence of the unconditioned, even from a theoretical point of view.[52] In other words, on this reading, the rational status of Supreme Principle-1 is sufficient to provide us with theoretical grounds for assenting to the existence of the unconditioned. It is just that those grounds, while rationally mandatory for us, are nonetheless (in Kant's terminology) merely subjectively, as opposed to objectively,

---

[51] This, indeed, is one way to read (Willaschek 2018) here.
[52] Conversations with Nick Stang have been particularly important for my thoughts about this issue. For more on this sense of "belief", see (Chignell 2007a, 2007b, 2014). For some of Stang's work on these issues, see (Stang 2016, 2019). In this sense, I disagree with (Neiman 1994) when she claims that the root of transcendental illusion lies in reason's tendency to "reify the Unconditioned" *insofar* as this simply means positing the existence of the unconditioned. Rather, on my account, the root of transcendental illusion lies in an unlicensed slide from a justified belief (*Glaube*) in the bare existence of the unconditioned to the belief that reason can provide us with cognition of the same. This deserves to be called a *transcendental* illusion in Kant's technical sense of "transcendental" precisely because it involves an error about the scope and sources of a priori cognition.

sufficient. That is, these grounds are grounded in our form of reason and *its* needs, as opposed to any *cognition of the objects* we are positing the existence of.

That having been said, I want to be cautious about this last point, since the status of this sort of "doctrinal belief" in Kant is the subject of considerable controversy. For example, it is not difficult to find passages in Kant that seem to describe "belief" (*Glauben*) as a phenomenon that is only possible on practical as opposed to theoretical grounds, which would seem to rule the possibility of the sort of theoretically grounded "doctrinal belief" I am appealing to here. For example, when he introduces the category of belief in the first *Critique*, Kant writes that:

> In the transcendental use of reason, on the contrary, to have an opinion is of course too little, but to know is also too much. In merely speculative regard, therefore, we cannot judge at all here, for subjective grounds for taking something to be true, such as those that can produce belief, deserve no approval in speculative questions, where they neither remain free of all empirical assistance nor allow of being communicated to others in equal measure. Only in a **practical relation**, however, can taking something that is theoretically insufficient to be true be called believing. This practical aim is either that of **skill** or of **morality**, the former for arbitrary and contingent ends, the latter, however, for absolutely necessary ends. (A823/B852, compare 9:67)

But Kant goes on shortly thereafter to complicate this picture by introducing a "theoretical analogue of this form of practical belief":

> ... thus there is in merely theoretical judgments an **analogue** of practical judgments, where taking them to be true is aptly described by the word **belief**, and which we can call **doctrinal beliefs**. (A825/B854)

Kant's view in these passages seems to be that there is a strict or narrow sense of "belief" in which belief is only on practical grounds but that there is *also* a "theoretical analogue of this form of practical belief", which we can call "doctrinal belief". What, then, is this "analogue"? Well, what we are dealing with in the case of Supreme Principle-1 is an assent to the existence of something (the positing of something) which is necessary for theoretical reason to successfully engage in its essential activities. This, then, is an act of assent that is grounded in the fact that it is a *necessary means* to a rationally mandatory end—namely, finding the unconditioned in the manner the logical maxim demands. In this sense, the grounds for assent at issue would be similar in structure to those involved in the moral proof of God's existence, and indeed they have a structure that is recognizably practical in nature (a means-ends structure). *But*, at the same time, the ends or needs or interests that provide the basis for these grounds are ends and needs and interests of *theoretical*, and not practical reason. So, are the grounds that result from these arguments theoretical or practical? In a certain sense, the answer must be both. They are theoretical insofar as it is theoretical reason's needs/interests/ends that are driving this story. But they are practical insofar as we are still dealing with necessary means to a necessary end, which is a *practical relationship*. This may explain why Kant seems uncertain about how to locate this sort of assent. But the important thing for present purposes is not how we categorize it, but rather the general idea that theoretical reason's ends and interests are sufficient to ground a certain sort of commitment to the existence of the unconditioned and so to the truth of Supreme Principle-1.

g. Further Complications

Again, this is compatible with Kant's rejection of rationalist metaphysics precisely because this acceptance of Supreme Principle-1 does not commit us to the sort of *cognition* of the unconditioned the rationalist metaphysician claims to be able to attain through pure reason[53] (A329/B386). Similarly, consider Kant's claim that the "supreme principle" should be regarded as a "merely regulative" as opposed to a "constitutive" principle. Contrary to how it is often read, Kant's point in making this distinction is not to say that we should *merely* reason *as if* the unconditioned existed without thereby positing its existence. Rather, his point is that we should not confuse the bare act of positing the existence of the unconditioned as a mere "Something" (per Supreme Principle-1) with the "constitutive" use of the "supreme principle" that would be involved if the "supreme principle" could indeed (per Supreme Principle-2) be used to *constitute a given object of cognition* for us:

> Nevertheless, the systematic connection that reason can give to the empirical use of the understanding furthers not only its extension but also guarantees its correctness, and the principle of such a systematic unity is also *objective but in an indeterminate way* (*principium vagum*): not as a constitutive principle for determining something in regard to its direct object, but rather as a merely regulative principle and maxim.... (A680/B708, my emphasis)

As such passages make clear, in saying that principles like the "supreme principle" are "merely regulative" and not "constitutive", Kant's point is that these principles are not suitable "for determining something in regard to" an *object of cognition*. But, again, this does not mean that we should not posit the bare existence of the unconditioned. It only means that we should not take this bare act

---

[53] For similar readings on this point, see (Gardner 1999; Ameriks 2006; Watkins 2016, forthcoming-a, forthcoming-b) My account of these issues is especially indebted to Watkins on this score.

of positing to provide us with anything like a determinate "given object of cognition". Thus, while there is a clear sense in which principles like Supreme Principle-1 lack "objective validity" for Kant, this is because these principles do not "give" us anything like a determinate object of cognition, and not because Kant rejects the demand to posit the bare existence of the unconditioned as a *mere* "Something". For, once again, he takes theoretical reason's need for systematic comprehension of what is to provide us with rationally mandatory, if merely subjective, grounds for positing just this.

Of course, there are certainly other texts that one could point to as counting against this reading of Kant. Perhaps most notable are passages like the following, which could be read as implying a rejection of both Supreme Principle-1 and Supreme Principle-2:

> Systematic unity (as mere idea) is only a projected unity, which one must regard not as given in itself, but only as a problem; this unity, however, helps to find a principle for the manifold and particular uses of the understanding, thereby guiding it even in those cases that are not given and making it coherently connected. (A647/B676)

The phrasing in such passages might suggest that we are not *really* committed to the existence of the whole series of conditions in the manner that Kant's discussion of the "supreme principle" might seem to imply. For doesn't Kant say here that we shouldn't regard this "systematic unity" as something that is "given in itself"? And doesn't mean precisely that we shouldn't assume that this unity is something that actually exists? Fortunately, while we could read this passage in this way, given the other passages noted above, it seems to me more plausible to read Kant as using this term in a slightly different way in this passage, according to which something is "given in itself" just in case we can cognize its intrinsic features as opposed to, say, merely positing it in relation to appearances.[54]

On this interpretation, the point Kant is making here concerns, not whether this systematic unity should be assumed to exist, but rather whether, in assuming its existence, it is thereby given to our faculties for theoretical cognition as a determinate cognizable object. In other words, on this reading, the "problem" at issue in this passage is not *whether* (say) the whole series of conditions exists, but rather, *what* this series of conditions *is like*—and, in particular, what it is like "in itself" as opposed to in its relation to appearances. If that is right, then the "problem" in this passage is not to discover whether some condition for every conditioned exists (up to and including the entire series of conditions), but rather to determine what these conditions are like in the manner cognition of them

---

[54] See again A677/B705 and A520/B548. And compare (Watkins and Willaschek 2017) on this issue.

requires. Only insofar as we have done this, I would suggest, will this systematic unity be "given in itself" in the manner Kant has in mind.[55]

At this stage, the reader is likely to want to know more about the nature of the "unconditioned Something" that, if I'm right, we must posit according to Kant. But if these arguments are correct, there is in fact rather little of a substantive sort that we can say in response to this question, at least from a theoretical point of view. For, as we just saw, the primary barrier to cognition of the unconditioned for Kant is precisely that our conception of the nature of this "unconditioned Something" remains almost wholly indeterminate. For this reason, at least according to Kant, it is only by drawing on the resources of practical reason that we can make our conception of this "unconditioned Something" determinate.

As we will see in the next chapter, this is one of the central functions of Kant's discussion of the "highest good" in the second *Critique*. But for the moment the important point is simply to stress how little we can say about the nature of the unconditioned from a theoretical perspective. This, once again, is one of the primary ways in which Kant resists the metaphysical excesses he associates with Leibniz and (especially) Spinoza. For Kant, the primary problem with the rationalist's use of the PSR is not that they see theoretical reason as implicitly committed to the existence of the unconditioned—for Kant would agree with a version of this thought. Rather, the basic mistake of the rationalists lies in their attempt to *use* this basic commitment to ground robust metaphysical conclusions about the nature of reality, even from a theoretical point of view. It is this illusion about our own ability to gain a priori cognition of things in themselves that constitutes the core of the "transcendental illusions" Kant critiques in the Dialectic. For, as the name "transcendental illusion" itself implies, these illusions are first and foremost illusions, not about *whether* the unconditioned exists, but rather about *our* capacity to *cognize* the unconditioned *via* a priori means.[56]

That having been said, it is important to stress (once again) that Supreme Principle-1 is *only* acceptable for Kant insofar as the "whole series of conditions" it refers to is understood to include *both* appearances and things in themselves within its scope. Indeed, if Supreme Principle-1 is limited *only to appearances*, then we should in fact reject it as well. This is a product of the fact that, given transcendental idealism, when these principles are limited to appearances, there is much less space for a view that accepts Supreme Principle-1, while also rejecting Supreme Principle-2. Without going deeply into the details here, we can see that

---

[55] Something similar is also true of passages like A609–10/B637–8, which seem to claim that the "transcendental principle of inferring from the contingent to a cause" lacks all "significance" and "sense" when applied to things other than appearances. Once again, I think such passages are most charitably read as articulating conditions on cognition of objects, but there is no doubt that they could also be read as making stronger claims.

[56] See again, "I call all cognition transcendental that is occupied not so much with objects but rather with our a priori concepts of objects in general." (A11–12)

this follows from the fact that (for Kant) appearances are *essentially* such that they could (at least in principle) be given to finite cognizers like us as objects of empirical cognition. Thus, to say of an appearance that it is "given" in the first sense (in accordance with Supreme Principle-1) is always also to say that it could (at least in principle) be "given to us" in the second sense as well (in accordance with Supreme Principle-2). For this reason, in the case of appearances, we can only accept that some appearance is "given" in the sense relevant to Supreme Principle-1 insofar as we *also* accept the (in principle) possibility of the same appearance being given in the sense relevant to Supreme Principle-2.

For this reason, if we treat Supreme Principle-1 as limited to a series of conditions that lies *wholly* within the domain of appearances, there is much less logical space for a view that accepts Supreme Principle-1 while rejecting the possibility of Supreme Principle-2 being true. We can coherently accept Supreme Principle-1, while rejecting the possibility of any cognition of the unconditioned, *only* insofar as we take the "series of conditions" at issue in Supreme Principle-1 to include both appearances and things in themselves within its scope. As a result, cases in which we consider a series of conditions that are defined so that they must lie *wholly within* the world of appearances—like those under discussion in the first and second Antinomies—require special treatment here, something that has sometimes caused confusion in interpretations of the Transcendental Dialectic.[57]

If this is right, then it also implies that Supreme Principle-1 should be entirely unproblematic for Kant *so long as* we restrict its application to pure concepts of the understanding—that is, to concepts that do not have the connections with intuition that make cognition of objects possible for us. Once again, this fits very well with what Kant says about this matter. For example, he writes that:

> *If one represents everything through mere pure concepts of the understanding, without the conditions of sensible intuition, then one can say directly that for a given conditioned the whole series of conditions subordinated one to another is given; for the former is given only through the latter.* But with appearances a special limitation is encountered in the way conditions are given, namely through

---

[57] Indeed, as Kant indicates at A673/B701, the Antinomies are in general a dangerous guide to Kant's attitudes with respect to the "supreme principle", since issues of this sort arise to some degree in each of them. For example, similar issues arise in the discussion of the Fourth Antimony, where Kant writes, "Anything taken as condition must be viewed precisely in the same manner in which we viewed the relation of the conditioned to its condition in the series which is supposed to carry us by continuous advance to the supreme condition" (A458/B486). Contrary to the suggestion of (Boehm 2014), it seems to me that Kant merely intends this principle to show that the existence of such a conception of the unconditioned cannot be established *via* a regression along the series of empirical conditioning relations in space and time. In other words, Kant's point here is that if the existence of the unconditioned were to be established by such an argument, the resulting conception of the unconditioned would have to be immanent to the spatial-temporal world—but this does not amount to a general argument for this conception of the unconditioned.

> the successive synthesis of the manifold of intuition, which is supposed to be complete in the regress. Now whether this completeness is sensibly possible is still a problem. (A417/B444, my emphasis)

As passages like this seem to say quite plainly, when restricted to the pure or *unschematized concepts* of the understanding, there is *nothing* problematic about the "supreme principle" from Kant's perspective, provided that we do not take it to provide us with anything like genuine cognition or knowledge of the unconditioned—provided, that is, that we read it as Supreme Principle-1.

If this is right, then Kant only takes issue with the "supreme principle" insofar as this principle is regarded as committing us to the possibility of genuine theoretical *cognition* of things in themselves (i.e. Supreme Principle-2). In this way, we have arrived at the result that Kant accepts a version of the PSR as valid *even for theoretical reason*. For, once again, that is just how Kant would understand Supreme Principle-1's commitment to the existence of a condition for every condition, when this includes within its scope the whole series of such conditions as an unconditioned whole. In other words, on this reading, Kant does not take issue with the PSR with respect to its commitment to the bare existence of the unconditioned. Rather, he takes issue with it *only* with respect to the further claim that it is possible for us to achieve cognition of the unconditioned through use of this principle (as a principle for cognition).

6
Practical Reason's Supreme Principle, the Moral Law, and the Highest Good

As we've just seen, even in the theoretical sphere, Kant's attitude towards at least a version of the Principle of Sufficient Reason (PSR) is considerably more positive than has generally been assumed. Nevertheless, it remains true that in the theoretical domain Kant rejects the rationalist's characteristic emphasis on the possibility of *using* the PSR as a source of theoretical cognition from absolute principles. Thus, the traditional reading is right to emphasize that, in the theoretical sphere, Kant restricts the proper *cognitive use* of principles like the PSR to the regulation of our endless search for ever more fundamental, but ultimately merely "comparative", principles within nature. In this sense, we should indeed see Kant as rejecting the hopes of the rationalists to use the PSR as a source of theoretical cognition from first principles.

In this chapter, I want to turn to the role that this principle plays for Kant within the context of practical reason.[1] In doing so, I will argue that, for Kant, the supreme principle of practical reason—the moral law—expresses the same principle we have been discussing above, only as applied to the sort of *practical cognition from principles* that is characteristic of practical, as opposed to theoretical, reason. We will thus see that the moral law is itself another expression of the very same principle that the "supreme principle" expresses in the theoretical sphere, only now in the form it takes when it is applied to distinctively practical questions. As we will see, the practical use of this principle is especially important, because while this principle fails to provide us with a source of *theoretical* cognition from absolute principles, things look quite different in the practical domain. For in its practical use, reason is able to make use of this principle (in the guise of the moral law) to provide us with something very like cognition from absolute principles or cognition of the unconditioned, albeit in a distinctively practical form. Thus, while the role of this principle in theoretical reasoning remains merely regulative, in practical reasoning and practical cognition it is able to serve as the basis for something like genuine practical cognition from absolute principles of just the sort that reason seeks.[2]

---

[1] For more on the role of the PSR in a practical context, see the insightful discussion in (Nisenbaum 2018, forthcoming).

[2] In attempting to understand the nature of the moral law in terms of the requirements that arise out of the nature of practical reason as the capacity for a form of practical cognition, my approach here is greatly indebted to Engstrom's groundbreaking discussion of the categorical imperative as arising out of the nature of "practical reason, conceived of as a faculty of practical knowledge" (Engstrom 2009, 8).

Such practical cognition from principles is ultimately made possible, for Kant, by our practical understanding of our dignity as rational beings. And moreover, as we will see, this provides us with a practical principle that can ground not only a systematic body of practical cognition, but also (*via* the various practical postulates) a practically enriched body of theoretical beliefs as well. Thus, while reason's basic drive for cognition from absolute principles (or complete comprehension) is frustrated in the theoretical sphere by the limits on our capacities for theoretical cognition, the same is not true in the practical domain. Or at least it is not to the same degree. For, in the practical domain, it is possible for the "supreme principle" (in the guise of the moral law) to serve as a source of practical cognition from absolute principles. And this, in turn, provides us with a practical basis for extending, if not our theoretical cognition (*Erkenntnis*) or knowledge (*Wissen*) of things in themselves, then at least our rationally grounded beliefs (*Glauben*) about them. Thus, as we will see, it is here, in Kant's account of the highest good, and his related accounts of natural and aesthetic teleology, that reason's drive for complete comprehension (of *both* a theoretical and practical sort) is most fully satisfied.

a. The Supreme Principle in a Practical Context: Universal Law

But let's begin with Kant's conception of the supreme principle of practical reason or the moral law. As I've just suggested, I believe that Kant's discussion of the moral law is best viewed as part of a systematic attempt to explain how it is possible for practical reason to generate the sort of practical cognition from absolute principles that practical comprehension or wisdom requires. In this chapter, I want to lay out some of the elements of this approach to Kant's practical philosophy, focusing on its application to the two most famous formulations of the moral law: the Formula of Universal Law (FUL) and the Formula of Humanity (FH), saving a detailed discussion of Kant's conception of practical reason as autonomous for the next chapter. This focus is natural, in part, because it is these two formulas that correspond most naturally to the two expressions of theoretical reason's principle we focused on above: the "logical maxim" and the "supreme principle".

To understand why this is the case, it will be helpful to begin by considering which formulation of practical reason's principle plays the role that the "logical maxim" played in the theoretical sphere. These, once again, will be formulations of

---

For another recent exploration of this approach to the "unity of reason as a faculty", see the very important discussion in (Merritt 2018). But despite the many similarities between these views, the details of our respective development of this basic idea diverge in many respects. For instance, I see the moral law as closely tied with reason's drive for complete *comprehension* or *cognition from principles*, while Engstrom tends to tie it more closely Kant's account of *judgment*. For more on the importance of this difference, see below and (Schafer 2022a).

practical reason's principle that can be placed under the first of our three main headings in Chapter 5—that is, formulations that characterize practical reason's principle primarily in terms of what it aims to achieve with respect to our practical representations considered *as representations* in the subject.

The practical principle that plays this role is sometimes thought to be the (so-called) "hypothetical imperative" or "imperatives":

> Whoever wills the end, also wills (insofar as reason has decisive influence on his actions) the means that are necessary to it that are in his control. (GMS 4:417)[3]

Plainly, there are similarities between this principle and the logical maxim. After all, just as the logical maxim asks us to *ascend* higher in the sequence of theoretical cognitions by searching for the condition of the conditioned, the hypothetical imperative requires us to *descend* lower in the sequence of practical cognitions by willing whatever is a necessary means to our willed ends. So, if the logical maxim merely demanded that we find the condition for any conditioned cognition, the analogy between these principles would be quite strong. In other words, if the logical maxim merely demanded the following, it would correspond quite naturally to the "hypothetical imperative":

Maxim of Conditional Thought$_{Seek}$:   Seek the condition for every conditioned cognition of the understanding.

But, as we have already seen, the logical maxim demands considerably more than this. In particular, the full logical maxim also demands that, in so ascending, we seek the *particular sort of systematic unity* that is required for reason to satisfy its aims, or "with which its unity will be completed". Indeed, as we saw in the last chapter, in its strongest formulation, the logical maxim demands even more than this, for it demands not just that reason seek the unconditioned, but also that reason *find it*:

Logical Maxim$_{Find}$:   Find the *unconditioned* for every conditioned cognition of the understanding, *with which reason's unity will be completed.*

---

[3] There is considerable debate in the literature about whether we should speak of a single "hypothetical imperative" in this context or whether it might be better instead to speak of a variety of more specific "hypothetical imperatives". And there is also considerable debate about whether such imperatives are "genuine imperatives" at all for Kant. But I will set these issues aside here, since they are mostly incidental to my aims. Still, as should be obvious, I have a good deal of sympathy of this sort of skepticism of the hypothetical imperative, at least if it is considered in isolation from the moral law. See (Kohl 2018) and compare the helpful discussion of these issues in (Tenenbaum 2019, 2021). For a recent argument that Kant shifts his views on this point, see (Papish 2018).

In other words, in commanding us to "ascend" upwards in the sequence of conditions *in the manner it does*, the logical maxim effectively commands us to continue this inferential activity until all the cognitions of the understanding have been placed within a single, unified system, one that terminates in absolute theoretical principles. In this way, the logical maxim, once again, expresses not just the *understanding's* demand for logical consistency, but *reason's* demand for systematic unity as well.

In other words, as we saw above, the logical maxim expresses reason's demand for cognition from absolute principles, albeit in a "merely logical" form—a form, that is, which focuses on the nature of our representation as such. And however we interpret the "hypothetical imperative" in Kant, *this* goes well beyond anything we might reasonably associate with that principle considered on its own. Rather, for Kant, practical reason's demand for practical cognition from *absolute principles* is expressed not by the hypothetical imperative or imperatives, but by the moral law in its various formulations. Thus, to locate a practical principle that corresponds to the full logical maxim, we need to find a principle that expresses *practical reason's* demand for *complete systematic unity* in a "merely formal" fashion—that is, in a manner that focuses on the systematic unity of the subject's *practical representations* considered as such.[4]

I think it is obvious which practical principle best meets this description for Kant. After all, this is just how Kant characterizes the formulation of the moral law that, like the logical maxim, comes first in his presentation—namely, the Formula of Universal Law (FUL):

> Act only in accordance with that maxim through which you at the same time can will that it become a universal law. (GMS 4:421)

I will thus interpret the FUL as providing us with a merely formal characterization of the sort of systematic unity that is distinctive of practical cognition from absolute principles or practical comprehension. To understand why the FUL has this status, let's run through what must be true if a practical cognition or maxim is to count as an instance of practical cognition from absolute principles. First of all, a maxim can only count as practical cognition *from principles* if it is derived from a practical principle—a principle that provides the subject with a grasp of why this maxim is valid in the way they take it to be. But in order to count as an instance of practical cognition from *absolute* principles, something stronger than this must be true—namely, this maxim must ultimately be derived from a principle that has the status of a "practical principle", not just "comparatively" or relative to some

---

[4] Contrast (Engstrom 2009, 151) which sees the FUL as more closely associated with the "object-directed" side of the demand for universality, although note that this apparent difference made be a product of the different ways Kant uses terms like "objective" in this context.

further body of maxims or ends, but "absolutely". In other words, to count as an instance of practical cognition from absolute principles, our maxim must ultimately be derived from a principle whose validity is not conditional on any further, more fundamental practical principle or end. Thus, as we noted in Chapter 4, a principle or ground can have the status of being an "absolute principle" in the full sense of this term only insofar as its status as a principle or ground is not itself derived from something even more fundamental.[5]

Now, and this is the first important point here, this will be true only if *this* absolute practical principle itself passes the FUL test. For, contrary to (say) self-effacing forms of consequentialism, Kant's conception of reason as essentially self-conscious requires that practical reason be conscious (at least implicitly or potentially) of the principles that govern its own activities. Thus, if X is an absolute practical principle in Kant's sense, any being with practical reason must (at least implicitly or potentially) be consciousness of it as unconditionally valid for practical reason as such. In other words, for Kant, X can be an absolute practical principle only if every practically rational being is (at least implicitly or potentially) conscious of X as having universal validity for all rational subjects. And, for Kant, to be conscious of the *universal practical validity* of a principle of practical reason just is to will that that principle holds with full universality for all practically rational beings—which, of course, is just what the FUL demands of our maxims. So, X can be an absolute practical principle only if X *itself* would pass the FUL test.

Given this line of argument, a maxim of our will M can be an instance of practical cognition from absolute principles only if it is *based* on a principle X that *itself* passes the FUL. Although the details of this story are the subject of much controversy, I think this basic connection between the FUL and Kant's conception of absolute practical principles should be relatively uncontroversial. The more difficult question is whether being *derived* in this way from an absolute principle is sufficient to entail that the "maxim of my will" or "maxim of one's action" *itself* passes the FUL in the manner the FUL seems to demand.[6] The secondary literature with respect to this question is vast. But it is not too difficult to provide a reading of phrases like "the maxim of my will" on which this conclusion follows naturally from our setup. For suppose that we interpret the "maxim of one's will" to refer, not to any "plan" or "intention for action" in the contemporary sense of those terms, but rather to the full system of maxims and principles that forms an

---

[5] As we noted there, Kant also generally claims that grounding relations must be irreflexive and so rejects the idea that something could be a ground of itself in the sense that one might associate with Spinoza's God. For more discussion of this, see (Chaplin forthcoming). As we will see in the next chapter, I don't think we should understand Kant's claims about the autonomy of reason to conflict with this basic commitment.

[6] Compare (Wood 1999; Hill, Jr 2012). For recent discussion of this issue see (M. C. Timmons 2008; Nyholm 2015; Kleingeld 2017). My reading here is in some ways closest to Kleingeld's.

agent's (implicit or explicit) grasp of the reasons why they are acting as they do.[7] Such a reading of this phrase has been endorsed by many interpreters as a way of dealing with some of the purported counterexamples to the FUL, so it has a long interpretative pedigree. But it is significant here because if we read the "maxim of one's will" in this way, it is relatively easy to see that any maxim that is properly derived from an absolute practical principle will pass the FUL test. After all, as we have just seen, any such absolute principle must *itself* pass that test. And so too must any maxim M that is properly derived from such a principle *insofar as* we understand this maxim to encode within itself how it is derived from that absolute principle, and any conditions on that action that follow from this derivation. For once all of this is encoded in our maxim, this maxim will pass the FUL test just in case it is properly derived from a principle that itself passes this test.

In this way, on my reading, the FUL can be understood as expressing a necessary condition on practical cognition from absolute principles or practical comprehension or wisdom, a condition that emphasizes how this practical-cognitive achievement requires systematicity in my practical representations or maxims. More precisely, the FUL does this by focusing on the relationships between these practical representations or maxims considered merely *as such*, and not in relation to their objects. The FUL is thus the formula of the moral law that best corresponds in Kant's sense to the "logical maxim" in the theoretical sphere.[8]

---

[7] Returning to Engstrom's discussion, it is important to stress that the present focus on practical cognition *from absolute principles* allows us to explain why the FUL for Kant plays more than the merely "expository function" it does on Engstrom's account. Contrast again (Engstrom 2009, 18).

[8] Contrast (Guyer 2019)'s treatment of these issues. Much as is true of my account, Guyer's account focuses on reason as a faculty that consistently seeks sufficient reasons or conditions for conditioned cognitions so as to arrive at a fully systematic body of both theoretical and practical cognition. But Guyer's understanding of the connection between this and the moral law is nonetheless quite different from my own. In particular, Guyer believes that only the Principle of Non-Contradiction is directly relevant to Kant's derivation of the moral law. Thus, Guyer writes that:

> Kant's derivation of the foundational principle of morality proceeds by the application of the principle of non-contradiction to the fact that every human being has a will of his or her own, in the form of the idea that to act immorally is both to assert and deny that the object of such an action, whether oneself or another, has its own will. This is a fact, in Kant's own terminology a "fact of reason", but it is not a mysterious moral fact, or a blue that somehow exists in the universe independently of our act of valuing it. It is simply a fact that cannot be denied on pain of self-contradiction.... (Guyer 2019, 64)

Obviously, there's much in what Guyer says here that I agree with. But I do not agree with him that we can derive the validity of the moral law *solely* from the principle of non-contradiction, together with theoretical and non-moral claims about my nature and the nature of those around me. Indeed, it seems to me that Kant would deny that any *practical* principle follows *logically* from these theoretical claims considered merely on their own. Rather, to move from a theoretical conception of myself and others to a practical conception of how I *should* treat such beings requires some appeal to a principle of practical reason—that is, to a principle that governs reason in its practical use. And while I agree with Guyer that the principle of non-contradiction applies equally to theoretical and practical reason, it does not seem to me that this principle, *on its own*, can bridge this gap in Guyer's argument. For these reasons, it seems to me much more plausible to follow Kant in viewing the moral law as the practical analogue of something like the Principle of Sufficient Reason (albeit, once again, not in a Leibnizian form).

b. The Supreme Principle in a Practical Context: Humanity and Autonomy

With that in mind, I want next to extend this analogy between theoretical and practical reason by considering the transition in the practical sphere that corresponds to the transition we discussed in the last chapter from the "logical maxim" to the "supreme principle". To do so, we will need to consider how Kant's discussion of the FUL lays the groundwork for the introduction of a further formula of the moral law, one that characterizes practical reason's aims in the second of the three ways noted above. This is a formulation of the moral law that focuses on the "objects" of practical reason or the *ends* that practical reason treats as valuable—namely, the Formula of Humanity (FH):[9]

> So act that you use humanity, as much in your own person as in the person of every other, always at the same time as an end and never merely as a means.
> (GMS 4:429)

Much like the FUL, I believe that this principle is best understood as specifying a requirement on practical cognition from absolute principles or practical comprehension. But, whereas the FUL focuses on how practical cognition from absolute principles constrains the relations between our representations or maxims, the FH focuses on how it constrains the proper *objects* of these representations—that is, the *ends* that form the objects of a body of practical cognition from absolute principles.[10]

To understand how the FH performs this function, we need to return to one of the basic features of Kant's general account of the nature of rational capacities. This is the broadly Aristotelian idea that every rational capacity must treat its own proper activity or exercise as its "formal end"—that is, as the abstract end that gives teleological structure to all of the various activities of that capacity.[11] Applied to practical reason, this means that practical reason must treat its own proper form of activity as its most basic "formal end".[12] In this way, for Kant, every rationally permissible maxim can be thought of as a way of making more determinate the very abstract idea of practical reason respecting itself as an "independent end" (*selbstständiger Zweck*) in itself.

---

[9] Again contrast (Engstrom 2009, 153), which seems to me to reverse Kant's understanding of the relationship between the FUL and the FH on this point—although in the end, since we agree that both formulas are equivalent, this may not be terribly significant.

[10] Contrast Timmerman's claim that "the purpose of the Formula of Humanity... is not cognitive ...but metaphysical, motivational, and educational" (Timmermann 2012, 224). Needless to say, I would reject the division of labor between the cognitive and motivational that this presupposes.

[11] For this idea, see (Engstrom 2009; Reath 2010, 2013) among others.

[12] Compare again (Schafer 2019a; Tenenbaum 2019).

As this suggests, on my interpretation, what reason must respect is, on the most fundamental level, *just reason itself* in general—a respect that naturally manifests itself in reason's respect for its own form of exercise.[13] Such respect certainly involves a form of "recognition respect" in Darwall's classic sense of this term—namely, a recognition of the foundational normative authority of reason over its own activities.[14] But, as discussed above, it also involves a *striving* on the part of reason to realize itself in its own characteristic mode of activity—a striving that expresses this recognition of reason's significance for itself. Thus, for example, practical reason's (or the will's) respect for itself *as a capacity* will be expressed for Kant in its striving to realize itself in its proper form of activity—namely, that form of activity that is characteristic of the *good will*. In this way, it is a mistake to think (as some commentators have) that Kant must choose between (i) treating respect for the *capacity of reason* as what is fundamental here or (ii) treating respect for the realization of this capacity in the *good will*.[15] Rather, these two forms of respect are, for Kant, a package deal: they are simply two aspects of what is it is for reason to treat itself as an independent end in the manner any rational capacity must.

Given this point, we can extract one very abstract end from the bare idea of pure practical reason as a rational capacity—namely, that practical reason in me must, at the very least, have the formal end of respecting its own actualization in its proper form of activity. But the FH, of course, demands something that seems considerably more robust. For the FH demands, not just that *my* faculty of reason "respect" *its own* actualization in its proper form of activity, but also that *everyone's* faculty of reason "respect" the actualization of *everyone's* rational capacities in the same manner. Once again, there are countless accounts in the literature of how this gap might be closed.[16] Indeed, there is perhaps no more discussed question in Kantian ethics. But I believe that the key to closing it is already implicit in our discussion of the FUL. For, as we noted there, our maxims will only constitute genuine practical cognition from absolute principles insofar as

---

[13] This, it is important to stress, will be true of both practical and theoretical reason. Thus, contrary to the suggestions of (Sylvan 2020; Sylvan and Lord forthcoming), what theoretical reason owes "respect" to (at least in the first instance) is, not "the truth" or "the value of the truth", but rather simply *itself*. On my account, theoretical reason must "respect the truth" and "respect the evidence" because that is what it means for it to respect itself (given its proper relationship to its objects). Once again, there are interesting connections between this and the idea of "respecting reason" in the mass sense discussed by (Fogal 2016).

[14] (Darwall 1977). Note here Darwall's later remark that, "In a sufficiently broad sense of 'power,' recognition respect may always be for a power of some kind or other" (Darwall 2021, 195).

[15] See for example (Dean 2021), which attempts to characterize this feature of Kant's teleological conception of reason as an ambiguity that is fatal to the appeal of the very idea of respect for a rational capacity.

[16] As we will see in the next section, this way of presenting things is, in some ways, deeply un-Kantian, but it's familiar enough that I will begin by setting things up in this way here. For other attempts to bridge this gap, see (O'Neill 1989; Herman 1996; Korsgaard 1996a; Wood 1999; Engstrom 2009). See also the helpful discussions in (Parfit 2011) and (Moran 2022).

they are based on principles that apply to all practical reasoners *unconditionally*. And this point applies equally to the ends that these maxims treat as valuable. Thus, as Kant writes, "... if all worth were conditional and therefore contingent, then no supreme practical principle for reason could be found anywhere" (4:428). In other words, for Kant, practical cognition from absolute principles is possible only if some of our ends have their worth unconditionally.[17] And if any end is unconditional in this sense, it must be the formal end that is characteristic of practical reason as such. So, if practical cognition from absolute principles is to be possible, this must be because reason demands that *everyone* "respect" the actualization of *everyone's* rational capacities in the same way they "respect" their own rationality.

This can be developed into an argument from the FUL to the FH, once we recognize that implicit in the FUL *as the principle of a rational capacity* is the idea that that capacity must treat its own proper exercise as its formal end. In saying this, it is important to stress that I am *not* claiming that the FH is implicit in the FUL when the latter is read as an abstract principle, in isolation from Kant's account of the nature of rational capacities or powers. Rather, on my reading, the FH can *only* be derived from the FUL when the FUL is understood *as the principle of a rational capacity or power*. In other words, on my view, to appreciate the connection that Kant establishes between the FUL and the FH, we need to consider what a rational capacity would have to be like in order to have the FUL as *its* principle. Thus, while there is a sense in which we can regard the FUL and the FH as "equivalent" to one another, on my account, this equivalence runs *through* the idea that they are both expressions of the principle of practical reason *as a rational capacity*.[18]

To better understand this connection, let's spell out how this argument from the FUL to FH would work in more detail. In doing so, we can begin, once again, with the idea that every rational capacity aims (as its formal end) at its own

---

[17] It is common to talk of the unconditional value of humanity in this context, but there is considerable controversy in the literature about whether the significance of humanity as an end in itself for Kant involves a form of *value* in a strict sense of this term (as opposed to some related notion of moral worth). Since I don't mean to take a stand on this issue here, I will mostly refer to the status of humanity or our rational nature in terms that are neutral with respect to this debate, such as "worth", "end in itself", and "independent end". For some of the complexities here, see (Bader 2023; Fix forthcoming), although note that I disagree with Bader (for example) with respect to whether there is a sense in which ends in themselves can be regarded as part of the "matter" of what we will. Nonetheless, given the flexible fashion in which Kant makes use of the form/matter contrast in different contexts, it's not clear how deep this difference goes. If there is a substantive issue here, I believe it has to do with Bader's insistence that "ends-in-themselves are not being determined. They are not the determinable. Instead, it is their maxims, in particular the matter of their maxims, that is being determined" (Bader 2023, 22). Once again, it seems to me that Kant's considered view allows for us to say that there is a sense in which ends-in-themselves are themselves determinable precisely in virtue of how their maxims are determinable.

[18] This is another illustration of the foundational role that rational capacities play within Kant's philosophical project. Compare again (McDowell 2011; Kern 2017; Land 2018; Schafer 2019a, 2021b, 2022a; Pendlebury 2022) among many others.

actualization through its characteristic mode of activity. It is this, I want to suggest, that licenses Kant's claim that every rational being, simply in virtue of being rational, must treat *its own* rational nature as an end in itself. For Kant, every human being must necessarily represent their own rational nature as an end in itself *because* this is simply part of what it is to be a creature who possess the capacity of practical reason. In this way, by considering the nature of practical reason, we can extract from Kant's general account of our rational capacities the claim that, whatever else it wills, practical reason is always (at least implicitly) willing that it actualize itself *via* its own characteristic form of activity, or, alternatively, that practical reason must treat its proper actualization in this way as an "independent end" (*selbstständiger Zweck*):

Own Rationality: Practical reason must always treat its own proper exercise as an independent end. In doing so, whatever else it is willing at any given time, practical reason (implicitly) wills that it actualize itself in its own characteristic mode of activity.

As we have just seen, Own Rationality is a consequence of Kant's general conception of the nature of rational capacities. But how does Kant move from this principle to the FH? Once again, this is one of the most debated questions in Kant's practical philosophy, and I won't attempt to consider all the answers to it here. Instead, I want to simply describe *one* way in which we might move from Own Rationality to the FH, making use of the fact that we have already established the FUL at this stage of Kant's argument. I think this argument is clearly available to Kant, given his other commitments. But I don't want to claim that it is the *only* plausible way of making this transition.

On my interpretation, what is crucial here is how a principle like Own Rationality affects our understanding of the FUL as a principle of practical reason. In particular, given Own Rationality, no matter what else I am willing at a given moment, I must always also be willing that I treat my own rationality as an independent end. Accordingly, this end will always be implicit in the full "maxim of my will" once it is completely spelled out. As a result, whenever I test a maxim M using the FUL test, what I *really* need to test for universalizability is ultimately not just M alone, but rather M plus the maxim that I treat my own current rationality as an end in itself. In other words, once we consider it in the context of Own Rationality, the FUL test becomes the following:

Expanded FUL: Act only in accordance with that maxim through which you can at the same time will that it *and* the maxim that one treats the proper exercise of one's practical reason as an independent end *both* become universal laws.[19]

---

[19] Although developed independently, my reading of this principle is, in many ways, similar to the reading of the FUL defended by (Kleingeld 2017).

But now suppose that I want to see whether some maxim M of mine passes the Expanded FUL test. Then I will need to consider whether it is possible for me to consistently will M while willing that it *and* the maxim that one treat the proper exercise of one's practical reason as an independent end both become universal laws. That is, I must consider whether it is possible for me to consistently will M while willing that it *and* the maxim that *one's practical reason actualize itself in its characteristic mode of activity* both are universally willed. Or, more simply, I must consider whether it is possible for me to consistently will M while willing that it *and* the maxim that *one act in accordance with the principles of practical reason* both become universal laws.

So, when is *this* something that one consistently will? Well, if some maxim X is to be a universal law, it must at the very least be the case that every rational will conforms to X. Thus, a maxim M will pass this test only if everyone can (i) will M, and (ii) will that M is a universal law, and also (iii) treat their own rationality as an end in itself. But if everyone can do this, then it must also be true that everyone can simultaneously will *that I will M* while treating *their own rationality* as an end in itself. Or, alternatively, it must also be true of every rational being that they can (i) will that I will M (ii) while properly exercising their capacity for practical rationality. For this is just a particular case of these more general claims. Thus, if my maxim M passes the Expanded FUL test, it will only do so because every other rational being can "rationally accept" that I adopt this maxim in this manner. In other words, the following principle follows from the Expanded FUL:

Universal Rational Acceptance: Act only in accordance with a maxim that every rational being could will that I act upon while fully exercising their capacity for practical rationality.

This, in effect, is what the "merely formal" FUL becomes if we enrich it through making explicit the implicit "matter" (or end) that is built into it, in virtue of Kant's general conception of the nature of our rational capacities.[20]

But, as readers will have surely noted, Universal Rational Acceptance is very close to *both* the second *and* the third main formulations of the moral law. For

---

[20] Compare (O'Neill 1989; Korsgaard 1996a; Guyer 2000; Rawls 2000; Timmermann 2007). Here I disagree with (Bader 2023) who denies that ends in themselves contribute to the matter of the will (or practical cognition more generally). Although I'm sympathetic to much of Bader's discussion, on this point he seems to me to have an overly inflexible and narrow understanding of Kant's use of "matter" in this context. Nonetheless, I agree with Bader that one crucial role that this "matter" plays in this context is that it fixes more determinately the scope of the domain over which universalization principles like the FUL range. In other words, the move from the FUL to the FH is significant here in part because the FH makes explicit the domain with respect to which some maxim must be able to become a "universal law". Bader and I agree on this; we simply disagree about whether there is a sense in which this involves making explicit the matter implicit in the idea of the FUL (again, *as a principle of practical reason*). Nonetheless, I do think that this represents a boundary case that Kant is not completely sure how to classify.

example, if my actions are in accordance with Universal Rational Acceptance, then every rational being will be capable of willing that I act as I do, without in any way deviating from the demands that practical reason places upon their will. In this way, Universal Rational Acceptance is very close to the ideal of "universal legislation" that Kant associates with the third formula of the moral law—in particular, with the variant of that formula known as Formula of the Realm of Ends:

> Act in accordance with maxims of a universally legislative member for a merely possible kingdom of ends. (GMS 4:439)

But for present purposes, the most important point is that Universal Rational Acceptance also provides us with a basis for deriving what seems to be the core of the FH for Kant. For Kant generally seems to regard the core of the FH as involving something very close to Universal Rational Acceptance as well.[21] For example, in discussing how to derive a prohibition of false promises from the FH in the *Groundwork*, Kant writes that:

> ... he who has it in mind to make a false promise to others sees at once that he wants to make use of another human being *merely as a means*, without the other at the same time containing in himself the end. For, he whom I want to use for my purposes by such a promise cannot possibly agree to my way of behaving toward him, and himself contain the end of this action. (GMS 4:429–30)

And in a related discussion in the second *Critique*, he writes:

> Just because of this every will, even every person's own will directed at himself, is restricted to the condition of agreement with the *autonomy* of the rational being, that is to say, such a being is not to be subjected to any purpose that is not possible in accordance with a law that could arise from the affected subject himself. (KpV 5:87)

As such passages indicate, Kant often seems to think of the essence of the FH (and, by extension, the FA and FKE) as lying in the idea that one should adopt a maxim only if every other rational being could will that one do so while properly exercising their own capacity for practical rationality. And this is precisely the principle that we have just shown to follow from the FUL, once it is interpreted in the context of Kant's background understanding of the nature

---

[21] Compare (O'Neill 1989; Engstrom 2009; Sensen 2011). For a contrary view, see (Wood 1999, 2007).

of rational capacities. Thus, given that background, we have seen how to derive the FH (on one plausible interpretation of it) from the FUL, when the latter principle is interpreted as the principle of practical reason or the will as a rational capacity.[22]

On this reading, the FH, like the FUL, primarily characterizes a constraint on any system of practical comprehension of what ought to be. But, unlike the FUL, the FH brings out that this constraint is not *merely formal*. Rather, it can also be thought of in terms of practical reason itself providing us with a certain sort of end—albeit not an end-to-be-effected, but an independent end that deserves our respect in just the manner Universal Rational Acceptance articulates. Thus, the FH characterizes a constraint on the ends that constitute *the objects* of any system of practical comprehension or practical wisdom.

As this should indicate, Korsgaard and Wood, in their famous readings of the argument for the FH as a "regress of conditions", are right to see a close connection between the possibility of the moral law as an absolute practical principle and the possibility of unconditioned ends.[23] Where readings like theirs go wrong is in imaging this relationship to be something we *discover via a regress of such conditions*. For to think of practical reason in this way is to model practical reason's operations on the operations of theoretical reason, which does, of course, regress on conditions in this fashion. But while this sort of "regress" is characteristic of theoretical reason in its canonical form, the canonical activities of practical reason move in precisely the opposite direction. In other words, unlike theoretical reason, practical reason has no need to "regress on conditions" in *search* of its fundamental principle; rather, its reasoning *begins* with a basic consciousness of this principle (as we saw in our discussion of the *Faktum der Vernunft*). Thus, while the FH does connect the possibility of practical cognition from absolute principles with the existence of unconditional ends, we should not see this connection as the product of the sort of regress of conditions that Korsgaard and Wood describe. Rather, the transition at issue here generally moves in the opposite direction: from practical reason's grasp of its own internal principle to practical cognition of particular actions as good.

---

[22] It might be objected that this interpretation does not do sufficient justice to the "value of humanity" in this context. (For some of the complexities here, see (Timmons 2017).) But this will only be true if we understand that phrase in terms that Kant himself would have rejected. Once again, the role of humanity here is to serve as an independent end to be respected (something that has dignity, that is). And this is very different from having value in the sense that ends-to-be-effected do. Once we keep this in mind, I think we can see that the present account does justice to the sense in which humanity has unconditional worth for Kant. For more discussion of this issue in particular, and a compelling case against treating humanity as having value in an overly strict sense of "value", see (Bader 2023).

[23] See (Korsgaard 1996a; Wood 1999, 2007). For some criticism, see (Hills 2005; Timmermann 2006).

c. Interlude: Is Kant's Ethics Too Individualist, or Not Individualist Enough?

In presenting this argument from the FUL (viewed as a principle of practical reason) to the FH and the FA, I have followed the interpretative literature in focusing on the question of how Kant might bridge the alleged gap between (on the one hand) the "first-personal" relationship I have with my own rationality and (on the other) the "second-" or "third-personal" relationship I have with the rationality of other persons around me. As we have seen, this does provide one helpful way of understanding the potential relevance of the FUL in this context. Indeed, when viewed in this light, and properly contextualized, the FUL plays this role quite well. For, as we have seen, when we enrich the FUL with the ends that are implicit in the very idea of it as the principle of a rational capacity, we arrive at something very like the FH and the FA (on one reading of them).

But in fact I think this way of presenting Kant's conception of practical reason is importantly misleading in certain important respects that matter for understanding the relationship between these formulas. Moreover, as we will see, I think this matters for properly understanding Kant's relationship with many of his immediate critics, such as Fichte and Hegel, as well as the broader philosophical importance of Kant's conception of the moral law. The first of these points should not be terribly surprising. After all, as already noted, on my interpretation, what reason must respect is mostly fundamentally *just reason itself in general*—a respect that naturally manifests itself in reason's respect for its own form of proper exercise or activity. So the fundamental sort of "respect" at issue in Kant's account of practical reason is the respect that reason in general owes *to itself*. And the respect that *reason owes particular rational individuals*, in virtue of their possession of reason as a capacity, or the respect that *one rational individual owes another*, are ultimately downstream from the more fundamental respect that *reason in general* owes itself in general.[24]

Thus, on my reading, it is this relation of reason in general to itself that is fundamental here. Of course, since reason in us is realized by a diverse community of particular rational individuals, reason's basic respect for itself will express itself, in part, in terms of the demand that each of us, as rational, should respect every other rational individual as such.[25] We have begun to discuss this connection

---

[24] Thus, as Kant says, "Inclination is never its own object, for it makes us dependent, but a moral will is its own object, for such a will is not conditional, but unconditional" (V-Met/Mron 29:610). Compare here Timmerman's interpretation of such passages to mean that for Kant: "We must treat human beings as 'ends in themselves' because they possess a pure will, which literally *is* its own end (as well as law unto itself)" (Timmermann 2012, 217).

[25] I should note that the resulting account of respect resonates nicely in many ways with that developed in (Sensen 2021). This also, I think, helps to explain why it is natural to appeal to idealized versions of us in trying to spell out the implications of this sort of respect, as in, for example, (Hill, Jr 2000). Such idealizations are natural insofar as it is really reason itself that is the ultimate target of our respect here.

above, and will turn to some other reasons why this is the case in the next section. But nonetheless it is crucial to stress that the fundamental target of Kant's account is the relationship that *reason in general* should have to itself.[26]

This marks one respect in which Kant's views are quite different from those of many contemporary Kantians, especially those with Korsgaard's rather existentialist leanings. Many contemporary Kantians do, following Korsgaard, conceive of "Kantian constitutivism" as concerned primarily with the "self-constitution" of particular rational individuals or agents. As we will discuss below, such views are naturally subject to the worry that they do not give us the materials we need to cross the gap *between individuals*—the worry, in effect, that their account of rationality and agency is caught in an individualistic trap that leaves each rational individual hopelessly alienated from those around them. Those, as Jack Samuel writes, "To start with an individualistic account of the source of normativity and wind up with a full-throated vindication of normative facts as facts about concrete others appears to involve crossing a gap" (Samuel forthcoming-b, 23). And this has led many in the recent literature to argue that we must go beyond a Kantian approach to these issues. For example:[27]

> I propose that we discard Korsgaard's individualistic view of autonomy.... To count as autonomous, on this sort of view, we must be moved to act by our appreciation of the normative force of a principle that we have imposed on ourselves—or, at least, of one that stands in a suitable relation to some duly self-imposed principle; otherwise, we count as heteronomous.... It is this sort of view that should be resisted. On the contrary, in affirming that other persons can obligate us directly, we must also insist that the claims of others—specifically, their needs, aims, and interests—can just as directly *move* us to act for their benefit. So, along with a more thoroughly social conception of authority, we need an equally social view of autonomy, so that it turns out that our being moved immediately by the claims of others does not constitute a threat to our freedom but rather an expression of it, perhaps even a condition of it.
>
> (Tarasenko-Struc 2020, 90)

---

[26] For a helpful articulation of why this step from respect for reason as a capacity to respect for rational individuals is more complicated than it might seem, see (Dean 2021). But note that Dean's objections take for granted a background metaphysical picture that is quite different from Kant's own, ignoring as they do the relationship capacities like practical reason have to their own proper actualization in, say, the good will. In any case, Dean takes it for granted that capacities are first introduced in this context to explain why individuals deserve our respect, whereas for my Kant, things are rather the other way around. It is reason (as a capacity) that most fundamentally deserves respect, and then this respect turns out to require a respect for various rational individuals in keeping with the arguments above. In any case, I do ultimately agree with many of Kant's critics (notably Fichte and Hegel) that his account of how the respect of reason for itself in general relates to our respect for rational individuals is not entirely compelling. But this is not for the reasons Dean cites.

[27] For other versions of the basic worry here, see (Walden 2017, 2020; Samuel and Peterson 2021; Samuel forthcoming-b).

Now, I think such worries are apt with respect to many forms of contemporary Kantianism like Korsgaard's, and I'm very sympathetic to their conclusion, once it is placed in its proper context. But we have already seen some reason to be suspicious of them as applied to Kant's own philosophy. After all, as I've been presenting it here, there is nothing particularly "individualistic" about Kant's conception of reason. Rather, the target of Kant's account is a general capacity for comprehension. And this capacity is necessarily one that involves all rational individuals to an equal degree. Indeed, as we have been stressing, one of the strengths of Kant's focus on reason as a capacity or power is the fundamental metaphysical flexibility of this view.[28] So nothing in our presentation would conflict in the slightest with the plausible idea that human forms of rationality can only be realized by social collectives as opposed to isolated individuals.[29] In this sense, Kant's focus on reason as a rational capacity is (at worst) neutral with respect to the questions that drive objections that Kantian ethics is individualistic.

In this sense, then, the charge that Kant's own ethics is individualistic involves a quite fundamental misinterpretation of Kant. Rather, if there is an issue for Kant in this area, it lies somewhere else. Indeed, it seems to me that the real worry here is not that Kant's ethics is "too individualistic", but rather that it is, in a sense, "not individualistic enough". After all, if our presentation is correct, the real question for Kant is not how we bridge the gap separating one rational individual from another, but rather how we get from reason in general (as a capacity) to particular rational individuals at all. In other words, if I am correct, the real concern here is not how we turn a "fundamentally individualistic Kantian ethics" into something social and intersubjective, but rather how we turn a general account of reason as a rational capacity into an account of how this capacity is realized, *either* by particular rational individuals in isolation from one another *or*, more plausibly, by communities of rational individuals standing in various social relations.

Although there is no space to defend this claim in detail here, it is important to stress that this is just how Kant's immediate critics like Fichte and Hegel understood their criticisms of Kantian ethics. For contrary to how this story is often told today, for both Fichte and Hegel, the fundamental question is not whether Kant can bridge an alleged gap between the "first-person" and "second-person" standpoints, but rather whether he can provide us with a philosophical account of the relationship between *reason in general* and *particular rational individuals*.[30] This,

---

[28] Compare here the insightful discussion of (Walden 2020).

[29] Indeed, something like this appears to be Kant's own view in passages like this one: "In the human being (as the only rational creature on earth), those predispositions whose goal is the use of his reason were to develop completely only in the species, but not in the individual." (IAG 8:18–19)

[30] For examples of the contemporary focus on the second-person, see (Thompson 2004; Darwall 2006; Haase 2014; Zylberman 2018; Wallace 2019; Rödl 2021; Zylberman 2021). Once again, I think all this work points in the right direction, but in a manner that disguises what Hegel at least would have regarded as the fundamental issue here. The interpretation error here with respect to Hegel goes back at least to (Pinkard 1994), but it is so widespread that it is difficult to read Hegel in any other way.

to be sure, is an issue that arises within Kant's ethics with respect to second-personal relations between individuals. But it also arises *just as much* with respect to my own first-personal relationship *to myself*. For the fundamental issue here is not anything to do with first- or second-personal relations per se, but rather with the relationship between reason *in general* and my or your or anyone else's determinate individuality as one rational individual among many. Thus, Rödl is right to say that, according to Fichte and Hegel, "The moral law, as Kant understands it, is no relation of me to you" (Rödl 2021). But it is equally true, from this perspective, that the moral law is *no relation of me to me* either. Rather, for both Fichte and Hegel the fundamental problem for Kant is to provide a philosophical account of how reason in general relates to me and you and everyone else *as individuals* who realize this capacity.

This, it is important to stress, is fundamentally a *logical point*, and not one that is distinctive of the second-personal perspective in particular. So, for example, it is not second-personal relations as such that open the door to the importance of social life and relations for Hegel. Rather, for Hegel, social life matters fundamentally because social life, like life in general, provides a model for thinking about the logic of the relationship between reason *in general* and particular *rational individuals* in the manner philosophy demands. Once again, this is a logical point: one that is grounded, not on the worry that Kantian ethics is "too individualistic", but rather on the more basic concern that Kant's philosophy (in both the theoretical and the practical domains) fails to explain how reason in general relates to determinate individuals. Indeed, on this point, a capacities-focused reading of Kantian ethics might be even seen as inviting a "no self" approach to ethics of the sort often associated with Buddhism.

d. Transition: The Maxims of Common Understanding

Unfortunately, pursuing such thoughts would lead us beyond Kant and so beyond the scope of the current essay. So I want to set them aside here to return to our discussion of Kant's conception of the fundamental principle of practical reason: the moral law. In a moment, I'll connect this discussion of the moral law to the last chapter's discussion of the PSR in a theoretical context so as to give a systematic picture of how all of these principles fit together for Kant. But before doing so, I want to briefly discuss a further set of principles or "maxims" that Kant associates with the correct use of reason—namely, what he calls the "maxims of common understanding". As we will see, consideration of these maxims points us towards just such a systematic picture of *all* these principles, theoretical and practical. For they provide us with an important case in which Kant treats the theoretical and the practical cases in relation to one another.

The first of these maxims, the Maxim of the Universal Use of Reason, reads as follows:

To make use of one's own reason means nothing more than to ask oneself, with regard to everything that is to be assumed, whether he finds it practicable to make the ground of the assumption or the rule which follows from the assumption, a universal principle of the use of his reason.   (O 8:146)

As O'Neill has stressed, Kant's statement of this first "maxim" is plainly meant to echo the first formulation of the moral law, the Formula of Universal Law (FUL). But, contrary to what O'Neill suggests, the nature of this "maxim" is importantly different from the FUL. In particular, while the FUL demands that we act *only* on maxims that we can will to be universal laws for all rational beings, this first "maxim of common understanding" demands only that whenever make an assumption, we *ask* ourselves *whether* it is possible to make the ground of that assumption a universal principle for the use of reason. Thus, contrary to what readings like O'Neill's imply, the demand that this first maxim places upon us is weaker in one crucial respect than the FUL.

In the context of our discussion, it should be easy to understand why this is the case. For in demanding that we always *ask* whether our assumptions are grounded in a universal principle of reason, the Maxim of the Universal Use of Reason is, in effect, demanding that we proceed in accordance with the "logical maxim" discussed above. For example, suppose I make some assumption about the world. Then this first maxim of common understanding will demand that I ask myself whether this assumption is grounded in a universal principle of reason. If it is, it will represent an instance of theoretical cognition from absolute principles. And so theoretical reason's work will be done. But, of course, this is a standard that very few, if any, of our theoretical cognitions will reach. So, the normal case will be one in which I cannot yet see how my assumption can be grounded in such a universal principle. In this case, the work of reason here must continue by searching for ever more fundamental grounds for my assumption, in the hope of uncovering a ground for this assumption that does have the relevant status.

In this way, what the first maxim of common understanding demands of us is that we continually *search* for ever more general principles or grounds for our assumptions, in exactly the manner we have discussed above. This, in turn, explains why Kant formulates this "maxim" in weaker terms than the FUL. For while, according to Kant, it is possible for to achieve genuine practical cognition from absolute principles, it is not possible for us to achieve theoretical cognition from absolute principles in the same way (even if this is possible for some more idealized form of theoretical reason). So, a principle (like this maxim) that is meant to apply to human cognition of both a theoretical and a practical sort cannot demand all of what the FUL demands of us. For to do so would be to demand a form of theoretical cognition from us that we are simply incapable of.

Nonetheless, O'Neill is surely correct to see this first maxim of common understanding as expressing the same basic principle that the FUL does. Both express reason's interest in systematic cognition from principles or comprehension, but only in a fashion that focuses on the proper relationships between our representations. In this way, both are most naturally grouped with the "logical maxim" under the heading of formulations of the principle of reason that focus on the subject's internal state as opposed to on the objects it thereby cognizes. With that in mind, let's turn to the second of Kant's maxims of common understanding. This "Maxim of Enlarged Thought" demands that one:

> ... detaches himself from the subjective personal conditions of his judgment, which cramp the minds of so many others, and reflects upon his own judgment from a universal standpoint (which he can only determine by shifting his ground to the standpoint of others). (KU 5:294–5)

As is familiar, this principle is closely associated with Kant's second main formulation of the moral law, the Formula of Humanity, but we can also approach it from the more general perspective of our discussion of reason as the capacity for cognition from principles and comprehension. In doing so, it is crucial to remember that cognition (*Erkenntnis*) is always of *objects*—that is, it is a form of representation that makes us conscious of objective things, which place correctness conditions on our representation that go beyond anything internal to our own subjective mental state. Thus, we can only cognize an object for Kant insofar as our consciousness of that object extends beyond our merely subjective experience of it. In this sense, the very idea of cognition already carries with it a demand to go beyond a merely subjective point of view so as to achieve a consciousness of intersubjectively available objects from a sort of "universal standpoint".

Given this, the proper use of any of our cognitive faculties requires what Kant sometimes (somewhat metaphorically) calls a "*sensus communis*":

> By '*sensus communis*,' however, must be understood the idea of a communal sense, i.e. a faculty for judging that in its reflection takes account (a priori) of everyone else's way of representing in thought, in order as it were to hold its judgment up to human reason as a whole and thereby avoid the illusion which, from subjective private conditions that could easily be held to be objective, would have a detrimental influence on the judgment. (KU 5:293–4)

Thus, a requirement to transcend our merely subjective point of view on the world is already built into Kant's conception of cognition. And this demand to "transcend the merely subjective" is only intensified by the further demands that reason's characteristic search for *comprehension* brings with it. For in order to comprehend something, we must cognize both its features and whatever it is that explains those features. In this way, as we have seen, comprehension requires, not just cognition of an object, but also a cognition of that object that is itself based on further objective grounds.

Given this, cognition and (even more so) comprehension are always at least potentially intersubjective. For Kant, we can only be said to grasp something objective insofar as that grasp is not limited to our own particular subjective point of view. In this way, as Kant notes, there is a tight connection between the idea of objective truth and the "possibility of communicating" that truth "and finding it to be valid for the reason of every human being to take it to be true" (A821/B849). At the same time, picking up on our discussion in the last section, it is important to stress that the importance of this form of intersubjectivity is ultimately *derivative* here. For example, the "possibility of communicating" something is described by Kant as an "external touchstone" of objective validity and not as its essence. Rather, the essence of this sort of objectivity consists instead in the presence of a "common ground" for agreement in the object itself. As this indicates, at the deepest level, what really matters most for Kant here is less the "intersubjective agreement" of different cognitive subjects *as such* and more the agreement of some representation with the nature of our rational powers—or, more simply, with reason itself. For, in keeping with our discussion of Kant's "capacities-first" method above, it is ultimately the nature of these capacities that constitutes the nature of the "universal standpoint" that Kant appeals to in such passages.[31] Thus, once again, it is just *reason itself* that is the most fundamental object of respect for Kant. And this is true in both the practical and the theoretical domains.[32]

So, for example, Kant is clear that a concern for the viewpoint of other rational subjects is only necessary for us because we are subject to a constant temptation towards what he calls "logical egoism":[33]

> The logical egoist considers it unnecessary also to test his judgment by the understanding of others; as if he had no need at all for this touchstone (*criterium veritatis externum*)'.... the logical egoist values his own judgment over and above everyone else's, thereby subordinating the interest of truth to his subjective point of view.... The opposite of egoism can only be pluralism, that is, the way of

---

[31] Of course, there is a very close connection here between the sort of "objectivity" or "objective truth" that cognition aims at and the possibility of intersubjective agreement for Kant. And this connection becomes tighter when we turn from these abstract claims to consider how they might be applied to objects, like appearances, whose nature (and in particular, form) is constituted in part by their relationship to our cognitive faculties. For in this case, of course, to say that the ground of judgments lies in the "object itself" is *not* to say that this ground does not ultimately *also* lie in the nature of our cognitive faculties. But, again, this fact plays this role only because we take the form of the relevant objects to *itself* be grounded in the nature of these faculties.

[32] Once again, this conflicts to some degree with the focus in (K. L. Sylvan 2020; K. L. Sylvan and Lord n.d.) on the foundational significance of "respect for the truth" or "respect for the value of the truth" in theoretical epistemology. On my reading, such forms of respect must be seen as derivative from the more fundamental sense in which reason owes respect to itself for Kant.

[33] Compare the discussion in (Mudd 2017) on this point. And see also the discussion of self-conceit in (Russell 2020).

thinking in which one is not concerned with oneself as the whole world, but rather regards and conducts oneself as a mere citizen of the world.

(Anth 7:128–30)

As this indicates, "logical egoism" in Kant's sense is just the tendency to treat features of our merely subjective point of view as if they were features of the "universal standpoint" that is constituted by reason (and our other rational capacities). Thus, the real problem with the logical egoist, for Kant, is that they have an unreasonable degree of confidence in their own ability to determine which of their views follow from the universal perspective of reason and which are merely idiosyncratic to their own subjective perspective on the world. In this way, the logical egoist effectively treats their judgments about what agrees with the nature of our cognitive faculties as authoritative, *even* when other rational subjects disagree with them about this.

Now, if we had perfect and infallible access to the nature of our rational capacities, there would not necessarily be any problem with this sort of self-confidence. But unfortunately, given our limitations, we are constantly tempted to deceive ourselves about exactly this question. And given our propensity to self-deception on this score, the logical egoist's attitude towards the views of others must be regarded as deeply unreasonable, according to Kant. For in that case, this attitude represents a failure to take others seriously as beings who are equally in possession of the same rational faculties we possess. In this way, while the fundamental question for Kant is always the relationship between our representations and our rational capacities, consideration of whether other rational subjects agree or disagree with us is an essential tool for avoiding the vice of "logical self-conceit".

With that in mind, let's turn to the third of Kant's "maxims of common understanding". Kant claims that this third maxim is "only attainable by the union of both the former" (KU 5:295) and that it is the "hardest of attainment". So here, much as with his various formulations of the moral law, Kant seems to be thinking of these three "maxims" as three formulas of a single principle, where the third of these formulas unites the first two in some sense. Such claims seem, at first glance, to be belied by the simplicity of the third "maxim", which simply demands that one "always think consistently". For if this is read merely as a demand to be logically consistent, it is quite mysterious how this third "maxim" could unite the other two, or why this principle would in some sense be the most complete of the three. Thus, it is fortunate that, as Wood notes, Kant's reference to "consistency" can be understood to involve something much more robust than mere logical consistency:

My being consistent in this sense requires that my conduct flow from a common principle or coherent set of principles—coherent not merely in the sense that the

> principles do not contradict one another but in the deeper sense that the principles are all systematically connected and mutually supporting.
>
> (Wood 2007, 19)

As this indicates, what Kant has in mind in this third maxim is much more robust than a mere demand for logical consistency. Rather, it is best understood as demanding from us the sort of "consistency in thought" that can only be achieved insofar as our thoughts form a genuine systematic unity. And when it is read in this way, the connections between this third maxim and our discussion of reason as the faculty for comprehension should be obvious. For, as we have discussed at length, we can achieve comprehension only through bringing our cognitions into this sort of systematic unity. So, the demand for "consistency in thought" at issue in this third maxim just is the demand for a certain sort of systematic understanding of things in just the sense that comprehension involves. And, in describing this as the most "complete" of the three maxims, Kant is again pointing our attention to the role that the idea of comprehension plays in characterizing the essential aims of reason as a capacity.

e. A Systematic Presentation of Reason's Principle

With this in mind, let's conclude our discussion of reason's principle by bringing the discussion of the last two chapters together to provide a systematic presentation of all the formulas and principles we have been discussing. For, as should hopefully be clear, we are now in position to see how *all* these principles follow from the basic idea of reason as the faculty for theoretical and practical comprehension (or cognition from principles). More precisely, as discussed above, it follows from Kant's basic conception of cognition that any cognitive faculty's proper exercise can be characterized in three interrelated ways. First, we can characterize the proper exercise of the faculty in question formally by focusing on how it would establish internal relations between its own representations and activities. Second, we can characterize it materially in terms of the nature of the objects of cognition that it would cognize if it were exercised correctly. And third, we can characterize it in terms of its characteristic union of form and matter—that is, in terms of the relationship between subjects and objects its proper exercise would bring about. Given this way of characterizing things, it should be obvious why this third approach to the nature of a faculty is, for Kant, the most complete. For this third perspective on a faculty's proper exercise involves the other two and brings them into a systematic relationship to one another. Thus, another way to think about this third perspective on the proper exercise of a cognitive faculty is in terms of a characterization of this in terms of a genuine system of relations between subjects and objects.

In order to arrive at Kant's various formulas of the principles of reason as a faculty, we need to pair this tripartite division of perspectives on a faculty's fundamental principle with two further ideas: First, the idea of reason as the faculty for comprehension; and second, the distinction between theoretical and practical forms of cognition. For then we can see each formulation of reason's fundamental principle as characterizing what either theoretical or practical comprehension requires from one of these three basic perspectives.

For example, if we adopt the first "more formal" perspective and focus on the relations between representations that comprehension requires, we will be led to the ideas expressed, in turn, by the "logical maxim" in the theoretical case and the Formula of Universal Law in the practical case. For, as we have seen, the "logical maxim" simply characterizes the relationships that must obtain between our representations (considered as such) insofar as these representations constitute theoretical comprehension. The Formula of Universal Law similarly characterizes the internal structure of the will that is required for us to achieve practical comprehension of our actions.[34] And finally, the first maxim of common understanding expresses the same basic idea as the Formula of Universal Law, only in a less demanding form that makes this idea compatible with the limits of both theoretical and practical reason.

In a similar vein, if we approach the nature of theoretical comprehension materially–that is through the question of what the objects of such comprehension must be like, we quickly arrive at the idea that we must assume that these objects comply with what Kant calls the "supreme principle" of theoretical reason—that is, that the objects of ideal comprehension must obey a (weakened) version of the Principle of Sufficient Reason. In the three ideas of theoretical reason, we find this general idea in a more precise form that articulates its demands with respect to the three basic forms that our thought about such conditioning relations can take. Similarly, the Formula of Humanity articulates a basic constraint on the objects of practical comprehension—namely, that any such system of "practical objects" or ends must treat rational nature as an end in itself. As we will discuss in a moment, this general idea can be further developed by bringing it together with the three ideas of theoretical reason, and the practical significance of happiness, so as to form our conception of what Kant calls "the highest good", which (as we will discuss in the next section) provides us with our best overall grasp of what the objects of ideal theoretical and practical comprehension must be like. Finally, the same idea is expressed in a more general way in the second of Kant's maxims of common understanding—the "maxim of enlarged thought"—which expresses the

---

[34] That having been said, the correspondence between these principles should not be overstated. For, of course, the logical maxim and the FUL express this demand for systematicity among our representations in rather different ways. Indeed, in its focus on finding the unconditioned, the logical maxim is in some ways superficially more akin to the FH than it is to the FUL, but in its focus on finding the *logically* unconditioned, it is more akin to the FUL.

manner in which the "objectivity" involved in comprehension is connected to a certain sort of intersubjectivity.

These various principles are then given their most systematic expression when we turn to the third perspective on reason. Here we notably do not find any principle in the theoretical domain that fits neatly into this category. But this is no surprise since Kant's view is that it is strictly speaking impossible for us to achieve the sort of relationship to the objects of theoretical cognition that ideal theoretical comprehension requires. Fortunately, things are more promising when we turn to the practical point of view. For here we do have a grasp of the relationship that ideal practical comprehension requires between the subject and the object—namely, that this relationship obtains whenever we have an instance of genuine "autonomous action" from the moral law. This, of course, is what is expressed in the Formula of Autonomy. Here we also find this idea given a more explicitly systematic form in the Formula of the Realm of Ends, which makes explicit the systematic relationships between all rational beings, as *both* the subjects *and* the objects of practical cognition, which genuine practical comprehension requires. Finally, we find the same basic idea expressed in a manner that fits both the theoretical and the practical cases in the third maxim of common understanding, whose demand for "consistency" is (as we saw) best understood in terms of the demand for a certain sort of systematic unity in our (theoretical and practical) cognition.

Taking all this together, we can see why *all* of these various formulas express a single fundamental idea—namely, the idea of reason as the faculty for comprehension—from a variety of different perspectives and with respect to a variety of different forms that comprehension can take. We can summarize these results in the form of the following Table of Principles of Reason:

	Principle of Theoretical Reason	Principle of Practical Reason	Maxims of Common Understanding
Subject-Focused (Formal)	The Logical Maxim	The Formula of Universal Law (The Formula of the Law of Nature)	The Maxim of the Universal Use of Reason
Object-Focused (Material)	The Supreme Principle (Supreme Principle-1) (The Ideas of Theoretical Reason)	The Formula of Humanity (The Highest Good)	The Maxim of Enlarged Thought
Complete System of Subjects and Objects (Union of Form and Matter)		The Formula of Autonomy (The Formula of the Realm of Ends)	The Maxim of Consistency in Thought

In accordance with this table, both the moral law and the various principles that Kant associates with the theoretical use of reason can be thought of as expressing (in different forms) reason's demand for systematic unity in (theoretical and practical) cognition or, more simply, its quest for theoretical and practical comprehension.[35] In this way, as we have seen, in both the theoretical and the practical spheres, these principles can be thought of as giving expression to the same fundamental demand (of reason) that the PSR expresses within more "dogmatic" forms of rationalism. Thus, as we have seen, even in the theoretical case, Kant's attitude towards the PSR is considerably more positive than is generally assumed. And that is only truer in the practical domain, where the "supreme principle" takes on the distinctively practical form of the moral law, thereby making possible a genuine form of practical cognition from absolute principles for Kant.

f. The Ultimate Object of Human Comprehension and the Highest Good

In this way, on my reading, where the theoretical and practical cases differ most clearly is with respect to the degree to which reason is capable of achieving the sort of cognition from principles or comprehension it seeks. In the theoretical domain, while reason does demand a sort of "doctrinal belief" in the unconditioned, it is incapable of translating this belief into *genuine cognition of the unconditioned*. Rather, for Kant, the theoretical cognition from absolute principles that theoretical reason seeks is forever beyond our grasp. In the practical case, on the other hand, reason is considerably more successful. For here practical reason can achieve a very significant degree of practical cognition of the practical unconditioned—namely, cognition of the unconditional worth of humanity as an end in itself.

But the practical case does not merely provide us with a grasp of the unconditioned good in this way, it also thereby provides us with a basis for enriching theoretical reason's grasp of the unconditioned objects whose existence the "supreme principle" posits. In this way, practical reason not only provides us with practical comprehension or wisdom, it also extends our grasp of what is, albeit on distinctively practical grounds and for practical purposes. This extension of our theoretical beliefs on practical grounds is central to Kant's conception of the "highest good". For this provides us with a unified conception of the proper objects, not just of practical comprehension or wisdom, but of theoretical comprehension as well.[36] Thus, the "highest good" in many ways represents the

---

[35] Compare the table in (Cohen 2014), but note that this (crucially) neglects the relationship between the first of my categories and the other two categories. This neglect, it seems to me, leads Cohen to overstate the degree to which the "maxims of common understanding" are derived from practical *as opposed to* theoretical principles, and so leads Cohen to a conception of the unity of reason as a faculty that over-emphasizes the practical side of this unity over the theoretical.

[36] See (Gardner 1999; Wood 1999; Guyer 2005; Fugate 2014).

farthest we can penetrate into the nature of things, not just with respect to practical questions, but with respect to theoretical questions as well.

More precisely, as Kant uses the term, the "highest good" is that good which is complete along all relevant dimensions.[37] Thus, as Kant writes in the second *Critique*, practical reason "seeks the unconditioned totality of the object of pure practical reason, under the name of the highest good" (KpV 5:108). In this way, the idea of the highest good goes beyond the idea of the good will as something that possesses unconditional value. For while the good will has unconditional value according to Kant, it does not exhaust the "totality" of the good *qua* the proper object of practical reason. Instead, in order to arrive at the idea of this "totality" (the highest good), we must place the unconditional value of the good will within a larger system of conditional goods, which encompasses all other forms of value or worth and their various relations of dependence. Only by doing this will we arrive at the idea of the "unconditioned totality of the object of pure practical reason".[38]

Thus, while Kant's account of the highest good begins with the unconditional value of the good will and the associated worth of rational nature, it does not end there. Rather, it extends this unconditioned value to include all the forms of value that are conditional upon it. So, in particular, the highest good involves not merely the unconditioned value of rational wills freely willing the good, but also the derivative value of a natural world that is systematically related to these wills such that (i) what they will is made actual and (ii) happiness is apportioned to them in accordance with their degree of moral worth.[39] It is this system of ends, according to Kant, that forms the proper object of "wisdom"—or, in other words, of the sort of "practical comprehension" which represents the most perfect form of practical cognition we are capable of as human beings (KpV 5:108, 5:130–1).

Not surprisingly, for Kant the fact that the highest good involves *both* morality *and* happiness in a systematic relationship follows from the fact that we are both rational and sensible beings. Thus, while Kant insists that rationality demands that we treat the value of happiness as merely conditional on its relationship with the moral law (and so pure practical reason), he does not deny that all of us necessarily have a practical concern for our own happiness. As a result, although the value of happiness is merely conditional, and in particular is conditional on whether this happiness is deserved, finite agents will necessarily experience a lack of deserved happiness as a way in which the world is less good that it ought to be.

As this indicates, happiness is far from irrelevant to Kant's conception of the good. Rather, it plays a crucial role in *making determinate* the abstract demands of

---

[37] For a much more detailed discussion of the highest good in Kant and its relationship to the PSR as a practical principle, see (Nisenbaum 2018, forthcoming).

[38] In effect this involves completeness with respect to both the ascending and descending series of conditions here.

[39] See (Engstrom 1992; Reath 2006; Nisenbaum 2018, forthcoming).

the moral law as characterized above. After all, to understand the implications of the moral law for sensible creatures like ourselves, we need to take into account the basic practical significance of happiness for such creatures. Once again, this significance will always be qualified by the relationship between the happiness in question and the moral law. But nonetheless, we cannot make determinate sense of what the moral law demands *of us* without recognizing the importance that creatures like us necessarily attach to our own happiness.[40] It is this sort of a picture of the good—one that begins with the abstract principles of pure practical reason but then determines these principles in accordance with the practical significance of happiness for creatures like us—that reaches its most complete form in the idea of the highest good.[41]

Once again, this idea is particularly important for us here because Kant claims that the idea of the highest good represents, in some sense, the highest object of reason in general. This is sometimes taken to indicate that reason is, for Kant, fundamentally concerned with practical matters *as opposed to* (say) cognition from principles or comprehension. But, as we have already seen, this way of describing the relationship between theoretical and practical reason rests on a conception of cognition that Kant himself would reject. Rather, such claims are best understood not as asserting that reason is *fundamentally practical as opposed to cognitive*, but rather as another way of understanding the underlying unity of reason's practical and cognitive dimensions.

To see how this is possible, we need to connect Kant's claims about the highest good with the last chapter's discussion of theoretical belief in the unconditioned. For one of the most important roles of the highest good within Kant's system is to provide us with our best grasp of what the *object of complete theoretical and practical comprehension* would have to be like for such comprehension to be possible. The highest good is thus not only the highest object of practical reason; it also gives our theoretical conception of the unconditioned a determinacy of content that it would otherwise lack, thereby taking us as close as we can come to an understanding of the unconditioned Something that the supreme principle posits the existence of.

In particular, as we saw above, as long as we limit ourselves to a purely theoretical perspective, our best grasp of what this object is like is provided by the three ideas of theoretical reason—namely, the soul, the world, and God. But our theoretical grasp of the nature of these things is so indeterminate that we

---

[40] Of course, to say this is to leave the details of how this occurs very much open. I won't say much about this here, in part because I agree with (Bremner forthcoming) that Kant is in some ways closer than one might imagine to contemporary forms of "particularism" about this question than one might have thought—even though the resulting sort of "particularist universalism" is quite different from the particularism one finds in, say, (Dancy 2018). Contrast, to some degree, the attempts to account for this sort of determination in more explicitly rule-governed terms in (Timmons 2017).

[41] See also (Guyer 2000).

cannot be said to have any sort of theoretical cognition of them. Thus, it is fortunate for theoretical reason's aims that, in addition to giving us a grasp of what the ideal object of *practical* comprehension must be like, the idea of the highest good also brings these three ideas into a systematic relationship with one another and, by doing so, provides us with a richer and more determinate grasp of their objects.

More precisely, the essence of the idea of the highest good lies precisely in a system of relationships between these three ideas. After all, as understood by Kant, the idea of the highest good consists precisely in the idea of (i) God establishing certain systematic relations between (ii) immortal rational subjects and (iii) the world of appearances. Thus, in thinking of God, the soul, and the world in the terms required by the highest good, we not only make more determinate our practical conception of what ought to be, we also make more determinate *our theoretical conception of what is*, albeit on distinctively practical grounds. In this way, as Kant stresses, the comprehension or "wisdom" that our grasp of the highest good brings with it has both a theoretical and a practical dimension: "*wisdom* theoretically regarded signifies *the knowledge of the highest good* and practically *the uniformity of the will to the highest good* (KpV 5:130–1). In short, for Kant, the highest good provides us with our best grasp of the system of objects (both theoretical and practical) that would satisfy reason's drive for maximally systematic and unified comprehension in *both* the theoretical and practical domains. Thus, as Gardner points out, it is the idea of the highest good that best "satisfies reason's 'architectonic' interest".[42] For it is the idea of the highest good that provides us with our most fundamental model for thinking about the objects of both theoretical and practical comprehension. In this sense, the highest good truly is the highest idea or end of reason in *both* its theoretical and its practical manifestations.[43]

---

[42] (Gardner 1999). Note again that the third *Critique*'s "transcendental principle of purposiveness" further extends the resulting conception of the "highest good" by adding to it the idea of God as creating a system of natural laws that has the unity that "they would have if an understanding (even if not ours) had likewise given them for the sake of our faculty of cognition" (KU 5:180). Compare the discussion in (Bowman 2021).

[43] Compare the excellent discussion in (Fugate 2014): "Presumably, in view of what we saw with the previous two meanings, this unity of reason would presuppose an idea by means of which the unity of reason in the service of the understanding (theoretical) and the unity of reason commanding in the moral law (practical) are somehow brought into an overarching systematic unity of all possible cognitions of whatever kind (wisdom)... this idea is precisely that of the highest good as the *bonum consummatum*."

7
The Autonomy of Reason and the Capacity for Autonomy

Our account of the unity of reason thus far has focused on Kant's conception of reason as the highest of our cognitive powers. In developing this account, we began with the observation that Kant's conception of cognition is a conception of *both* theoretical cognition of what is—that is, cognition that aims to be responsive to existing objects—*and* practical cognition of what ought to be—that is, cognition that aims to make its objects actual. Given this, as we explored in Chapter 4, Kant's references to reason as the capacity for "cognition from principles" or "comprehension" can be made more determinate in at least two ways. First, we can consider this capacity in the guise of a capacity for *theoretical* cognition from principles or comprehension. And second, we may consider it in the guise of a capacity for *practical* cognition from principles or comprehension—that is, what Kant often describes as "wisdom" (*Weisheit*).

Then, in Chapters 5 and 6, we discussed how we can make use of this conception of reason as the capacity for comprehension to explain why Kant associates both theoretical and practical reason with the principles he does. In this way, while our discussion thus far has focused on the "more cognitive" dimensions of reason, one of its consistent themes has been that these dimensions apply *equally* to theoretical and practical reason, thus providing us with a powerful way of developing a unified conception of both in Kantian terms. But, nonetheless, partisans of "more practical" or "agentive" conception of reason may feel neglected by our discussion so far. For while we have constantly emphasized the practical dimension of Kant's characterizations of reason as a cognitive capacity, we have not yet given much space to the "more practical" or "agentive" characterizations of reason that Kant also provides. So, to see why *all* that Kant says about reason is rooted in a single, unified conception of this capacity, I want now to discuss these "more agentive" characterizations of reason more explicitly and to explain how they fit into the account of reason and its unity we have been developing.

To do so, in this chapter I'll build on the last chapter's discussion of the moral law to focus more explicitly Kant's claim that reason is a genuinely *autonomous* capacity or faculty—and, indeed, that reason is autonomous in a deeper and more complete sense than any other such capacity. In considering this, my aim will be to argue that, far from conflicting with the idea of reason as the capacity for comprehension, the idea of reason as autonomous represents another way of presenting the same fundamental conception of reason. Indeed, one of my central claims in this chapter will be that one of Kant's deepest insights lies precisely in his recognition that these two basic ways of conceiving of reason's function—comprehension and autonomy—are ultimately equivalent. For example, as we will see, we can achieve genuine comprehension only through the autonomous exercise of reason. And similarly, reason can be conceived of as an autonomous capacity only insofar as it is a capacity for certain forms of comprehension.

Moreover, we will see that reason, as the capacity for cognition from principles or comprehension, forms the essential core of our capacity to exercise autonomy in a broader sense. That is, it is the core of our capacity to be the source of the principles, reasons, and ends that govern our actions, choices, and beliefs. Thus, far from conflicting with the idea that reason has an especially close relationship with autonomy, our discussion of the kind of cognitive capacity reason is lays the groundwork for a richer and more precise understanding of *why* Kant connects reason and autonomy in the manner he does.

a. Kant's Conception of Capacities as Autonomous

Let's turn now to Kant's conception of reason as autonomous and its connections with his conception of reason as the capacity for comprehension. In doing so, it is important to begin by clarifying exactly what Kant means when he speaks of the *autonomy of reason*.[1] This is crucial because in the contemporary philosophical debate, autonomy is often thought of primarily as a property of individual agents or actions.[2] As we will see, those sorts of questions are hardly absent from Kant's thought. But nonetheless it is important to begin by stressing that Kant generally treats autonomy, at least in the first instance, as a property of faculties or capacities, as opposed to a property of individuals or individual actions.[3] Thus,

---

[1] This idea is, of course, not wholly novel to Kant. Nor is it wholly due to the influence of Rousseau on him. For example, compare Wolff: "Since we cognize through reason what the law of nature wants, a rational human being needs no further law, but by means of his reason he is a law for himself" (1720, 18).

[2] For an excellent overview, see (Buss 2008).

[3] (O'Neill 2002) argues that autonomy is not primarily a property of individual agents, but rather a property of principles. In doing so, she agrees with my negative point here but disagrees (to some degree) with my positive one. In response, I would simply stress that while Kant will sometimes speak of autonomy as a property of principles, this attribution is ultimately downstream from the more fundamental notion of capacities as autonomous. In particular, for Kant, a principle will count as autonomous just in case it is the principle of a (possible) autonomous capacity: "Autonomy of the will is the property of the will through which the will is a law to itself (independently of any property of the objects of the will)" (4:440). Interestingly, neither "capacity" nor "faculty" appear in (O'Neill 2002), excepting a reference to Kant's *Conflict of the Faculties*.

the primary notion for Kant is not the idea of *me* or *my actions* as autonomous, but rather the notion of *reason itself* as autonomous.[4]

Of course, as we will discuss, since rational capacities are always realized in some agent or agents, we can extend this account of the autonomy of reason so that it applies to agents and their actions. But it is important to begin with what, for Kant, is most fundamental—namely, the notion of a capacity or faculty or power as autonomous. Once again, this focus is important, in part, because it allows us to be flexible about how reason (as a capacity or power) is realized by imperfectly rational creatures like us. For example, in a broadly Hegelian vein, it might be that this capacity can be fully realized, not by individual human beings, but only by collectives or societies that are organized in a rational fashion. One of the attractions of a focus on the nature of rational powers, as opposed to the individuals or other substances that realize these powers, is that it allows us a great deal of flexibility with respect to this question and others like it.[5] This flexibility, it seems to me, represents one of the attractive features of a Kantian approach to these issues.

But what does it mean to say of a capacity or power that it is autonomous? As I understand Kant's account, to say this is just to say that a capacity's *proper exercise* involves a form of activity *whose law or principle is given by the capacity itself.*[6] In this sense, the question of whether a capacity is autonomous for Kant is always, in the first instance, a question about how its proper exercise is best understood and explained—that is, a question about whether the proper exercise of this capacity is captured by the idea of that capacity as being "a law to itself...independently of any property" of its objects (GMS 4:440). Thus, when Kant speaks of autonomy as a matter of *Selbst-Gesetzgebung* (GMS 4:431; V-Met/Mron 29:629) or *eigene Gesetzgebung* (KpV 5:33), what is at issue in the first instance is whether a capacity like reason (or the will) "gives a law to itself", and not whether (say) an individual agent does.[7]

To understand what this means, it is important to distinguish the autonomy of a capacity from the related notion of a capacity as spontaneous. As I understand

---

[4] Compare (Reath 2006; Timmermann 2010; Sensen 2012). For a recent example of how this can generate confusions about Kant's conception of autonomy, see (Larmore 2021).

[5] For related discussion, see (Pippin 2018). Once again, this is especially important in the context of passages like the following: "In the human being (as the only rational creature on earth), those predispositions whose goal is the use of his reason were to develop completely only in the species, but not in the individual." (IAG 8:18–19).

[6] Compare the reading of "autonomy of the will" as "the sovereignty of the will over itself" in (Reath 2006). It is important to distinguish this general notion of autonomy from the Formula of Autonomy. Plainly these are closely connected in some way, but their relationship is not as simple as it might at first seem. For an example of the potential complexities here, see (Kleingeld 2018), which argues that the Formula of Autonomy loses its centrality within Kant's conception of his moral philosophy over time due to a shift in Kant's conception of the nature of legitimate legislation. But, as Kleingeld notes, even if this is true, it does not mean that Kant ceases to be committed to the idea of reason as autonomous. Thus, even if Kant does indeed end up rejecting or the Formula of Autonomy, we should not see this as a rejection of the idea of reason as autonomous.

[7] Compare (Reath 2019): "the nature of the will, or (equivalently) the nature of practical reason, is by itself the source of its own fundamental principle—the basic principle according to which the faculty operates."

Kant's use of these terms, to say that capacity is spontaneous—or, perhaps better, that it is capable of spontaneous forms of activity—is simply to say something about *the form of causality* that is characteristic of that capacity. A capacity is spontaneous for Kant just in case it is capable of acting in a manner that is independent of any external influence.[8] Kant's conception of autonomy, as I understand it, is related to this notion but distinct from it. For to say that a capacity is autonomous is, for Kant, to say something about this capacity's *proper* form of exercise. More precisely, it is to say that this capacity's proper exercise can be characterized in terms of this capacity's acts being subject only to a law or principle that it gives to itself. In other words, insofar as a capacity is autonomous, this capacity *ought* to function in a manner that consists solely in it being governed by its own internal principle(s). In this sense, while questions about the spontaneity of a capacity are always merely causal, questions about the autonomy of a capacity are always in part normative or evaluative: they always address the question of how that capacity is *properly* exercised.

As this indicates, the sort of "self-lawgiving" involved in autonomy has a number of different aspects for Kant: explanatory, normative, *and* cognitive.[9] First, the role of this sort of "self-legislation" is always, in part, explanatory, although since, as just noted, what is at issue here is the *proper* exercise of some faculty, questions about the autonomy of a faculty are always in part normative as well. Still, insofar as a faculty is autonomous, we can explain its proper form of activity through reference to its internal principle (so long as nothing external to that faculty interferes with it).[10] But because the possibility of such "hinderance" or "interference" always exists in finite, imperfectly rational creatures like ourselves, the "law-giving" at issue here is not merely explanatory for Kant. Rather, because of this, the "law" that these capacities "give to themselves" also plays a *normative* role, characterizing how they *ought* to operate in creatures in whom such interference is possible.[11] Finally, as we discussed above, this normative or teleological dimension of a capacity's "self-legislation" is closely associated for Kant with the idea that such capacities must represent their own characteristic

---

[8] See, for example, the extremely helpful discussion in (Brink forthcoming).

[9] Compare (Watkins 2019). In treating these different aspects of autonomy as forming a package, I am (to some degree) taking issue *both* with readings of "autonomy" like that of (Reath 2006), which emphasize the normative dimension of autonomy over the explanatory dimension, *and* readings of "autonomy" that emphasize the explanatory dimension of autonomy over the normative dimension, although obviously my reading is heavily influenced by Reath's work on these topics.

[10] Note again that these sorts of explanatory claims do not require Kant to deviate from his general commitment to the idea that real grounding relations between things are always irreflexive. In other words, the sense in which reason is autonomous for Kant does not require that reason be self-causing or self-necessitating in the manner one might associate with Spinoza's God. For more discussion of this, see again (Chaplin forthcoming). Note also that I must leave to the side here the complicated question of whether Kant's account of radical evil in the *Religion* represents a break with his earlier work on this score.

[11] Again compare (Reath 2006).

forms of activity to themselves in some sense. Thus, when any capacity fails to act in accordance with its own internal principles, it is failing to act in accordance with its own representation of how it ought to function. In this sense, a capacity that fails to act as it ought to acts in a manner that conflicts with its own implicit "self-understanding".

As this should indicate, there is a sense in which the basic conceptual framework at work in Kant's conception of reason as autonomous can be applied to *any* rational capacity.[12] For all our higher rational capacities are capable of spontaneous forms of activity. And in any case of spontaneous activity, it is the internal principle of the relevant faculty that provides the activity in question with its distinctive form. So, for Kant, any rational capacity is "self-legislating" with respect to some of the (formal) features of its objects. In this way, there is a sense in which the proper exercise of any rational capacity can be described in terms of a contrast between proper (and so "autonomous") exercise and improper (or "heteronomous") exercise. None of our rational faculties should, according to Kant, operate in a manner that involves simply "following the lead" of a law that is provided by something *wholly external* to them.[13]

But this does not mean that these capacities are all equally "autonomous" in the fullest sense of this term. For while there is a sense in which every rational capacity ought to function "autonomously", there is also a sense in which some capacities (or systems of capacities) are more autonomous than others. To see why there is a contrast between rational capacities to be drawn on this score, consider, for example, the understanding. On Kant's account, the understanding is a *spontaneous* capacity, and so does have the capacity to function in a "free and yet lawful by itself" fashion (KU 5:241). For example, the understanding manifests this sort of "pure spontaneity" when it forms mere thoughts involving the unschematized categories. For in this case, the understanding's activities are governed solely by its own internal principles (considered on their own).[14]

If this were all the proper exercise of the understanding involved, we would have no reason to treat it as "less autonomous" than any other faculty. But, of course, it is not. For example, consider the relationship between the understanding and theoretical reason. When viewed as a part of the larger system of rational capacities, the understanding's activities are oriented not merely towards the *internal* ends of the understanding *itself*, but rather towards the more demanding

---

[12] In this sense, I agree with (Cohen 2014) that a version of Kant's conception of autonomy applies both to theoretical and practical reason, although I also think she overstates the similarity of these cases.
[13] See, for example, Kant's comment that "to think for oneself" is "the maxim of reason that is never *passive*. The tendency [to passivity], hence to heteronomy of reason, is called *prejudice*; and the greatest prejudice of all is representing reason as if it were not subject to the rules of nature, i.e. *superstition*" (KU 5:294f).
[14] Similarly, the understanding manifests this sort of "pure spontaneity" insofar as we are concerned only with its legislation of the abstract form of laws—a form that, again, is grounded solely in features of the understanding as such.

ends that are characteristic of theoretical reason as the highest theoretical faculty.[15] In this way, while the understanding's activities are of course governed by its own internal principles, when viewed as a part of this larger system of faculties, these principles are themselves best understood as standing in the service of theoretical reason's aims, aims that provide our *ultimate* ends as theoretical cognizers. As a result, the proper exercise of the understanding is only *fully* intelligible insofar as we view the understanding as subject to a law or standard that is imposed upon it by theoretical reason.

This points to the limits on the autonomy of the understanding from a "top-down" direction, but similar considerations also arise from a "bottom-up" perspective as well. For while the understanding is capable (at least in principle) of forming *mere thoughts* in a purely spontaneous fashion, in doing so it has no hope (at least for creatures like us) of achieving the understanding's own internal aims. For, at least in us, such thoughts on their own can never amount to *cognition of objects* for Kant.[16] Rather, at least in our case, the understanding can only successfully achieve its aim of cognizing objects insofar as it is responsive to the deliverances of sensibility. And this dependence of the understanding (as a cognitive faculty) on sensibility relates, not merely to the matter the understanding operates on, but also to the form of the understanding's own acts, at least insofar as these are guided by the *schematized categories*. For when the understanding synthesizes some intuition in accordance with a schematized category, its activities are guided by a principle that is grounded in *both* the nature of the understanding *and* our particular form of sensibility.[17] Thus, in these cases, "the law" that governs the understanding's activities cannot be regarded as given to the understanding *solely* by itself.[18] In this way, in the theoretical sphere, what is *fully* autonomous for Kant is not so much the understanding considered in isolation from our other faculties, but rather the *entire system* of faculties under reason's guidance, or "reason" in the broad, as opposed to the narrow, sense. For it is only this system of faculties that represents a capacity whose proper exercise can be *fully* characterized in terms of it *solely* "giving a law to itself".

---

[15] See (Schafer 2022a).

[16] Compare: "To be able to abstract from a representation, even when it forces itself upon a human being through sense, is a much greater ability than the ability to attend: because it proves a freedom of the capacity for thought and the power of the mind to control the state of its representations" (Anth 7:131). Note that the freedom of the understanding at issue here is plainly insufficient for genuine cognition on its own. (But contrast GMS 4:290, which suggests a more robust form of freedom with respect to the understanding.)

[17] As I discuss in (Schafer 2022a), this means that the nature of the understanding (as a faculty of theoretical cognition) is in some sense "transformed" by its relationship with sensibility. In other words, in sensibly conditioned creatures like us, we can only understand how the understanding can function as a source of genuine *cognition* insofar as we understand the understanding's own internal principles to be informed by the understanding's relationship with sensibility.

[18] My main point of disagreement with (Kohl 2015)'s excellent treatment of these issues lies in his relevant neglect of this crucial point. Compare (McLear forthcoming).

Something broadly similar is true in the practical case as well. For there too, it is really the full *system* of faculties under practical reason's governance that is best regarded as governed *only* by a law it has given to itself. This remains true, even though practical reason can achieve a greater degree of practical cognition in its own terms than theoretical reason can. For in order to fully achieve its aims, practical reason must still draw on the resources provided to it by a host of other rational capacities. For instance, in order to translate its general principles for action into more specific maxims, practical reason must draw on theoretical reason's grasp of causal facts about the world, and this, as just noted, will require a use of the schematized categories. Similarly, given the practical significance of my own happiness and the happiness of others, practical reason's verdicts about what I should do will also be determined, in part, by the sensible inclinations of myself and others. And, of course, practical reason's ability to translate its own internal "law-giving" into effective action in the world requires that our power of choice (*Willkür*) be properly responsive to practical reason *and* that our lower "executive powers" be properly responsive to our power of choice. Thus, the full realization of practical reason's aims will only be possible insofar as its acts are informed in various ways by the nature of these other faculties. In short, the *full* realization of practical reason's aims requires, not only the sort of abstract practical cognition that the autonomous operation of practical reason "on its own" provides, but also the proper operation of a host of other faculties under practical reason in accordance with the sort of virtue that Kant sometimes refers to as "autocracy".[19]

Once again, what this indicates is that what *really* deserves to be called "autonomous", in the fullest sense of this word, is not practical reason considered in isolation from our other faculties, but rather the full system of these faculties insofar as it functions in accordance with practical reason's aims—that is, "practical reason" in the broad sense. But nonetheless, if what we have argued above is right, there is a sense in which practical reason (in *both* the narrow and the broad senses of the term) has a special status with respect to the autonomy of our faculties.[20] After all, all our theoretical faculties are ultimately governed by theoretical reason and its end, so none of them is truly autonomous in the fullest sense of this term. Rather, each of them functions as it should insofar as it heeds the laws that theoretical reason lays down for the entire system of theoretical faculties. But, as we say in Chapter 4, at least in us, theoretical reason's own end—namely, theoretical comprehension—is itself relativized to our proper ends as the rational beings we are. And this, as we saw there, places theoretical reason in certain ways under the governance of practical reason as the faculty for the determination of such final ends. Thus, there is a sense in which only reason in its practical use can

---

[19] My thought about this is indebted to some of Tolley's work in progress on this issue.
[20] Compare the insightful discussion in (Timmermann 2012).

be said to be fully autonomous for Kant. For it is only in practical reason, as the capacity to freely determine our ends, that we locate a capacity that is not governed by a law whose origins lie outside of the capacity in question.

b. Autonomy and Practical Comprehension

Let's turn now to Kant's claims about the autonomy of reason in particular. Here my focus will be on the idea that, far from conflicting with the idea of reason as the capacity for comprehension, the idea of reason as autonomous is another way of presenting to us the same fundamental conception of reason we have been exploring above. To develop this idea, I will begin here by discussing the connections between the idea of practical cognition from absolute principles (or practical comprehension or practical wisdom) and the autonomy of practical reason. Then, in the next section, I will turn to the relationship between reason's autonomy and its capacity for a certain sort of self-comprehension (in both the theoretical and the practical cases).

As just discussed, for Kant, practical reason is autonomous insofar as its proper exercise is constituted by it acting in a manner that it is determined by its own internal a priori principle. Thus, as Kant says about practical reason:

> ... it is requisite to reason's lawgiving that it should need to presuppose only *itself*, because a rule is objectively and universally valid only when it holds without the contingent subjective conditions that distinguish one rational being from another.   (KpV 5:21)

But what exactly is involved in practical reason being "self-legislating" in this sense? As we've seen, practical reason is a faculty for practical cognition—that is, it is a faculty for forming representations of what ought to be, representations that (when all functions as it should) make the actions and objects represented by them actual. As such a faculty, if practical reason is to be autonomous in its proper exercise, its own internal a priori principles must provide it with a basis for drawing conclusions about what ought to be. As a result, for practical reason to be autonomous is just for its own internal a priori principles to provide it with a sufficient basis for this sort of practical cognition. Thus, practical reason can be autonomous only insofar as it is a faculty for *practical cognition from principles*.[21]

---

[21] Of course, in ordinary practical thought, such practical cognition from principles will not normally take the form of an explicit inference, which takes the relevant principles as its premises. But, if Kant is right, the structure of ordinary practical thought can always be made explicit through a representation of that thought in terms of such an inference from principles.

But if practical reason is to be truly autonomous, the sort of practical cognition from principles at issue here must not merely be a form of cognition from *comparative* principles, but a form of cognition from *absolute* principles as well. For, as principles of practical reason, the principles at issue must be ones that apply to the faculty of practical reason without any further conditions or restrictions. Indeed, as we have seen, for Kant, the status of these principles as unconditionally valid for practical reason is one aspect of the manner in which they are constitutive of practical reason itself. And this, as we have seen, is the deepest our insight into such principles can reach. Moreover, this appears to be more than a merely epistemic point for Kant. Rather, Kant's view seems to be that the validity of such principles must be unconditional in a stronger sense, such that there is simply no further explanation that *anyone* could give of why they hold unconditionally for practical reason in general, over and above their status as constitutive of practical reason.[22]

Thus, for Kant, if practical reason is to be a genuinely autonomous faculty, this can only be because it is a capacity for *practical cognition from absolute principles*—principles, that is, which hold unconditionally for practical reason, not just relative to our understanding of things but also in general. And, as we've discussed above, this just is what *practical comprehension* or *wisdom* consists in. So, to say that practical reason's proper mode of activity lies in its autonomous exercise is just to say that its proper mode of activity consists in a form of practical comprehension. Making these steps more explicit we arrive at the following argument:

1. The proper exercise of practical reason is autonomous if and only if this exercise is determined by practical reason's own internal principle.
2. An exercise of practical reason is determined by practical reason's internal principle if and only if this exercise consists in practical cognition from absolute principles.
3. An exercise of practical consists in practical cognition from absolute principles if and only if this exercise consists in practical comprehension.
4. Therefore the proper exercise of practical reason is autonomous if and only if the proper exercise of practical reason consists in practical comprehension.

This argument establishes an abstract equivalency between practical comprehension and the autonomy of practical reason. Given it, for reason's practical activities to be autonomous just is for these activities to provide us with practical

---

[22] Note, though, that there is a weaker fallback position available to a Kant here—namely, a position on which these principles would count as "absolute" or "unconditioned" only relative to the purposes and needs of our form of practical reason and not in this more general sense. I'll return to this below.

comprehension of what ought to be.[23] Once again, in practical contexts, Kant often prefers to speak of "wisdom" when this sort of systematic practical cognition from principles or practical comprehension is at issue. So, for example, Kant will speak of "wisdom" as involving the "perfection of [practical] cognition in the derivation of an end from the system of all ends" (V-Phil-Th/Pölitz 28:1065, compare KpV 5:108). Given this, it should come as no surprise to find Kant insisting that this sort of wisdom can only be the product of the autonomous activity of reason, as he does in the *Anthropology*: "not even the slightest degree of wisdom can be poured into a man by others; rather he must bring it forth from himself" (Anth 7:200).

c. Autonomy and the Self-Comprehension of Reason

This establishes one connection between autonomy and comprehension. But it is only the most obvious of several.[24] For a broadly similar line of argument applies not just to practical reason but to reason in both its practical and its theoretical manifestations. Insofar as either theoretical or practical reason operates in an autonomous fashion, the activities of these faculties can be regarded as a product of what we might call reason's "self-comprehension".[25] To see this, let's begin again with reason in its practical use. We just saw that activities of practical reason are autonomous only insofar as those activities provide us with practical cognition from absolute principles. But *this* requires that the agent (at least implicitly) be conscious of those fundamental principles and how the act in question follows from them. In other words, to have this sort of practical cognition from principles, we must grasp the fundamental principles that characterize the essence of practical reason, and we must (at least implicitly) appreciate how these principles ground the "to-be-done-ness" of the acts we practically cognize. In this sense,

---

[23] Once again, as (O'Neill 1989) has stressed, the conception of "practical reason" that is treated as autonomous here is not, in the first instance, the practical reason of this or that *individual* agent. Rather, the fundamental notion here is the autonomy of the *capacity of practical reason*, which (as such) is something that can be shared by more than one individual agent. But this does not mean that the autonomy of individual practical reasoners is *irrelevant*—only that the general notion of "the autonomy of practical reason" does not on its own determine how practical reason is realized by individuals. To determine exactly how it is realized, we need to turn from these abstract questions about the "autonomy of practical reason" in general to investigate what the moral law has to tell us about the attributability of practical actions to practical agents (given the other facts). For related discussion, see (Sensen 2012).

[24] There is *also* an important connection between practical autonomy and *theoretical* comprehension here. In order to know how to best realize the principles of practical reason within empirical reality, we need to understand empirical objects and they can be acted upon in an efficacious fashion. Thus, practical autonomy generally requires theoretical comprehension of the things it takes as its objects. It is this sort of *theoretical comprehension for practical purposes* that is the focus of works like the *Anthropology*.

[25] Compare (O'Neill 2002; Cohen 2014; Mudd 2017).

practical cognition from absolute principles necessarily requires a considerable (although normally implicit) understanding of the nature of practical reason itself.[26] The autonomy of practical reason is thus, for Kant, essentially connected with practical reason's self-consciousness—in particular, its consciousness of the fundamental principles at work in its acts.

But such self-consciousness is not *mere* self-consciousness. Rather, given Kant's purpose-relative definition of "comprehension", it is also appropriate to regard it as a form of *self-comprehension* as well. After all, given this definition, to decide whether the self-consciousness of practical reason at issue here counts as self-comprehension, we need to consider whether this consciousness is sufficient for the purposes of pure practical reason. And the fundamental purpose of practical reason just is to determine the will in accordance with its own principle (the moral law)—which, of course, is just what has occurred here insofar as practical reason has functioned in an autonomous fashion. So, at least in this sense, it seems that practical reason's consciousness of its own principles is indeed *sufficient for its purposes.*[27]

The attribution of this sort of self-comprehension to us might seem to run afoul of Kant's insistence that we cannot have any insight (*Einsehen*) into how freedom or pure practical reason is possible in us: "But among all the ideas of speculative reason freedom is the only one the possibility of which we *know* a priori, though without having insight into it, because it is the condition of the moral law, which we know" (KpV 5:2, compare GMS 4:463). But perhaps surprisingly, such claims do not mean that practical reason cannot achieve self-comprehension in Kant's *purpose-relative* sense of this term. For these sorts of deeper "insight" into the possibility of freedom or practical reason are incidental to the purposes of *practical reason*. Thus, relative to those purposes, our limited insight into the nature of practical reason need not translate into a failure on practical reason's part to achieve self-comprehension. In other words, for Kant, the self-comprehension of practical reason doesn't require further insight into practical reason's *ratio essendi*. Nor, by the same lights, does the self-comprehension of practical reason require that we

---

[26] Compare (Reath 2013).

[27] Of course, we might understand practical reason's purposes in a more demanding fashion. After all, as we have discussed above, practical cognition of some object is only *fully* successful (by reason's own standards) insofar as that object is made actual by our representation of it. And for this to occur, it is not enough that practical reason merely determine *itself* in an autonomous fashion; it must also be the case that these acts of self-determination determine our power of choice and our "executive capacities" to function in accordance with practical reason's conclusions. Obviously, as the various forms of *akrasia* make clear, this is not always the case. But once again, insofar as it *is* the case, practical reason's consciousness of its own principles is sufficient for its ends. So, while things are more complicated here, when we *are* able to translate practical reason's conclusions into effective actions in the world, we can say that practical reason's consciousness of its own principles is sufficient to its ends. Here too, then, there continues to be a tight connection between the degree to which practical reason can realize itself in autonomous action and the degree to which its self-consciousness should count as a form of self-comprehension. Compare (Korsgaard 1996b)'s discussion of the relationship between autonomy and what she calls self-conceptions.

comprehend *how* practical reason is possible. For while such insights are, of course, of interest to *theoretical* reason, they are not of interest to practical reason in the same way, since they are not a condition on practical reason achieving its distinctive ends. As above, we can make this argument more explicit as follows:

1. Practical reason is autonomous if and only its proper exercise is determined by practical reason's own internal principles.
2. An exercise of reason is determined by practical reason's own internal principles if and only if practical reason can provide us with conscious of its activities as grounded in its own internal principles.
3. If reason's consciousness of its own activities as grounded in its own internal principles is sufficient for its purposes, then reason provides us with comprehension of its own principles and activities.
4. In cases of autonomous action, practical reason's consciousness of its own activities as grounded in its own internal principles is sufficient for its purposes.
5. Thus, in cases of autonomous action, practical reason is autonomous if and only if practical reason can provide us with comprehension of practical reason's principles and activities (relative to practical reason's ends).

This establishes a second connection between autonomy and comprehension with respect to practical reason. But does anything similar apply to theoretical reason? In one sense, the connection between the autonomy of theoretical reason and comprehension should already be obvious. After all, as we discussed above, although there are important differences between the theoretical and practical cases for Kant, there is also a sense in which the proper use of theoretical reason is autonomous.[28] In particular, as Kant stresses, it remains true in the theoretical case that reason ought, as much as possible, to function in a "free" or "autonomous" fashion. In this sense, all thought ought to be as free as possible: "[F]reedom in thinking signifies the subjection of reason to no laws except those which it gives itself; ... if reason will not subject itself to the laws it gives itself, it has to bow under the yoke of laws given by another" (O 8:145).

As noted above, the sense in which theoretical reason's proper exercise is autonomous is somewhat weaker or more constrained than the sense in which this is true of practical reason. Nevertheless, it remains true that, insofar as theoretical reason functions in this autonomous manner, it will be guided by its own internal principle. And this internal principle, as we have seen, itself aims at theoretical comprehension. So, given this, theoretical reason will function autonomously only insofar as it *seeks* theoretical comprehension, just as practical reason's autonomy necessary involves striving for practical comprehension:

---

[28] Compare (O'Neill 1989; Cohen 2013; Mudd 2017; Smit 2019; McLear forthcoming).

1. Theoretical reason is autonomous if and only if its proper exercise is determined by theoretical reason's own internal principle.
2. Theoretical reason's own internal principle demands of us that we strive for theoretical comprehension.
3. Theoretical reason is autonomous if and only if its proper exercise involves striving for theoretical comprehension.

But is it *also* true that the autonomous activities of theoretical reason can regarded as, in some sense, an expression of theoretical reason's *self-comprehension* in the manner that we just outlined in the case of practical reason? Given the ends of theoretical reason, and our limitations with respect to them, one might well have one's doubts. And yet, much as was true in the practical case, insofar as the activities of theoretical reason *are* autonomous, we can regard them as rooted in something like theoretical reason's comprehension of itself.

More precisely, theoretical reason's activities will (again) be autonomous just in case these activities are determined by theoretical reason's internal principles. What this means is somewhat different in the case of theoretical reason than it was in the case of practical reason, for here, unlike in the practical case, reason does not ever *fully* achieve its own internal ends, even in a particular case. Rather, the activity that theoretical reason demands of us consists in an endless search for ever more systematic cognition from principles, a search that never fully achieves a *complete* system of theoretical cognition from *absolute* principles. Even so, much as in the practical case, this activity will be autonomous just in case it is determined by theoretical reason's self-understanding as the *faculty for theoretical cognition from principles*.

The question is whether this "self-consciousness of theoretical reason" should count as an instance of self-comprehension in Kant's sense of this term. If we took reason's interest to lie in *complete theoretical comprehension*, then theoretical reason's activities would never fully achieve these aims, according to Kant. In other words, if we conceived of the ends of theoretical reason in the inflationary terms familiar from "dogmatic rationalism", we would have to regard the self-consciousness of theoretical reason as insufficient with respect to these ends. But one of the main points of the critical philosophy is to bring about a *re-conception* of the proper ends of theoretical reason in us, so that we conceive of them in a more modest fashion. For one of the primary lessons of the *Critiques* is precisely that we should re-conceive of the proper use of theoretical reason as aiming, not at complete theoretical comprehension, but rather at the continual extension of our cognition of appearances, a cognition that will never arrive at cognition from absolute principles.[29] And once we have internalized *this* lesson about how to

---

[29] Despite appearances to the contrary, this point is wholly compatible with our discussion above of the transition from the logical maxim to the supreme principle. For that argument focused on the ability of theoretical reason in general to achieve its aims, and not on the ends that are characteristic of theoretical reason in a specifically human form.

properly conceive of theoretical reason's purposes, we can see that theoretical reason's self-understanding may (in some cases) be sufficient to these purposes once they are properly understood. For while theoretical reason's consciousness of its own principles does not give anything like the sort of cognition from absolute principles that we can achieve in the practical case, it is sufficient to guide the characteristic activities of theoretical reason once they are understood in the more modest terms Kant recommends. Thus, here too, there is at least *a sense* in which theoretical reason's self-consciousness can be regarded as sufficient to its purposes. And insofar as this is the case, we can again regard the self-understanding of theoretical reason at work in its activities as a form of *self-comprehension*:

1. Theoretical reason is autonomous if and only its proper exercise is determined by theoretical reason's own internal principles.
2. An exercise of reason is determined by theoretical reason's own internal principles if and only if reason can provide us with consciousness of its activities as grounded in its own internal principles.
3. If reason's consciousness of its own activities as grounded in its own internal principles is sufficient for its purposes, then reason provides us with comprehension of its own principles and activities.
4. If we restrict ourselves to the more modest ends Kant recommends to theoretical reason, theoretical reason's consciousness of its own activities as grounded in its own internal principles is sufficient for its purposes.
5. Thus, if we restrict ourselves to the more modest ends Kant recommends to theoretical reason, theoretical reason is autonomous if and only if theoretical reason can provide us with comprehension of theoretical reason's principles and activities.

d. Comprehension and the Capacity for Autonomous Action

Thus, there are several ways in which the idea of reason as an autonomous faculty is closely connected, for Kant, with idea of reason as the faculty for cognition from principles or comprehension. First, practical reason is only autonomous insofar as it provides us with a form of practical cognition from principles, and thus a form of practical comprehension. And second, reason acts autonomously only insofar as its activities are grounded in its own self-comprehension (in Kant's purpose-relative conception of the same). These arguments form the core of Kant's understanding of the relationship between comprehension and autonomy. For it is the notion of a capacity or power as autonomous that is primary for Kant. But it is also important to discuss a third way in which autonomy and comprehension are closely related, given Kant's views. To do so, we need to turn from our focus on the autonomy of practical reason as a capacity to the more familiar notions of "autonomous action" and the capacity for a certain sort of "autonomy as agents".[30]

In this section, then, I want to turn from the sense in which reason is an *autonomous capacity* to the sense in which this capacity forms the core of our broader *capacity for autonomous action*. As we will see, these two notions are closed connected.[31] For, given how Kant conceives of the ends of practical reason as a capacity, practical reason can only realize these aims insofar as its autonomous exercise grounds, not just practical reason's autonomous activity of *self-determination*, but also "autonomous actions" in the world in very much the sense that many contemporary authors have in mind when they speak of "autonomous agency". In this sense, although Kant generally treats autonomy as a property of faculties, it is not at all unreasonable to see this notion of autonomy as providing a basis for an account of autonomous agency in much the manner many Kantians have done.[32]

In other words, reason is not only an autonomous capacity for Kant; it also forms the core of Kant's conception of our capacity for autonomous agency or our autonomy as agents. To discuss why this is true, we need to turn from our prior focus on practical reason's autonomy with respect to its own internal activities, to consider the broader question of when some internal or external action can be said to be "autonomous". Fortunately, it would be a mistake to treat these questions as unrelated. After all, as a capacity for practical cognition, practical reason's interests extend to include within their scope, not just its own internal activities and representations, but also the *realization* of these representations in the form of *efficacious actions* in the world. As practical cognitions, the practical representations that practical reason forms will only achieve the relationship to their objects that they ought to have (by their own internal standards) insofar as they make

---

[30] Here my discussion links up again with the recent discussion of "self-formation" in (Kraus 2020); See also Schapiro's discussion of the proper role of our "inner animal" in (Schapiro 2021).

[31] This connection is important for Kant in part because of how he conceives of the conditions on the "imputability" of responsibility for actions to agents. In his discussion of this question, Kant stresses that an action can only be imputable to us in this sense insofar it lies "under our control" in a certain sense. As (McLear forthcoming) has recently argued, the notion of an action being "under own one's control" at issue here seems to involve the following idea: "a subject is in control of their acts when the determining grounds of those acts are not independent of any exercise of the capacities for so acting". Ultimately this means that, for Kant, actions are only attributable to us insofar as they result from the (pure or impure) self-activity of our rational capacities. Thus, for actions to be imputable to us, they must count as "autonomous" in at least this sense. Crucially, this means that, contrary to (Cohen 2013), we do not need to search for forms of "indirect control" that our will can exercise over our beliefs in order to make sense of our responsibility for these beliefs, on Kant's account. On the most fundamental level, the "control" we have over our beliefs and cognition is, for Kant, not a product of the relationship between them and our will, but 'rather a product of the spontaneity of our cognitive faculties themselves.

[32] Similarly, (Reath 2019) recommends a "narrow" or "strict" reading of Kant's core conception of autonomy, but also acknowledges that the significance of this notion brings into play a larger complex of ideas.

their objects actual. In this way, the full perfection of practical reason's characteristic form of activity will only be realized insofar as practical reason succeeds in making these actions and objects real. Thus, while there is a minimal form of practical cognition (and, indeed, practical comprehension) that is secured by practical reason's own autonomous activities on their own, practical reason's interests extend well beyond this to include within their scope everything that is required in order to translate what it wills into effective actions that make a difference in the larger world.

In this way, while practical reason's autonomy is, in the first instance, a matter of its relationship to its own activities and representations, the *complete* realization of practical reason's autonomous ends requires that these activities' influence extends beyond practical reason to make a difference in the larger world.[33] Thus, the complete realization of practical reason's own autonomy requires that practical reason (in a narrow sense) form the core of a broader capacity for autonomous action. For just as the realization of theoretical reason's interest in genuine theoretical comprehension requires the cooperation of a system of "lower" powers for theoretical cognition, the realization of practical reason's interest in genuine practical comprehension (and so action) requires the cooperation of a system of "lower" practical faculties.[34] In this way, consideration of the autonomy of practical reason *over itself* leads naturally to the idea of a general *capacity for autonomy* in a broader sense: a capacity that stands under practical reason but extends beyond the bounds of practical reason proper to involve a system of "lower" capacities, insofar as these are properly responsive to practical reason itself.[35]

---

[33] (Tolley 2017b).

[34] Compare: "The inner perfection of the human being consists in having in his control the use of all of his faculties, in order to subjugate them to his free choice" (Anth 7:144). Compare the discussion of this in (Schapiro 2021).

[35] For example, there are at least three stages of this process at which forms of *akrasia* (in a broad sense) can arise for Kant (Pasternack 1999; Guevara 2009; Hill, Jr 2012). First, we can be *akratic* insofar as our power of choice is insufficiently responsive to practical reason or the will. This, in turn, can occur in two basic ways for Kant. First, our power of choice can adopt an evil maxim by simply prioritizing our own happiness over the demands of morality. In this case, our choice of maxim will display the form of "evil" that Kant calls the "depravity of human nature"—that is, "the propensity to adopt evil maxims" simply out of our own overweening self-love (RGV 6:29). But our power of choice can also be unresponsive to practical reason insofar as it manifests our "propensity to adulterate moral incentives with immoral ones (even when it is done with good intention, and under maxims of the good)" (RGV 6:29). In this case, we will be subject to the second form of "evil" that Kant identifies in the *Religion*—namely, what he calls "impurity". Here, the power of choice does respond to practical reason by adopting a general maxim of action that is moral, but it then deviates from the dictates of practical reason in the manner in which it derives more particular choices from this general maxim. In this way, this second form of "evil" essentially involves the corruption of our powers for practical judgment. Finally, we can also be *akratic* insofar as our powers for action are insufficiently responsive to our power of choice. It is this that Kant describes as the third main form of evil—that is, "the general weakness of the human heart in complying with the adopted maxims, or the frailty of human nature" (RGV 6:29). Here, the corruption at issue is not located in our power of choice but rather in our lower

It is this *system of faculties* under the guidance of practical reason that forms Kant's conception of our more general capacity for autonomous action, or "practical reason" in the broad sense. Once again, in thinking about this system of faculties, it is important to remember that, in it, the *ultimate end* of all the acts of these faculties will be determined by their relationship to reason and its ends.[36] This is most obvious in the case of the faculty of desire, which functions properly for Kant only insofar as it acts in the service of reason's autonomous self-determination. But the same is true of the various elements in the faculty of cognition, whose activities ought to be in the service of reason's end of comprehension. And although we have not had time to discuss this in detail, the proper exercise of the faculty of pleasure and displeasure is also best understood in reference to the aims of reason. For its proper role within this system is to provide us with forms of feeling that appropriately correspond to and reinforce the proper exercise of our faculties. Thus, not only is each of these different capacities a necessary condition on reason, but their proper use is organized around the ends that reason provides to the whole system.

Relatedly, in considering this more general capacity for autonomous action in the world, it is crucial to remember that the actions at issue here are themselves constituted in part by the *grounds* and *maxims* on which the agent acts, and thus by the agent's practical cognition of their ends. For this reason, we should be careful not to conceive of this move from the internal autonomy of practical reason to the realization of practical reason's ends in a broader capacity for autonomous action in the terms of a reductive, causal account of action of the sort that dominated much of twentieth-century action theory.[37] For while practical reason requires the cooperation of various other cognitive faculties in order to realize its aims in action, this cooperation brings about a constitutive relationship between practical reason and these actions, as opposed to a merely causal one. In other words, human action, for Kant, is best understood as the shape that practical reason's attempts at practical cognition take insofar as these attempts are successful at making their objects actual.[38] For Kant, autonomous action just is the form that practical cognition takes when it makes its object real in action. Thus, the development of the capacity for autonomous action in the world is a necessary condition on the full realization of practical reason's interest in practical cognition

executive powers, the function of which is to translation our choices into effective action. As Clinton Tolley has pointed out to me, this threefold division of our practical powers in some ways corresponds to the three basic powers that Kant assigns to God: omniscience, omnibenevolence, and omnipotence.

[36] For more discussion, see (Schafer 2022a).
[37] For criticism of such accounts, see, for example, (Thompson 2008; Lavin 2015; Ford 2018).
[38] In forthcoming work, Tolley challenges this by claiming that practical reason's interest in practical cognition only extends to practical reason's internal acts of self-determination. On this view, all the phenomenal consequences of our acts of self-determination lie outside of the scope of genuine practical cognition. But this view seems to me to restrict the scope of practical cognition too narrowly, both for Kant's purposes, and for the purposes of developing a plausible version of Kant's account.

from principles. And achieving this will require the cooperation of a variety of capacities beyond practical reason in a narrow sense, as well as the cooperation of the larger world. Indeed, the full realization of the ends of practical reason will often involve an explicitly political dimension for Kant.[39]

Moreover, in this sense, actions can be *more or less* autonomous. An action will be *fully* autonomous just in case it *fully* expresses the autonomy of my capacity of practical reason. And this will be true only when the action is a successful realization of a piece of practical cognition from absolute principles. So, for Kant, *fully* autonomous action in this sense will only be possible insofar as I am acting out of my grasp of the moral law. But, of course, many human actions do not rise to this standard, as is true whenever my grounds for action are ultimately heteronomous. Crucially, such actions will still be imputable to me here so long as they express the maxim of my will. So, while all human action *ought* to be *fully* autonomous for Kant, this does not mean that I am not responsible for the less than fully autonomous actions that I perform. Nonetheless, when all goes well, the actions of such an autonomous capacity are best understood not as metaphysically distinct from the practical representations or principles which sit at that capacity's core, but rather, as more perfect or successful forms of these very representations— forms of them that are constituted in part by the relationship between these representations and the events in the world they make actual.

This is crucial, in part, because it allows Kant to make sense of how any human action can itself be conceived of in terms of a unified system of further (sub-)actions that are done for the sake of the more general action.[40] Whenever we act, we perform the action we are doing by doing many other things. And most of the actions we perform are done for the sake some larger action that they support in this way. I break the eggs and mix them together with some cream *in order to* make an omelet, which I in turn prepare *in order to* bring my sick partner something to eat in bed. Any ordinary human action involves a system of different actions—a system that places the various actions one performs into teleological relations to one another. In this sense, almost every human action involves a *teleological system of actions and ends*—that is, a system of actions that are done for the sake of doing other things.

As this makes clear, even the most ordinary human actions necessarily involve some degree of "systematic unity" in the sense characteristic of practical comprehension. Given Kant's conception of an end, this unity must be something that the agent is, in some sense, conscious of in performing the action in question. In this way, these reflections lead us to the idea that even the most ordinary forms of human action are partially constituted by a modest form of "systematic practical cognition from principles" or "practical comprehension" or "practical wisdom".

---

[39] For the importance of this for the moral law, see (O'Neill 1989; Pallikkathayil 2010).
[40] Compare (Thompson 2008; Korsgaard 2009).

For the performance of *any* human action appears to require, not just a grasp of "what to do", but also a grasp of why the action's various "sub-actions" are to be done—a grasp that places these sub-actions within the context of a larger teleological system of actions and ends. So in any instance of complex human action, there is already a connection between human action and a (very modest) form of "practical comprehension" or "practical wisdom".

Of course, there is no guarantee at this stage that this amounts to *full-fledged* practical comprehension in the sense discussed above. For while this shows that any agent, in acting, must have some grasp of why they are doing the sub-actions that are part of this local system of actions and ends, this does not mean that they will be able to answer questions about why some action is to be performed all the way to the limit of such questions, and nor does it mean that they will be able to answer these questions insofar as they are relevant to the purposes of *practical reason itself*. If they cannot accomplish these further tasks, they will not truly have practical comprehension of their actions *relative* to these aims. In other words, while any human action must involve some degree of practical cognition from principles, this cognition does not rise to the level of practical cognition from *absolute* principles in most cases. Rather, it often simply bottoms out in practical cognition from *comparative* principles. But when we do have an instance of *fully autonomous action*, the agent's practical cognition must extend beyond this so that it ultimately represents an instance of practical cognition from absolute principles as well. For an action can only be fully autonomous, for Kant, insofar as it is grounded in a genuinely autonomous exercise of practical reason. And, as we have seen, an exercise of practical reason will be autonomous insofar as it represents an instance of practical cognition from absolute principles. Thus, at least for Kant, any instance of fully autonomous action is also (at least implicitly) an instance of practical cognition from absolute principles, and so, of practical comprehension of (the goodness of) the action in question.

Fully autonomous action, in other words, requires that the agent act out of a grasp of reasons for action that ultimately terminate in an absolute practical principle—a principle, that is, characteristic of practical reason in general.[41] This might sound like an extremely demanding sense of "autonomous action", but I don't think that Kant would have viewed it in this way. For all it really requires is a view of one's action on which one's reasons for acting ultimately terminate in a grasp of the status of this action as the thing do under one's circumstances, given the relevant moral and non-moral considerations. And, in order to have *this*, at least in the sense relevant to *ordinary* practical comprehension or wisdom, we do

---

[41] Once again, it is worth stressing that Kant also has a weaker position available to him here, on which these principles would count as "absolute" or "unconditioned" only relative to the purposes and needs of our form of practical reason and not in this more general sense. But Kant's own view seems to be stronger than this more modest form of Kantianism.

not need have a sophisticated grasp of the moral and rational principles that stand beyond this action. Rather, we must only be acting as we do *because* the action in question is consistent with the demands of morality and rationality as they apply to our situation.[42]

Thus, the sort of "practical comprehension" at issue here should not be taken to require a hyper-reflective attitude towards our reasons for action. Rather, in ordinary agents, this sort of practical comprehension generally takes the form of a systematic and often tacit grasp of how one's actions ought to be sensitive to one's circumstances. It is crucial, for Kant, that this sensitivity be encoded in one's full maxims for action, and that these maxims, at least in principle, generally be available to more explicit forms of conscious reflection like those involved in moral philosophy. But none of this requires that ordinary agents engage in such explicit reflection. Rather, just as reasoning in a healthy fashion does not require the ability to write a handbook of abstract logical rules, the sort of practical comprehension that autonomy requires does not require each of us to write our own personal work of Kantian moral philosophy in our head.[43]

Nonetheless, as the previous reflections should make plain, there is a sense in which any human action does require placing one's action in a more systematic context. Indeed, in the case of truly autonomous action, this context will involve an implicit relationship between one's action and, *via* the FUL and the FH, literally all the actions that any human agent may perform. But establishing this relationship between one's action and these other actions does not require that one think of all these other actions. It only requires that one's action be grounded in one's (often tacit) grasp of a practical principle—like the moral law—that ensures that one's actions are responsive to these other considerations insofar as they are relevant to what one chooses to do. In this sense, this conception of autonomous action does not require that every autonomous moral agent be anything like a systematic moral philosopher.

e. Comprehension as a Guide to Autonomy

With this in mind, I want to close this chapter by briefly discussing the contemporary relevance of the connections between Kant's conception of reason as the

---

[42] Of course, having a sense of which considerations are relevant in one's situation is far from trivial. But Kant is consistent in maintaining that ordinary agents are highly sophisticated with respect to the first-order task of responding in an appropriate fashion to the morally relevant factors in their own environment. What ordinary agents do not possess, and what is not required here, is any sort of explicit or reflective grasp of this system of morally relevant considerations. It is the task of the moral philosopher, and not the ordinary moral agent, to develop a "moral theory" in this sense. But Kant believes that all the materials needed to do so are already implicit in how ordinary agents systematically respond to their own concrete situations.

[43] For a helpful discussion of why Kant's conception of reflection and virtue does not demand this sort of explicit, philosophical reflection of ordinary moral agents, see (Merritt 2018). Compare again (Bremner forthcoming) here.

capacity for comprehension and his conception of reason as autonomous. To do so, I'm going to begin by illustrating the intuitive force of these ideas by connecting them to Jaeggi's recent revival of the traditional complaint that certain social practices or forms of life are objectionably "alienating" for those involved in them. Jaeggi summarizes the core of this worry as follows:

> Alienation means indifference and internal division, but also powerlessness and relationlessness with respect to oneself and to a world experienced as indifferent and alien. Alienation is the inability to establish a relation to other human beings, to things, to social institutions and thereby also—so the fundamental intuition of the theory of alienation—to oneself. An alienated world presents itself to individuals as insignificant and meaningless, as rigidified or impoverished, as a world that is not one's own, which is to say, a world in which one is not "at home" and over which one can have no influence. The alienated subject becomes a stranger to itself; it no longer experiences itself as an "actively effective subject" but a "passive object" at the mercy of unknown forces. (Jaeggi 2014, 3–4)

As this indicates, for Jaeggi, to speak of "alienation" is to speak of a seemingly diverse range of complaints whose relationship is often difficult to completely and precisely explain. Given this, I don't want to claim that everything that might reasonably be regarded as a form of alienation can be understood as a failure of practical comprehension. But I think it is striking that so many of the phenomena that Jaeggi cites as forms of alienation are captured very naturally in this way.

For example, consider a sense of indifference with respect to one's life and the choices one faces in that life. This form of alienation plainly represents a failure of practical comprehension in our sense. For it involves a failure to fully appreciate or grasp what is to be done and why. Similarly, finding "meaning" or "purpose" in the world is plainly one central element in having practical comprehension as defined above. So, forms of alienation that involve a failure to find this sort of meaning in life are captured very well by the present account. And much the same is also true of a sense of powerlessness or mere passivity. For this sort of self-consciousness is also incompatible with practical comprehension in our sense. After all, part of what it is for practical comprehension to be successful is for it to self-consciously manifest itself in effective action in the world. Successful practical comprehension requires a recognition that one has this sort of efficacy, and it requires that this recognition makes a difference to the way things are. Thus, a failure to represent oneself as powerful or active must involves a defect of practical comprehension. Finally, as discussed above, in order to comprehend something, we must be able to place what we comprehend within a larger, more unified context that allows us to answer why- and how-questions with respect to it. Thus, insofar as the world or oneself appears to one to be deeply fragmented or disunified, this too will represent a dimension along which our practical comprehension is defective. In all these ways, the present focus on practical comprehension seems perfectly placed to capture the concerns traditionally associated with "alienation critique".

As this indicates, I believe these connections between comprehension and autonomy can help to illuminate the sort of autonomy that is rationally significant on a post-Kantian account of these issues.[44] But this can also be seen with respect to recent debates about the foundations of Kantian moral philosophy. For example, a familiar difficulty with respect to Kant's appeals to autonomy in a moral context is the worry that this appeal is "too thin" or "formal" to provide morality with the positive content it intuitively possesses. The difficulties with respect to this issue were, of course, noted by many of Kant's early critics.[45] But they have also bedeviled more recent attempts to revive a Kantian conception of autonomy within moral philosophy. For example, neo-Kantians like Korsgaard have argued that autonomous agency is possible only insofar as one satisfies the demands of a broadly Kantian conception of morality on which one ought to act only on *principles* that *could be accepted by all rational agents*.[46] But many philosophers of action have been skeptical about whether it is plausible that the mere idea of autonomous agency requires something this robust. For does autonomous agency really requires *lawfulness* in the sense that we act only on *general principles* or laws? And even if autonomous agency does require this, does that require that these laws be *intersubjectively valid*, in the sense that we must treat them as principles that every rational agent could join us in accepting?[47]

One might respond to such concerns by invoking a more robust conception of autonomy from which they clearly do follow. But we would then face the challenge of why *this* (robust) conception of autonomy should have the importance we claim it does from either a rational or a moral perspective. As a result, if we go in this direction, the Kantian's claims about the significance of autonomy (in this robust sense) could easily seem to be nothing but another substantive foundational normative claim just like any other, in which case, the Kantian view of the foundations of moral philosophy would be much less distinctive than many Kantians have claimed.[48]

Although they will not completely respond to such worries, the connections between practical comprehension or understanding and autonomy can, I think, help Kantians to respond to *some* of them. For the idea of practical comprehension and the idea that autonomy requires comprehension are ideally suited to help the Kantian establish that autonomy (in this sense) requires many of the elements

[44] This section draws on (Schafer 2018b).
[45] This complaint goes back at least to Hegel. For an overview of some of these concerns see (Wood 2007).
[46] See e.g. (Wood 2007; Korsgaard 2009).
[47] For a pointed expression of this objection, see (Setiya 2010). For an extreme version of it, see (Gingerich forthcoming).
[48] This would return us to the concerns discussed in the "shmagency" literature. See Chapter 3 for more discussion.

that Kant's critics have been suspicious of. For example, as we have seen, the idea of practical comprehension plainly does bear a tight connection with the ability to place one's views in a more systematic and explanatorily deep context. For, if we are to comprehend what to do, we must be able to explain why some action is indeed the thing to do under the circumstances. In the absence of this ability, we may "know" in some sense *which* action is the right one to perform, but we will have no genuine practical understanding of this, and so will fail to be fully autonomous in our actions. In such cases, there will be a clear sense in which we are still "flying blind" in our practical deliberations.

In this way, as we have explored above, there is a tight connection between comprehension and the availability of *principled explanations* in both the theoretical and practical domains. Thus, if we think of autonomy through the lens of its relationship with practical comprehension, we can more easily appreciate why genuine autonomy requires the sort of "generality" in practical thought that is so central to Korsgaard's account of these issues. Indeed, as we have also seen above, if such explanations are to be satisfactory from the point of view of achieving comprehension, they must (at least in principle) be shareable with other rational subjects. For insofar as they fail to meet this criterion, they will fail to transcend our own, merely subjective perspective in the manner that genuine comprehension does (KU 5:293-4). In this way, theoretical and practical comprehension requires having a perspective on what one understands that is not simply an expression of one's own *idiosyncratic* perspective but rather represents a point of view that is responsive to the perspective of *any* possible rational subject whatsoever.

Thus, this too seems to be a fundamental aspect of comprehension: insofar as we grasp something only from *this or that* perspective, our understanding of it will necessarily be partial and imperfect.[49] And so, when we apply these ideas to practical comprehension, we find that practical comprehension—and so, by extension, autonomy—requires, not just a certain sort of "generality" or "lawfulness" in our practical thought, but also a view of these laws or principles that treats them as following from features of rationality that are common to all rational agents as such.[50] In this way, the idea of practical comprehension seems to me to have a more direct and compelling connection with *both* lawfulness and intersubjectivity than our intuitive (and vague) notion of autonomous agency. So, by connecting autonomy together with practical comprehension, we can motivate many of the traditional Kantian claims about what autonomous agency requires of us. But, at the same time, I think that comprehension or understanding also has a compelling connection with our intuitive understanding of rationality itself. After

---

[49] This, we should note, is one of the reasons that our comprehension of most things is imperfect for Kant.
[50] Compare Nagel's classic discussion in (Nagel 1986).

all, our intuitive conception of rationality or reason is precisely the conception of something like *the capacity to make sense of things* (in both the theoretical and practical spheres). And this is just to say that our intuitive notion of rationality is as the capacity for what Kant calls comprehension. Thus, the intuitive connection between rationality and the project of comprehending things seems to much more obvious and robust sense than the (true, but nonetheless contentious) claims Kantians make about the relationship between rationality and autonomy.[51]

---

[51] Indeed, Kant's view seems to be that only skeptics whose skepticism is motivated by the aim of better understanding things are truly worth responding to. It is this, in part, that makes Hume such an important interlocutor for Kant. For more discussion, see (Goldhaber forthcoming.; Schafer 2021a).

Conclusion

Reason, Reasons, and the Future of the Critical Project

In Part I, we developed a reading of the foundations of Kant's philosophy which characterized it as rooted in the self-consciousness of our basic rational powers, or, more simply, in the self-consciousness of reason itself. Since these powers are all capacities for some form of cognition—that is, for consciousness of something objective—this locates the foundations of Kant's philosophy in the form of self-organizing self-consciousness that is distinctive of the human form of cognition. In this way, as we saw, Kant's philosophy can be seen as an attempt to develop our human cognitive capacities as far as possible, given the limitations placed on those capacities by our nature as finite, sensible beings.

When applied to the meta-normative domain, this approach resulted in a form of what is today called "meta-normative constitutivism"—that is, an attempt to ground the fundamental norms that apply to us as finite rational beings in our particular form of rationality and the capacities that make this form of rationality possible. At the core of this form of constitutivism was the idea that the fundamental norms that apply to us as rational beings are rooted in our rational capacities, and (in particular) in the standards that these capacities set for their own proper functioning:

Rational Constitutivism: The fundamental norms that apply to us are grounded in our nature as *finite rational beings* or *sensibly conditioned beings with the capacity of reason*.

This idea, if I am right, sits at the heart of Kant's meta-normative philosophy. But in order to understand the implications of it, we needed to understand the conception of reason that forms its core. Through the course of Part II, we have seen that Kant characterizes the proper function of reason in several different, but ultimately interdependent ways, the most important of which are (i) as the capacity for (theoretical and practical) cognition from principles, (ii) as the capacity for (theoretical and practical) comprehension, (iii) as autonomous, and (iv) as the core of what we might call the capacity for autonomous agency. Moreover, through our discussion, we saw that a variety of different principles for how reason ought to function can be derived from this conception, including both a modest version of the Principle of Sufficient Reason and the various formulations that Kant provides of the moral law.

The result has been a more determinate form of Rational Constitutivism that includes both of the following forms of constitutivism within its scope as two expressions of the conception of reason that sits at the core of Kant's philosophy:

Comprehension-First Constitutivism: The most fundamental norms that apply to us are grounded in our nature as sensibly conditioned creatures with the *capacity for (theoretical and practical) comprehension*.

Autonomy-First Constitutivism: The most fundamental norms that apply to us are grounded in our nature as sensibly conditioned creatures with the *capacity for autonomous self-determination*.

More precisely, we have seen that reason is not merely one cognitive capacity among many; it is the capacity for the highest form of cognition human beings are capable of: comprehension. And, as we saw in the last chapter, in order to play this role, reason must also be autonomous and so self-governing and self-organizing. Taking these two facets of reason together, we can arrive at the idea of reason as *a self-organizing power for understanding*—at the idea, that is, of reason as a capacity that realizes itself through the development of a system of theoretical and practical comprehension that allows it to make sense of both what is and what ought to be (insofar as this is necessary for its ends).

In other words, like any rational power, reason's activities are governed and informed by how it represents its characteristic mode of activity. And it is this basic "self-understanding of reason" that realizes itself insofar as it organizes our mind and the world around us in the manner that genuine (theoretical and practical) comprehension requires. So since the core of this capacity or power lies in its own *formative self-understanding*, we might also gloss our conception of reason in terms of the idea of reason as nothing other than *self-organizing understanding* itself. At its foundations, then, reason for Kant is nothing more or less than this sort of self-organizing understanding taken to its limit—a form of understanding, that is, which strives to realize itself through further acts of understanding that allow it to make sense of ever greater parts of both the natural and the normative world.

With that in mind, in this conclusion, I hope to accomplish four main tasks. First, I want to bring out some of the general lessons of my interpretation of Kant's conception of reason for our understanding of his critical project by relating my interpretation to Longuenesee's foundational work on these topics. Second, I want to emphasize two areas of contemporary philosophy where I believe this conception of reason remains significant: contemporary debates about the nature of reasons and the recent revival of interest in social and political critique. These will point to areas in which I think these ideas can be further developed in a productive fashion. But I want then to close our discussion by raising some worries about whether Kant's account is ultimately adequate to these tasks, even by its own lights. So, despite my general optimism about the Kantian conception of reason I have been developing, I'm going to end on a note of mild pessimism, although I will leave it up to the reader whether this is a pessimism about Kant's account of reason or a pessimism about the reach of our finite cognitive capacities, which are (sadly) accurately represented by Kant's account.

a. Generalized Longuenessianism

As we've seen, given Kant's understanding of reason, it must be the faculty of reason, and reason in its practical use in particular, that provides the ends around which the system of our faculties in general is organized.[1] Thus, once again:

> To every faculty of the mind one can attribute an *interest*, that is, a principle that contains the condition under which alone its exercise is to promoted. *Reason, as the faculty of principles, determines the interest of all the powers of the mind but itself determines its own.* The interest of its speculative use consists in the *cognition* of the object up to the highest a priori principles; that of its practical use consists in the determination of the *will* with respect to the final and complete end.... (KpV 5:119–20, my emphasis)

In our discussion here, I've focused on reason as the highest of these capacities. But what would this mean for our understanding of this system of faculties more generally?

To consider this, I want to shift focus for a moment to Longuenesse's groundbreaking discussion of the unity of the acts of the understanding. In that account, Longuenesse focuses on the idea of the understanding as *the capacity to judge*. On this basis, she traces how the acts that Kant attributes to the understanding may be understood as contributing to this basic aim. In this way, she argues that the idea of the understanding as the capacity to judge "provides [us with] a definition of the original capacity from which all aspects of the understanding are developed" (Longuenesse 2005, 19). As she shows, this perspective on the function of the understanding provides a powerful lens through which to interpret Kant's arguments in both the Metaphysical and Transcendental Deductions. The result is a view of the understanding on which:

---

[1] This section adapts portions of (Schafer 2022a).

... in order to understand Kant's doctrine of the categories, and in order to understand Kant's argument to the effect that such concepts have applications to objects of experience (i.e. that all objects of experience fall under the categories), one needed to take seriously the origin Kant assigns to these concepts in logical functions of judgment. (Longuenesse 2005, 4)

Given our discussion above, Longuenesse's teleological account of the acts of the understanding can be seen as an application of certain basic features of Kant's general account of rational capacities to the understanding in particular. For example, as we have seen, a central element of Kant's general account of rational capacities is that the acts of any rational capacity form a teleological system in which these acts are done *for the sake* of the ends or interests of the capacity in question. But if this is right, then Longuenesse's account of the teleological unity of the *understanding* is only the beginning of the story. For, in order to develop a full account of the teleological unity of our faculties, we need both an account of the teleology at work in *each* of these faculties and an account of how *all* of them fit together into a single, unified teleological system. In preceding chapters, I have tried to contribute to the first of these projects by providing an account of the teleological unity of the faculty of reason in both its theoretical and its practical manifestations. But here I want to briefly consider the second.

As discussed above, this unity is essential to the viability of Kant's critical project. For, according to Kant, philosophy can achieve a rationally satisfying form only insofar as it forms a systematic whole, unified by some idea or principle. And at least within the bounds of the critical philosophy, this idea or principle can only be provided to us by our rational capacities. Thus, for Kant, the success of that project is ultimately conditional on our rational capacities themselves forming a unified system—a system, that is, which has the sort of unity that allows it to provide philosophy with the unity it needs. None of this, of course, would come as any surprise to Longuenesse. Indeed, in her work since *Kant and the Capacity to Judge*, she has attempted to generalize the results of her investigations there to apply them to the entire system of rational capacities. As should be clear, I have a great deal of sympathy with that discussion. But, when viewed against the background we have been developing, we can also see that the manner in which she attempts this extension is not always unproblematic. For example, in discussing the relationship between the various faculties that comprise the intellect for Kant—the understanding, the power of judgment, and reason—Longuenesse writes the following:

The understanding is a capacity for concepts. But we form concepts only for use in judgments. And all forms of judgment govern possible forms of syllogistic inference. The understanding, then, or the intellect as a whole—our capacity to form concepts, to combine them in judgments, and to infer true judgment from true judgment in syllogistic inferences—is nothing other than a "capacity to judge" (*Vermögen zu urteilen*).... (Longuenesse 2005, 18)

In such passages, Longuenesse plainly appreciates the need to be sensitive, not just to the internal teleological unity of each faculty considered on its own, but also to the teleological unity of the entire system of faculties. As I hope is clear, I am very sympathetic with what I take to be the spirit of her approach to this. But, at the same time, I worry that the letter of what Longuenesse says in passages like this one does not represent the best version of this idea. For passages like this one suggest a picture of the teleological unity of the system of faculties on which Longuenesse's focus on *judgment* is extended so that the nature of judgment becomes the lens through which the unity of *this entire system* is best understood.

Whether or not Longuenesse is best read as engaged in this project, it is undeniable that some of those influenced by her work have attempted just this.[2] For example, in his insightful discussion of these issues, (Engstrom 2009) focuses on the idea that "judgment includes...the awareness of itself as positively self-sustaining". As should be clear, I think that Engstrom is onto something very deep about Kant's views in making such claims. But, at the same time, in making this an issue primarily about *judgment*, as opposed to the more ambitious ends of reason, I think that his discussion makes Kant's views about this issue more mysterious than they need to be. After all, if anything is "self-consciously self-sustaining" for Kant, it must be the activities of the *faculty of reason* that has this status.

As this suggests, I believe the focus on judgment that characterizes Longuenesse's account, and many of those influenced by her, does not represent the most compelling way the spirit of that account might be developed. This, again, is for two basic reasons. First, focusing just on the understanding, while we can of course characterize the understanding as the capacity to judge, this does not fully capture the ultimate ends of the understanding as a *cognitive* faculty. After all, the teleological point of the understanding's activities (in judgment or otherwise) is not merely to generate judgments for their own sake, as if *mere* judgment *as such* were a primary cognitive good. Rather, the point of these activities, and indeed judgment in general, is to give us *cognition*. Thus, from a teleological point of view, the most fundamental of Kant's characterizations of the understanding's activity is not his characterization of the understanding as the capacity to judge, but rather his characterization of the understanding as the capacity for *discursive cognition*—that is, for cognition through concepts and judgments.[3]

---

[2] See, for example, (Kern 2006; Rödl 2007; Engstrom 2009).
[3] Authors in the Pittsburgh tradition might respond to this by insisting that the significance of cognition is something that is internal to judgment itself. But while I agree with them about this, this seems at best an unnecessarily confusing way of conceding my fundamental point.

To be clear, I suspect that Longuenesse would agree with this. And this point in no way undermines the importance she attaches to judgment in her discussion of the Metaphysical and Transcendental Deductions. For the purpose of her focus on judgment *there* is to provide us with a *Leitfaden* for understanding the structure of Kant's arguments in those sections of the first *Critique*. As long as it is used for *this* purpose, a focus on judgment seems to me quite appropriate. Nonetheless, I think it is fair to say that some readers of Longuenesse have made more of her focus on judgment than this. And these worries only become more pressing when we turn from the understanding *in particular* to consider the full system of rational capacities. Here, Longuenesse's tendency to conceive of this system as a *system for judgment* threatens to leave us with a distorted picture of how Kant conceives of this system's teleology. For, in understanding this larger system of capacities, it is crucial that we keep in mind that its activities do not aim at mere judgment, or even mere cognition, but at something much more demanding, namely, cognition from principles or comprehension.

For example, on Kant's account, the significance of the inferential activities of reason is not merely that they produce more judgments, or even more cognitions, but rather, as we have seen, that the system of inferentially-related judgments that reason thereby produces is constitutive of genuine comprehension. Thus, if we continue to focus our attention on judgment, we will lose track of Kant's account of the ends at which this system of capacities ultimately aims. Indeed, Longuenesse's focus here on unifying not just the understanding in particular, but also the entire system of rational capacities around the idea of judgment threatens to present us with a picture of this system on which it is, not reason, but rather the understanding that is ultimately responsible for the ends that give this system its unity. But any such conception of the relationship between the ends of reason and the ends of the understanding would necessarily undermine one of the most central commitments of the critical system—namely, the autonomy of practical reason as a capacity for setting and cognizing ends.[4]

For these reasons, I believe that Longuenesse's fundamental insights are best developed not through a focus on judgment, but through the idea of our rational capacities as a system that aims at comprehension, the sort of comprehension that is only possible insofar as reason functions in an autonomous fashion. When viewed in this way, we can see that judgment is ultimately of rational significance for Kant because, given the nature of our cognitive capacities, we can only achieve

---

[4] Here one might look to (Engstrom 2009)'s attempt to derive something like the requirements on genuine comprehension from the idea of judgment for assistance. But I think Engstrom's attempts in this vein only make sense insofar as they begin by assuming that judgment in some sense aims at the more demanding cognitive achievements involved in full comprehension. If so, Engstrom's claims about judgment in effect take for granted the more fundamental point I am making here about the need to focus our attention not on mere judgment but rather on comprehension, in attempting to understand the teleology at work for Kant in our cognitive capacities.

cognition, and so comprehension, *via* it. But judgment per se is hardly the point of the teleological story here. Rather, when we form judgments in a proper fashion, we are always doing so for the sake of a more general cognitive achievement—namely, comprehension (of both a theoretical and a practical sort).[5]

b. Reasons-First or Reason-First

With that in mind, let's return to the meta-normative significance of Kant's account of reason. As noted above, I believe that something like Kant's form of constitutivism offers us the prospect of developing a deep and unified account of the normative domain. To further illustrate this, I'm going to focus here on one recent style of account—namely, the sort of "reasons fundamentalism" which is currently very much in vogue in ethics, epistemology, and beyond. In considering such views, my main goal with be to illustrate how reasons fundamentalism naturally finds itself under pressure to acknowledge that something like the capacity of reason plays an *even more* fundamental explanatory role than reasons do. Thus, I want to suggest that, as one develops the view, reasons fundamentalism naturally tends to transform into a view on which it is *really reason*, and not reasons, that is truly fundamental. To illustrate this point, I'm going to focus on one of the most prominent and careful recent attempts to defend reasons-first-ism, Errol Lord's recent *The Importance of Being Rational*.[6] I believe that much of what I say about Lord's views will generalize to other forms of reasons fundamentalism, but I will not argue for that here.

For Lord, "reasons fundamentalism" consists in the view that, "reasons are normatively fundamental because we can provide real definitions of all of the complex normative properties in terms of normative reasons".[7] Lord's book does not attempt to give a complete defense of this view, but it *is* meant to provide a central element in its defense by providing an account of one other central normative property—namely, rationality—in terms of reasons. In this way, the aim of Lord's book is to defend a real definition of rationality in terms of reasons.

The core of Lord's account is the following simple idea:

---

[5] For my attempt to develop this line of thought, see (Schafer 2022a). For an alternative in a similar general spirit, see (McLear 2022). For a more metaphysically ambitious version of the line I am attracted to here, see (Brink forthcoming). For classic statements of the "transformative view" at the root of this discussion, see (Boyle 2016; Conant 2016).

[6] This discussion draws on my comments on (Lord 2018) in (Schafer 2020). But also compare (Setiya 2014; McHugh and Way 2018; Schafer 2018a). For other prominent recent "reasons-first" accounts, which share many features with Lord's account, see (Kiesewetter 2017; Schroeder 2021). For important precursors to such views, see (Parfit 2011; Scanlon 2014; Dancy 2018) among many others.

[7] (Lord 2018, 12).

Reasons Responsiveness: What it is to be rational is to correctly respond to possessed normative reasons.

Thus, Lord spends much of his book developing detailed accounts of two crucial pieces of ideology in this definition: (i) what it is to *possess* a normative reason and (ii) what it is to *correctly respond* to a reason one possesses. The core of these, in turn, is as follows:

Possession: What it is for agent A to possess reason R to X provided by fact F is for A to be in a position to manifest knowledge about how to use R to X.

Correctly Responding: What it is for A's x'ing to be *ex post* rational is for A to possess sufficient reason S to X and for A's X-ing to be a manifestation of knowledge about how to use S as sufficient reason to X.

As this makes plain, Lord's account of both these properties gives a central role to the notion of *knowing how to use facts as reasons.* In this way, Lord's view of rationality is built from two main components: (i) normative reasons and (ii) this distinctive sort of know-how. Lord's account is thus both a form of *reasons fundamentalism* and an instance of the *knowledge-first* program in epistemology.[8] As such, Lord's account differs from the view I am attributing to Kant both in its *reasons fundamentalism* and in its focus on *knowledge* as opposed to *understanding* (or comprehension). But Lord is an interesting case to discuss in this regard, because, while he is a reasons fundamentalist, he is not a *reasons primitivist*. That is, although Lord takes reasons facts to be fundamental *within* the normative domain, he does not assume that they are fundamental *simpliciter*. Thus, he does not rule out the possibility of a further reduction of reasons facts to naturalistic or other non-normative facts of some sort. This, as we will see, raises the question of whether a view like Lord's is best developed as a form of reasons fundamentalism or whether it is best developed as a version of the sort of *reason-first constitutivism* I have attributed to Kant.

Lord's book provides an excellent opportunity to discuss this issue because much of its discussion proceeds in ways that seem quite friendly to a "reason-first" approach. For instance, Lord's discussion gives a basic role to virtue- or capacity-theoretic notions such as "know-how" or "competence". And someone attracted to a "capacities-" or "reason-first" approach would also be quite happy with how Lord first introduces us to the notion of rationality that forms his subject matter. For example, right at the beginning of his book, Lord approvingly quotes Parfit's claim that "rational" expresses "the kind of approval that we can also express with

---

[8] Given this, one natural set of questions concerns how these two elements of Lord's account fit together. But while I have raised questions about this in (Schafer 2020), I want to focus on Lord's "reasons fundamentalism" here.

words like 'sensible', 'reasonable', 'intelligent', [and] 'smart'".[9] And he goes on to write that:

> The sort of credit or blame one is open to when one is rational or irrational is thus a very personal evaluation. To react rationally is to show good sense; to react in a fully irrational way is to be stupid or crazy.[10]

Once again, these comments tie rationality quite closely to faculties such as "good sense", "judgment", "intelligence", or (quite simply) *reason*, and to the virtues characteristic of the proper functioning of these faculties. Given this, a natural question about Lord's approach is why he chooses to approach giving a real definition of rationality by taking reasons as fundamental, as opposed to *reason* (as a faculty) or reasoning (as an activity).

I take it that the appeal of reasons fundamentalism is (in considerable part) a product of its promise to reduce the diverse variety of normative facts to a simple and unified set of facts about reasons. But this promise will only be fulfilled insofar as the domain of reasons-facts is *itself* relatively simple and explanatorily unified. And it is not clear that this is the case for Lord. For example, as Lord notes, the domain of reasons facts involves, not just facts about the *existence* of reasons of various sorts, but also facts about the relative *weights* of these reasons, *and* facts about a variety of other ways in which such reasons can *interact* with one another.[11] In short, as Lord's discussion makes clear, the plausibility of reasons fundamentalism often rests on the existence of quite complicated interactions between the reasons the view takes as basic. And the more complicated these interactions, the less plausible it becomes that a reduction of rationality to reasons reduces complexity in the manner characteristic of good explanations.

Lord is well aware of such concerns, and my sense is that he would (quite reasonably) respond to them by reminding us that his form of reasons fundamentalism only commits him to treating reasons as fundamental with respect to other *normative* properties, and not to the view that reasons facts are fundamental *simpliciter*.[12] In other words, while Lord is a committed reasons fundamentalist, he is not a committed reasons primitivist. Thus, it's open to Lord to reduce any complexity at the level of reasons-facts by giving a further reductive account of reasons in non-normative terms. In this way, Lord's account of rationality seems most promising to me when it is paired with a further account of the nature and weight of reasons *in other terms*.

---

[9] (Lord 2018, 4).   [10] (Lord 2018, 4).
[11] Compare the discussion in (Maguire and Lord 2016). The complexity of these phenomenon is also stressed in (Dancy 2018).
[12] See, for example, (Lord 2020).

Given this, it is no surprise to find Lord attracted to such a view in some of his other work.[13] But the idea that we might explain reasons in terms of something more fundamental brings us back to the comparison between reasons-first accounts of rationality and reason-first accounts like Kant's. For it is not at all clear how we might develop a reductive account of *reasons* which does not appeal in some way to the nature of *reason* as a capacity, *reasoning* as an activity, or something else closely related to these concepts.[14] The problem this raises for reasons-first accounts of rationality is simple: If the reasons facts themselves are explained by facts about the capacity of reason or the activity of reasoning or something else of that sort, why not explore the possibility that rationality might be explained *directly* in terms of those more fundamental facts? After all, as we've seen, this sort of reason-first view of rationality is suggested by the way reasons-firsters like Parfit and Lord themselves introduce their topic, so it's only natural to wonder whether their attempts to define rationality in terms of reasons might be a detour from a simpler account of rationality that ties rationality *directly* to the capacity/activities of reason.

Of course, Lord might respond to this by insisting that we *can* develop a reductive account of reasons without appealing to the capacity of reason, or the activity of reasoning, or anything like them. But it is telling that this is not the direction Lord takes in his other work on these topics. Rather, in that work (with Kurt Sylvan), Lord tentatively endorses a form of *constitutivism about reasons* that appeals to a naturalistic conception of *agency*. But when Lord and Sylvan go on to define what "agency" is, they write that "To engage in deliberation is *just what it is* to be an agent".[15] So, as they are using it, to be an "agent" is just to be a deliberator, or (in other words) to be a reasoner in at least one sense of this term. Thus, Lord's full account of the nature of rationality seems to ultimately involve *two* steps: first, a reduction of rationality to reasons, and second, a further reduction of reasons-facts to facts about reason or deliberation. If that is his position, then Lord's full account of rationality would indeed be a version of the *reason*-first project, albeit one that connects reason with rationality *via* claims about reasons.

Again, one question about this strategy is why the connection between reason (or reasoning) and rationality needs to travel *via* claims about reasons. I take it

---

[13] Compare (K. Sylvan and Lord forthcoming) and see the replies in (Lord 2020).

[14] For example, (Schroeder 2007) appeals to activities like reasoning or deliberating in providing an account of the weight of reasons, and (Schroeder 2021) applies this to facts about the nature of belief that could be seen as bringing in similar considerations. See also (Kauppinen 2021) here. And compare the treatment of coherence in (Lasonen-Aarnio 2021), although note that I'm far more sympathetic to internalism than they are.

[15] (K. Sylvan and Lord forthcoming, 14). In (Lord 2020), Lord resists this charge by emphasizing that his form of constitutivism focuses on *standards* (and not capacities) and that these standards are *purely naturalistic* in their origins. But nonetheless it remains true that his account rests on "standards of the activities that are constitutive of agency" and "deliberation," so it is unclear to me whether this really avoids the charge that this view is ultimately a form of reason- or agency-first constitutivism—even if (unlike Kant) he understands the nature of reason and agency in purely naturalistic terms.

that at least part of the answer to this question lies in the idea that all-things-considered evaluations like "rational" need to be explained by contributory notions, and that these contributory factors must either be reasons or something structurally isomorphic to them.[16] But even if this is correct, it is natural to wonder whether Lord's account might have been different if he had conceived of the role of reasons within it not in terms of a form of reasons fundamentalism, but rather as providing the *connective tissue* necessary to complete a (fundamentally) reason-first account of rationality. And this remains true *whether or not* we conceive of the relevant notion of "reason" as something that can be captured in purely naturalistic terms. Thus, even if we accept that an appeal to reasons is inevitable at *some* point in the development of an account of rationality, this does not settle the question of whether they should play the role that Lord assigns to them, and it leaves open how this role should be shaped by the (arguably) more fundamental role of a notion of reason in such an account.

In this way, close study of one of the most sophisticated forms of reasons fundamentalism supports the idea that the reasons-first program is itself best developed in the context of a view that takes the faculty of reason to be what is *really* fundamental. If this is right, then reasons fundamentalism may be best developed as a form of Rational Constitutivism of the sort I have been attributing to Kant. Of course, saying this leaves many questions open about how someone who accepted Kant's conception of reason might explain *reasons-facts* in terms of that account. Perhaps the most obvious possibility would be to adapt one of the contemporary attempts to reduce reasons-facts to facts about *reasoning* so as to fit better with Kant's account of reasoning or inference.[17] This is promising in some ways, but at least if "reasoning" is taken to mean *mediate inference* in the sense that is distinctive of reason (in the narrow sense) for Kant, we have already seen reason to be cautious about this approach. After all, as we saw above, Kant's account of mediate inference is only one part of a more general account of how acts of assent can ground one another. And it is really *this* more general account of "objective and subjective grounds" for assent that seems relevant to thinking about reasons. Nonetheless, if this is right, the most obvious path to a Kantian account of reasons might travel from Kant's account of reason to reasons-facts *via* Kant's account of "objective and subjective grounds" for assent or willing. Interestingly, this path would be similar, in some respects, to the one Mark Schroeder is traveling along in his recent defense of a "reasons first" approach to epistemology.[18] So, if this is right, then there is some reason to think that, once it is fully developed, Schroeder's own "Kantian" account of knowledge will *also* be

---

[16] (Maguire and Lord 2016), and see (Lord 2020) for confirmation of this.

[17] For some accounts in this vein, see (Setiya 2014; Asarnow 2016; Asarnow 2017; Way 2017; Hieronymi forthcoming).

[18] See (Schroeder 2021).

most plausible not as a form of *reasons* fundamentalism, but rather as a view that treats *reason* as what is fundamental. This would vindicate Schroeder's self-description as a Kantian, but only at the cost of his deeper commitment to reasons fundamentalism.

At the same time, I think we have seen some reasons to be cautious about this way of thinking about reasons within the context of Kant's account of reason. For, as we saw above, Kant's primary interest is not in reasons as "grounds for assent" or "justifiers" but rather in reasons as something like "sense-makers"—that is, as considerations that add to our systematic comprehension of what is and what ought to be. Thus, one of the lessons of our discussion, I think, is that an exclusive focus on "reasons" in the sense of "justifying considerations" providing a potentially misleading way of thinking about reasons in general. Rather, if we follow Kant, we will tend to see the fundamental notion here as being the idea of reasons as sense-makers, and see the justificatory role they play as a secondary consideration to this primary role. And this would push us away from views like Schroeder's that focus on the justificatory role of reasons in a "competition" for our assent.[19]

c. Practical Understanding as a Tool for Social and Political Critique

Obviously, there is much more to be said about these issues. But as this hopefully indicates, one potential source of optimism about the continuing relevance of Kant's conception of reason is its potential power in the meta-normative domain. But this is hardly the only area in which this is true. For example, the resulting conception of reason also provides us with a potentially quite powerful basis for social or political critique. This is important here, not just because it brings out the potential political implications of the conception of reason we have been exploring, but also because it illustrates the flexibility of the conception of reason as a capacity we are working with—demonstrating once again how it can be applied, not just to individual rational subjects, but also to various social collectives or groups.

At the heart of this conception of critique lies the idea that social practices may be thought of as *attempts at realizing a shared form of practical understanding*. To see why this is plausible, let's begin by briefly introducing the notion of a "social practice". In the sense I am interested in here, social practices are constituted by networks of social conventions, customs, institutions, and the like—networks that

---

[19] For the centrality of "competition" in Schroeder's account, see (Schroeder 2021). We might try to model this sort of view using the sort of "directed support relations" that are the focus of Fogal's recent account of "rational pressure." See, for example, (Fogal 2020; Fogal and Risberg 2021).

both structure and are structured by the practical deliberation and choices of the agents who participate in them. Social practices thus involve more than mere patterns of behavior: they also involve patterns of reasoning, feeling, attention, and deliberation, which are internalized (to at least some degree) by those who participate in the practices in question. In other words, social practices or forms of life represent social or shared "forms of practical consciousness". They are not blind patterns of behavior; rather, the patterns of action that they involve are dependent upon certain patterns of thought, feeling, and reasoning. In this way, "social practices" in my sense always involve some form of shared "practical ideology," in the broad, non-pejorative sense of "ideology" in which an "ideology" is just a system of shared attitudes and concepts that help to determine what the participants in some practice do.[20]

In saying this, it is important to stress that the attitudes and concepts involved in this sort of "shared practical consciousness" will often not be "shared" in the strong sense of being possessed by every individual participant in the social practice in question. Rather, what makes these attitudes and concepts an essential element of the social practice is the *explanatory role* they play with respect to what goes on within that practice. What distinguishes "social practices" or "forms of social life" (in the sense at issue here) from blind patterns of behavior is precisely that the behavior of those involved in a genuine social practice is guided by a set of (implicit or explicit) practical attitudes that embodies a shared sense of "what to do" that is characteristic of the social practice in question.

Thus, as defined here, it is distinctive of social practices that they involve patterns of actions that are guided by a shared sense of what to do. But what must this conception of "what to do" be like if a social practice is to be successful? Well, in any meaningful social practice, this sense must extend beyond (say) a piecemeal list of actions to be performed under certain circumstances. Rather, in order to motivate participants to act in accordance with its demands, this grasp of what to do must embody some sense of *why* these actions are to be done. And, moreover, in order to be effective across a variety of circumstances, this conception of what to do must also be able to draw on some further sense of *how* these things are to be done. Finally, if a practice or way of life is to have any flexibility or ability to adapt to new situations, it will have to place these "things to do" within a *broader context* that allows for the reinterpretation of them under changing circumstances. Only in this case, will a social practice or way of life really have any "life" at all.[21]

In all these ways, a social practice must be based around not just a shared conception of what to do, but also some degree of *shared understanding* of this—some degree, that is, of what we have been calling "practical comprehension". And

---

[20] For this conception of social practices, see (Haslanger 2017; Jaeggi 2018).
[21] Compare (Jaeggi 2018).

this understanding plays a certain sort of explanatory role within a properly functioning social practice. When they function properly, social practices achieve what they do *in virtue of* the effectiveness of this shared understanding of what to do. In this way, the success or failure of a social practice will be a function of the degree to which it is successful at providing its participants with an effective, shared practical understanding. In this sense, we can regard any social practice as *an attempt to achieve a form of shared practical understanding*, albeit one limited to the goals or areas of life that are distinctive of the social practice in question.

If something like this line of thought is correct, then a conception of rationality that focuses on the connections between rationality and (theoretical and practical) understanding or comprehension would provide us with a powerful framework for criticizing not only the attitudes of individuals, but also the social practices, institutions, and forms of life in which those individuals live their individual lives. As we've already suggested, the idea that rationality has this sort of social dimension is already present in Kant's discussion. For Kant is clear that the abstract demands of the moral law can only be give the determinacy of content they need in order to guide our actions insofar as these demands are realized in shared systems of law and other institutions.[22] Thus, in order to achieve the sort of practical understanding that practical reason demands of us, we must for Kant engage in a *social and practical practice* that *realizes* the demands of practical reason not *only* in our individual actions, but also through the development of social practices and institutions that make it possible for individuals to act in accordance with the demands of morality. Thus, for Kant, there is a very deep sense in which the whole point of social practices, laws, and institutions is to translate the abstract demands of morality into concrete patterns of actions in the world in the manner that fully realized practical understanding requires. In other words, social practices are in the "practical comprehension business" from the very start.

Given this, the standards of success that apply to all forms of practical understanding as such provide us with an important lens through which to evaluate the success or failure of social practices on rational grounds that are (in some sense) immanent to the practices we are criticizing. In saying this, it is important not to overstate the sense in which the resulting form of critique is "internal" or "immanent" to the practices in question. For none of this means that the standards we derive from the role that practical understanding plays in a practice will seem obvious or "inescapable" from within that practice. Rather, these standards are best regarded as describing the "form" a social practice must have in order to be successful, as opposed to describing the objects it explicitly treats as important or valuable. For this reason, it is not hard to imagine social practices that treat

---

[22] See again (Pallikkathayil 2010).

practical understanding as having very little explicit or first-order value or importance. The important point about such social practices is not that they are impossible, but rather that they involve an implicit conflict between the form common to all successful social practices and the values that particular social practices treat as important.

Given this, there is a sense in which no functional social practice can be completely indifferent to the project of achieving practical understanding. For it is only through some form of such understanding that social practices manage to function at all. So, a form of critique that is grounded in the notion of practical understanding should always be able to get *some* non-trivial foothold within any meaningful social practice. In this sense, such critique is never one that operates "wholly from the outside". Rather, a form of critique that focuses on practical understanding *in general* can be seen as operating with a *natural generalization* of a notion of rationality that is already operative within the social practice being critiqued. Of course, those involved in a particular social practice can resist the pressure to generalize their implicit concern for certain forms of practical understanding in this way. But this is no surprise. For one can always resist the pressure to become more consistent or more rational, however these notions are understood.

As our discussion of alienation above should already have indicated, I believe that many of the familiar forms of social critique can be helpfully placed within this general perspective. In particular, as we saw in Chapter 7, if we conceive of reason as a capacity for both theoretical and practical comprehension, the realization of reason's own ends will be possible only insofar as reason transforms itself into the centerpiece of a much more general capacity for autonomous action in the world. Thus, beginning with Kant's basic conception of reason and its ends, we are led to a conception of reason and rationality on which the satisfaction of reason's needs will only be possible insofar as we realize this broader capacity for autonomous practical understanding. And while such ideas are often more closely associated with post-Kantian philosophers like Hegel or Marx, this task—of realizing reason's proper form of activity *within the world*—is also a deeply political and social project for Kant as well.[23] Thus, while we can of course think about the conception of reason we have been exploring in terms of its implications for individuals, it is best seen as laying the groundwork for a larger social and political project—the project, that is, of fully realizing this capacity of reason through the reform of actual human societies so that they fit with its twin aspirations of (theoretical and practical) understanding and autonomy. It is this

---

[23] Compare the "capabilities approach" to political philosophy pioneered by Nussbaum and Sen in e.g. (Sen 2004; Nussbaum 2011). See also (McNulty 2022) for a related discussion of this sort of "left Kantianism."

"left Kantian" project that I believe Kant's conception of reason most naturally leads us towards.

d. Realizing Reason—The Future of the Critical Project?

The question, of course, is whether Kant's conception of reason really puts us in a position to succeed at this task. This is crucial here, for only insofar as it does so will we be able to truly vindicate the claim that our form of reason, despite its many limitations, can provide us with comprehension—that is, insight which is sufficient to our purposes. In other words, does Kant's account of reason really provide us with the grasp of the unity of reason that reason *itself* demands?

Unfortunately, on this point, I think it is only fair to say that there remains considerable room for doubt, even given all we have said. For example, there are questions concerning the relationship between our intellectual powers and our form of sensibility—questions that have long been the focus of various Hegelian critiques of Kant's commitment to an allegedly dualistic conception of our cognitive faculties.[24] And there are, of course, familiar worries about whether transcendental idealism's distinction between appearances and things in themselves necessarily implies that reason will never be able to achieve the sort of self-comprehension it seeks. But there is also the related but perhaps less familiar worry that Kant's account of irrationality as the product of the "unnoticed influence" of our "lower" faculties (like sensibility) on our "higher" ones (like reason) remains objectionably hierarchical in ways that echo the least progressive parts of his philosophy, such as his views about the sexes or "races". All these considerations should, I think, push us towards the development of a less hierarchical conception of reason than Kant's own. This would require the development of a picture of human reason on which it is realized by a system of capacities, where each capacity is a potential source of irrationality and error to the same basic degree.

Thus, one might still worry that Kant's account of the unity of the full system of rational capacities "under reason" remains unacceptably authoritarian in some sense. And there is also another sense in which Kant's account of reason might leave us dissatisfied that is more directly relevant to our discussion here—namely, the question of whether the very distinction between theoretical and practical cognition that Kant is working with fails to fully do justice to the interdependence of these two aspects of understanding. For here, too, the Hegelian critic is likely to

---

[24] It might be thought that these issues could be avoided through the development of what has come to be called a fully "transformative" reading of the relationship between sensibility and intellect in Kant (Boyle 2016; Conant 2016; Land 2018). I discuss such views in my (Schafer forthcoming), but while I'm quite sympathetic to their claims, I doubt that they provide a fully satisfying Kantian solution to these issues. Compare (McLear 2022) here.

feel that Kant fails to fully account for the sense in which "the theoretical is essentially contained in the practical" and vice versa (*PR* 4). Thus, much like Kant's treatment of the relationship between sensibility and the understanding, the significance that Kant continues to assign to the distinction between theoretical and practical reason is likely to seem to the Hegelian to be a symptom of Kant's failure to provide us with an account of reason on which reason can *fully* comprehend itself.

Above, we tried to respond to worries like these by focusing on Kant's purpose-relative conception of "comprehension," arguing that this end- or purpose-relativity opened space for Kant to insist that reason can "comprehend itself," even though it does not really achieve full insight into its underlying nature. But while this maneuver may allow Kant to insist that reason can "comprehend" itself in a technical sense, it will only do so insofar as reason's self-understanding *actually is sufficient* for its most basic ends and purposes. And here it is hard not to agree with Kant's idealist followers that Kant's account of reason leaves reason fundamentally frustrated in its drive for comprehension of what is and what ought to be.

Whether this is ultimately fatal to Kant's account depends, of course, on one's level of optimism about the reach of our form of rationality. For example, it may be that Kant's modesty on this score expresses basic limitations on our cognitive powers. And here, it must be said, the attempts of those who followed in Kant's wake to do better on this score do not fill with one tremendous confidence. But it is worth stressing that Kant's conception of human reason is the conception of a power or capacity that is, in certain very deep ways, *fundamentally incomplete*. As noted above, it is this that provides Kant's philosophy with much of its continuing relevance. Indeed, as I've argued elsewhere, the idea of rational order, not as something already present in this "best of all possible worlds," but rather as a *task to be accomplished* is crucial to the significance of Kant's conception of reason to contemporary debates about these issues.[25] In this sense, it is no surprise that Kant himself continued to be dissatisfied with his account on this score throughout his life. The only real question is whether this dissatisfaction is something we should strive to overcome or whether it represent a sense in which our human form of reason is sentenced to a frustrated fate by its fundamental limitations.

---

[25] I develop this thought further in my work in progress on this topic.

References

Abaci, Uygar. 2019. *Kant's Revolutionary Theory of Modality*. Oxford University Press.
Abaci, Uygar. 2022. "Noumenal Freedom and Kant's Modal Antinomy." *Kantian Review* 27 (2): 175–94.
Adams, Robert Merrihew. 1997. "Things in Themselves." *Philosophy and Phenomenological Research* 57 (4): 801–25.
Adorno, Theodor W., and Max Horkheimer. 1997. *Dialectic of Enlightenment*. Verso.
Allais, Lucy. 2015. Manifest Reality: Kant's Idealism and his Realism. Oxford University Press.
Allison, Henry E. 1990. *Kant's Theory of Freedom*. Cambridge University Press.
Allison, Henry E. 2004. *Kant's Transcendental Idealism*. Yale University Press.
Ameriks, Karl. 2000. *Kant's Theory of Mind: An Analysis of the Paralogisms of Pure Reason*. Clarendon Press.
Ameriks, Karl. 2003. *Interpreting Kant's Critiques*. Clarendon Press.
Ameriks, Karl. 2006. "The Critique of Metaphysics: The Structure and Fate of Kant's Dialectic." In *The Cambridge Companion to Kant and Modern Philosophy*, edited by Paul Guyer, 269–302. Cambridge University Press.
Ameriks, Karl. 2012. *Kant's Elliptical Path*. Oxford University Press.
Amijee, Fatema. 2021. "Principle of Sufficient Reason." In *Encyclopedia of Early Modern Philosophy and the Sciences*, edited by Dana Jalobeanu and Charles T. Wolfe, 1–10. Springer International Publishing.
Anderson, R. Lanier. 2015. *The Poverty of Conceptual Truth: Kant's Analytic/Synthetic Distinction and the Limits of Metaphysics*. Oxford University Press.
Arruda, Caroline T. 2016. "Constitutivism and the Self-Reflection Requirement." *Philosophia* 44 (4): 1165–83.
Arruda, Caroline T. 2017. "Why Care about Being an Agent?" *Australasian Journal of Philosophy* 95 (3): 488–504.
Asarnow, Samuel. 2016. "Rational Internalism." *Ethics* 127 (1): 147–78.
Asarnow, Samuel. 2017. "The Reasoning View and Defeasible Practical Reasoning." *Philosophy and Phenomenological Research* 95 (3): 614–36.
Bader, Ralf M. 2009. "Kant and the Categories of Freedom." *British Journal for the History of Philosophy* 17 (4): 799–820.
Bader, Ralf M. 2023. "The Dignity of Humanity." In *Rethinking the Value of Humanity*. Oxford University Press.
Bagnoli, Carla. 2011. "Constructivism in Metaethics." In *Stanford Encyclopedia of Philosophy*, edited by E. Zalta. Stanford University. https://plato.stanford.edu/entries/constructivism-metaethics/
Bagnoli, Carla. 2013. "Constructivism about Practical Knowledge." In *Constructivism in Ethics*, edited by Carla Bagnoli, 153–82. Cambridge University Press.
Bagnoli, Carla. 2021. *Ethical Constructivism*. Cambridge University Press.
Beck, Lewis White. 1963. *A Commentary on Kant's Critique of Practical Reason*. University of Chicago Press.
Beizaei, Banafsheh. forthcoming. "Establishing the Existence of Things in Themselves." *History of Philosophy of Quarterly* 39 (3): 257–74.

Bengson, John. 2017. "The Unity of Understanding." In *Making Sense of the World: New Essays on the Philosophy of Understanding*, edited by Stephen R. Grimm, 14–53. Oxford University Press.
Bengson, John, Cuneo, Terence & Shafer-Landau, Russ. forthcoming. *The Moral Universe*. Oxford University Press.
Benzenberg, Christopher. forthcoming a. "Two Demands, One Goal: Kant's Principle of Theoretical Reason".
Benzenberg, Christopher. forthcoming b. "From Opinion to Knowledge: Kant's Infallibilism and the Specter of Skepticism."
Boehm, Omri. 2014. *Kant's Critique of Spinoza*. Oxford University Press.
Boehm, Omri. 2016. "The Principle of Sufficient Reason, the Ontological Argument and the Is/Ought Distinction." *European Journal of Philosophy* 24 (3): 556–79.
Boer, Karin de. 2020. *Kant's Reform of Metaphysics: The Critique of Pure Reason Reconsidered*. Cambridge University Press.
Boghossian, Paul. 2008. "Epistemic Rules." *Journal of Philosophy* 105 (9): 472–500.
Boghossian, Paul. 2012. "Blind Rule-Following." In *Mind, Meaning, and Knowledge: Themes From the Philosophy of Crispin Wright*, edited by Crispin Wright and Annalisa Coliva, 27–48. Oxford University Press.
Boghossian, Paul. 2014. "What Is Inference?" *Philosophical Studies* 169 (1): 1–18.
Bommarito, Nicholas. 2020. *Seeing Clearly: A Buddhist Guide to Life*. Oxford University Press.
Bowman, Caroline. 2021. "Purposiveness, the Idea of God, and the Transition from Nature to Freedom in the Critique of Judgment." In *Purposiveness, the Idea of God, and the Transition from Nature to Freedom in the Critique of Judgment*, 931–40. De Gruyter.
Boyle, Matthew. 2009. "Two Kinds of Self-Knowledge." *Philosophy and Phenomenological Research* 78 (1): 133–64.
Boyle, Matthew. 2011. "'Making Up Your Mind' and the Activity of Reason." *Philosophers' Imprint* 11 (7): 1–24.
Boyle, Matthew. 2016. "Additive Theories of Rationality: A Critique." *European Journal of Philosophy* 24 (3): 527–55.
Boyle, Matthew. forthcoming. "Kant and the Significance of Self-Consciousness." *Philosophy*.
Breitenbach, Angela. 2013. "V—Aesthetics in Science: A Kantian Proposal." *Proceedings of the Aristotelian Society* 113 (1): 83–100.
Breitenbach, Angela. 2014. "Biological Purposiveness and Analogical Reflection." In *Kant's Theory of Biology*, edited by Eric Watkins and Ina Goy, 131–48. De Gruyter.
Breitenbach, Angela. 2016. "Normativity and Purposiveness." *British Journal of Aesthetics* 56 (4): 405–8.
Bremner, Sabina Vaccarino. forthcoming. "Practical Judgment as Reflective Judgment: On Moral Salience and Kantian Particularist Universalism." *European Journal of Philosophy*.
Brink, Claudi. forthcoming. *Spontaneity and Teleology in Kant's Theory of Apperception*. University of California Press.
Broome, John. 1999. "Normative Requirements." *Ratio* 12 (4): 398–419.
Brueckner, Anthony. 1996. "Modest Transcendental Arguments." *Philosophical Perspectives* 10: 265–80.
Buss, Sarah. 2008. "Personal Autonomy." In *Stanford Encyclopedia of Philosophy*. https://plato.stanford.edu/entries/personal-autonomy/
Carroll, Lewis. 1895. "What the Tortoise Said to Achilles." *Mind* 4 (14): 278–80.
Cassam, Quassim. 1997. *Self and World*. Oxford University Press.

Chaplin, Rosalind. forthcoming. "Is Kant's Supreme Principle of Pure Reason the Principle of Sufficient Reason?"
Chignell, Andrew. 2007a. "Belief in Kant." *Philosophical Review* 116 (3): 323-60.
Chignell, Andrew. 2007b. "Kant's Concepts of Justification." *Noûs* 41 (1): 33-63.
Chignell, Andrew. 2012. "Kant, Real Possibility, and the Threat of Spinoza." *Mind* 121 (483): 635-75.
Chignell, Andrew. 2014. "Modal Motivations for Noumenal Ignorance: Knowledge, Cognition, and Coherence." *Kant-Studien* 105 (4): 573-97.
Chignell, Andrew. 2017. "Noumenal Ignorance: Why, For Kant, Can't We Know Things in Themselves?" In *The Palgrave Kant Handbook*, edited by Matthew Altman, 91-116. Palgrave Macmillan.
Chignell, Andrew. 2021. "Kantian Fallibilism: Knowledge, Certainty, Doubt." Midwest Studies in Philosophy 45: 99-128.
Chignell, Andrew, and Derk Pereboom. 2010. "Kant's Theory of Causation and Its Eighteenth-Century German Background." *Philosophical Review* 119 (4): 565-91.
Cicovacki, Predrag. 2006. "Kant's Debt to Leibniz." In *A Companion to Kant*, edited by Graham Bird, 79-92. John Wiley & Sons, Ltd.
Cleve, James Van. 2003. *Problems from Kant*. Oxford University Press.
Cohen, Alix. 2013. "Kant on Doxastic Voluntarism and Its Implications for Epistemic Responsibility." *Kant Yearbook* 5 (1): 33-50.
Cohen, Alix. 2014. "Kant on the Ethics of Belief." *Proceedings of the Aristotelian Society* 114 (3): 317-34.
Cohen, Alix. 2020. "A Kantian Account of Emotions as Feelings." *Mind* 129 (514): 429-60.
Conant, James. 2016. "Why Kant Is Not a Kantian." *Philosophical Topics* 44 (1): 75-125.
Dancy, Jonathan. 2018. *Practical Shape: A Theory of Practical Reasoning*. Oxford University Press.
Darwall, Stephen. 1977. "Two Kinds of Respect." *Ethics* 88 (1): 36-49.
Darwall, Stephen. 2006. *The Second-Person Standpoint: Morality, Respect, and Accountability*. Harvard University Press.
Darwall, Stephen. 2021. "On a Kantian Form of Respect: 'Before a Humble Common Man...My Spirit Bows.'" In *Respect: Philosophical Essays*, edited by Richard Dean and Oliver Sensen, 192-204. Oxford University Press.
Dean, Richard. 2021. "The Peculiar Idea of Respect for a Capacity." In *Respect: Philosophical Essays*, edited by Richard Dean and Oliver Sensen, 140-56. Oxford University Press.
Della Rocca, Michael. 2010. "PSR." *Philosopher's Imprint* 10 (7): 1-13.
Della Rocca, Michael. 2020. *The Parmenidean Ascent*. Oxford University Press.
DeWitt, Janelle. 2014. "Respect for the Moral Law: The Emotional Side of Reason." *Philosophy* 89 (1): 31-62.
DeWitt, Janelle. 2018. "Feeling and Inclination: Rationalizing the Animal Within." In *Kant and the Faculty of Feeling*, edited by Kelly Sorensen and Diane Williamson, 67-87. Cambridge University Press.
Dogramaci, Sinan. 2013. "Intuitions for Inferences." *Philosophical Studies* 165 (2): 371-99.
Dogramaci, Sinan. 2017. "Why Is a Valid Inference a Good Inference?" *Philosophy and Phenomenological Research* 94 (1): 61-96.
Elizondo, E. Sonny. 2013. "Reason in Its Practical Application." *Philosophers' Imprint* 13: 1-17.
Elizondo, E. Sonny. 2014. "More Than a Feeling." *Canadian Journal of Philosophy* 44 (3-4): 425-42.

Elizondo, E. Sonny. 2022. "Kantian Eudaimonism." *Journal of the American Philosophical Association*, Firstview: 1–15.
Engstrom, Stephen. 1992. "The Concept of the Highest Good in Kant's Moral Theory." *Philosophy and Phenomenological Research* 52 (4): 747–80.
Engstrom, Stephen. 2002. "Kant's Distinction between Theoretical and Practical Knowledge." *Harvard Review of Philosophy* 10 (1): 49–63.
Engstrom, Stephen. 2006. "Understanding and Sensibility." *Inquiry* 49 (1): 2–25.
Engstrom, Stephen. 2009. *The Form of Practical Knowledge: A Study of the Categorical Imperative*. Harvard University Press.
Engstrom, Stephen. 2016. "Self-Consciousness and the Unity of Knowledge." In *Bewusstsein/Consciousness*, edited by Dina Emundts and Sally Sedgwick, 25–48. De Gruyter.
Enoch, David. 2006. "Agency, Shmagency: Why Normativity Won't Come from What Is Constitutive of Action." *Philosophical Review* 115 (2): 169–98.
Enoch, David. 2011. "Shmagency Revisited." In *New Waves in Metaethics*, edited by Michael Brady, 208–30. Palgrave-Macmillan.
Enoch, David. 2013. *Taking Morality Seriously: A Defense of Robust Realism*. Oxford University Press.
Ferrero, Luca. 2009. "Constitutivism and the Inescapability of Agency." *Oxford Studies in Metaethics* 4: 303–33.
Ferrero, Luca. 2019. "The Simple Constitutivist Move." *Philosophical Explorations* 22 (2): 146–62.
Fix, Jeremy David. 2020. "The Error Condition." *Canadian Journal of Philosophy* 50 (1): 34–48.
Fix, Jeremy David. 2021. "Two Sorts of Constitutivism." *Analytic Philosophy* 62 (1): 1–20.
Fix, Jeremy David. forthcoming. "Grounds of Goodness." *Journal of Philosophy*.
Fogal, Daniel. 2016. "Reasons, Reason, and Context." In *Weighing Reasons*, edited by Errol Lord and Barry Maguire, 74–103. Oxford University Press.
Fogal, Daniel. 2020. "Rational Requirements and the Primacy of Pressure." *Mind* 129 (516): 1033–70.
Fogal, Daniel, and Olle Risberg. 2023. "Explaining Normative Reasons." *Noûs* 57 (1): 51–80.
Foot, Philippa. 2003. *Natural Goodness*. Clarendon Press.
Ford, Anton. 2011. "Action and Generality." In *Essays on Anscombe's Intention*, edited by Anton Ford, Jennifer Hornsby, and Frederick Stoutland, 76–104. Harvard University Press.
Ford, Anton. 2018. "The Province of Human Agency." *Noûs* 52 (3): 697–720.
Förster, Eckart. 2011. *Die 25 Jahre der Philosophie: Eine systematische Rekonstruktion*. Vittorio Klostermann.
Franks, Paul W. 2005. *All or Nothing: Systematicity, Transcendental Arguments, and Skepticism in German Idealism*. Harvard University Press.
Friedman, Michael. 1992. *Kant and the Exact Sciences*. Harvard University Press.
Friedman, Michael. 2013. *Kant's Construction of Nature: A Reading of the Metaphysical Foundations of Natural Science*. Cambridge University Press.
Frost, Kim. 2014. "On the Very Idea of Direction of Fit." *Philosophical Review* 123 (4): 429–84.
Fugate, Courtney D. 2014. *The Teleology of Reason: A Study of the Structure of Kant's Critical Philosophy*. De Gruyter.
Gardner, Sebastian. 1999. *Routledge Philosophy Guidebook to Kant and the Critique of Pure Reason*. Routledge.
Gardner, Sebastian. 2007. "The Primacy of Practical Reason." In *A Companion to Kant*, 259–74. John Wiley & Sons, Ltd.

Garrett, Don. 2008. "Should Hume Have Been a Transcendental Idealist?" In *Kant and the Early Moderns*, edited by Daniel Garber and Béatrice Longuenesse, 193–208. Princeton University Press.
Gibbard, Allan. 1999. "Morality as Consistency in Living: Korsgaard's Kantian Lectures." *Ethics* 110 (1): 140–64.
Gibbard, Allan. 2003. *Thinking How to Live*. Harvard University Press.
Ginsborg, Hannah. 2014. *The Normativity of Nature: Essays on Kant's Critique of Judgment*. Oxford University Press.
Gingerich, Jonathan. forthcoming. "Stop Making Sense."
Gledhill, James, and Sebastian Stein. 2020. *Hegel and Contemporary Practical Philosophy: Beyond Kantian Constructivism*. Routledge.
Goldhaber, Chuck. forthcoming. "Kant's Offer to the Skeptical Empiricist." *Journal of the History of Philosophy*.
Gomes, Anil, Andrew Stephenson, and A. W. Moore. 2022. "The Necessity of the Categories." *Philosophical Review* 131(2): 129–68.
Grier, Michelle. 2001. *Kant's Doctrine of Transcendental Illusion*. Cambridge University Press.
Grier, Michelle. 2008. "Kant's Critique of Metaphysics." In *Stanford Encyclopedia of Philosophy*. https://plato.stanford.edu/entries/kant-metaphysics/
Grüne, Stefanie. 2009. *Blinde Anschauung: Die Rolle von Begriffen in Kants Theorie sinnlicher Synthesis*. Klostermann.
Guevara, Daniel. 2009. "The Will as Practical Reason and the Problem of Akrasia." *Review of Metaphysics* 62 (3): 525–50.
Guyer, Paul. 1987. *Kant and the Claims of Knowledge*. Cambridge University Press.
Guyer, Paul. 1990. "Reason and Reflective Judgment: Kant on the Significance of Systematicity." *Noûs* 24 (1): 17–43.
Guyer, Paul. 2000. *Kant on Freedom, Law, and Happiness*. Cambridge University Press.
Guyer, Paul. 2005. *Kant's System of Nature and Freedom: Selected Essays*. Clarendon Press.
Guyer, Paul. 2006. *Kant*. Routledge.
Guyer, Paul. 2019. *Kant on the Rationality of Morality*. Cambridge University Press.
Haase, Matthias. 2009. "The Laws of Thought and the Power of Thinking." *Canadian Journal of Philosophy* 39 (S1): 249–97.
Haase, Matthias. 2014. "For Oneself and toward Another: The Puzzle about Recognition." *Philosophical Topics* 42 (1): 113–52.
Habermas, Jürgen. 1981. *Theorie des kommunikativen Handelns*. Suhrkamp.
Hanna, Robert. 2006. *Kant and the Foundations of Analytic Philosophy*. Repr. Clarendon Press.
Hannon, Michael. 2021. "Recent Work on the Epistemology of Understanding." *American Philosophical Quarterly* 58 (3): 269–290.
Haslanger, Sally. 2017. *Critical Theory and Practice*. Koninklijke Van Gorcum.
Heide, Dai. 2021. "Rationalism and Kant's Rejection of the Ontological Argument." *Journal of the History of Philosophy* 59 (4): 583–606.
Heis, Jeremy. 2014. "The Priority Principle from Kant to Frege." *Noûs* 48 (2): 268–97.
Henrich, Dieter. 1994. *The Unity of Reason: Essays on Kant's Philosophy*. Harvard University Press.
Herman, Barbara. 1996. *The Practice of Moral Judgment*. Harvard University Press.
Herman, Barbara. 2007. *Moral Literacy*. Harvard University Press.
Hieronymi, Pamela. 2021. "Reasoning First." In *Routledge Handbook of Practical Reasoning*, edited by Ruth Chang and Kurt Sylvan, 349–65. Routledge.
Hill, Jr, Thomas E. 2000. *Respect, Pluralism, and Justice: Kantian Perspectives*. Oxford University Press.

Hill, Jr, Thomas E. 2012. *Virtue, Rules, and Justice: Kantian Aspirations.* Oxford University Press.
Hills, Alison. 2005. "Rational Nature as the Source of Value." *Kantian Review* 10: 60–81.
Hills, Alison. 2015. "Understanding Why." *Noûs* 49 (2): 661–688.
Hlobil, Ulf. 2019. "Inferring by Attaching Force." *Australasian Journal of Philosophy* 97 (4): 701–14.
Hogan, Desmond. 2009. "Three Kinds of Rationalism and the Non-Spatiality of Things in Themselves." *Journal of the History of Philosophy* 47 (3): 355–82.
Hogan, Desmond. 2013. "Metaphysical Motives of Kant's Analytic–Synthetic Distinction." *Journal of the History of Philosophy* 51 (2): 267–307.
Horst, David. 2022. "In Defense of Constitutivism about Epistemic Normativity." *Pacific Philosophical Quarterly* 103 (2): 232–58.
Horstmann, Rolf-Peter. 2012. "The Unity of Reason and the Diversity of Life: The Idea of a System in Kant and in Nineteenth-Century Philosophy." In *The Cambridge History of Philosophy in the Nineteenth Century (1790–1870)*, edited by Allen W. Wood and Songsuk Susan Hahn, translated by Allen W. Wood, 61–92. Cambridge University Press.
Jaeggi, Rahel. 2014. *Alienation.* Translated by Frederick Neuhouser and Alan E. Smith. Columbia University Press.
Jaeggi, Rahel. 2018. *Critique of Forms of Life.* Belknap Press of Harvard University Press.
James, Aaron. 2007. "Constructivism about Practical Reasons." *Philosophy and Phenomenological Research* 74 (2): 302–25.
Jauernig, Anja. 2008. "Kant's Critique of the Leibnizian Philosophy: Contra the Leibnizians, but pro Leibniz." In *Kant and the Early Moderns*, edited by Daniel Garber and Béatrice Longuenesse, 41–63. Princeton University Press.
Jauernig, Anja. 2021. *The World According to Kant: Appearances and Things in Themselves in Critical Idealism.* Oxford University Press.
Kain, Patrick. 2010. "Practical Cognition, Intuition, and the Fact of Reason." In *Kant's Moral Metaphysics: God, Freedom, and Immortality*, edited by Benjamin Lipscomb and James Krueger, 211–30. De Gruyter.
Katsafanas, Paul. 2013. *Agency and the Foundations of Ethics: Nietzschean Constitutivism.* Oxford University Press.
Kauppinen, Antti. 2021. "Rationality as the Rule of Reason." *Noûs* 55 (3): 538–59.
Kelly, Thomas. 2003. "Epistemic Rationality as Instrumental Rationality: A Critique." *Philosophy and Phenomenological Research* 66 (3): 612–40.
Kern, Andrea. 2006. *Quellen des Wissens: Zum Begriff vernünftiger Erkenntnisfähigkeiten.* Suhrkamp.
Kern, Andrea. 2017. *Sources of Knowledge: On the Concept of a Rational Capacity for Knowledge.* Harvard University Press.
Kiesewetter, Benjamin. 2017. *The Normativity of Rationality.* Oxford University Press.
Kitcher, Patricia. 2011. *Kant's Thinker.* Oxford University Press.
Kleingeld, Pauline. 1998. "Kant on the Unity of Theoretical and Practical Reason." *Review of Metaphysics* 52 (2): 500–28.
Kleingeld, Pauline. 2017. "Contradiction and Kant's Formula of Universal Law." *Kant-Studien* 108 (1): 89–115.
Kleingeld, Pauline. 2018. "The Principle of Autonomy in Kant's Moral Theory: Its Rise and Fall." In *Kant on Persons and Agency*, edited by Eric Watkins, 61–79. Cambridge University Press.
Kohl, Markus. 2015. "Kant on the Inapplicability of the Categories to Things in Themselves." *British Journal for the History of Philosophy* 23 (1): 90–114.

Kohl, Markus. 2018. "Kant's Critique of Instrumental Reason." *Pacific Philosophical Quarterly* 99 (3): 489–516.
Kolodny, Niko. 2005. "Why Be Rational?" *Mind* 114 (455): 509–63.
Korsgaard, Christine. 1996a. *Creating the Kingdom of Ends*. Cambridge University Press.
Korsgaard, Christine. 1996b. *The Sources of Normativity*. Cambridge University Press.
Korsgaard, Christine. 2008. *The Constitution of Agency: Essays on Practical Reason and Moral Psychology*. Oxford University Press.
Korsgaard, Christine. 2009. *Self-Constitution: Agency, Identity, and Integrity*. Oxford University Press.
Kraus, Katharina. 2020. *Kant on Self-Knowledge and Self-Formation: The Nature of Inner Experience*. Cambridge University Press.
Kreines, James. 2008. "Metaphysics without Pre-Critical Monism: Hegel on Lower-Level Natural Kinds and the Structure of Reality." *Bulletin of the Hegel Society of Great Britain* 57: 48–70.
Kreines, James. 2009. "Kant on the Laws of Nature: Laws, Necessitation, and the Limitation of Our Knowledge." *European Journal of Philosophy* 17 (4): 527–58.
Kreines, James. 2015. *Reason in the World: Hegel's Metaphysics and Its Philosophical Appeal*. Oxford University Press.
Kreines, James. 2022. "For a Dialectic-First Approach to Kant's Critique of Pure Reason." *Open Philosophy* 5 (1): 490–509.
Land, Thomas. 2018. "Conceptualism and the Objection from Animals." In *Natur Und Freiheit. Akten des Xii. Internationalen Kant-Kongresses*, edited by Violetta L. Waibel, Margit Ruffing, and David Wagner, 1269–76. De Gruyter.
Land, Thomas. 2021. "Epistemic Agency and the Self-Knowledge of Reason: On the Contemporary Relevance of Kant's Method of Faculty Analysis." *Synthese* 198: 3137–54.
Larmore, Charles. 2021. *Morality and Metaphysics*. Cambridge University Press.
Lasonen-Aarnio, Maria. 2021. "Coherence as Competence." *Episteme* 18 (3): 453–76.
Lavin, Douglas. 2004. "Practical Reason and the Possibility of Error." *Ethics* 114 (3): 424–57.
Lavin, Douglas. 2015. "Action as a Form of Temporal Unity: On Anscombe's Intention." *Canadian Journal of Philosophy* 45 (5): 609–29.
LeBar, Mark. 2008. "Aristotelian Constructivism." *Social Philosophy and Policy* 25 (1): 182–213.
Lewis, David K. 1971. "Immodest Inductive Methods." *Philosophy of Science* 38 (1): 54–63.
Lindeman, Kathryn. 2017. "Constitutivism without Normative Thresholds." *Journal of Ethics and Social Philosophy* 3 (XII): 231–58.
Longuenesse, Béatrice. 1998. *Kant and the Capacity to Judge: Sensibility and Discursivity in the Transcendental Analytic of the "Critique of Pure Reason."* Princeton University Press.
Longuenesse, Béatrice. 2005. *Kant on the Human Standpoint*. Cambridge University Press.
Longuenesse, Béatrice. 2017. *I, Me, Mine: Back to Kant, and Back Again*. Oxford University Press.
Lord, Errol. 2018. *The Importance of Being Rational*. Oxford University Press.
Lord, Errol. 2020. "Replies to Schafer, Schroeder, and Staffel." *Philosophy and Phenomenological Research* 100 (2): 476–87.
Lu-Adler, Huaping. 2018. *Kant and the Science of Logic: A Historical and Philosophical Reconstruction*. Oxford University Press.
Lu-Adler, Huaping. 2021. "Kant and the Principle of Sufficient Reason." *Review of Metaphysics* 74 (3): 301–30.
MacFarlane, John. 2002. "Frege, Kant, and the Logic in Logicism." *Philosophical Review* 111 (1): 25–65.

Maguire, Barry, and Errol Lord. 2016. "An Opinionated Guide to the Weight of Reasons." In *Weighing Reasons*, 3–24. Oxford University Press.

Makkreel, Rudolf A. 2018. "Kant on Cognition, Comprehension, and Knowledge." In *Natur Und Freiheit. Akten des Xii. Internationalen Kant-Kongresses*, edited by Violetta L. Waibel, Margit Ruffing, and David Wagner, 1269–76. De Gruyter.

Marcus, Eric. 2021. *Belief, Inference, and the Self-Conscious Mind*. New edition. Oxford University Press.

Marshall, Colin. 2022. "Kant's Derivation of the Moral 'Ought' from a Metaphysical 'Is.'" In *The Sensible and Intelligible Worlds: New Essays on Kant's Metaphysics and Epistemology*, edited by Karl Schafer and Nicholas F. Stang, 382–404. Oxford University Press.

Matherne, Samantha. 2021. "Cognition by Analogy and the Possibility of Metaphysics." In *Kant's Prolegomena: A Critical Guide*. Cambridge University Press.

McDowell, John Henry. 2009. *Having the World in View: Essays on Kant, Hegel, and Sellars*. Harvard University Press.

McDowell, John Henry. 2011. *Perception as a Capacity for Knowledge*. Marquette University Press.

McHugh, Conor, and Jonathan Way. 2018. "What Is Reasoning?" *Mind* 127 (505): 167–96.

McLear, Colin. 2011. "Kant on Animal Consciousness." *Philosophers' Imprint* 11 (15): 1–16.

McLear, Colin. 2018. "Motion and the Affection Argument." *Synthese* 195 (11): 4979–95.

McLear, Colin. 2019. "The Mind's 'I.'" *European Journal of Philosophy* 27 (1): 255–65.

McLear, Colin. 2020. "'I Am the Original of All Objects': Apperception and the Substantial Subject." *Philosophers' Imprint* 20 (26): 1–38.

McLear, Colin. 2022. "Rationality: What Difference Does It Make?" *Philosophy and Phenomenological Research*. Online first.

McLear, Colin. forthcoming. "On the Transcendental Freedom of the Intellect." *Ergo: An Open Access Journal of Philosophy* 7 (2): 35–104.

McLear, Colin. forthcoming. *Reason's Order*. Oxford: Oxford University Press.

McNulty, Jacob. 2022. *Hegel's Logic and Metaphysics*. Cambridge University Press.

McNulty, Jacob. 2022. "Historical Materialism as Transcendental Philosophy: The Frankfurt School Synthesis of Kant and Marx." *Journal of the History of Philosophy*. 60 (3): 475–501.

Mensch, Jennifer. 2013. *Kant's Organicism: Epigenesis and the Development of Critical Philosophy*. University of Chicago Press.

Mercier, Hugo, and Dan Sperber. 2017. *The Enigma of Reason*. Harvard University Press.

Merritt, Melissa. 2018. *Kant on Reflection and Virtue*. Cambridge University Press.

Merritt, Melissa. 2021a. "Kant and Stoic Affections." *Canadian Journal of Philosophy* 51 (5): 329–50.

Merritt, Melissa. 2021b. "Nature, Corruption, and Freedom: Stoic Ethics in Kant's Religion." *European Journal of Philosophy* 29 (1): 3–24.

Moore, A. W. 2012. *The Evolution of Modern Metaphysics: Making Sense of Things*. Cambridge University Press.

Moran, Kate. 2022. *Kant's Ethics*. Cambridge University Press.

Mudd, Sasha. 2016. "Rethinking the Priority of Practical Reason in Kant." *European Journal of Philosophy* 24 (1): 78–102.

Mudd, Sasha. 2017. "The Demand for Systematicity and the Authority of Theoretical Reason in Kant." *Kantian Review* 22 (1): 81–106.

Müller, Andreas. 2020. *Constructing Practical Reasons*. Oxford University Press.

Murdoch, Iris. 1970. *The Sovereignty of Good*. Routledge.

Mylonaki, Evgenia. 2018. "Action as the Conclusion of Practical Reasoning; The Critique of a Rödlian Account." *European Journal of Philosophy* 1: 30–45.
Nagel, Thomas. 1986. *The View from Nowhere*. Oxford University Press.
Nagel, Thomas. 2012. *Mind & Cosmos: Why the Materialist Neo-Darwinian Conception of Nature Is Almost Certainly False*. Oxford University Press.
Neiman, Susan. 1994. *The Unity of Reason: Rereading Kant*. Oxford University Press.
Neta, Ram. 2018. "Rationally Determinable Conditions." *Philosophical Issues* 28 (1): 289–99.
Neta, Ram. 2019. "The Basing Relation." *Philosophical Review* 128 (2): 179–217.
Newton, Alexandra. 2019. "Kant and the Transparency of the Mind." *Canadian Journal of Philosophy* 49 (7): 890–915.
Newton, Alexandra. 2015. "Kant on the Logical Origin of Concepts." *European Journal of Philosophy* 23 (3): 456–484.
Nisenbaum, Karin. 2018. *For the Love of Metaphysics: Nihilism and the Conflict of Reason from Kant to Rosenzweig*. Oxford University Press. Nisenbaum, Karin. forthcoming. "Realizing Our Capacity to Know the Good: Kant on the Dialectic of Pure Practical Reason."
Nunez, Tyke. 2014. "Definitions of Kant's Categories." *Canadian Journal of Philosophy* 44 (5–6): 631–57.
Nunez, Tyke. 2019. "Logical Mistakes, Logical Aliens, and the Laws of Kant's Pure General Logic." *Mind* 128 (512): 1149–80.
Nussbaum, Martha C. 2011. *Creating Capabilities*. Harvard University Press.
Nuzzo, Angelica. 2005. *Kant and the Unity of Reason*. Purdue University Press.
Nyholm, Sven. 2015. "Kant's Universal Law Formula Revisited." *Metaphilosophy* 46 (2): 280–99.
O'Neill, Onora. 1989. *Constructions of Reason: Explorations of Kant's Practical Philosophy*. Cambridge University Press.
O'Neill, Onora. 2002. *Autonomy and Trust in Bioethics*. Cambridge University Press.
Owen, David. 1999. *Hume's Reason*. Oxford University Press.
Paakkunainen, Hille. 2018. "The 'Just Too Different' Objection to Normative Naturalism." *Philosophy Compass* 13 (2): e12473
Pallikkathayil, Japa. 2010. "Deriving Morality from Politics: Rethinking the Formula of Humanity." *Ethics* 121 (1): 116–47.
Papish, Laura. 2018. "Kant's Revised Account of the Non-Moral Imperatives of Practical Reason." *Ergo, an Open Access Journal of Philosophy* 5 (11): 289–317.
Parfit, Derek. 1984. *Reasons and Persons*. Oxford University Press.
Parfit, Derek. 2011. *On What Matters: Two-Volume Set*. Oxford University Press.
Pasnau, Robert. 2018. *After Certainty: A History of Our Epistemic Ideals and Illusions*. Oxford University Press.
Pasternack, Lawrence. 1999. "Can Self-Deception Explain Akrasia in Kant's Theory of Moral Agency?" *Southwestern Philosophical Review* 15 (1): 87–97.
Pendlebury, T. A. 2022. "The Shape of the Kantian Mind." *Philosophy and Phenomenological Research* 104 (2): 364–87.
Pinkard, Terry. 1994. *Hegel's Phenomenology: The Sociality of Reason*. Cambridge University Press.
Piper, Adrian M. S. 2012. "Kant's Self-Legislation Procedure Reconsidered." *Kant Studies Online* 2012 (1): 203–77.
Piper, Adrian M. S. 2013. *Rationality and the Structure of the Self, Volume II: A Kantian Conception*. APRA Foundation.

Pippin, Robert B. 2018. *Hegel's Realm of Shadows: Logic as Metaphysics in "The Science of Logic."* University of Chicago Press.
Pollok, Konstantin. 2017. *Kant's Theory of Normativity: Exploring the Space of Reason.* Cambridge University Press.
Proops, Ian. 2003. "Kant's Legal Metaphor and the Nature of a Deduction." *Journal of the History of Philosophy* 41 (2): 209-29.
Proops, Ian. 2010. "Kant's First Paralogism." *Philosophical Review* 119 (4): 449-95.
Proops, Ian. 2014. "Kant on the Cosmological Argument." *Philosophers' Imprint* 14: 1-21.
Proops, Ian. 2015. "Kant on the Ontological Argument." *Noûs* 49 (1): 1-27.
Proops, Ian. 2021. *The Fiery Test of Critique: A Reading of Kant's Dialectic.* Oxford University Press.
Rauscher, Frederick. 2010. "The Appendix to the Dialectic and the Canon of Pure Reason: The Positive Role of Reason." In *The Cambridge Companion to Kant's Critique of Pure Reason*, edited by Paul Guyer, 290-309. Cambridge University Press.
Rawls, John. 2000. *Lectures on the History of Moral Philosophy.* Edited by Barbara Herman. Harvard University Press.
Reath, Andrews. 2006. *Agency and Autonomy in Kant's Moral Theory: Selected Essays.* Oxford University Press.
Reath, Andrews. 2010. "Formal Principles and the Form of a Law." In *Kant's Critique of Practical Reason: A Critical Guide*, edited by Andrews Reath and Jens Timmermann. Cambridge University Press.
Reath, Andrews. 2012. "A High Plains Drifter: Remarks on Engstrom's the Form of Practical Knowledge." *Analytic Philosophy* 53 (1): 79-88.
Reath, Andrews. 2013. "Formal Approaches to Kant's Formula of Humanity." In *Kant on Practical Justification*, edited by Mark Timmons and Sorin Baiasu, 201-28. Oxford University Press.
Reath, Andrews. 2019. "Autonomy and the Idea of Freedom: Some Reflections on Groundwork III." *Kantian Review* 24 (2): 223-48.
Rescher, Nicholas. 2000. *Kant and the Reach of Reason: Studies in Kant's Theory of Rational Systematization.* Cambridge University Press.
Rinard, Susanna. 2017. "No Exception for Belief." *Philosophy and Phenomenological Research* 94 (1): 121-43.
Rödl, Sebastian. 2007. *Self-Consciousness.* Harvard University Press.
Rödl, Sebastian. 2010. "The Form of the Will." In *Desire, Practical Reason, and the Good*, edited by Sergio Tenenbaum, 138-60. Oxford University Press.
Rödl, Sebastian. 2018. *Self-Consciousness and Objectivity.* Harvard University Press.
Rödl, Sebastian. 2021. "Freedom as Right." *European Journal of Philosophy* 29 (3): 624-33.
Rohlf, Michael. 2010. "The Ideas of Pure Reason." In *The Cambridge Companion to Kant's Critique of Pure Reason*, edited by Paul Guyer, 190-209. Cambridge University Press.
Rosati, Connie S. 2016. "Agents and 'Shmagents': An Essay on Agency and Normativity." *Oxford Studies in Metaethics* 11: 182-213.
Rosefeldt, Tobias. 2000. *Das logische Ich: Kant über den Gehalt des Begriffes von sich selbst.* Philo.
Rosefeldt, Tobias. 2019. "Kant über Sollen als Wollen." In *Natur Und Freiheit. Akten des Xii. Internationalen Kant-Kongresses*, edited by Violetta L. Waibel, Margit Ruffing, and David Wagner, 1269-76. De Gruyter.
Rosenblueth, Arturo, Norbert Wiener, and Julian Bigelow. 1943. "Behavior, Purpose and Teleology." *Philosophy of Science* 10 (1): 18-24.

Russell, Francey. 2020. "Kantian Self-Conceit and the Two Guises of Authority." *Canadian Journal of Philosophy* 50 (2): 268–83.
Samuel, Jack. forthcoming a. "Alienation and the Metaphysics of Normativity: On the Quality of Our Relations with the World." *Journal of Ethics and Social Philosophy*.
Samuel, Jack. forthcoming b. "Toward a Post-Kantian Constructivism." *Ergo, an Open Access Journal of Philosophy*.
Samuel, Jack, and Christa Peterson. 2021. "The Right and the Wren." In *Oxford Studies in Agency and Responsibility VII*, edited by David Shoemaker, 81–103. Oxford University Press.
Scanlon, Thomas. 2014. *Being Realistic about Reasons*. Oxford University Press.
Schafer, Karl. 2013. "Perception and the Rational Force of Desire." *Journal of Philosophy* 110 (5): 258–81.
Schafer, Karl. 2014a. "Constructivism and Three Forms of Perspective-Dependence in Metaethics." *Philosophy and Phenomenological Research* 89 (1): 68–101.
Schafer, Karl. 2014b. "Doxastic Planning and Epistemic Internalism." *Synthese* 191 (12): 2571–91.
Schafer, Karl. 2014c. "Knowledge and Two Forms of Non-Accidental Truth." *Philosophy and Phenomenological Research* 89 (2): 373–93.
Schafer, Karl. 2015a. "Hume's Unified Theory of Mental Representation." *European Journal of Philosophy* 23 (4): 978–1005.
Schafer, Karl. 2015b. "Realism and Constructivism in Kantian Metaethics 1: Realism and Constructivism in a Kantian Context." *Philosophy Compass* 10 (10): 690–701.
Schafer, Karl. 2015c. "Realism and Constructivism in Kantian Metaethics 2: The Kantian Conception of Rationality and Rationalist Constructivism." *Philosophy Compass* 10 (10): 702–13.
Schafer, Karl. 2016. "The Modesty of the Moral Point of View." In *Weighing Reasons*. 241–56. Oxford University Press.
Schafer, Karl. 2017. "Intuitions and Objects in Allais's Manifest Reality." *Philosophical Studies* 174 (7): 1675–86.
Schafer, Karl. 2018a. "A Brief History of Rationality: Reason, Reasonableness, Rationality, and Reasons." *Manuscrito* 41 (4): 501–29.
Schafer, Karl. 2018b. "Constitutivism about Reasons: Understanding and Autonomy." In *The Many Moral Rationalisms*. Vol. 1. Oxford University Press.
Schafer, Karl. 2019a. "Kant: Constitutivism as Capacities-First Philosophy." *Philosophical Explorations* 22 (2): 177–93.
Schafer, Karl. 2019b. "Rationality as the Capacity for Understanding." *Noûs* 53 (3): 639–63.
Schafer, Karl. 2020. "The Scenic Route? On Errol Lord's The Importance of Being Rational." *Philosophy and Phenomenological Research* 100 (2): 469–75.
Schafer, Karl. forthcoming b. "Kant on Method." In *The Oxford Handbook of Kant*, edited by Andrew Stephenson and Anil Gomes. Oxford University Press.
Schafer, Karl. forthcoming c. "Reason as the Capacity for Comprehension in Kant." *Australasian Journal of Philosophy*.
Schafer, Karl. 2021a. "The Beach of Skepticism: Kant and Hume on Skepticism and Philosophy." In *The Cambridge Companion to the Prolegomena*, edited by Peter Thielke, 111–32. Cambridge University Press.
Schafer, Karl. 2021b. "Transcendental Philosophy as Capacities-First Philosophy." *Philosophy and Phenomenological Research* 103 (3): 661–86.
Schafer, Karl. 2021c. "A Kantian Virtue Epistemology: Rational Capacities and Transcendental Arguments." *Synthese* 198: 3113–36.

Schafer, Karl. 2022a. "A System of Rational Faculties: Additive or Transformative?" *European Journal of Philosophy* 29 (4): 918-36.
Schafer, Karl. 2022b. "Kant's Conception of Cognition and Knowledge of Things in Themselves." In *The Sensible and Intelligible Worlds*, 248-78. Oxford University Press.
Schafer, Karl. forthcoming. "Practical Cognition and Knowledge of Things-in-Themselves." In *Kantian Freedom*, edited by Evan Tiffany and Dai Heide. Oxford University Press.
Schapiro, Tamar. 2021. *Feeling Like It: A Theory of Inclination and Will*. Oxford University Press.
Schellenberg, Susanna. 2018. *The Unity of Perception: Content, Consciousness, Evidence*. Oxford University Press.
Schönecker, Dieter. 2013. "Kant's Moral Intuitionism: The Fact of Reason and Moral Predispositions." *Kant Studies Online* 2013 (1).
Schönecker, Dieter, and Christoph Horn. 2006. "How Is a Categorical Imperative Possible?" In *Groundwork for the Metaphysics of Morals*, edited by Dieter Schönecker and Christoph Horn, 301-24. De Gruyter.
Schroeder, Mark. 2007. *Slaves of the Passions*. Oxford University Press.
Schroeder, Mark. 2015a. "In Defense of the Kantian Account of Knowledge: Reply to Whiting." *Logos and Episteme* 6 (3): 371-82.
Schroeder, Mark. 2015b. "Knowledge Is Belief for Sufficient (Objective and Subjective) Reason." *Oxford Studies in Epistemology* 5: 226-52.
Schroeder, Mark. 2021. *Reasons First*. Oxford University Press.
Sen, Amartya. 2004. *Rationality and Freedom*. Belknap Press of Harvard University Press.
Sensen, Oliver. 2011. "Kant's Conception of Inner Value." *European Journal of Philosophy* 19 (2): 262-80.
Sensen, Oliver. 2012. *Kant on Moral Autonomy*. Cambridge University Press.
Sensen, Oliver. 2017. "Kant's Constitutivism." In *Realism and Antirealism in Kant's Moral Philosophy: New Essays*, edited by Elke Elisabeth Schmidt and Robinson dos Santos, 197-222. De Gruyter.
Sensen, Oliver. 2021. "How to Treat Someone with Respect." In *Respect: Philosophical Essays*, edited by Richard Dean and Oliver Sensen, 99-118. Oxford University Press.
Sethi, Janum. 2020. "'For Me, in My Present State': Kant on Judgments of Perception and Mere Subjective Validity." *Journal of Modern Philosophy* 2 (9): 20.
Setiya, Kieran. 2007. "Cognitivism about Instrumental Reason." *Ethics* 117 (4): 649-73.
Setiya, Kieran. 2010. *Reasons without Rationalism*. Princeton University Press.
Setiya, Kieran. 2012. *Knowing Right from Wrong*. Oxford University Press.
Setiya, Kieran. 2014. "What Is a Reason to Act?" *Philosophical Studies* 167 (2): 221-35.
Shafer-Landau, Russ. 2003. *Moral Realism: A Defence*. Oxford University Press.
Silverstein, Matthew. 2015. "The Shmagency Question." *Philosophical Studies* 172 (5): 1127-42.
Small, Will. 2019. "Basic Action and Practical Knowledge." *Philosophers' Imprint* 19 (19): 1-22.
Smit, Houston. 1999. "The Role of Reflection in Kant's Critique of Pure Reason." *Pacific Philosophical Quarterly* 80 (2): 203-23.
Smit, Houston. 2000. "Kant on Marks and the Immediacy of Intuition." *Philosophical Review* 109 (2): 235-66.
Smit, Houston. 2009. "Kant on Apriority and the Spontaneity of Cognition." In *Metaphysics and the Good: Themes from the Philosophy of Robert Merrihew Adams*, edited by Samuel Newlands and Larry M. Jorgensen, 188-251. Oxford University Press.
Smit, Houston. 2010. "Apriority, Reason, and Induction in Hume." *Journal of the History of Philosophy* 48 (3): 313-43.

Smit, Houston. 2019. "Kant's 'I Think' and the Agential Approach to Self-Knowledge." *Canadian Journal of Philosophy* 49 (7): 980–1011.
Smith, Michael. 2012. "XV—Agents and Patients, or: What We Learn about Reasons for Action by Reflecting on Our Choices in Process of Thought Cases." *Proceedings of the Aristotelian Society* 112 (3): 309–31.
Smith, Michael. 2015. "The Magic of Constitutivism." *American Philosophical Quarterly* 52 (2): 187–200.
Smith, Michael. 2017. "Constitutivism." In *The Routledge Handbook of Metaethics*, edited by Tristram McPherson and David Plunkett, 371–84. Routledge.
Smithies, Declan. 2019. *The Epistemic Role of Consciousness*. Oxford University Press.
Sommerlatte, Curtis. 2018. "Erkenntnis in Kant's Logical Works." In *Natur und Freiheit: Akten des XII. Internationalen Kant-Kongresses*, edited by Margit Ruffing and Violetta Waibel, 1413–20. De Gruyter.
Stang, Nicholas. 2016. *Kant's Modal Metaphysics*. Oxford University Press.
Stang, Nicholas. 2017. "Transcendental Idealism without Tears." *In Idealism: New Essays in Metaphysics*, edited by Tyron Goldschmidt, Oxford: Oxford University Pres: 82–103.
Stang, Nicholas. 2018. "Kant's Transcendental Idealism." In *The Stanford Encyclopedia of Philosophy*, edited by Edward N. Zalta. Stanford University Press. https://plato.stanford.edu/entries/kant-transcendental-idealism/
Stang, Nicholas. 2019. "A Guide to Ground in Kant's Lectures on Metaphysics." In *Kant's Lectures on Metaphysics: A Critical Guide*, edited by Courtney Fugate, 74–101. Cambridge University Press.
Stang, Nicholas. forthcoming. "Bodies, Matter, Monads and Things in Themselves." In *Leibniz and Kant*, edited by Brandon Look, 132–42. Oxford University Press.
Stephenson, Andrew. 2021. "How to Solve the Knowability Paradox with Transcendental Epistemology." *Synthese* 198: 3253–78.
Stephenson, Andrew. forthcoming. "Kant and Kripke: Rethinking Necessity and the A Priori." In *The Palgrave Handbook of German Idealism and Analytic Philosophy*, edited by James Conant and Jonas Held. Palgrave MacMillan.
Stern, Robert. 2011. *Understanding Moral Obligation: Kant, Hegel, Kierkegaard*. Cambridge University Press.
Stratmann, Joe. forthcoming. "The End of Explanation: Kant on the Unconditioned." *Philosophy and Phenomenological Research*.
Strawson, Galen. 1989. *The Secret Connexion: Causation, Realism, and David Hume*. Oxford University Press.
Strawson, Peter. 1990. *Bounds of Sense*. Routledge.
Stroud, Barry. 1968. "Transcendental Arguments." *Journal of Philosophy* 65 (9): 241–56.
Sturm, Thomas. 2020. "Kant on the Ends of the Sciences." *Kant-Studien* 111 (1): 1–28.
Sussman, David. 2008. "From Deduction to Deed: Kant's Grounding of the Moral Law." *Kantian Review* 13 (1): 52–81.
Sylvan, Kurt L. 2020. "An Epistemic Nonconsequentialism." *Philosophical Review* 129 (1): 1–51.
Sylvan, Kurt L., and Errol Lord. 2022. "On Suspending Properly." In *Propositional and Doxastic Justification*, edited by Luis Oliveria and Paul Silva, 234–46. Routledge.
Sylvan, Kurt, and Errol Lord. forthcoming. "Prime Time (for the Basing Relation)." In *Well-Founded Belief: New Essays on the Basing Relation*, edited by J. Adam Carter and Patrick Bondy. Routledge.
Tarasenko-Struc, Aleksy. 2020. "Kantian Constructivism and the Authority of Others." *European Journal of Philosophy* 28 (1): 77–92.

Tenenbaum, Sergio. 2007. *Appearances of the Good: An Essay on the Nature of Practical Reason.* Cambridge University Press.
Tenenbaum, Sergio. 2012. "The Idea of Freedom and Moral Cognition in Groundwork III." *Philosophy and Phenomenological Research* 84 (3): 555-89.
Tenenbaum, Sergio. 2019. "Formalism and Constitutivism in Kantian Practical Philosophy." *Philosophical Explorations* 22 (2): 163-76.
Tenenbaum, Sergio. 2021. *Rational Powers in Action: Instrumental Rationality and Extended Agency.* Oxford University Press.
Thompson, Michael. 2004. "What Is It to Wrong Someone? A Puzzle about Justice." In *Reason and Value: Themes from the Moral Philosophy of Joseph Raz*, 333-84. Clarendon Press.
Thompson, Michael. 2008. *Life and Action: Elementary Structures of Practice and Practical Thought.* Harvard University Press.
Thomson, Judith Jarvis. 2008. *Normativity.* Open Court.
Tiffany, Evan. 2012. "Why Be an Agent?" *Australasian Journal of Philosophy* 90 (2): 223-33.
Timmermann, Jens. 2006. "Value without Regress: Kant's 'Formula of Humanity' Revisited." *European Journal of Philosophy* 14 (1): 69-93.
Timmermann, Jens. 2007. *Kant's Groundwork of the Metaphysics of Morals: A Commentary.* Cambridge University Press.
Timmermann, Jens. 2010. "Reversal or Retreat? Kant's Deductions of Freedom and Morality." In *Kant's Critique of Practical Reason: A Critical Guide*, edited by Andrews Reath and Jens Timmermann, 73-89. Cambridge University Press.
Timmermann, Jens. 2012. "Autonomy and Moral Regard for Ends." In *Kant on Moral Autonomy*, 212-24. Cambridge University Press.
Timmermann, Jens. 2018. "A Tale of Two Conflicts: On Pauline Kleingeld's New Reading of the Formula of Universal Law." *Kant-Studien* 109 (4): 581-96.
Timmons, Mark. 2017. *Significance and System: Essays on Kant's Ethics.* Oxford University Press.
Timmons, Mark C. 2008. "The Categorical Imperative and Universalizability (GMS, 421-424)." In *Groundwork for the Metaphysics of Morals*, edited by Christoph Horn and Dieter Schönecker, 158-99. De Gruyter.
Tolley, Clinton. 2006. "Kant on the Nature of Logical Laws." *Philosophical Topics* 34 (1/2): 371-407.
Tolley, Clinton. 2012. "The Generality of Kant's Transcendental Logic." *Journal of the History of Philosophy* 50 (3): 417-46.
Tolley, Clinton. 2014. "Kant on the Content of Cognition." *European Journal of Philosophy* 22 (2): 200-28.
Tolley, Clinton. 2017a. "Hegel and Kant on Reason and the Unconditioned." *Hegel Studien* 50: 131-41.
Tolley, Clinton. 2017b. "Kant on the Place of Cognition in the Progression of Our Representations." *Synthese* 197: 3215-44.
Valaris, Markos. 2014. "Reasoning and Regress." *Mind* 123 (489): 101-27.
Valaris, Markos. 2017. "What Reasoning Might Be." *Synthese* 194 (6).
Velleman, David. 2000. *The Possibility of Practical Reason.* Vol. 106. Oxford University Press.
Velleman, David. 2009. *How We Get Along.* Cambridge University Press.
Walden, Kenneth. 2017. "Mores and Morals: Metaethics and the Social World." In *The Routledge Handbook of Metaethics*, edited by Tristram McPherson and David Plunkett, 417-30. Routledge.

Walden, Kenneth. 2018. "Practical Reason Not as Such." *Journal of Ethics and Social Philosophy* 13 (2): 125–53.
Walden, Kenneth. 2019. "Reason Unbound: Kant's Theory of Regulative Principles." *European Journal of Philosophy* 27 (3): 575–92.
Walden, Kenneth. 2020. "Reason and Respect." *Oxford Studies in Metaethics* 15: 1–23.
Wallace, R. Jay. 2019. *The Moral Nexus*. Princeton University Press.
Ware, Owen. 2014. "Rethinking Kant's Fact of Reason." *Philosophers' Imprint* 14 (32): 1–21.
Ware, Owen. 2021. *Kant's Justification of Ethics*. Oxford University Press.
Watkins, Eric. 2005. *Kant and the Metaphysics of Causality*. Cambridge University Press.
Watkins, Eric. 2010. "The Antinomy of Practical Reason: Reason, the Unconditioned and the Highest Good." In *Kant's Critique of Practical Reason: A Critical Guide*, edited by Andrews Reath and Jens Timmermann. Cambridge University Press.
Watkins, Eric. 2016. "The Unconditioned and the Absolute in Kant and Early German Romanticism." *Kant Yearbook* 8 (1): 117–42.
Watkins, Eric. 2017. "The Unconditioned Goodness of the Good Will." In *Kant on Persons and Agency*, edited by Eric Watkins, 11–28. Cambridge University Press.
Watkins, Eric. 2019. *Kant on Laws*. Cambridge University Press.
Watkins, Eric. forthcoming a. "Kant on the Pretensions of Metaphysics."
Watkins, Eric. forthcoming b. "Kant on the Unconditioned."
Watkins, Eric, and Joe Stratmann. 2021. "Kant on the Principle of Sufficient Reason." In *The Principle of Sufficient Reason*, edited by Michael Della Rocca and Fatema Amijee. Oxford University Press.
Watkins, Eric, and Marcus Willaschek. 2017. "Kant's Account of Cognition." *Journal of the History of Philosophy* 55 (1): 83–112.
Way, Jonathan. 2017. "Reasons as Premises of Good Reasoning." *Pacific Philosophical Quarterly* 98 (2): 251–70.
Willaschek, Marcus. 2018. *Kant on the Sources of Metaphysics: The Dialectic of Pure Reason*. Cambridge University Press.
Wodak, Daniel. 2020. "Who's on First." *Oxford Studies in Metaethics* 15: 49–71.
Wood, Allen W. 1999. *Kant's Ethical Thought*. Cambridge University Press.
Wood, Allen W. 2007. *Kantian Ethics*. Cambridge University Press.
Worsnip, Alex. 2021. *Fitting Things Together: Coherence and the Demands of Structural Rationality*. Oxford University Press.
Worsnip, Alex. forthcoming. "Epistemic Normativity Is Independent of Our Goals." In *Contemporary Debates in Epistemology (3rd Ed.)*, edited by Blake Roeber, Matthias Steup, Ernest Sosa, and John Turri. Wiley-Blackwell.
Ypi, Lea. 2021. The Architectonic of Reason: Purposiveness and Systematic Unity in Kant's Critique of Pure Reason. Oxford University Press.
Zinkin, Melissa. 2017. "Kantian Constructivism, Respect, and Moral Depth." In *Realism and Antirealism in Kant's Moral Philosophy*, edited by Robinson dos Santos and Elke Elisabeth Schmidt, 21–45. De Gruyter.
Zinkin, Melissa. 2022. "Kant on Wonder as the Motive to Learn." *Wiley: Journal of Philosophy of Education* 55 (6): 921–34.
Zylberman, Ariel. 2018. "The Relational Structure of Human Dignity." *Australasian Journal of Philosophy* 96 (4): 738–52.
Zylberman, Ariel. 2021. "Relational Primitivism." *Philosophy and Phenomenological Research* 102 (2): 401–22.

Index

For the benefit of digital users, indexed terms that span two pages (e.g., 52–53) may, on occasion, appear on only one of those pages.

Action 224–30
Agency 109, 224–30
Aim, *see also* End 92, 189–95
Alienation 115, 230–4
Akrasia 221, 226
Analytic vs. synthetic, cognition 124–6
Anscombe, Elizabeth 74–5, 77
Antinomies 180–2
Aquinas 65, 74–5, 77
A priori, *see also* Cognition from principles 121, 141
Aristotle 108–9
Autocracy 217
Autonomy 20–1, 24–5, 27, 41–3, 212–34
　Autonomy, and comprehension 212–34
　Autonomy, of reason 41–3, 218–24
　Autonomy, of agents 224–30

Basing relation, *see also* Grounds for assent 123
Baumgarten 129–30
Belief, *see also* Grounds for assent 23–4, 69–73, 149–50, 172–8
　Belief, doctrinal 149–50, 172–8
Buddhism 51–2, 199

Capacity 4, 21, 31–2, 38–41, 120, 151–2
　Capacity, rational 4–5, 21, 91–2, 120–1
Capacities-first 31–2, 35–41
Choice, power of 217
Cognition 21–2, 32–3, 48–52, 56–90, 151–2, 201
　Cognition, formal 48–9
　Cognition, theoretical vs. practical 33, 73–9
Cognition from principles, *see also* Comprehension 123–30, 184–8, 200, 219
Communication 201–3
Comprehension, *see also* Cognition from Principles 23–5, 33–4, 130–41, 201, 204–7, 218–24
　Comprehension, theoretical vs. practical 143–5, 204–7, 218–24
Condition, *see also* Grounds 124–30, 152–82, 195
　Condition, logical 127–8, 152–4

Condition, real 128–30, 154–9
Consciousness, *see also* Self-Consciousness 21–2, 58–60, 62, 67–8, 79–81
Constitutivism 22, 91–100, 106–15, 166–8, 227–8, 241–6
　Constitutivism, agential 22, 108–9, 241–6
　Constitutivism, rational 22, 110–12, 241–6
Contradiction 103–4, 168
Coordination 135–6
Critique 42–3
　Critique, social 246–50
Critique of the Power of Judgment 26–7

Deduction, metaphysical 162–3
Determinateness 62–9
Disagreement 202–3
Dogmatism 141–3

Egoism, logical 201–3
Ends 11–17, 189–95, 207–10, 214–18, 237–41
Engstrom, Stephen 19–20, 75–7, 184
Explanation, *see also* Grounds, Comprehension 40–1, 214–18
Evil 226

Fact of reason 40–1, 95–101
Faculty, *see* Capacity
Fichte 51, 198–9
Finitude 93–5
Form 39–40
Foundations, *see also* Grounds, Principles, System, Systematic Unity 35–41, 44–8
Freedom 17–18, 95–101, 218–34

Generality, *see also* Principle and Comprehension 233
Givenness 88–90, 157–9
God 85–6, 94–5, 173–5, 207–10, 227
Guyer, Paul 44–5, 98, 169, 188
Grounds 35–41, 135–7, 141
Grounds for assent 69–73, 78–9, 139–41, 149–50, 168–82
Groundwork for the Metaphysics of Morals 27

INDEX

Habermas, Jürgen 10–11
Hegel 47, 56, 81, 198–9, 249–51
Heteronomy 214–18
Hierarchy 250–1
Highest Good 207–10
Hope 176
Hume 98, 108–9, 164, 174–5
Hylomorphism 74, 83, 151–2, 186–7, 195

Idealized epistemology 134
Idealism, German 51, 250–1
Idealism, transcendental 48, 68–9, 141–3, 157–9, 168–82
Ideas 207–10
Imperative 92–5, 166–8, 184–8
Imperative, hypothetical 184–6
Indeterminacy 48–9, 174–8, 207–10
Inference, see also Syllogism 121–30, 184–6
Inquiry 115
Insight, see also Cognition from Principles, Comprehension 18–19, 23, 135–6, 221–2
Instrumental reason 177–8, 184–6, 228–9
Interests, see also Ends 11–17, 92, 130, 237–41
Intersubjective 51–2, 196–204, 230–4

Jaeggi, Rahel 230–4
Judgment 237–41

Kreines, Jim 120
Kitcher, Patricia 105–6
Korsgaard, Christine 10–11, 52–3, 111–12, 195, 197–9, 232–4
Knowledge (Wissen) 33–5, 69–73, 139–41
Know how, see also Practical understanding, Wisdom 143–5, 242

Legislation 214–18
Leibniz 141, 169–72
Logic 101–3, 152–4
Logical Maxim 152–4, 160–8, 184–6
Longuenesse, Béatrice 237–41

Marx 249–50
Maxims 184–8, 229–30
Maxims of common understanding 199–204
McLear, Colin 49–52, 67–8
Meier 132–3
Moral Law 24, 93–101, 183–210, 218–34
  Moral Law, Expanded Formula of Universal Law 192
  Moral Law, Formula of Universal Law 184–8
  Moral Law, Formula of Humanity 189–95
  Moral Law, Formula of the Realm of Ends 194
  Moral Law, Universal Rational Acceptance 193

Meaning, see also Sense-making 231–2
Merritt, Melissa 19–20, 104, 184
Metaethics 95–101, 106–15, 235–7, 241–6
Metaphysics 43, 49–52, 168–82, 207–10
Method 42–8
Moral Theory 229–30

Naturalism 54–5, 241–6
Neiman, Susan 10–11, 146–7
Neta, Ram 83–4
Normativity 95–101, 105–6, 166–8, 218–34
  Normativity, epistemic 105–6

O'neill, Onora 10–11, 146–7

Passivity 231–2
Perspective 199–204, 233
Philosophy 21, 42–3
  Philosophy, critical 42–8
  Philosophy, cosmopolitan 147–8
  Philosophy, doctrinal 43
  Philosophy, transcendental 44–8
Pleasure, see also Interest 11–17, 92, 227–8
Possibility, real 62–4
Power, see Capacity
Power of judgment 104–5, 237–41
Primacy of practical reason 8, 11–17, 105–6, 145–8, 218–34
Primacy-first 8–12
Principle 23–4, 35–41, 78, 123–30, 149–210
  Principle, absolute 124–6, 219
  Principle, comparative 126–30
  Principle, constitutive 178–9
  Principle, regulative 178–9
  Principle, Supreme 154–82
Principle of Sufficient Reason 23–4, 149–83
Proops, Ian 161–4

Ratio cognoscendi 40–1, 95–101
Ratio essendi 40–1, 95–101, 221–2
Rational individuals, relation to reason 15, 50–2, 115, 196–203, 212–13, 232–4, 246–50
Rationality, see also Reason 142–3, 241–6
Reason 20, 119–48, 241–6
  Reason, multiply-realizable 50–2, 196–203, 246–50
  Reason, practical 183–210
  Reason, theoretical 149–82
  Reason, unity of 3–8, 143–8, 204–7, 215–18, 235–46
Reason-First 2, 241–6
Reasoning, see also Reason 121–30, 142–3, 241–6
Reasons, see also Grounds, Principles 139–41, 241–6

Reasons fundamentalism 2–3, 25, 241–6
Reduction 107–8
Regress 195
Respect 189–91, 196–9
Responsibility 225
Rödl, Sebastian 46

Schapiro, Tamar 80–1
Schematized concepts 214–18
Science 35–48
Second-person 198–9
Sensibility 81, 214–18, 239–41
Shmagency 112–15
Self-effacing 187
Sense-making, *see also* Understanding, Comprehension 139–41, 233–4
Sensus Communis 201
Self-consciousness 21–2, 44–8, 95–101, 220–4
Skepticism, moral 114–15
Social practices 196–9, 246–50
Spinoza 171–2
Spontaneity 213–16
Standard of correctness 59–65
Stang, Nicholas 101–2
Subordination 135–6
Substance 49–52
Syllogism 122–3, 126–7, 152–4
System, *see also* Principles 17–18, 21, 35–6, 131–3, 142
System of faculties 215–18, 237–41
System of principles 204–7

Systematic unity 5–6, 35–6, 131–3, 142, 152–4, 179, 184–6

Taking condition 81–4
Teleology 12–17, 56, 81, 92, 218–24, 235–41
Things in themselves, *see also* Transcendental Idealism 48, 68–9, 141, 157–9, 168–82, 207–10
Tolley, Clinton 85–7, 103–4
Transcendental arguments 44–8
Transcendental dialectic 169–82
Transcendental illusion 176, 180

Unconditioned 152–82, 207–10
Understanding, *see also* Comprehension 130–41
Understanding, shared 246–50
Understanding, theoretical vs. practical 143–5
Understanding (faculty) 214–18, 237–41
Unity 131–3, 151–2, 204–7, 231–2
Unity, objective 151–2, 204–7
Unity, relational 151–2, 204–7
Unity, subjective 151–2, 204–7
Unity-First 11–12

Values, *see also* Ends 189–95, 207–10, 218–24

Watkins, Eric 88–90
Willaschek, Markus 88–90, 160–1
Wisdom, *see also* Comprehension 144–5, 207–10, 218–24, 228–30
Wolff 129–30, 141, 169–70, 212–13
Wood, Allen 52–3, 195